SOCIAL CHANGE IN
DEVELOPING AREAS

SOCIAL CHANGE IN DEVELOPING AREAS

A Reinterpretation of Evolutionary Theory

Edited by

HERBERT R. BARRINGER · *University of Delaware*

GEORGE I. BLANKSTEN and

RAYMOND W. MACK · *Northwestern University*

SCHENKMAN PUBLISHING COMPANY · Cambridge · Massachusetts

CONTENTS

PREFACE

Each of the editors of this volume has wrestled with the problem of a systematic theoretical framework for the analysis of social change in a developing area. In the course of seeking ideas from each other, we have been stimulated to discover a shared conviction that a number of scholars, deliberately or accidentally, are employing a model of social evolution to order their data on underdeveloped areas. Despite the lip service paid in social science theory seminars to Talcott Parsons' querulous "Who now reads Spencer?," a clear-cut assumption of social evolution seems to undergird work ranging from Rostow's *The Stages of Economic Growth* to Moore and Feldman's *Labor Commitment and Social Change in Developing Areas*. Indeed, the assumption that one can make social scientific generalizations about *patterns* of urbanization, industrialization, or political development as processes suggests sequence—an evolutionary model.

A review of the literature convinced us that this was such a promising theoretical frontier that at least a preliminary stocktaking was appropriate. Our excitement was fed as we learned that our enthusiasm for examining this idea was shared by other scholars interested in social change in underdeveloped areas. We invited 22 men to prepare or discuss papers and attempt to organize what is thought or known about the usefulness of evolutionary theory for contemporary social science; every one accepted enthusiastically and took three days out of busy schedules to participate in a discussion of the manuscripts and their implications.

The conference, which resulted in this volume, was held at Northwestern University.[1] The conference enabled the authors of the papers presented here to exchange views with each other and with other interested participants.

Papers were mimeographed and circulated among the participants during the month before the conference. Each author was allowed to present a fifteen

[1] June 8–10, 1961.

1

minute summary or amplification of his paper. A discussant was assigned two papers, and was also allowed fifteen minutes for a formal critique, after which the session was opened for general discussion of the question which inspired the conference: Does the tenor of current social science research in the under-developed areas constitute a revival of evolutionary theory?

We are grateful to the men who prepared papers for the meeting and participated so enthusiastically in the dissection of their own as well as their colleagues' manuscripts. We thank, too, the discussants who brought fresh ideas to the work sessions, and whose views are reprinted in the introductory discussions.

HERBERT R. BARRINGER
GEORGE I. BLANKSTEN
RAYMOND W. MACK

Evanston, Ill.,
October, 1965

INTRODUCTION

HERBERT R. BARRINGER
GEORGE I. BLANKSTEN
RAYMOND W. MACK

Recent studies by social scientists of emergent or "underdeveloped" areas are characteristically concerned with the dynamics of change. When these studies are compared with, for example, sociological studies of the United States, it is apparent that essentially static models are employed for the familiar. In contrast, among studies of emergent areas, and peculiar to them, is a concern with change. The theories employed in the latter appear to share some aspects in common with evolutionary theory.

Given the low esteem of evolutionary theory among social scientists, we believe it worthwhile to examine the possibility that evolutionary theory, either unconsciously or surreptitiously, may be accompanying explicit theories of change. To that end, members of various academic disciplines represented at the conference were asked to discuss the possible relationship of evolutionary theory to their particular theoretical and substantive interests, and to examine the possibility of making any evolutionary undertones explicit.

Some of the specific problems of concern were: (1) To what extent are studies in underdeveloped areas operating in a theoretical framework of determinism? (2) What are the steps or stages prescribed by theories of change? (3) To what extent do these studies involve a "from-simple-to-complex" model? (4) Do social-scientific theories of change assume the value position that change is good; or that increased complexity, or industrialization, or political sophistication, or technological change, is desirable? (5) To what extent are theories of change in underdeveloped areas similar to earlier evolutionary theories in social science?

It was immediately apparent to members of the conference that even this last question was not an easy one to answer. Participants represented eight academic disciplines: anthropology, economics, history, philosophy, political

3

science, psychology, sociology, and zoology. As our discussion proceeded, it became clear that not only did the methodological and theoretical approaches of these disciplines differ from one another, but considerable variation existed within the ranks of any one discipline. Consequently, a considerable portion of the discussion involved clarification and explication of the various formal theoretical approaches to studies of emergent areas. Furthermore, a number of interpretations or definitions of evolutionary theory arose during the course of the conference, ranging from the lucid explanations of modern biological theories by Alfred Emerson and the similar selective retention model of Campbell on the one hand, to the older theories of Lamarck and Spencer, on the other. As will be seen, a further complication arose from differences in conceptualization of the basic problem. For example, anthropologists and historians tended to view evolutionary theory as an aspect of culture, or as a theory of culture. Sociologists and economists tended to look for evolutionary theory within the other scientific theories of change themselves. Finally, it was not always clear as to whether the major problem of the participants was to determine the relationship of evolutionary theory to their explicit theories of change, or to point out the utility of evolutionary theory for future use in the social sciences. The latter interpretation held its own during the conference with some very useful, if unintended, consequences.

The preceding paragraph may give the reader the impression that very little progress was made toward answering our questions. Actually, the conference resulted in a clarification of the main question, and opened many new avenues for thought. To those familiar with interdisciplinary investigations of such a controversial subject as the present one, it may come as a surprise that civilized communication took place at all.

Specifically, the conferees dissected the problem, and addressed the following issues: (1) What are the characteristics of various social-scientific studies of underdeveloped areas? (2) What is meant by evolutionary theory? (3) How are various definitions of evolutionary theory related to theoretical approaches to the study of social change? (4) What utility has evolutionary theory for studies of emergent areas? (5) What are some of the problems inherent in the use of evolutionary theory?

CHARACTERISTICS OF DISCIPLINARY APPROACHES TO THE STUDY OF UNDERDEVELOPED AREAS

A considerable portion of discussion at the conference was spent in clarifying some of the objectives of the various disciplines involved. Following are some of the highlights of these discussions, together with an analysis of interdisciplinary differences as manifested at the conference. It should be pointed out that these generalizations are approximations: they do not necessarily represent the individual approaches of any one participant.

Anthropology

The first, most obvious characteristic of anthropological approaches to the study of underdeveloped areas is a concern with culture. In effect, the problem for the anthropologist is to build a cultural model for the society under investigation in order to view the world as members of that society would see it, before proceeding to further analysis. Throughout the conference, the anthropological representatives maintained the position that change or stages of change must be formulated in such a way as to be consistent with the culture in question. During discussions of decision-making models, for example, Bohannan insisted that "choice" must be investigated in terms of the culture in question: "*Who* is making a choice about *what*?" Bohannan felt that choice can be made on many levels, but that the level of greatest scientific value is that of culture.

This concern with the cultural perspective is, of course, related to the standpoint of cultural relativism. At one stage in a discussion of economic models, Opler objected strenuously to Rottenberg's contention that modern industrial societies are more proficient technically than underdeveloped areas. Opler felt that societies such as Haiti, for example, are just as proficient, given their geographic, climatic and cultural uniqueness, as is a society such as Switzerland. Further, he indicated that such societies may encounter severe difficulties in attempting to adopt modern Western technology. Rottenberg countered with the suggestion that modern technology allows societies to become less dependent upon their natural environment than is true with pre-technological societies. To this, Opler retorted with examples of China and Japan, who attempted to convert to Western technology, only to find themselves without an outlet for their knowledge *or* their produce.

The problem in the above exchange, as Moskos pointed out, was that Opler based his analysis upon a cultural-environmental model, while Rottenberg employed technical change as the major consideration. Bohannan indicated that both parties were probably correct, and added that in cases of technological change, "Persons entering a modern industrial society do tend to become more secondary in their social relationships. However, when we are concerned about the effects of these people becoming like us, we should remember that they need not become like us in all respects. Technical knowledge may bring technical change, but it need not reach all levels of society." Opler agreed in general with Bohannan, but went on to point out examples where technical change did disrupt the social and cultural life of peoples in underdeveloped areas. The point to be made here, of course, is that the anthropological approach to emergent areas tends to emphasize the importance of culture, and is therefore led to view change as it affects this culture.

A third characteristic of the anthropological approach is a pronounced reliance upon an open-minded induction unprejudiced by *a priori* theory. This appears to follow from the aforementioned concern with the reconstruction of a culture before analyzing it. Bohannan, in his discussion of the papers of Opler and Moskos, objected to the use of rigid *a priori* stages in research. Bohannan felt that "stages" are best represented by inductively-ascertained points in change where a major stimulus is noted. For example, the introduction of a new idea into a culture may result in a "stage." The exact nature of this change, or where it comes from is not particularly important. Bohannan indicated his agreement that stages are artificial constructs of the scientist, but he objected to the deductive method in formulating them. Here Herskovits noted that such a view might lead one to describe a series of historical accidents without any unifying element. Merriam agreed, but suggested that one might find unifying elements for seemingly accidental events in evolutionary theory. Opler appeared more interested in loose theoretical categories for studying change than did Bohannan, but insisted that these categories take into account the peculiarities of the cultures involved. The categories Opler would employ, however, would be similar to the "functional equivalents" presented by Ralph Linton in his *Tree of Culture*. It should be indicated that although the anthropologists rejected the notion of rigid *a priori* stages for the examination of change, they did recognize the need for theoretical links between whatever categories the social scientist decides to employ. Their arguments were decidedly not the arguments of raw empiricism.

Economics

Economists attending the conference, with the possible exception of Spengler, represented positions almost completely antithetical to those of the anthropologists. If one were to construct a continuum of views expressed at the conference, anthropology would almost certainly be placed at one pole and economics at the other. There were, of course, some convergences, but these were comparatively few and far between.

First, as might have been expected, economists viewed the study of social change in underdeveloped areas as an examination of changes in technology or in the production and distribution of goods and services. In contrast to sociologists and anthropologists, the economists tended to treat social and cultural changes as consequences of economic changes. For example,

Spengler indicated that "social evolution" is not much help in analyzing the phenomena of interest to an economist. The most "sociological" of the economists present, Spengler, did indicate an interest in problems such as institutionalization of inventions or innovations, criticizing older economic models for treating change linearly. Rottenberg and Spengler disagreed over the problem of incorporating change into economic models, as will be indicated, but there was no question throughout the conference as to the major categories of interest to economists. If social or cultural concepts could assist in understanding economic growth, one had the impression that Spengler would be willing to incorporate them, but primarily as "intervening" variables. Moskos—a sociologist—indicated during the conference that Spengler tended to view change itself as integrative for society, while Feldman and Opler treated change as disruptive for the social and cultural systems respectively. De Schweinitz pointed out, however, and Rottenberg agreed, that "some stability" is generally considered necessary for economic growth. It was not always clear as to whether economists viewed change as beneficial for the society as a whole, or whether this was confined to the economic system alone. Rottenberg's exchange with Opler, however, indicates that "what is good for the economic system is good for society" may still characterize economic analysis.

Unlike the anthropologists, economists tended not to be cultural relativists. Spengler did indicate that independent variables affecting economic development might not be the same for underdeveloped areas as for Western societies. Even here, however, Spengler did not refer so much to cultural perspectives but rather to factors such as climate, geography, and standard economic variables. The difference appears to be that anthropologists view the whole problem of change from the cultural perspective, while economists tend to employ "objective" conceptual models directly.

Exchanges between Spengler and Rottenberg, plus additional comments by de Schweinitz, indicated clearly their favorable attitude toward *a priori* theoretical categories. However, all three pointed out that present economic models are not entirely satisfactory for the examination of change, and particularly in underdeveloped areas. It was striking that the complaints of economists about their models was not that they were not dynamic but that the dynamics involved were not completely satisfactory. Spengler indicated concern with both static models and linear dynamic models. Rottenberg defended static models as being useful for some purposes, but both agreed that dynamics must be examined. To those who have had an opportunity to compare economic models with other social-scientific models, it will come as no surprise that economics is head and shoulders above other disciplines in its attempts to deal with the time dimension. In Blanksten's words, "They have done their homework."

With respect to the problem of stages, economists agreed that the constructs employed do not represent "reality." In Rottenberg's terms, "I join with (Professor Spengler) in his healthy skepticism about the merit of Rostow on stages. I am even doubtful of the value of a perception of history that sees stages marching across the proscenium of time . . . . Change occurs in small steps. It is continuous and not linked, autonomous and not imposed. . . . If a stage is only an intellectual construct it is potentially dangerous because it blinds the observer . . . ." However, Rottenberg did advocate the use of intellectual constructs which would *not* "blind the observer." He and Spengler agreed that a dynamic model of "equilibrium and equilibrium changes" is needed. This would not be a purely inductive model, however, but rather a different form of the theoretical construct than has been employed in the past.

History and Political Science

The only reason for lumping together these two disciplines for analysis is that their respective representatives tended to be more concerned with social science in general than with any more restricted disciplinary approach. Consequently, the reader is referred to papers appearing elsewhere in this volume by Professors Brace and Weiner for more specific disciplinary problems.

Brace's approach as a historian is similar to that of the anthropologists with respect to culture. Brace's analysis of the Algerian elite was based entirely upon the point of view of the Algerians themselves. On the other hand, his paper and further remarks during the conference indicate that he is not at all opposed to the use of *a priori* theoretical categories for analysis. His interest in F. S. C. Northrop's analysis of evolutionary theory and Aristotilean logic can hardly be considered inductive. Brace clearly viewed change within an abstract theoretical framework, with an equally clear empirical reference.

If the foregoing approach to history does not reflect the common stereotype of historians, the political scientists at the conference appeared to be even further removed from their popular image. Snyder's concluding remarks, which will be examined in more detail subsequently, indicated quite clearly that any social-scientific concepts or theories of heuristic value to the political scientist are of interest as defining or independent variables. For example, Blanksten pointed to his interest in employing economic variables as predicting variables for political change in emergent societies. Weiner expressed interest and decided familiarity with functional social system theory, though he indicated that functional analysis is not sufficient for the understanding of social change. All three agreed that newer or more refined theories are needed for the investigation of social change in underdeveloped areas.

Sociology

Sociologists composed the largest contingent at the conference, with six members attending. Their approaches to the study of underdeveloped areas varied widely, from Cottrell's emphasis on "technology" to Feldman's and Mack's concern with definitional or "cultural" problems. Cottrell's approach bordered economics closely, while Feldman, particularly, demonstrated substantive theoretical interests similar to anthropology. Nevertheless, a common interest in types of social organization (as a dependent variable) appeared to unite the sociologists present.

Cottrell's comments about technology complemented portions of his paper. In general, he indicated a belief that technological progress has been so rapid that social organization or culture lose much of their predictive power in studies of decision-making. Modern computers make decisions so rapidly and efficiently that men do well just to keep up. Where technology has "taken over" in this manner, rational decision-making models are of little utility. Cottrell also indicated that democracy may be in process of becoming less of a decision-making process and more of an adaptive process. However, he qualified these generalizations by acknowledging that not all aspects of modern life are permeated by this phenomenon. Condit, in his critique of Cottrell's paper, indicated some dissatisfaction with the notion that technology has displaced "purposeful action." However, he agreed that modern technology has brought with it substantial changes. Both agreed that the question of the effect of technology remains open, but Cottrell remained closer to viewing technology itself as an independent variable, while Condit seemed to be in favor of employing it as an "intervening variable" between purposeful action and result.

Another block of sociologists, notably Bell, Greer and Moskos, appeared particularly concerned with the transition of societies from the *Gemeinschaft* to *Gesellschaft* orientation. Unlike economists or anthropologists, however, their concern was with "increasing scale through time and space." Greer included in this concept such variables as ecological pressures. The problem presented here is the determination of functional adaptations of societies to increasing scale. Both Mack and Feldman cautioned that such an approach can lead to "taking a manager's view of society," but both agreed that it is necessary to go beyond cultural differences to explain or predict differential social action. In general, Bell found in his studies of Jamaica that increasing scale was accompanied by increased internal inclusiveness, *plus* increasing heterogeneity. Expanding scale appeared to result in more and more diverging groups, each "agreeing to hate one another." This diversity set the pattern for a new kind of consensus, a procedural consensus setting the limits upon intergroup interaction. Bell and Moskos, however, indicated that values or cultural definitions could not be ignored. They appeared to view increasing scale as an independent variable, cultural definitions as intervening variables, and types of social organization as consequent variables. Feldman, while acknowledging some utility in the concept of increasing scale, found it imprecise. Furthermore, he indicated that studies employing the concept did not deal adequately with the conflict between older *Gemeinschaft* values and the contractual values accompanying increased industrialization. His position, and that of Mack, were not radically different from those of Bell and Moskos, but demonstrated a much greater concern with cultural definition.

In general, sociologists appeared to agree on the utility of *a priori* categories in research, though it was indicated again that present theories are not sufficient, and need modification. Sociologists seemed not so committed to the inductive method as anthropologists, but were perhaps more interested in modifying their conceptual schemes than were the economists present. Feldman, particularly, expressed dissatisfaction with the structural-functional, or equilibrium, models of society, maintaining that models of social change must be incorporated. He disagreed sharply with Rottenberg on the latter's contention that static models were useful for studies of developing areas. Feldman indicated that sociological theory has avoided the problem of violence or disintegration in change, and has been led by equilibrium models to view change as peaceful and integrative. He maintained that from other theoretical perspectives, e.g., "the bottom levels of societies," systems *do* break up violently and change *is* disintegrative. Moskos, in discussing his work with Albanian elites, indicated that inductively derived results correspond quite closely to the ideal types of Max Weber, and some of the theoretical notions of Pareto. However, he agreed with Herskovits that these stages of change did not incorporate an *adequate* underlying dynamic action system. Addressing the same problem, Feldman and Bell noted that categories or "stages" of change are merely theoretical artifacts, substituted for sufficient knowledge of the underlying processes.

Summary

Interdisciplinary differences were evident. Discussions at the conference pointed up the wide disparity of viewpoints among social scientists, particularly with respect to theory and methodology. These differences in approach resulted in rather different views concerning the status of evolutionary theory in the study of underdeveloped areas.

The foregoing discussion, however, indicates clearly that the social scientists attending the conference were united in a recognition of the need for more adequate theories with which to study social change. Furthermore, they were unanimously concerned with this problem as it applies to the study of emergent areas. Some conferees considered static models to be of some value, but all agreed that improved models of change were needed.

Part I

THEORIES OF SOCIAL EVOLUTION

INTRODUCTION TO PART I

As the conference proceeded it became evident that the term "evolutionary theory" incorporated many theories, ranging from Darwin's and Spencer's contributions to the concept of change itself. Fortunately, Professor Emerson's explication of modern biological versions of evolution opened the conference, making other conferees aware of the widely divergent definitions of evolution.

As Emerson indicated at the beginning of his discussion of evolutionary theory, Darwin's theories are largely of historical interest to biologists. Nevertheless, his theoretical contributions formed the basis for newer theories. His chief contribution was the notion of random variation and adaptive selection to the environment among these variations. Campbell, in essential agreement with Darwin, emphasized that this concept of natural selection is essential to modern evolutionary theory and is worth careful consideration in the study of socio-cultural evolution. There was apparent agreement on the part of most of the other members of the conference, however, that Darwinian theory was not of direct relevance to social science.

Condit, in his discussion of Emerson's paper, indicated that cultural evolution appears more analogous to Lamarck's theories than to Darwin's. Lamarck conceived of the variation process itself as adaptive, while Darwin indicated that variation is blind, but selection of variations is adaptive. Condit indicated that cultural systems, including language, emerge or change as the result of purposeful adaptations to the environment, and therefore fit the Lamarckian model. Cottrell maintained that rapid technological change called "purposeful action" into question. Lamarck was not mentioned again at the conference, but it should be pointed out that social scientific debates concerning purposeful or rational adaptation to an environment as opposed to "unconscious" or irrational adjustment are somewhat analogous to the Lamarckian and Darwinian models respectively. Campbell

13

evades the problem, or unifies the approaches, by interpreting purposeful problem-solving as a trial-and-error process at a substitute level.

The direct application of Darwinian-type theory to social phenomena is best known through the writings of Spencer and Tylor, although many other 19th century social scientists elaborated such theories, and they dominated sociological thinking up to around 1920. Spencer, though an enthusiastic publicist for Darwin, had been an evolutionist before Darwin and incorporated many of the ideas of Lamarck into his theories of society.

Both Emerson and Campbell appeared to be somewhat more sympathetic to the social evolutionists than did other conferees. Emerson's opening remarks indicated that the wide schism between the biological and social sciences came about, in part, by the fact that biologists built upon Darwin, while contemporary social scientists tended to reject Spencer and his followers outright. Campbell, both in his paper and during the conference, pointed to useful concepts in socio-cultural evolution. He took pains to distinguish between this and unilinear stage theories on the one hand and social Darwinism of the eugenicist type on the other. He suggested that one of the problems facing social scientists is the explanation of convergent evolutions, such as "air conditioning" in termite societies as well as human societies. He felt that many of Spencer's analogies between organisms and societies were still useful, particularly if they could be explained by analogies in process or in selective systems. He quoted Spencer as maintaining (here in substance) that cooperation of parts is the only trait common to all animals and societies. Despite Campbell's "defense" of aspects of socio-cultural evolution, the negative attitude of some of the conferees was apparent. Herskovits, in reply to Campbell, pointed out that Spencer's methodology was poor. He tended to set up theoretical models, and then select only favorable empirical documentation. Young indicated that the simplistic notion of unilinear stages is untenable, and at several points the notions of "from-simple-to-complex" came under attack as being too simplistic.

Opler did point out some theorists, including Redfield and Radcliffe-Brown, who were definitely not social Darwinists, however. He suggested Freud and the neo-Freudians as examples of social evolutionists (considering the super-ego as an adaptation to the libido).

Newer Biological Models of Evolution

Emerson felt that it was not necessary to argue about evolutionary theory because we are always involved in change. We want to know the order of the time dimension involved in this change. A new notion in the biological sciences is that function (effect) determines the cause (evolutionary feedback). A self-regulatory process of production of optimal conditions is involved, for perpetuation of the system. In biology, the mechanism for allowing this repeatability is the gene. Its counterpart in the social world is symbolic (language, primarily). In biological models, the gene is not simply the cause, but rather repeatability allows effects to precede cause, so the evolutionary process is not linear. In other words, effects become the cause of cause in a self-regulatory system. Such a view leads to problems of teleology, but Emerson indicated that end-directedness is seen every day. Organisms are selected in terms of future goals. They are fitted to adapt to something in the future. They are selected for variability and change itself. The sexual process, for example, produces controlled variation which allows organisms to change. This is known as the homeostatic regulation of the change process. In addition, group systems and group integration have become important in biology, moving much of evolutionary analysis from the individual organism to the generic level.

Emerson indicated that some concepts of biology are not applicable to social phenomena. For example, mutation is a process requiring longer time spans than are available for an analysis of social change. On the other hand, the "freedom to change," while very slow on the biological level, is much more rapid on the social level, and is much more applicable for social analysis. In reply to a criticism of Condit, Emerson indicated that biological evolution is not rigidly deterministic. In fact, considerable uniqueness exists, requiring the use of probability statistics. For the same reason, the theory is not mechanistic. Emerson further indicated that the utility of biological evolutionary theory lies in analogies with social phenomena. The mechanisms of adaptation may be different, but the analogies yield rough exploratory hypotheses for explanation of social change.

Among other points made by Emerson is one which more or less follows from his remarks about the generic nature of modern evolutionary theory, and bears directly upon the question of increased integration and division of labor accompanying the breakdown of international isolation. To Emerson, a higher level of integration on the societal level does not negate (though it may modify) lower levels of integration (groups, individuals, etc.). The integration of subsystems for the adaptation of the entire system to its environment is not complete. Organisms can subdivide functions and "give" some to a higher level of organization, thus becoming simpler themselves. Tighter and tighter organization, therefore, is not necessarily a consequence of change. Furthermore, subsystem incompatibility in complex organisms can be regulated by, (1) separation of functions (the testicles of mammals are exterior to the body because body heat destroys spermatozoa) and (2) by periodicity or cyclic variations in function as a compromise with the optimum (breathing cycles, etc.).

One of the most striking departures of modern evolutionary theory from older models is the change in levels of abstraction. Substantive categories have been replaced by more abstract concepts. For example, Emerson emphasized several times that change is now viewed as directed toward more complete homeostatic regulation (greater regulation of adaptation) rather than to some given end. In other words, the "ends" are seen as changes in the basic processes of evolution themselves, rather than in some concrete future states of affair. Consequently, greater complexity may not come about with change, but greater regulation may. This aspect is unquestionably a departure from social Darwinism of considerable significance.

Selective Retention Systems

Professor Campbell proved to be the most sympathetic to evolutionary theory of the social scientists at the conference. His views, in general, were quite similar to those of Emerson, although they differed upon a number of specific points. The effect of pointing up these differences in this introduction may be to exaggerate them. Consequently, it should be indicated that he and Emerson presented a position quite favorable to evolutionary theory, differing primarily on problems of applying it to social phenomena.

"Selective retention," as employed by Campbell, refers to adaptive processes of social systems which retain those structures, processes, etc., which lead to greater adaptation to the environment. Campbell indicated that this general notion should be of help in directing research on social change. He felt, however, that analogy should be to the process of biological evolution (i.e., natural selection) rather than to the course of biological evolution (i.e., increased homeostasis, complexity, and division of labor). The analogies at the course-of-evolution level should be viewed as convergences to be explained, rather than as suggestive hypotheses or predictive devices. He indicated an anxiety lest the analogy to the course of evolution introduce teleological pseudo-explanations into social theory. For this reason, Campbell felt that a tendency toward "social-homeostasis" should not be assumed, but rather needs to be explained by social scientists: "The wisdom of evolution is retrospective. If the environment changes, the products of past selection may be stupid." The analogies made between biological and social phenomena need to be examined more carefully.

The problem for the social scientist, then, is to attempt to understand the selective systems involved in any observed similarities. For example, he felt that the notion of "division of labor" has had great utility in both the social and biological sciences. Campbell viewed this phenomenon as an indicator of powerful selective retention systems, systems which need to be examined. But whereas the course of biological evolution is toward a more and more rigid, immutable specialization among the cells, the trend within modern industrial societies is toward increased flexibility in the labor market—a disanalogy in *course* of evolution, but quite understandable from the analogy to the natural selection *process*.

Campbell maintained that rigid homeostatic devices in animals are the result of a relatively stable environment. He felt that the social environment is much less stable, so that homeostasis may not be a useful device or concept for the social sciences. He pointed to India as an example of a highly specialized society adapted to one environment but misadapted to recent changes. Again, the problem for the social scientist, in Campbell's view, is to indicate the selective retention systems of a society, and to determine how they react to change.

Cultural Change

All of the anthropologists and, to some extent Brace, were interested in evolutionary theory as cultural change. Bohannan, Condit, Herskovits and, to a lesser extent, Opler were primarily concerned with the mechanisms of change in culture. The essence of the approach was demonstrated in Bohannan's suggestion that ideas are the greatest impetus to cultural change. Herskovits pointed out that Marxian theories of progress, rather than evolutionary theories, are providing the directions of change throughout most of the world.

Social Change

Although none of the conferees directly equated social change with evolutionary theory, there were a number of exchanges which left the impression that a clear distinction had not been made explicit. Opler indicated some divergences from classical evolutionary theory such as the work of Boas, which he termed "neo-evolutionary." Herskovits indicated that Stewart used "evolution" to mean simply "change," while Tylor used the term to mean "development." As the conference proceeded, however, it became evident that the conferees were aware of differences. At one point Feldman stated unequivocally that his interests were in social change, which had little or no bearing upon "classical" evolutionary theory. Mack agreed, but indicated that Campbell's notions about convergences were of interest to him. Merriam then asked Moskos if his work was really concerned with evolutionary theory or with "regularities in behavior." Moskos indicated interest in the latter, to which Mack and Feldman agreed.

In other words, no single definition of "evolutionary theory" emerged from the conference. The question posed in the title of the conference, therefore, may be answered best by referring to any one of the specific definitions which did emerge. Although it may be difficult to locate the place of formal evolutionary theory in the views of, for example, Feldman and Bell, if one means by "evolutionary theory" social change, then it is central to their approach.

VARIATION AND SELECTIVE RETENTION IN SOCIO-CULTURAL EVOLUTION

DONALD T. CAMPBELL

Northwestern University

This essay will present an advocacy of one type of social-evolutionary theory. While there is currently a revival of interest in theories of socio-cultural evolution[1], the rejection of such theories in the recent past has been so overwhelming[2] that it seems desirable to distinguish carefully among types of evolutionary doctrines, only one of which is being advocated here, and also to examine reasons for the rejection of the once dominant thesis of social evolution. Of the sections which follow, the first two will be devoted to these preliminary tasks.

TYPES OF EVOLUTIONARY THEORY IN SOCIAL SCIENCE

1. Interaction of culture and social organization with man's biological evolution.

Here the word "evolution" refers to transformations in man's biological make-up. Two sub-types may be delineated:

1a. *Genetic influence upon culture.* There is first of all an emphasis upon man's biological evolution as making possible (or causing) his cultural

---

[1] This revival is illustrated or documented in the following: MacIver and Page (1949), Childe (1951), Steward (1955a, 1955b), Greenberg (1957), Roe and Simpson (1958), White (1959a), Meggers (1959), Sahlins and Service (1960), Tax (1960), Cohen (1962), Eisenstatt (1964), Parsons (1964) among others.

[2] For evidence of the rejection, note the record as reported by Becker and Barnes (1952) or by Herskovits (1948). The Boaz, Lowie, Goldenweiser, etc. rejection for anthropology is documented by White (1959a; 1959b; 1960). For sociology, Hofstadter (1944) provides the record. The rejection is also documented by Spengler (1950), and its flavor represented, without documentation, by Faris (1950). Becker and Barnes (1952) also give ample evidence of the earlier prevalence of social-evolutionary theories, a record enhanced by their generous attention to non-Anglo-Saxon sources.

achievements, his use of tools and language, etc. Along with this goes a tendency to regard members of "advanced" cultures as biologically superior to the members of more "primitive" ones, and the members of the "upper classes" as innately superior to those of the "lower classes."

1b.   *Cultural influence upon genetics.* Secondly, there is an emphasis on the effect of social organization and custom upon the genetic stock, leading often to recommendations of social policy. This, combined with the genetic superiority arguments, constitutes that syndrome known as "social Darwinism"[3], generally rejected by social scientists today, independently of their increasing tolerance of other forms of social-evolutionary theory. Social Darwinism was demonstrated in the opposition of Spencer and Sumner to social welfare legislation on the grounds that it weakened the biological race by encouraging the unfit to reproduce. The eugenics movement is an outgrowth of this view, as are the pseudo-scientific rationalizations for racist political ideologies. While outside the topic of this volume, there is an active and respectable form of this culture-affects-genetics interest today, for example, in the Washburn and Howell (1960) hypothesis as to the effect of tool-using upon the evolution of bipedal locomotion and expanded cranial size, and in Sir Charles Galton Darwin's (1960) speculations about the effect of contraceptives upon the future form of innate sexual motives in man. Further, an emphasis upon the social unit as the unit of biological survival, as by Kropotkin (1902, 1924), makes the individualistic dog-eat-dog social Darwinism unnecessary, and provides an evolutionary genetic base for altruism, sympathy, group solidarity, and other social-welfare motives.

2.   Socio-cultural evolution of socio-cultural forms independent of changes in genetic stock.

In this second major form of evolutionary theory in social science, it is technology, language, social organization, and culture that are doing the evolving, through processes that, while perhaps made possible by a certain level of biological evolution, can take place without biological change. To such socio-cultural evolution is attributed the most conspicuous changes on the face of the earth since the dawn of civilization. Evolutionary theories of this form are the concern of the present volume. In further classifying such theories, it will be useful to distinguish between theories describing the course of evolution and theories focusing on social processes that lie behind social evolution. While the greatest elaboration to date has been in the first of these, this article emphasizes the second.

[3] It would seem that the term "social Darwinism" has usually implied social-biological interaction (e.g. Brougle, 1909; Hofstadter, 1944; Banton, 1961; Ginsberg, 1961). However, occasionally it is used to connote purely social evolutionary processes (e.g. Bock, 1963).

2a. *Theories descriptive of the fact and course of socio-cultural evolution.* Such theories are much older than Darwin. They occur in some form in the Greek recognition that their own civilization had evolved from a barbarian-like past. In the hypothesis of continuity in a divergent speciation of the Indo-European languages, the concept is present in the science of linguistics at least by 1788 (Greenberg, 1959; Ginsberg, 1961). It is also this focus which is receiving the most attention in the revival of evolutionary theory in cultural and social anthropology today. Three further subtypes may be usefully distinguished.

2a1. *Non-valuational transformation theories.* These emphasize continuity or gradation in change and the effects of isolation and time upon the differentiation of cultures, without any commitment to the superiority of later forms over earlier ones. This point of view is characteristic of evolutionary thinking in linguistics, (e.g., Greenberg, 1957; 1959). It is Darwinian in sharing the 19th century revolt against the preformationist notions as to the separate creation of each language and species. While this opponent now seems thoroughly routed, the implied commitment of the transformationists in favor of a single source of language or cultural advance may need to be modified to admit of independent invention.

2a2. *Unilinear progress theories.* The social evolution doctrines of Spencer, Tylor, and Morgan which dominated social thought at the turn of the century were by-and-large of this type, even though close reading would show much more complexity and subtlety. In extreme form, such theories posit (a) that all changes in specific cultures or societies represent progress (e.g., advances in complexity of organization, division of labor, size, and energy utilization), (b) that all societies, in the course of their advance, go through the same stages, and hence (c) that the less advanced societies in the contemporary world are similar to earlier stages of the more advanced peoples. It is against such a version of socio-cultural evolution that the overwhelming rejection of the older theories was focused, as well as most current opposition. But, as many have pointed out (e.g., Lesser, 1952; Stewart, 1955; Goldman, 1960, p. 711), the unilinear progress model is not at all typical of evolutionary models, certainly not Darwin's, and the case for socio-cultural evolution should not hinge on its acceptability.

In understanding how such a view could have become dominant, it is well to remember that there were many sources of evolutionary thought in the 19th century besides Darwin. Herbert Spencer, for example, was a vigorous evolutionist before Darwin's *Origin of the Species* was published. His major source of analogical inspiration was embryology, and this model remained dominant in his thinking even though he recognized the greatness of Darwin's theory of natural selection. In the embryological model, the evolution from an "indefinite incoherent homogeneity to a definite coherent heterogeneity" takes place as a result of internal dynamics, independent of environmental contingencies. It is an orderly, progressive, goal-directed unfolding repeated in essential form time and again in widely varying circumstances. In contrast, evolution in the theory of natural selection is a meandering process almost entirely shaped by environmental contingencies, rather than insulated from them.

2a3. *Multilinear progress theories.* For these theories, the model is biological species formation rather than embryological development. Thus it is expected that developments from a common origin diverge in reflection of divergent environmental conditions. Parallel environmental conditions in widely differing locales would produce parallel evolutionary sequences (e.g., Steward, 1955), but parallels would only be expected under such conditions. In each of the multiple lines of speciation, there is progress or increasing adaptive adequacy, but along such divergent lines as the divergent environments make optimal. Such a speciation model is advocated in some degree by Lesser (1952), Steward (1955), Goldman (1960), and Sahlins (1958) in his concept of adaptive variation.

2b. *Theory descriptive of the process of evolution: variation and selective retention.* The above theories of socio-cultural evolution all focus on describing the course of such evolution, rather than describing the processes which produce it. More specifically, it is the variation-and-selective-retention process which seems appropriately borrowed from biological evolution, rather than analogues to the course of biological evolution. Thus while the speciation model is more appropriate for social evolution than is embryological development, there are still many important disanalogies, due to differences in the selection and retention processes involved.

Although the natural selection concept may seem an obvious tautology once formulated, it, rather than the concept of evolution, was Darwin's main theoretical contribution, as he himself recognized. By this process, concepts of planned shaping and teleological emergence became unnecessary. Instead, blind and haphazard variations, when differentially propagated due to the exigencies of different environments, could account not only for drift and divergent speciation, but also for the exquisitely purpose-like fit of organic form to environmental opportunity, and for progressive advance in adaptedness and complexity.

Therefore, it is odd that the Darwinian enthusiasm in social-evolutionary theorizing produced so little in the way of attention to variation, selection, and the transmission of selected variants. Although some slight attention was paid to such processes by Tylor and Morgan (Opler, this volume), and others (Childe, 1950; Ginsberg, 1961; Cohen, 1962), only in Keller's uneven but unduly neglected *Societal Evolution* (1915, 1931) does it become the focus of attention.

REASONS FOR THE REJECTION OF EVOLUTIONARY THEORY IN THE SOCIAL SCIENCES

The faults of the unilinear model were certainly an inadequate base for the overwhelming rejection by social scientists of all theories of social evolution. Better models were readily available from biology. Revision could have corrected the faults established by the critics without destroying the impressive scope of the theory. Yet the rejection was overwhelming, and persists in strength to this day. In attempting a revival of social-evolutionary theory, it is not enough to blame the past rejection upon the personal influence and unexplained idiosyncracy of Boas. White at times (e.g., 1945, 1959a, 1959b) comes near to such a "great-man" explanation, even though he argues against such explanations in principle. Instead, we have the problem of explaining why Boas had this reaction, and why these "erroneous" ideas proved to be so attractive to others as to make Boas a revered and honored scholar in his day. (White [1960] has indeed made a few comments on this problem, although not along the lines to be offered here.)

It seems to me that a major factor was the early contamination of the evolutionary perspective with the reactionary political viewpoints of the privileged classes and racial supremicist apologists for colonialism, exclusionist immigration laws, etc. While it is unfair to stereotype either Herbert Spencer or William Graham Sumner as conservatives (Spencer was a pacifist eager to advocate perspectives shocking to traditional beliefs; Sumner was willing to preach atheism from his classroom pulpit at Yale, and opposed the protective tariff at a time when Yale's industrial patrons favored it) yet by and large, the great bulk of their position favored the cause of the economic and social elite. Moreover, both were willing to meddle in politics as pamphleteers, speaking out vigorously against taxation and government protection of the weak. The vigor of their convictions came, I believe, from their enthusiastic adoption of the new evolutionary theory. It would be unfair, I believe, to portray them as the "kept" academic apologists for the powerful and greedy interests of their day. Nonetheless, they ended up in the position of justifying a generation of ruthless industrial exploitation too strong for the public conscience, or the social scientist's conscience, to bear.

This political ideology was the application of their social Darwinism, i.e., of theory of types 1a and 1b above, and an overly individualistic version even of that. It might seem incompatible with, or at least, independent of, the advocacy of the socio-cultural evolutionary theory, which is primarily at issue here. The contamination occurred, however, because the socio-cultural evolutionist was usually also a social Darwinist. The attraction of the evolutionary perspective was so great that the enthusiasts applied it concurrently at all levels. This is very clear in the case of Herbert Spencer, the most widely read of all in his day, and it holds true for Sumner and Keller as well. In the case of Keller, I should like to report some previously unrecorded field notes in the sociology of knowledge:

In the spring of 1955, Professor Richard D. Schwartz and I visited Keller in his home in New Haven. Keller was an old man, and had been Emeritus since 1942. He welcomed us as befitted a neglected emeritus professor and one who had been disregarded everywhere but at Yale even in his years of vigor. But whereas we saw him as one whose original contributions in *Societal Evolution* had been neglected due to the stereotyped expectation that he could do nothing but rehash Sumner, he himself had none of this feeling. Instead, he still played the disciple's role, proudly showing us Sumner's files of notes, still confident that much unexploited value lay in them (even after the tedious posthumous extraction of the 4 volumes of *The Science of Society* [Sumner, Keller, and Davie, 1927] from them).

In spite of the very old man's kindly hospitality, we—for the sake of science—were bold enough to probe his political beliefs. Expressing our admiration for his variation-and-selective retention model of societal change, we interpreted this to him as a justification of Roosevelt's New Deal policies: At a time when the old social system seemed to be working badly it would seem but applied Kellerism to strike out with innovative institutions in a variety of directions—their very ideological heterogeneity increasing the likelihood of encountering a useful social invention—to be followed (as had indeed been the case) by a perpetuation of those few innovations that seemed to work, retained even by the Republican successors.

Keller would have none of this. It was clear that his conservative political loyalties were much stronger than his loyalty to his own one original contribution to science. It also became clear that his careful distinction in *Societal Evolution* between increased adaptedness (toward which his theory pointed) and progress, had the role of expressing his conservative's conviction that whichever party was in power, society was currently changing for the worse. He turned out to be a stereotyped reactionary and a fan of Westbrook Pegler. He even went so far as to joke about Eleanor Roosevelt's teeth. He spoke with regret of how one of his former students, by the name of Reid, had allowed his *New York Tribune* to become a left-wing propaganda sheet, etc. In all, he was a convincing single case study of a correlation between social Darwinism and political conservatism which Hofstadter (1944)

309.1724 B277a
c.1

and Pastore (1949) have documented with persuasive numbers of instances.

In addition to social Darwinism, another aspect of early socio-cultural evolutionism furthered its alliance with a defense of the status quo. The cultural stages proposed uniformly placed the social scientist's own culture at the apex of the cultural ladder (even though in the Marx-Engels version this was but a predecessor of a still more perfect stage), providing "scientific" support to the natural ethnocentrism of the nation.

To complete the argument it is necessary to provide an explanation for the preponderant social-legal reformism or social ameliorism which, it is hypothesized, made the ideological overtones of evolutionary theories anathemas to the majority of the social scientists from 1900 to the present day. At the most general level, one could say that the social scientists held these attitudes because they were typical of (if a few decades ahead of) the general public of their time. This public in England and America has persistently and increasingly enacted the kind of restraints upon exploitation and the kind of welfare legislation which the social Darwinists opposed. The appearance of explicitly racist doctrines in the Nazi German dictatorship and the popular Anglo-American rejection of such doctrines has further consolidated this public sentiment. The social scientists can thus be seen as rejecting the social evolutionary doctrines as their part of a general public reaction to the excesses of a dog-eat-dog industrial and commercial era. Anti-trust legislation, the graduated income tax, the protective tariffs and social security provisions can be interpreted as cosymptoms of the general trends which also produced the rejection of evolutionary theories in the social sciences.

One can go further than this by noting special features in the recruitment of social scientists, leading them to be more hostile to the social status quo than are people in general. Participation in the social sciences would seemingly require a willingness to examine critically the culturally given and to consider alternatives. A profession with such prerequisites would tend to recruit persons who were not only willing to challenge the culturally given, but eager to do so. The zenophilia so often noted among anthropologists may be a symptom of a more basic ethnophobia. Some such orientation may be a prerequisite for a creative and open-minded participation in our profession. In the first generation, evolutionary theory was attractive to such social scientists through its shocking attack upon accepted cultural beliefs. As this wore off, as the perspective became generally accepted, its more specific role in apology for established special privilege became the dominant image to which the social scientist reacted.

It is intrinsic to the sciences of culture that a cultural provincialism is a liability to the scientist, and that a cultural heterogeneity of background gives an advantage (Veblen, 1919; Park, 1928; Seeman, 1956). But persons of such backgrounds, including minority group members, are often rejected by the entrenched ingroup, producing a resentment of the establishment on the part of those particularly apt to be creative social scientists. And for scholarly professions more generally, note that their relative objectivity in the evaluation of worth (as compared with the established social and business worlds) makes them favored channels for upward mobility for the industrious and talented from among the disadvantaged lower classes and segregated minority groups. All of these features support the expectation of a general recruitment to the leadership of the social sciences of those with a negative attitude toward the dominant powers of the status quo. Such a recruitment combined with the explicit ideological stance of the social Darwinists, makes understandable, and perhaps inevitable, the widespread acceptance of those such as Boas, who presented plausible criticisms.

These explanatory efforts are, perhaps, unnecessary both in detail and in kind. For I have attempted to explain a shift of fads in the social sciences in terms of the specific content of those fads. Perhaps no content-specific explanation is needed. Until the social sciences become more truly scientific than they were in 1900 or 1930, until, that is, they become truly cumulative, building upon past achievements, until then, boredom itself becomes an adequate explanation for the abandonment of any once-dominant theoretical point of view. In these terms, the great popularity of social-evolutionary theory is sufficient to explain its later rejection. The psychology of stimulus satiation, the need for new experience, provides the necessary motivating force for such a content-free explanation, as does the sociology of social science in terms of the rewards offered for pseudo-innovation.

VARIATION-AND-SELECTIVE-RETENTION IN SOCIO-CULTURAL EVOLUTION

Three basic requirements. Rather than an analogy to the course of organic evolution, this section offers an analogy between natural selection in biological evolution and the selective propagation of cultural forms. Analogies are, of course, not sources of proof, but sources of hypotheses. Even so, they are widely suspect. It may make the analogy less objectionable in the present case to make the analogy an indirect one. The analogy to cultural cumulations will not be from organic evolution *per se*, but rather from a general model for adaptive fit or quasiteleological processes for which organic evolution is but one instance.

Today, the most exciting current contribution of Darwin is in his model for the achievement of purposive or ends-guided processes through a mechanism involving blind, stupid, unforesightful elements. In recent years, the cyberneticist Ashby (1952), Pringle (1951) and others have pointed out anew the formal parallel between natural selection in organic evolution and trial-and-error learning. The common analogy also has been recognized in many other loci, as in embryonic growth, wound healing, crystal formation, development of science, radar, echo-location, vision, creative thinking, etc. (e.g., Mach, 1896; Spiegelman, 1948; Popper, 1959; Campbell, 1956, 1959, 1960). The three essentials are these:

1. The occurrence of variations: heterogeneous, haphazard, "blind", "chance", "random", but in any event variable. (The mutation process in organic evolution, and exploratory responses in learning).

2. Consistent selection criteria: selective elimination, selective propagation, selective retention, of certain types of variations. (Differential survival of certain mutants in organic evolution, differential reinforcement of certain responses in learning).

3. A mechanism for the preservation, duplication, or propagation of the positively selected variants (the rigid duplication process of the chromosome-gene system in plants and animals, memory in learning).

Given these conditions, an evolution in the direction of better fit to the selective system becomes inevitable. It is through such a process of selective cumulation of the unlikely that the extremely improbable and marvelous combinations found in plants and animals become, in fact, highly probable. As understood by present-day biologists, the elegantly engineered and complexly coordinated animals have been developed through this uncoordinated, unforesightful, unplanned, elementaristic process.

If there are representatives of these three requirements at the level of social forms and customs, then a socio-cultural "evolutionary" process, or a socio-cultural "learning" process is inevitable. If analogues of these three requirements are in operation, then there will occur drift pressures toward increased adaptedness, and toward increased complexity, size, and integration of social organizational units, if such increases give selective advantage. If these are granted, then the fact of socio-cultural evolution no longer remains problematic. It is not obvious, however, that these conditions do, in fact, hold. Accepting the theory it could still be that the requirements are not met and that societal evolution does not occur. This could happen because of the absence of any one of the requisites. Thus, there could be an absence of variation in the enactment of cultural forms in any one generation, although this is scarcely conceivable. Much more doubtful is the presence of consistent selection pressures operating over long enough periods and involving sufficiently large populations of social units to average out the purely fortuitous. It is also possible that positively selected variants might be lost through a social-reproduction (indoctrination, education) system too inaccurate to pass on the essentials of the innovation. It is with such problems, and with an attempt to be more specific as to possible details, that the following paragraphs deal.

Variation

It is obvious that variation in the execution of socio-cultural forms is continually taking place, so that this requirement is easily met. Such variations can be of several kinds: On the one hand, there can be variations between social groups, as in the form of social organization or some item of material culture. Equally relevant are internal variations such as differences between persons within a group in their execution of a common custom. Also usable are variations across occasions, as in the execution of some collective organizational problem. Such variations provide adequate raw materials for selective systems to operate on, whether the variations are deliberate or haphazard. The more numerous and the greater the heterogeneity among variations, the richer the opportunities for an advantageous innovation. Note, however, that at many levels of cultural development, and for organic evolution, variation is at the expense of jeopardizing the already achieved adaptive system. Too high a mutation rate threatens the preservations of the complexly adapted animal form. Nonetheless, other things being equal, those social-environmental settings providing the greatest range of variations, are the most likely to produce cultural advances. The heterogeneity of variants provided in the cultural crossroads and melting pots predisposes them to be the sites of novel emergents, as Teggart (1952), Park (1928), and others have pointed out. Similarly, a cultural norm valuing change, progress, and innovation should produce more variation.

If the same range of variations occur, it does not, of course, matter what the source of the variations is. "Deliberate" or "intelligent" variations would do as well as "blind," "haphazard," "chance," "random," or "spontaneous" ones. They might be better insofar as they could be pre-selected. But they might be worse in that they could be restricted to the implications of already achieved wisdom and would not be likely to go beyond it. One of the services of terms like "blind" and "haphazard" in the model is that they emphasize that elaborate adaptive social system, such as the priesthood dominated irrigation civilizations, (Steward, 1955) could have emerged, just as did termite societies, without any self-conscious planning or foresightful action. It provides a plausible model for social systems that are "wiser" than the individuals who constitute the society, or than the rational social science of the ruling elite. It provides an anticipation of powerful "in-advertent" social change processes in our own day which may be adaptive in unforeseen or unwanted ways.

Selective Systems

The potential selective systems are so numerous and so intertwined, and the selective criteria so difficult to specify, that quite respectable intellectual grounds are provided for a denial of the existance of a socio-cultural evolutionary process. Even if one does not go that far, one must nonetheless face up to the difficulties involved. It has seemed to reduce the complexity of the presentation to postpofie the discussion of selection criteria to a subsequent section, even though implicitly they will be involved all through this discussion. In this section some six selective systems will be discussed. But first here are some concrete examples to be held in mind while considering the systems.

The work Bavelas, Leavitt, Guetzkow and others (see Guetzkow, 1961) has made it seem likely that a social division of labor or differentiation of roles to provide a single coordinator or communications clearing-house has adaptive value. Thus in Guetzkow's laboratory experiments, groups having a limited hub-spokes pattern of communication channels among five persons are superior to those having all channels open. Further, the all-channel groups improve through a communications-delegation process in which many channels fall into disuse, evolving toward a hub-spokes pattern. Were this pattern be found to have general superiority in the coordination of information and action on the part of aggregates of persons, then the variation-and-selective-retention system would explain the ubiquitous presence of headship institutions, in groups capable of collective action, in indigenous cultures the world over. What selective systems would have made this possible? Aubert (1959) provides this example of an adaptive superstition: Norwegian fishing boats once located new fishing sites by the divination process of pouring water over a sand map of the sea and coastal areas, locating the new fishing site as the spot where bubbles first rose. Aubert points out two selective advantages. On the one hand, it is a randomization process insuring that a wide range of possibilities get explored (see also Moore, 1957). On the other hand, it has the social solidarity value of leaving no one fisherman to blame for suggesting a site upon which a tedious day's labor was wasted. What are the several selective systems that could have established this custom?

The organization of what follows is built upon the three modes of variation described above: variations among social units, variations among occasions within a social unit, and variations among the members of a social unit.

The selective survival of complete social organizations. The older discussions of socio-cultural evolution seem to overly depend upon the selective survival of total cultural systems, tribes, nations, etc., with elimination by biological death of the people, or the disappearance of the culture and/or social organization. Taking the society-organism analogy literally, this becomes the appropriate mode of selection. But the general model does not require this limitation, and it is a part of the disanalogy between organic and social evolution. Because of the differences in the social preservation system, and because of the greater variety of integrational organizations compatible with effective collective action, human social organizations, unlike the organizations of cells in the body and unlike the social organizations of insects, can be varied and eliminated and modified on a part-by-part basis (Childe, 1951). Nonetheless, it is conceivable that headship and fishing-site divination became dominant through the extinction of total societies lacking these customs. Furthermore, this selection system is somehow more fundamental and "direct" in its encounter with reality than are those listed below.

Selective diffusion or borrowing between social groups. Another selective system applicable to variations between social units is differential diffusion. Students of the diffusion process have regularly noted its selective nature. Groups seen as prospering would presumably be more borrowed-from. Compatibility with the borrowing culture also becomes a selective requirement. Thus, headship could have been spread and the fishing-divination become regionally dominant through the selective diffusion of these customs in competition with alternative customs. The historical presentation of evolutionist and diffusionist theories in anthropology as incompatible, is certainly wrong, as White (1945) has effectively argued. But it is diffusion that rules out both the embryological and the multilinear speciation models from biology as detailed analogies to socio-cultural evolution. Childe (1951), Ginsberg (1961) and Waddington (1961) have emphasized this point.

Selective propagation of temporal variations. If a given group of hunters tried out various coordination and decision systems on various hunting occasions, then the differential memories of pleasure and pain associated with each occasion would lead to a greater willingness to repeat those associated with success, and in this manner a headship system or a divination system could become established. This selective process is based upon individual pleasure-pain and memory systems. While it involves individual learning, it can provide for the selective retention of inter-personal arrangements or social system features.

Selective-imitation of inter-individual variations. Many aspects of an evolving culture are items of individual or subgroup performance. For these, variations within the group provide the raw material for several selective systems. At the psychological level, there are the laws of "imitation" or "conformity" which provide a selective process. In the "observation learning" processes, those acts of another most rewarding to the model tend to be imitated, and those acts most punished tend to be inhibited in future performances of the observer. This generalizes to a tendency to imitate even those acts for which the outcomes are not observed, with the most usually successful persons being most imitated (Campbell, 1961). Such processes could account for the selective evolution of fish-hook shape, and of divination procedures on the part of crews of fishing boats. As the boundary of the socio-evolutionary unit becomes arbitrary, between this selective system and selective diffusion disappears.

Selective promotion to leadership and educational roles. For those traits upon which intra-group variations can occur, the selective elevation to roles of differential influence of those persons who happen to vary customary usage in more adaptive fashion could lead to the general establishment of such variations.

Rational selection. In honor of older treatments such as Keller's (1915, 1931) and in honor of legislative planning, forecasting, simulating and rational decision-making processes on the part of modern societies, cognizance should be taken of rational, deliberate, or culturally-self-conscious selective processes. For these, the social group's knowledge of social process and its estimate of external selective factors would be employed as a substitute for the real selective factors, in an effort to think out in advance the relative adaptiveness of alternative cultural changes. While such selective systems undoubtedly cut down on the waste involved in the selective elimination of social systems, their efficacy is obviously limited by the state of knowledge. Furthermore, just because certain social institutions may seem to be "rational" solutions to complex problems is no indication that rational selection or planning was involved in their development. For note in contrast, the still more elegant "rational solutions" produced without rational selection in the course of organic evolution, as in the visual system.

Selective Criteria

There is bound to be a lot of the purely fortuitous or non-transferably specific in the life or death of a single biological individual or social system or culture item. For a systematic selective criterion to make itself felt above this "noise level," there must be numerous instances involved, and a high mortality rate. Thus we would be more apt to expect effective selective criteria to exist for neighborhood laundry organizations than for national organizational form. In the latter case, the environment or selective criteria may be too inconsistent, and the number of units too small, for any evolutionary process to take place.

How can we decide, for the social system, whether any persistent selective criteria have operated, or are now operating, to produce any consistent differential propagation of certain forms? Are there any "eternal verities" or external truths to which social organizations must conform? If survival or non-survival is a purely random matter, no evolution will take place. For organic evolution, we have our human common-sense and scientific understanding of much of the environmental selective system operating on lower animals. We know the physics of air, water and light to which the swimming, flying, and seeing apparatuses of the lower animals must conform. For the study of social evolution, we have no such semi-independent descriptions of the selective criteria.

This may be a major reason why the students of social systems have never been as awed by the adaptive fit, or the functional validity, of cultural products as biologists have been for biological products, even long before Darwin's day. If we assumed a social-evolutionary process, we might, as social scientists, examine each weird custom and incredible social belief with a little more of the respect shown by a biologist examining a strange form of life, the function of which he does not understand. The very fact that a custom goes against what would be the simple perceptions and rational constructions of a naive observer, means that it has withstood persistent selection pressures in the direction of more rational or hedonistically satisfying form (Jacobs & Campbell, 1961). The development of formal and compelling theories of organization, spelling out the requirements that have to be met for collectives of different sizes and degrees of coordination, may, in the end, provide a convincing picture of the selective system. However, this organizational "reality" to which social groups must conform may have, in the end, been inferred from an analysis of the social organizations themselves, providing an undesirable circularity. Something like this is also encountered on occasion in the study of biological evolution, in which the selective system is inferred from the organic form.

Another source of doubt regarding the evolutionary direction of social change comes from the very multiplicity of the social selection systems. The diffusion, imitation, and promotion systems are obviously capable of being selective in ways irrelevant to group effectiveness or social adaptedness. And if we exist in an epoch in which these mechanisms are unchecked for survival relevance, the total process may not be evolutionary in an adaptive sense. A distinction can be drawn between internal selectors and external selectors. The selective criterion whereby random processes form orderly crystals is the internal one of stable combinations among molecules. When such combinations occur by chance they tend to stay put, while others continue to change, thus leading to a biased accumulation of orderly arrangements. These internal stability requirements are one criterion in the formation of protein and DNA molecules. But external selective pressures enter the course of biological evolution, differentially modifying the reproductive opportunity of different molecules of equivalent internal stability.

Another type of internal selection criterion occurs when processes of evolution build in internal selective criteria which are vicarious representatives of external selectors. Thus the nutritiousness of foods represents an external criterion of direct survival relevance. It is represented in us by approximately appropriate internal selective criteria of taste buds and associated pleasure and pain mechanisms, which become the predominately effective selective criteria in our choosing of foods. The adaptive appropriateness of these vicarious criteria are to past ecologies, and if the environment has markedly changed, the vicarious selective system may operate in ways irrelevant to current adaptiveness.

Analogues of both kinds of internal selectors may be found in social selection systems. A process of habit-meshing takes place within any organization, in that each person's habits are a part of the environment of the others. Encounters which are punishing tend to extinguish both habit and maze. Rewarding encounters increase the strength of behavioral tendencies on the part of both parties. Thus any social organization tends to move in the direction of internal compatibility, independently of increased adaptiveness. Bureaucratic rigidity and inefficiency is one end product of a process in which internal selective criteria have operated, without the curb of external relevance. Of the selective mechanisms described above, selective diffusion, selective propagation of temporal and inter-individual variations, and selective promotion could all operate in the service of such internal goals. Analysis will be difficult in many cases because of the similar appearance but genuine survival-relevance of coordination *per se*, and of retention mechanisms which loyally preserve past adaptive achievements. Internal selective criteria vicariously representing past external criteria may also be expected at the social level, as in the group's ideal of leadership, as it is used in promotional systems, and in concepts of duty and virtue used in the selective reinforcement of individual actions.

At the level of human social organization, adaptive relevance will depend on the attribute in question, as well as the selective system. Where individual advantage and group advantage are clearly coordinate, as in systems of food gathering, for example, the less direct selective systems such as diffusion, emulation, and the selective propagation of intra-group variation, may be expected to have adaptive relevance. Where optimal group functioning requires curbs on individual advantage, selective criteria disfunctional at the group level may be expected.

Retention Systems

One of the things that impresses one in comparing biological evolution with socio-cultural evolution is the greater rigidity and loyalty of the biological retention system. Corresponding to this, no doubt, is the greater mutability and diversity of societal forms, so that in any modern society, by the time a total replacement of individuals has taken place (i.e., over the course of 50 to 100 years) the system has become a different "species," so to speak.

This may, of course, merely be a function of our point-of-observation from within the current system. There may be a great rigidity of form-preservation in which we unknowingly participate. And certainly, it does seem that in non-literate, non-industrial societies, an impressive rigidity of social institutions, a blind loyalty to past traditions, can be observed. The 19th century social scientists were very much impressed with the "dead hand of tradition," with the "cake of custom" (Bagehot, 1884). Nonetheless, the absence of an effective retention system would be grounds for rejecting the notion of socio-cultural evolution.

Retention systems themselves are subject to selective-retention editing. On these grounds we would expect the greatest rigidity, the greatest demand for conformity, on the part of those societies with the more elaborate adaptive systems, particularly when these systems demand restraint upon individual hedonistic impulse (which would represent a systematic selective force counter to the social institution). Consider, for example, a tillage society in which the seasonal rituals are carried out on superstitious, uncomprehending grounds. Individualistic impulse must be countered to preserve the seed for the spring planting against the hunger of winter famine. Planting and cultivation work must be done months ahead of the reinforcing results of the harvest. Barry, Child, and Bacon (1959) have compared the conformity pressures in child rearing of tillage and hunting cultures of comparable size and subsistence level. They find, as would be expected, the greater conformity pressure, the greater demand for unquestioning adherence to tradition, in the tillage cultures. The requirements of blind and loyal preservation of unrationalized cultural inventions makes understandable the important role of a priesthood and religious belief-system in each of the several independent developments of irrigation civilizations, as Steward (1955a, 1955b) has documented.

Such considerations alone might lead us to expect an increase in the degree of superstitious adherence to tradition with increasing elaborateness of culture. While this might well be true within the range of pre-literate societies, it would be hard to defend when encompassing the increasing elaborateness of modern industrial societies. However, in one broad sense, this truism may hold: the more elaborate the culture, the greater the amount of time devoted to passing on the cumulated tradition, i.e., the longer the educational process. There are probably grounds for surmising that some fundamental changes have taken place in the retention system. This paper can only point to the problem. There has probably been a progressive "externalization" of culture, so that there is less conflict between individualistic reward and punishment systems and societal demands. The increasing "rationalization" of culture may have similar effects. More and more of our tradition is embodied in our material culture rather than in our oral-mnemonic culture, not only in the form of written records, but also in the form of machinery, buildings, roads, etc., that become as coercive for individual learning as the physical realities of the natural environment.

There is, perhaps, always a potential conflict between the freedom to vary, which makes advance possible, and the value of retaining the cultural accumulation. But the invention of writing emancipates modern man from this to a remarkable degree. In a pre-literate society the cultural wisdom is preserved not only orally, but, more importantly, by that enactment of culture, which provides not only a model for the indoctrinees, but also a coercive set of other peoples' behaviors, with which the indoctrinee's own learned behavior must come to terms. At such a stage, each person varying the tradition is one less enacting it, thus reducing the likelihood of its transmission. Hence, no doubt, the strongly ingrained fear of innovation in many indigenous cultures. With the cultural wisdom in writing, such fears are less realistic. In addition, the written records make the temporal variations in the selection of adaptive forms more usable.

If the emphasis upon the adaptedness of cultures reduces the social scientist's authorization to stand in judgment of cultural institutions and call them evil, the emphasis upon the probable past selection for blindly rigid preservation systems gives him new authorization, wherever he can point to a change in the environmental realities. The "wisdom" produced by biological and societal evolution is retrospective, referring to past environments. It is only adaptive to the extent that these environments remain stable. Yet the rigid preservation systems essential for the process of evolution, also provide for a retention of these systems long beyond their usefulness. Where the social scientist can point to a modern change in the ecology or selective system, he can justify an assertion that the relevant institutions are inappropriate. Thus while in the past, man's capacity for ethnocentric loyalty, willingness for altruistic self-sacrifice in warfare, and capacity for out-group hate may have been positively selected, the changes introduced in the environment by modern weapons and increased national size may make the once-noble virtues self-destructive anachronisms. They may however, be so firmly embedded in the social-motivational nature of man that social planners will have to reckon with them for some time to come.

SOME IMPLICATIONS OF THE SELECTIVE RETENTION MODEL

Independent invention: The implications of the selective-retention model are, on some points, divergent from those often drawn from evolutionary theory. The blind-variation-and-selective-retention model strongly predicts independent invention for variations and variation-combinations of powerful selective advantage. Modern biochemical evolutionary theory predicts the "spontaneous generation" of nucleic acids, of protein molecules, of "life," wherever the physical conditions are appropriate for a long enough time. At a lower level, the repeated independent invention of the basic "elements" from hydrogen atoms is predicted, given appropriate temperature, pressure, and other conditions. The selective factors here are the conditions of stability. The basic elements of the periodic table are now seen as the loci of stable combinations of the subatomic particles. These "internal" selective criteria of stability, balance, resistance to disruption, can re-sort the subatomic materials into the chemical elements again and again. When "competitive" self-duplicating molecules occur, the external selective systems come into play. It is upon these natural selection or evolutionary grounds at the biochemical level that scientists are becoming increasingly convinced of the existence of independently invented life on other suitable planets of suitable solar systems of suitable galaxies. There are so many heavenly bodies, and so many temporal epochs for each, that it is incredible that none but Earth should be suitable.

In the traditional theory of biological evolution, this implication of the natural selection model is most clearly specified in the fact and concept of *convergent* evolution. Thus the aero-dynamic realities and the selective payoff have led winged flight to be independently invented by insects, pterodactyls, birds, and bats. There are apparently ecological niches for both meat eaters and vegetarians (note the convergent evolution of both marsupial wolves and herbivores in Australia). There is apparently an ecological niche for wood-peckers, and so, lacking rivals, Darwin's finches upon Galapagos convergently and independently evolved a pseudo-woodpecker, as well as a number of other non-finch-like forms. The complex eye in a very similar form has been independently invented by the octopus and the vertebrates. The image forming eye gives a tremendous selective advantage. There are, apparently, several lineages upon which variations in this direction are advantageous enough to "shape" development toward this common optical form. It is due to the convergence of forms upon the advantageous niches or nodes, that strongly functional characteristics often become unusable in the genealogical classification of plants and animals, while the irrelevant and vestigal incidentals carry the evidence of the history of descent, as

Darwin recognized. The great heterogeneity and the tremendous numbers of variations make almost inevitable the "accidental discovery" of any strongly adaptive form that lies "near" in number of mutation links to any prior form. It further makes it probable that any powerfully adaptive form will be approached from a variety of "directions", providing viable intermediaries exist.

Note the possibility here of arguing backwards: in those cases where we do not understand the selective system independently, but do find a convergent evolution on a common form we could argue a common advantageous selective system. The convergence would have provided independent triangulation on the functional reality, disentangling it from irrelevant genealogical carryover in each line. As will be pointed out below, it may be appropriate to use this argument for the selection of social forms, where we do not yet understand the environment, or the selective system, as well as we do the environments relevant to the forms of wings and eyes.

The fact that variation-and-selective-retention theory strongly predicts independent invention, makes it very appropriate to the data on independent discovery and invention in science and technology, as studied by Ogburn and Thomas (1922), Kroeber (1917) and Barber (1952). Here in a well studied field of culture history, the application of Darwin's specific contribution to evolutionary theory enables us to legitimately shift our language from cultural *history* to cultural *evolution*. If indeed many persons are, in thought or action, trying many variations on a common body of technology or science, and if a few variation-steps away there is indeed a marvelous device or conceptualization available, then many are likely to encounter it. This becomes no more incredible than that two rats in the same maze discover the same efficient running pattern. A reflexive example: Darwin's theoretical discovery was to him an emotionally exciting insight, so different from ordinary thought yet fitting the problem so well. Spencer and others in his day showed this great admiration for it, and wondered how, coming so close to it themselves, they had missed it. Yet it was so selectively advantageous and available to ordinary thought by such a few steps that it was almost inevitable that others would hit upon it, as indeed they had; not only Wallace, but, as Zirkle (1941) has so carefully documented, Empedocles and many more. The discovery was inevitable. The theory would have eventually become generally accepted, even if Darwin had never published. A variation-and-selective-retention theory makes us understand this inevitability. While such data series have been used to emphasize, correctly, a cultural reality independent of individual geniuses, they equally support a Darwinian analogue in socio-cultural evolution. And how much better it is to study the selective system than to impute causal status and free will to the "Zeitgeist" or "cultural bent."

If the natural selection model so strongly presages multiple independent lineages even for highly similar forms, how then has social evolutionary theory so frequently connoted unilinear sequences and a single common origin? The answer may perhaps lie in the almost forgotten background of ideas about creation against which Darwin argued.

Darwin had to make a case against a belief in the special creation of each species. A still-essential part of his argument was that behind each species lay a continuous ancestry of simpler and simpler forms back to some unicellular progenitor. In this sense, a line of stages is essential. Also essential was establishing that, through isolation and ecological diversity a wide variety of species could be developed from a single ancestry, and that this had in fact been so in specific cases. Both of these can be said without alleging that life was created only once, with all forms diversifying from this single spark. For those in Darwin's day who wished to soften the blow to religious belief, it may have seemed best to substitute the miracle of a single creation of life for the many separate miracles, one for each species. This single miracle might have seemed less miraculous had it been understood as liable to repeated occurrence. Today biologists and biochemists anticipate the "artificial" or "experimental" generation of life-like complex molecules in the laboratory. Probably most biological evolutionists would allow for multiple "spontaneous generations" for some virus species, even if perhaps only from once organic materials. Some virus are based upon simple enough and few enough molecule types so that independent inventions of "the same" virus is conceivable. At the same time, the shared intricacies of the gene-chromosome system, the elaborate ceremonies of mitotic cell division common to cellular plants and animals, probably carry conviction to biologists that these all diversified from a common ancestor. Strangely enough, however, were physicists and chemists working on the problem of large complexly coordinated self-duplicating molecule groups, to become convinced that the gene-chromosome mitotic cell division system was the only system *physically* possible, this would increase the likelihood of independent generation, in the sense that it would remove the strength of the argument for common ancestry based upon similarity in specific details.

For social evolution, the blind-variation-and-selective-retention model would seem to make plausible the multiple independent invention of tools, rope making, fire, spear, bow-and-arrow, monogamy, the avunculate, and headship in social organization. The case may be less clear for the compound bow, for soap, for first-fruits sacrifices, for wheat cultivation, and for enti-fying, noun-verb language. The more complex the cultural preconditions for the invention, the more variation-steps involved, and the rarer the ecological opportunities for its first appearance, the less plausible independent invention

becomes on purely *a priori* grounds. Archeological and geological reconstructions of diffusion opportunities are, of course, to be consulted when
specific cultural forms are at issue. The main point is that both from the
selective-retention theory, and from the European record for recent technological advances, independent invention seems more credible than it did to
some diffusionist theorists forty years ago.

Progress, adaptedness, and *niche-filling.* Do selective-retention processes
predict an inevitable progress in evolution? Biologists do not now answer
simply, as a reading of Simpson (1949) will show. Rather, the certain
prediction is that every ecological niche adjacent to any other ecological
niche will come to be filled. By an ecological niche is meant a viable mode
of living. Any mode of living that is near enough to another mode of living
to be entered by a blind mutation will be entered, for if the niche is empty,
if no other organism occupies it, the selective advantages of entering it are
initially very great. For the field of living forms the empty adjacent niches
have sometimes been in directions of reduced complexity, smaller size, etc.
Thus Darwin cited the case of the barnacle, whose immediate ancestors were
more complex swimming, seeing, animals. Thus in recent evolutionary developments, the many new viruses are very primitive forms filling ecological
niches not available prior to the evolution of warm-blooded animals.
Parasites in general show "degenerative" evolution. Since current forms at
all levels of complexity may be highly adapted to their niches, it is hard to say
that one is "fitter" or more "advanced" than another. Such are the sources
of the caution of biologists in pronouncing any dogma of evolution and
progress. This does not lead them to give up evolutionary theory, however.
Their sources of caution are quite comparable to the protests of the cultural
relativists in anthropology, who emphasize the excellent adaptedness and
internal coherence of simple cultures as of complex ones; who refuse to
identify size with excellence or moral worth; and who recognize the provincial
ethnocentrism of many social evolutionists in their assumption of their own
culture's superiority. Analogously, however, one may be a cultural relativist
within the framework of a correct social evolutionary theory. Indeed, the
relativist's frequent emphasis upon the adaptiveness or functional validity of
customs that seem bizarre to outsiders implies a selective retention and
elimination process.

But apart from this lessened dogmatism there remain senses in which a
progressive direction is indicated by the blind-variation-and-selective-
retention theory of evolution, for both organic and socio-cultural evolution.
Over the whole course of evolution, the simpler combinations come first, and
it follows that the great bulk of adjacent ecological niches are in the direction
of greater complexity—"there's always room on top" as it were. In general,

the "degenerative" ecological niches do not occur until created by the development of forms filling the "higher" ecological niches. It also becomes very generally true of any complex form that most, if not all, of its ancestors represented forms of less complexity, and in general, of uniformly ascending complexity. It also becomes true that the mean complexity of all occupied niches steadily increases from epoch to epoch. In this sense, the selective retention model predicts the over-all advance posited by White (1959a).

Transformation of function. Observers of culture history have noted instances in which a specific institution or cultural form changed function during the course of its history. Consideration of the requirement of adjacency for entering ecological niches makes such instances comprehensible under blind-variation-and-selective-retention theory. Because of the requirements of adjacency, there can exist unoccupied ecological niches, or ecological niches enterable only very indirectly. Often this process will involve a complete change in the form of utilization of an organ or institution. In recent years some of the most dramatic illustrations of this process have come from the behavioral zoologists (ethologists) such as Lorenz and Timbergen (see Thorpe, 1956, for exhaustive references). Working with closely allied species they have been able to reconstruct the evolutionary history of the ritual social behavior of birds and fish. In these histories, dramatic transformations of function occur. For example, a species with a highly elaborate courtship behavior may have evolved this through modifications of attack and defense gestures, or infant feeding reflexes, or nest building reflex elements.

The existence of this type of evolutionary sequence warns us away from blanket assumptions of structure-function continuity of development, and makes trouble for any simplistic use of evolutionary theory in comparative study. The most impressive aspect of modern evolutionary theory is not unilinearity, but the multi-dimensional opportunism of developmental processes.

Ecological pressure in the maintenance of consistent complexity. Another feature of the selective-retention model may be worth specifying for the societal analogue. In general, complex structures such as the vertebrate eye are only maintained by consistent ecological pressure. Without this, the cumulative occurrence of uneliminated mutations gradually destroys its functionality, and, combined with internal selection pressures in favor of simplicity, gradually removes its complexity. The more complex the structure the more statistically likely it becomes that random mutations will lessen rather than increase the adaptive adequacy. Or to revert to the learning model, the more the rat has learned of the maze, the more a random change in an element of his running pattern is likely to lead to increased error rather than to improvement. The maintenance of adequate complexity depends upon the continual elimination of such maladaptive variations. At the social level, a similar truism should hold. A formula for iron smelting, passed on orally from father to son, would tend to become unworkable if several generations went by without the reediting test of use, as a net result of the inevitable variations in transmission.

A backhanded use of this argument implies that where a complex structure seemingly persists, it is being sustained by an ecological pressure, even where the scientist does not yet understand what that pressure is. Such an argument seems a legitimate working hypothesis in dealing with persistent cultural items, even though it may seem to create more problems than it solves. It gives the social scientist more puzzles demanding explanation, as when he examines the stubborn persistence of "incredible" or "irrational" superstitions on the part of the exotic cultures he studies, or his own (Jacobs and Campbell, 1961). It opposes a parsimonious general law of cultural inertia. Instead, the inertia becomes something to be explained. Nonetheless, this seems to be the unavoidable implication.

Vicarious exploratory and selective systems. A major emphasis of the more general model (e.g. Campbell, 1956, 1959, 1960) is that in the course of evolution, both biological and social, more economical vicarious exploratory and selective systems have been evolved where they were possible. It is also important that each of these vicarious systems embody within themselves the three essentials of a blind variation process, a selective criterion, and a retention-propagation process. Thus instinct-formation involves a trial-and-error of the life and death of whole mutant animals. A learning process may end up providing a very comparable behavioral repertoire, but does so by trial-and-error of responses within the lifetime of a single animal, and using memory rather than genetic structure as the storage process. The encounter with environmental realities is now more indirect, being represented by pleasure and pain senses, the activation of which winnows out the responses. The indirectness is indicated by such illustrations as the rat's willingness to selectively retain responses leading to non-nutritive saccharine. Still more vicarious are exploration of memory representations of the environment by means of heterogeneous thought trials, selected through reactivation of memories of pleasure and pain, etc. Vision similarly substitutes for blind locomotor exploration. The accuracy or appropriateness of these indirect and vicarious processes is, of course, maintained only by the more fundamental selective pressure of differential biological propagation, but if they are maintained, they can lead to much more rapid adaptation than would otherwise be possible. Social processes of learning, as through profiting from the outcomes of another person's explorations, selective imitative tendencies, linguistic instruction, etc., can all be seen as such vicarious exploration processes.

Disanalogies between biological and socio-cultural evolution. Remembering that it is the general variation-and-selective-retention model that is being employed, one should also be alert to specific embodiments of the process in organic evolution which have no counterpart in socio-cultural evolution, and vice-versa. There is no need, for example, to search out the social analogue to bisexual reproduction, even though a loose analogue to heterozygosity might be of value. Heterozygosity, in particular the presence of recessives, represents a latent potentiality for rapid responses to a shift in environmental selection. In a similar way, dissident opinion, unexpressed while majority opinion is successful, represents a latent potentiality for change if group failure is encountered (Campbell, 1961).

The stringent restrictions against cross-lineage borrowing in organico evolution is necessitated by the rigid chromosome-gene preservation system, and becomes unnecessary in the social evolution of particular social groups. Childe (1951), Ginsberg (1961), Waddington (1961) and others have pointed out this as a major difference between organic and social evolution. This removes the requirement that advanced (complex) forms be achieved only by a complete set of viable intermediate forms in each specific cultural group. Thus, even if there were an unavoidable order of intermediate stages for the original achievement of an advanced one (even if, for example, a first manufacturing economy could only emerge from a cooperative agricultural economy) this sequence would not necessarily be required for all later social units moving into an industrial stage.

CONVERGENT EVOLUTION OF SOCIAL ORGANIZATION: PAYOFFS AND REQUISITE VALUES.

Where remote lines of descent converge on a similar functioning form, one can argue the strength of the selective system, i.e. the great advantages of the form, as well as the limited range of alternatives. Thus the similarity of the octopus and vertebrate eye argues both the great survival value of vision and the fewness of modes of achieving its equivalent. (Echolocation by bats does illustrate a partial alternate). Convergence in evolution can thus throw valuable light on selective systems, with a triangulation that is more convincing the more independent the lines of descent.

Urban social systems have been independently evolved on numerous occasions. Within the insect groups, ants, termites, and bees have quite independently evolved an apartment-house mode of living with the distinctive attributes of a storable food supply and a full-time division of labor, including members who are fed rather than gathering their own food (Allee, Emerson, Park & Schmidt, 1949). As Steward (1955b) has documented, where storable grains made a division of labor possible and where the tillage conditions made cooperation profitable, agriculturally based urban communities have, repeatedly, independently emerged. Common in the division of labor evolved among termites, ants, and irrigation civilizations, is a full time soldier caste, probably made necessary to protect the tempting food stores from out-group vandals.

There would thus seem to have been a convergent evolution in the direction of urban social life as defined in these minimal terms. Apparently there is in this system some pay off sufficiently compelling to shape by selection widely disparate forms in this common direction of increased sociality. The common selective system would be the requirements for the coordinated activity of individuals in a division-of-labor system. Among these requisites would be certain behavioral dispositions or values on the part of the individuals constituting the society. From such a theory of social organization, it would become reasonable to speak of the loyalty and self-sacrificial bravery of termite soldiers, of the honesty of scout bees, and the trust of worker bees, defining loyalty, honesty, and trust in terms of their functional roles in maintaining social organization rather than in terms of an introspective psychological analysis. The joint consideration of human and insect societies is distasteful to many, and the disanalogies between insect and human sociality are numerous and important. Yet the very remoteness of this convergence serves to free us from psychocentric presuppositions which stand in the way of a full understanding of the tremendous survival value of social life. Too often in contemporary social science analysis stops when it is traced back to individual motives, as though these were the prime mover, the uncaused beginning of causal sequences. The disanalogies are of course many. Insect sociality is a biological evolutionary achievement, human cities a socio-cultural cumulation. A given insect social form is found in numerous essentially identical replications of the same variety, in human social systems each exemplification fits its novel environment with unique adaptive details. But above this, a striking core of parallel devices and parallel survival-advantages over solitary species points to an important general principle of social organization.

There are a number of roots to this line of thought. One is functional requisite analysis in sociology, as exemplified by Bennett and Tumin (1948), Aberle *et al.* (1950) and Levy (1952) even though by including insect societies, which they did not do, a more minimal list of requisites results. Also highly relevant is Emerson's work on termite societies (1954), his and Gerard's (1942) comparisons of human societies, insect societies and biological organisms, and Herbert Spencer's (1896) very similar writings. However, by intent at least, this paper aspires to more specific and cautious generalizations than those offered by Emerson, Gerard and Spencer. By intent it stays closer to specifiable selection criteria. More specifically, the course of social evolution is not committed to such global goals as increased social homeostasis and integration. Further, the society-organism analogy is avoided except to the extent that the evolution of both can be shown to be under selection pressure from common principles of organization (Spencer, 1897, pp. 447–448). Increased human societal integration has not increased the immutability of the division of labor, for example, as the society-organism analogy would imply. While the social division of labor is increasing in specialization and range of interdependence, the amount of time required to learn these specialized roles is decreasing, and the freedom for the individual to change roles increasing. These developments are quite understandable in terms of selective retention mechanisms, but are contrary to the direction of organic development, in terms of the analogue to the increased specialization of cells within the body, which is accompanied by an increased irreversibility of specialization. While Emerson *et al.* start their analyses upon survival value and selective systems, the extrapolation seems to come more from the course of structural development rather than from considerations of selective pressures, implying in some of their writings a metaphysical or teleological value for increased societal integration *per se*. Further, even granting a general appropriateness to their position, the emphasis upon such abstract goals as social homeostasis and integration is deemed to be a poorer way of communicating with social scientists than would be a more specific analysis of the selective advantages of social coordination, and its results. There are also numerous evolutionary approaches to values, old and new, which, while less specific, differing in details, and frequently dealing with biological evolution in social man rather than with socio-cultural evolution, are nonetheless relevant (e.g. Pepper, 1958; Waddington, 1960; Quillian, 1950).

To return to our stored-food, division-of-labor, urban societies. What are the tremendous pay-offs of such an invention? What are the selective advantages that have made solitary species evolve toward the increasingly social, while no social species has evolved toward the solitary? Here are three, and some possibly requisite values.

Economy of cognition. From the standpoint of a psychologist interested in cognitive processes, one of the most obvious economies of social life is the economy of cognition, i.e. of processes whereby the trial-and-error explorations of one member serves to save others the trouble of entering the same blind alleys. In the social insects and man, such survival-relevant processes are readily observable, mediated by both observation and linguistic instruction. Asch (1950; Campbell, 1961) has called attention to the essential role played in social life of willingness to make use of the observations reported by others, and correspondingly, of reporting one's own observations so that others can depend upon them. Two requisite values emerge. On the one hand, there is a requirement of honesty by communicators. On the other hand, there is a requirement of trust in communication. These are presumably universal values in human societies.

The economy of cognition is clearly shown in the scouting activities of the social insects, in which the trial-and-error encounter of a food supply by one worker, leads to a direct locomotion to the food by the other workers. In the ants, this may be mediated by a scented back-tracking. In the honey bees, it is achieved by a linguistic instruction. Through the wagging-dance described by Frisch (1950) the successful scout indicates range and course, so that the other worker bees can fly directly to the new food source. Here too, honesty and trust, or their functional equivalents, are required. Hives with scout bees that keep the good news to themselves, or that dance of non-existent treasures, or that give erroneous bearing, undoubtedly occur from time to time, and fail to survive. Similarly, trust, gullibility, belief, or their functional equivalents, are required of the recipients of the messages, and have survival value even if occasionally deceived. The ecological pressure of the economy of cognition keeps honesty and trust as effective values. It is hard to see how it can be exploited without them.

Economy of specialization and the division of labor. The specialization of tasks and the division of labor is ubiquitous in complex social life. A minimal economic requirement is transportable foodstuffs, but the large-population division-of-labor complexes seem to have only been built up around food stuffs that are not only transportable, but also storable without spoilage. (Forde, 1934, p. 418; Steward, 1955 a, b). Requisite values related to this complex include industriousness, surplus production, hoarding, abstinence from indulgence, and obligation to share.

Economy of mutual defense. This selective criterion received great emphasis from Kropotkin (1902, 1924) in his effort to revise the erroneously individualistic hedonism assumed by the early interpreters of Darwinism. The concentrated defensive or offensive efforts of many individuals make them effective in instances where they would all be vanquished in a series of one-at-a-time encounters with the same foe. The requisite values are loyalty, altruistic willingness to sacrifice self for the group, etc. A division of labor along these lines allows for special armaments, which might interfere with work.

While these common requisites and convergences may be instructive, it is also important to note features shared by all human urban division-of-labor societies, which are missing from the social insects. For man, an early full time division of labor, away from food gathering, is in the priesthood or executive functions. There appear to be no corresponding castes among the social insects. There is apparently nothing like a communications clearing-house or coordinating role. This omission is, no doubt, related to the rigidly limited alternatives to individual and social behavior of termite societies. On this point, the analogy between organism and human society seems closer than between organism and termite society, in that termite society lacks anything corresponding to a central nervous system or brain cells. For human societies one may go on to other value requisites, such as the utility of preserving culture, with the requisite values of respect for authority and knowledge, which Waddington (1960) emphasizes, and in the social decision-making and coordination advantages, with the corresponding values of cooperativeness, and organizational loyalty. These brief illustrations have illustrated the utility of a focus upon selective systems and survival advantages in the analysis of social function.

SUMMARY

In reviewing the current relevance of the concept of socio-cultural evolution, the analogy to the variation-and-selective-survival mechanism is regarded as more valid and more valuable than the analogy to a progressive direction of increased size and complexity of integration *per se*. In line with this, an effort has been made to spell out the societal counterparts of variation, selection, and retention which would make an evolutionary process possible at the societal level. The primary sources of doubt lie in the selection process. This comes not only from the variety of intertwined selection processes, but also with the difficulty of specifying the selective criteria independently of what they seem to have selected. Nonetheless, the general tenor of the paper has been to assume that some socio-cultural evolutionary process takes place. Unavoidable organizational requirements in the coordination of individuals in collective action, and specific pay-offs from social life, are seen as part of the selective criteria involved. From these, certain requisite social values may be inferred. Incidental to this presentation, comments on the sociology of knowledge have been used to explain the rejection of earlier theories of social evolution.

References

Aberle, D. F., Cohen, A. K., Davis, A. K., Levy, M. J., & Sutton, F. X. The functional prerequisites of a society, *Ethics*, 1950, 60, 100–111.

Allee, W. C., Emerson, A. E., Park, O., Park, T., & Schmidt, K. P. *Principles of animal ecology*. Philadelphia: Saunders, 1949.

Asch, S. E. *Social psychology*. New York: Prentice Hall, 1952.

Ashby, W. R. *Design for a brain*. New York: Wiley, 1952.

Aubert, V. Chance in social affairs. *Inquiry*, 1959, 2, 1–24.

Bagehot, W. *Physics and politics*. New York: Appleton, 1884.

Baldwin, J. M. *Mental development in the child and the race*. New York: Macmillan, 1900.

Banton, M. The autonomy of post-Darwinian sociology. In M. Banton (Ed.) *Darwinism and the study of society*. Chicago: Quadrangle Books, 1961.

Barber, B. *Science and the social order*. Glencoe: Free Press, 1952.

Barry, H., Child, J. L., & Bacon, M. K. Relation of child training to subsistence economy. *American Anthropologist*, 1959, 61, 51–63.

Becker, H., & Barnes, H. E. *Social thought from lore to science*. Washington: Harren Press, 1952 (2nd. ed.).

Bennett, J. W., & Tumin, M. M. *Social life: structure and function*. New York: Knopf, 1948.

Bock, K. E. Evolution, function, and change. *American Sociological Review*, 1963, 28, 229–237.

Bougle, C. Darwinism and sociology, in A. C. Seward, Ed., *Darwin and modern science: Essays in commemoration of the centenary of the birth of Charles Darwin and of the fiftieth anniversary of the publication of the Origin of the Species*. Cambridge, England: Cambridge University Press, 1909.

Campbell, D. T. Adaptive behavior from random response. *Behavioral Science*, 1956a, 1, 105–110.

Campbell, D. T. Perception as substitute trial and error. *Psychological Review*, 1956b, 63, 330–342.

Campbell, D. T. Common fate, similarity, and other indices of the status of aggregates of persons as social entities. *Behavioral Science*, 1958, 3, 14–25.

Campbell, D. T. Methodological suggestions from a comparative psychology of knowledge processes. *Inquiry*, 1959, 2, 152–182.

Campbell, D. T. Blind variation and selective retention in creative thought as in other knowledge processes. *Psychological Review*, 1960, 67, 380–400.

Campbell, D. T. Conformity in psychology's theories of acquired behavioral dispositions. In I. A. Berg & B. M. Bass (Eds.) *Conformity and deviation*. New York: Harper, 1961.

Childe, V. G. *Social evolution*. London; Watts, 1951.

Cohen, R. The strategy of social evolution. *Anthropologica*, 1962, N. S. 4, 321–348.

Darwin, C. G. Can man control his numbers? In S. Tax, Ed., *Evolution after Darwin*. Vol. II. Chicago: Univer. Chicago Press, 1960.

Eisenstadt, S. N. Social change, differentiation and evolution. *American Sociological Review*, 1964, 29, 375–386.

Emerson, A. E. Dynamic homeostasis: a unifying principle in organic, social, and ethical evolution. *Scientific Monthly*, 1954, 78, 67–85.

Faris, R. E. L. Evolution and American sociology. In S. Persons, Ed., *Evolutionary thought in America*. New Haven: Yale University Press, 1950.

Frisch, K. von, *Bees, their vision, chemical sense, and language*. Ithaca: Cornell University Press, 1950.

Forde, C. D. *Habitat, Economy and Society: A Geographical Introduction to Ethnography*. London: Methuen, 1934.

Gerard, R. W. Higher levels of integration. In R. Redfield (Ed.) *Levels of integration in biological and social systems*. Biological Symposia No. 8, 1942, 67–87.

Ginsberg, M. Social evolution. In M. Banton, Ed. *Darwinism and the study of society*. Chicago: Quadrangle Books, 1961.

Goldman, I. The evolution of Polynesian societies. In S. Diamond, Ed. *Culture in history.* New York: Columbia University Press, 1960, pp. 677–712.

Greenberg, J. H. *Essays in linguistics.* New York: Wenner-Gren Foundation, 1957.

Greenberg, J. H. Language and evolution. In *Evolution and Anthropology: a centennial appraisal.* Washington, D. C. The Anthropological Society of Washington, 1959.

Guetzkow, H. "Organizational Leadership in Task-Oriented Groups", in B. Bass and L. Petrullo (eds.) *Leadership and Interpersonal Behavior,* New York: Holt, Rinehart and Winston, Inc., 1961, pp. 187–200.

Hawley, A. H. *Human ecology.* New York: Ronald Press, 1950.

Herskovits, M. J. *Man and his works.* New York, Knopf, 1948.

Hofstadter, R. *Social Darwinism in American Thought.* Boston: Beacon Press, 1955 (Revised ed. First ed., University of Philadelphia Press, 1944).

Jacobs, R. C., & Campbell, D. T. The perpetuation of an arbitrary culture through several generations of a laboratory microculture. *Journal of Abnormal and Social Psychology,* 1961, 62, 649–658.

Keller, A. G. *Societal evolution.* New Haven: Yale University Press, 1915 (revised edition 1931).

Kroeber, A. L. The superorganic. *American Anthropologist,* 1917, 19, 163–214.

Kropotkin, P. *Mutual aid: a factor in evolution.* New York: Double-day, Page, 1902.

Kropotkin, P. *Ethics: origin and development.* New York: Dial Press, 1924 (Tudor, 1947).

Lesser, A. Evolution in social anthropology. *Southwestern Journal of Anthropology,* 1952, 8, 134–146.

Levy, M. J. *The structure of society.* Princeton: Princeton University Press, 1952.

Mach, E. On the part played by accident in invention and discovery. *Monist,* 1896, 6, 161–175.

MacIver, R. M., & Page, C. H. *Society, an introductory analysis.* New York: Rinehart, 1949.

Meggers, B. (Ed.) *Evolution and Anthropology: a Centennial Appraisal.* Washington, D.C.: Anthropological Society of Washington, 1959.

Moore, O. K. Divination, a new perspective. *American Anthropologist,* 1957, 59, 72.

Muller, H. J. The guidance of human evolution, in S. Tax, Ed. *Evolution after Darwin.* Vol. II. Chicago: University of Chicago Press, 1960, pp. 423–462.

Ogburn, W. F. & Thomas, D. Are inventions inevitable? *Political Science Quarterly,* 1922, 37, 83–93.

Park, R. E. Human migration and the marginal man. *American Journal of Sociology,* 1928, 33, 881–893.

Parsons, T. Evolutionary universals in society. *American Sociological Review,* 1964, 29, 339–357.

Pastore, N. *The nature-nurture controversy.* New York: King's Crown Press, Columbia University, 1949.

Pepper, S. C. *The sources of value.* Berkeley: University of California Press, 1958.

Popper, K. R. *The logic of scientific discovery.* New York: Basic Books, 1959.

Pringle, J. W. S. On the parallel between learning and evolution. *Behaviour,* 1951, 3, 175–215.

Quillian, W. F. Evolution and moral theory in America. In S. Persons, Ed., *Evolutionary thought in America.* New Haven: Yale University Press, 1950.

Roe, A., & Simpson, G. G. *Behavior and evolution.* New Haven: Yale University Press, 1958.

Sahlins, M. D. *Social stratification in Polynesia.* Seattle: University of Washington Press, 1958.

Sahlins, M. D., & Service, E. R. (Eds.) *Evolution and culture.* Ann Arbor: University of Michigan Press, 1960.

Sandow, A. Social factors in the origin of Darwinism. *Quarterly Review of Biology,* 1938, 13, 315–326.

Seeman, M. Intellectual perspective and adjustment to minority status. *Social Problems,* 1956, 3, 142–153.

Sherif, M. *The psychology of social norms.* New York: Harper, 1936.

Simpson, G. G. *The meaning of evolution.* New Haven: Yale University Press, 1949.

Spencer, H. *Social statics.* London, 1850.

Spencer, H. *Principles of sociology.* New York: Appleton, 1897 (First edition, 1876).

Spengler, J. J. Evolutionism in American economics. 1800–1946. In S. Persons (Ed.) *Evolutionary thought in America.* New Haven: Yale University Press, 1950.

Spiegelman, S. Differentiation as the controlled production of unique enzymic patterns. In *Symposia of the society for experimental biology* II, *Growth in relation to differentiation and morphogenesis.* New York: Academic Press, 1948.

Steward, J. H. *Theory of culture change: the methodology of multilinear evolution.* Urbana: University of Illinois Press, 1955a.

Steward, J. H. (Ed.) *Irrigation civilizations: a comparative study.* Washington, D.C.: Pan American Union, 1955b.

Sumner, W. G. *Folkways,* Boston: Ginn, 1906.

Sumner, W. G., Keller, A. G., & Davie, M. R. *The science of society.* New Haven: Yale University Press, 1927 (4 vols.).

Tax, S. (Ed.) *Evolution after Darwin.* Vol. II. *The evolution of man.* Chicago: University of Chicago Press, 1960.

Teggart, F. J. *Theory of History.* New Haven: Yale University Press, 1925.

Thorpe, W. H. *Learning and instinct in animals.* London: Methuen, 1956.

Veblen, T. The intellectual preeminence of Jews in modern Europe. *Political Science Quarterly,* 1919, 34, 33–42.

Waddington, C. H. *The ethical animal.* London: George Allen & Unwin, 1960.

Waddington, C. H. The human evolutionary system, in M. Banton, Ed., *Darwinism and the study of society.* Chicago: Quadrangle Books, 1961, pp. 63–82.

Washburn, S., & Howell, F. C. Human evolution and culture. In S. Tax, Ed., *Evolution after Darwin.* Vol. II. Chicago: University of Chicago Press, 1960, pp. 35–56.

White, L. A. "Diffusion vs. evolution": an antievolutionist fallacy. *American Anthropologist,* 1945, 47, 339–356.

White, L. A. *The evolution of culture.* New York: McGraw Hill, 1959a.

White, L. A. The concept of evolution in cultural anthropology. In *Evolution and anthropology: a centennial appraisal.* Washington, D.C.: The Anthropological Society of Washington, 1959b.

White, L. A. Foreword in M. D. Sahlins & E. R. Service, Eds., *Evolution and culture.* Ann Arbor: University of Michigan Press, 1960, pp. V-XII.

Zirkle, C. Natural selection before the "Origin of Species". *Proceedings American Philosophical Society,* 1941, 84, 71–123.

HUMAN CULTURAL EVOLUTION AND ITS RELATION TO ORGANIC EVOLUTION OF INSECT SOCIETIES

ALFRED E. EMERSON

Department of Zoology
University of Chicago

The processes of cultural and organic evolution and their consequences are different, but they also have much in common. The biological scientist has much of significance to offer the social scientist, and the reverse is also true. We are at the threshold of a new multidisciplinary synthesis that may well prove to be as revolutionary as was Darwin's theory of evolution by natural selection.

There is a ferment of activity on the part of many investigators interested in the relationships between the sciences of life and of man. These studies center around the fields of organic and cultural evolution of man, behavior and psychology, population biology, and animal sociology. Basic principles are emerging, and it behooves each specialist to contribute what information he can to our understanding of social processes. Science is founded upon accurately observed sensory facts and their relationships. No interpretative generalization is worthy of the scientist's serious consideration unless it is substantiated by a wealth of detailed facts. At the same time, theories provide hypothetical meaning for the orderly facts and should indicate profitable directions for further investigation.

In a brief discussion, I shall have to skim lightly over quantities of details and profound philosophical implications. These together require both scientific knowledge and deep thought. Many statements are controversial and must remain tentative at present. However I hope that I can raise questions that will stimulate new ideas and inquiries.

We may begin with a few broad generalizations founded upon an abundance of evidence.

1. Population systems are highly evolved integrated biological entities,

ranking in importance with such analogous units as the gene, the cell, and the multicellular individual organism.

2. Population systems may be divided into two basic types: (a) intraspecies populations exhibiting genetic continuity, and (b) interspecies populations exhibiting ecological continuity.

Intraspecies populations include aggregations, flocks, herds, sex pairs, families, and societies with a division of labor between adults of the same sex. Interspecies populations are less well organized and show a variety of relations. They include exploited and exploiter species, such as predator-prey and parasite-host. They also include competing species for limited necessities of food and shelter within the same habitat. Toleration of other species is very common in nature. Cooperation between different species is often found in interspecies populations within biocoenoses, ecological communities, and ecosystems. However, on the whole, mutual cooperation is far more prevalent within intraspecies populations than in interspecies systems.

Each type of population system has adaptations between its individual components analogous to the adaptations between the parts of a proto-plasmically connected individual. Populations, therefore, have many organismic attributes and may be cautiously considered to be supraorganisms. Like an organism, a supraorganism is an open system with an export and import of materials and energy to and from an environment to which it is adaptively oriented; it exhibits a degree of self-regulation (homeostasis) of optimal conditions of existence and perpetuation; it exhibits functional division of labor between its parts, and an integration into an inclusive whole with emergent attributes not to be found in the separated parts by themselves; and it has a temporal ontogeny and a temporal phylogeny that incorporates time and spatial dimensions into a multidimensional system. Each unit of life from the gene to the ecosystem has boundaries that separate it from its environment and from other living systems. Boundaries may be scientifically detected for each level of biological organization. Each coordinated entity is an open system with certain factors that cross the borders in each direction, and certain factors, both internal and external, that are stopped or altered quantitatively or qualitatively at the border.

Many persons are opposed to some of the foregoing statements. As you know, some persons cannot see the forest for the trees, and some cannot see the trees when they view the forest. Or, to put it in more scientific language, some can see the borders of an individual, but fail to recognize the borders of a species, and some who recognize the species may be unaware of the interspecies community system. On the other hand, some biologists who are fully conscious of the assemblages of organisms in a coral reef or a tropical rainforest may treat the individual only as a statistic, and the species as a subjective figment of the imagination of the taxonomist. These differences in perspective are the bases of diverse political philosophies now plaguing human society and international relations. Overemphasis upon the state, to the exclusion of individual freedom, or overemphasis upon the rights of the individual, to the exclusion of his social responsibilities, are the ideological causes of both cold and hot wars.

Let us turn to animal societies for certain information that is relevant to the social scientist. Students of social insects know that each individual insect is separated from its fellows by nonliving space, but that across this space are transferred substances and sensory stimuli to which each individual reacts adaptively. There is communication between the individuals and an integration of behavior responses that may result, for example, in a nest construction exhibiting symmetry, orientation to the environment, replication of parts, functional differentiation of structure, regulation of its internal microclimate, protection from environmental fluctuations, such as heavy rain, protection from enemies, internal sanitation, regulation of plant or animal food by means of storage or cultivation, a development of the nest during the growth of the colony, and an evolution of the nest type with species and generic differentiation during phylogeny. All students of social insects know that the workers who build these nests are dependent upon the reproductive caste for the production of more workers and more colonies, and upon the defensive caste (worker or soldier) for protection from predatory enemies. (Please note that the enemies of social insects belong to other species and that intraspecies warfare is almost nonexistent among non-human societies.) Most of the nutriment for the entire colony is gathered by the workers from the feeding territory. The internal nest structure regulates the temperature, humidity, and ventilation so essential for the existence of these insects. This regulated nest environment is attractive to many different species of plants and animals that have evolved through the ages to fit the social behavior, nutritive physiology, and social homeostasis of their hosts. In many instances mutual interdependence of associated species has evolved. To the social level of integration, a community of different species adheres, together forming an ecosystem with ecological homeostasis.

The great principles of organic evolution are beautifully exemplified by the orderly progressive time sequences in the past history of the social insects. We have direct fossil evidence of the presence of various social insects in Eocene times (sixty million years ago) when the ancestors of man resembled lemurs. We have indirect evidence of the evolutionary radiation of some social insects by Cretaceous times about a hundred million years ago when our human ancestors were primitive insectivorous mammals. And we have bits of circumstantial evidence that indicate that some insect societies emerged at the end of Paleozoic or early Mesozoic times about two hundred million years ago when the ancestors of man were terrestrial reptiles. How does this range of time compare to the time scale of human social evolution?

In recent years we have learned much concerning the biological evolution of man. In 1959, Dr. L. S. B. Leakey discovered bones of a new form of Australopithecine hominid in Tanganyika. He found these remains in the culture site, and gave them the name of *Zinjanthropus boisei*. This man-like creature lived in early Pleistocene (probably more than one and a half million years ago); it possessed crude but stylized tools; it walked erect; it had large molars, small canines, and a carnivorous diet; its brain was roughly half the size of that of the Java man (*Pithecanthropus erectus*) or the Peking man (*Sinanthropus pekinensis*); and there is no indication that it used fire.

This species indicates the stage that biological evolution may have reached at the dawn of the cultural or social evolution of man. By means of upright locomotion, this hominid was adjusted to terrestrial life outside of forests, and the hands were freed from their previous locomotor function. The crude stylized implements indicate the beginnings of social communication, because we must assume that what was learned by one individual was passed along to others. Whether symbolic speech had been attained is not clear, but the imitation and social repetition of learned functions transcend the known abilities of any living non-human. The circumstantial evidence points to a crude social organization, possibly allowing cooperative hunting of animal food.

The absolute and relative size of the brain of *Zinjanthropus* was close to that of modern apes. Because this creature lived less than two million years ago, the evidence points to a relatively rapid evolutionary increase in the size of the brain in the hominid stock after other human traits had genetically evolved. There is a suggestion that the beginnings of cultural society may have exerted a strong selection pressure favoring the genetic basis for an advance of mentality.

The biological evolution of insect social organization is on the order of 200 times as long as the cultural evolution of human society. It appears to many modern scientists that the transition from nonhuman animals to man was not the result of any great qualitative or quantitative change in his individual biological functions and structures. True, there was probably an adaptive radiation from forests to grasslands together with some change in the genetic capacities for family and social organization beyond that seen in the baboons and apes of today. There was possibly some advance in mental ability at the earliest human levels, illustrated by the manufacture and use of crude tools. Size of brain and mentality seem to have progressed rapidly from the most primitive hominids to the origin of our own species, *Homo sapiens*. But none of these qualities indicates the enormity of the break-through apparent in the rapid evolution of the human species toward the exponential social advance of recent centuries, since Magdalenian man painted herds of extinct animals on the walls of caves in France and Spain about 15,000 years ago. I am inclined to the view that we must turn our attention to the processes of cultural evolution for an explanation, without negating the relatively slow advance through genetic change in man. At its inception, cultural evolution was also very slow. The Chellean hand axe remained the highest form of tool for at least 50,000 years of interglacial Neanderthal society. In contrast, modern technological advance is apparent from year to year, or even from month to month.

Insect society is not the result of the capacity of the individual to learn, to think abstractly, or to communicate individually acquired experience to others. There is no doubt that the insect does react somewhat differently after an experience than before. But insects have little ability to learn much or to transmit learned behavior to their fellows by means of symbols. Their behavior, their structure, their physiology, and their social adaptations are all dependent upon their genetic constitutions, and their social evolution is strictly dependent upon the processes of genetic change during the organic evolution of their social supraorganism.

By means of genetic mutation, genetic recombination, partial and complete reproductive isolation that divides and consolidates complex systems, and guidance through natural selection, insect societies (and all other biological systems) evolve division of labor between individual units, integration into inclusive entities, competition and cooperation between parts of each system, and dynamic homeostasis. Homeostasis may be defined as the self-regulation of optimal conditions for maintenance and continuation. Cybernetics and homeostasis are equivalent terms when used for biological processes. Increased homeostasis seems to be the adaptive direction of organic evolution at all integrative levels of biological organization. Homeostasis always involves feedbacks from effects to causes. Disequilibrium and unbalance, if functional, are regulated together with functional equilibrium and balance. The homeostatic mechanisms are themselves maintained and controlled. Evolutionary progress in time can be measured in terms of increase in homeostatic regulation. Perfection of homeostasis for all optima is an impossibility, but a decrease in the degree of incompatibility between optima for different processes in the same system can be accomplished by an evolution of spatial separation (structure), temporal separation (periodicity), and compromise adjustment. In the processes of evolutionary improvement of homeostasis, much conflict, competition, toleration, and cooperation may be detected. The trend often fluctuates. Death and extinction of subsystems within more inclusive systems occur. But the long-term trend seems to be clear. Regressions in subsystems are usually correlated with progress of the more inclusive system. Conflict at one end of the reaction gradient and cooperation at the other end are actions selected for optimal values. Competition between parts of an organism or supraorganism may have a degree of positive selection pressure. The trend is not rigidly deterministic. Chance and accident play a role in all processes involved. Prediction can only be made in terms of probability statistics.

Organic evolution is a changing sequence of hereditary components in time, but in living systems the time dimension becomes incorporated into the system. Each level of organization shows a short time dimension of stimulus and response, a somewhat longer time dimension of ontogenetic growth and differentiation, and a still longer time dimension of genetic change during evolution. Adjustment to the probable future (teleonomy) occurs in all time sequences, both short and long. All aspects of life represented by the various biological sciences have these time dimensions and each science is intricately interrelated to every other one.

Novel emergent properties appear with new associated units at each level of organization. Analysis of systems is a necessary scientific procedure, but analysis alone is insufficient for an adequate understanding of the characteristics of whole systems. Scientific synthesis and scientific analysis together are essential to comprehension. So far as man is concerned, human intellect, human emotions, and human values are all involved in a comprehensive awareness of reality, and should be integrated and harmonized in human wisdom and decision. Many current philosophies do not recognize the interrelatedness of different phases of either human personality or human society. Scientists themselves often present a picture of reality that is divisive, disjunct, and inadequate. They often fail to recognize that the relations of facts are as important as the facts that are related, and that the relations may be lost in the very process of analysis that is so fundamental to scientific method. Specialization is necessary for the accurate and comprehensive accumulation of related facts, but let us not forget its limitations.

Let us not be insensitive to holistic systems and their attributes. Let us foster an awesome regard of infinity. Let us, with Albert Schweitzer, have a reverence for life. Let us integrate the deepest emotional and intellectual concerns of man by means of art, religion, and science. When asked if anyone existed who was irreligious, my late friend, Edward Scribner Ames (Professor of Philosophy at the University of Chicago and minister of the Church of the Disciples) said, "Yes, there are two types—imbeciles and specialists." The imbecile cannot be intellectually sensitive to reality. The specialist may be blind to his place in the whole magnificent system of which he is a part and upon which he depends.

The great distinction of human society compared with insect society is in the acquisition of learned symbolic communication. Webster's dictionary defines a symbol as "that which stands for or suggests something else by reason of relationship, association, convention, or accidental but not intentional resemblance." And for Logic, Webster adds that a symbol is "any formed unit of expression, such as a term, proposition, or formal argument, which represents an aspect of thought capable of being dealt with as a unit."

Many animals can individually learn. They can communicate by means of signals and signs. They can live together cooperatively in organized societies. They can modify and regulate their physical and biotic environment to their own advantage. But they cannot symbolize their experiences and thoughts and communicate these to contemporary or future generations. They cannot accumulate social knowledge and correct the mistakes of others. In other words, they do not have a culture.

Therefore, evolution of civilization, including science, language, literature, art, and religion, rests upon a different mechanism than does organic or biological evolution. The two types of evolution are strictly analogous and definitely not homologous. Extrapolation from one to the other is suggestive, but not predictive. If valid, comparable evidence must be accumulated that indicates similar but not identical events, functions, and processes of change.

Cultural heredity is analogous to genetic heredity. Cultural heredity occurs by means of learned symbolic communication in contrast to the transmission of genetic molecular materials from generation to generation. Both cultural and genetic heredity involve conservative repetition of units, persistence of units over long periods of time through many generations, variation of units and transmission of the change, function of a degree of freedom, recombination of units that produce emergent properties of the combined systems, partial isolation of genetic "pools" or "pools" of symbols with consequent consolidation of complex systems, and selection for survival of the fit individual or group through time, accompanied by elimination of the less fit.

Of the various types of symbolization, possibly the easiest to understand is language, particularly written language. Written symbols, of course, evolved long after spoken symbols, but writing provides more concrete data for the study of function and evolution. For the moment, let me penetrate somewhat into the analogues to be found in genetic and symbolic systems. It should be noted that letters have often been used as symbols in genetic analysis as well as in mathematics, and the analogy between language (culture) and genetics (biological heredity) is highly significant.

Genes are composed of nucleic acid. Beadle (1959) says: "A DNA (deoxyribose nucleic acid) molecule represents a kind of code for which there is a counterpart in the amino acid sequence of a protein molecule. This permits the transfer of information from the four-symbol system of DNA to the 20-symbol system of protein in much the same way as the two-symbol Morse code is translatable into the 26-symbol code that is our written language."

We know that proteins consist, for the most part, of polypeptide chains made up of approximately 20 amino acids arranged in a specific sequence for each kind of protein. And we know that all enzymes that catalyze living processes are proteins. One cannot grow, differentiate, maintain bodily structure, feel an emotion (e.g. love), or think, without enzymes playing an essential role in the process. Our personalities, our social activities, and our advancing civilization are dependent upon nucleic acid genes that code 20 amino acids that in turn form an immense number of kinds of proteins including the enzymes vital to both insect and human social cooperation.

These facts have far-reaching importance for our understanding of human life and society. They mean that a dualistic separation of mind and body or a separation of personality from the biological organism, is quite impossible except by communication, utilizing the capacity to learn, reason, and think abstractly. It is necessary for the healthful advance of human society that we rid ourselves of false notions and discover truths that are better for the constructive integration of our emotional and intellectual natures, including compatibility of both of our individual and social personalities. Science communicates both its facts and its explanations by symbols, and these symbols have a highly significant relationship to scientific data. Let us summarize by stating that genes and symbols each transmit coded "information" to other individuals and that this communication occurs both between contemporary individuals and between generations. Both genes and symbols have the ability to repeat the codes. Both may vary by mutation or modification that produces new genes and new symbols from old ones. Both types of hereditary units may recombine to form new arrangements with emergent qualities. Systems of genes and systems of symbols may divide by partial or complete isolation to produce a branching evolutionary tree. Both become coordinated and coadapted within each population system. Each may be selected by either unconscious natural or conscious intelligent choices, and may thus be guided toward internal and external adaptation. Not only is there a cause leading to an effect in each system, but effects often influence repeated or continuous causes. Multiple negative feedbacks produce homeostatic regulations of optimal adjustments to varying conditions. In both genetic and symbolic systems we find an ever-increasing evolutionary diversity, division of labor, integration into more inclusive unitary entities, and control over the environment. Rigid determination and prediction are impossible in both organic and cultural evolution. Neither biology nor sociology will ever become an exact science that conforms to relatively simple mathematical formulae.

We may conclude that the symbol is a unit of cultural evolution, analogous to the gene unit in organic evolution. It is becoming increasingly apparent that numerous significant analogies occur between biological and cultural systems. These are based upon different mechanisms, but similar factors and processes result in time in a progressive advance in both types of evolution.

Progress is not just a subjective evaluation founded upon personal opinions or dogmatic assertions. We can scientifically measure evolutionary progress in terms of increased homeostasis, whether it be among individual organisms, social insects, or humans. We are coming to a mature understanding of biological evolutionary processes, and I think we are at the threshold of a far more mature understanding of cultural evolutionary processes as well. However, some concepts current in modern interpretations of cultural evolution seem to indicate a great need for better cooperation between social scientists and biologists. And productive investigations are by no means one-way from the natural sciences to the social sciences and humanities. The natural sciences are a product of cultural evolution and are motivated and stimulated by our emotional and intellectual responses to other aspects of our culture. I am confident that the geneticist can gain much perspective from a close study of linguistics and the evolution of language, and I think I have suggested how the linguist can borrow ideas from the theoretical models of the biochemical geneticist. The investigator of the social life of insects borrows many terms and concepts from the social scientist, and I am quite sure that the student of human society can find pertinent data and fundamental principles from researches on termite, wasp, bee, and ant societies. Let us not forget that both Darwin and Wallace independently discovered the guiding factor of organic evolution by reading Malthus on human populations. Natural science is intimately interdependent with all phases of human culture, including the social sciences, humanities, aesthetic arts, and religions.

Overpopulation is a major social problem of this century, and a sensible solution that avoids disaster will surely have to be worked out by many studies from multiple fields of inquiry. The investigation of the natural control of biological populations will contribute to the broad problem of the optimal control of human populations. Modern medicine has resulted in better control of health, infant mortality, and longevity. At the same time it is contributing to the "population explosion" that already produces poverty, misery, and degradation in large areas of the world (Vogt, 1960). This example of imperfection in balance between different optimal conditions necessitates drastic social action if overwhelming catastrophe is to be averted, and, so far, remedial programs are inadequate to meet this "problem of the century."

Another major social activity that is conspicuously the reverse of progress toward improved homeostasis is international war. Second only to overpopulation, war produces human misery and destroys many of the highest values of civilization. Mankind must learn what is obvious to the student of biological group systems. Human society the world over has species unity with interdependent parts, each with a contribution to make to the healthy progress of the whole. We need much more scientific knowledge of the evolution of human society, and we need social inventions that will apply this knowledge to human welfare and healthy survival of the whole species.

If the guiding factor of selection produces an evolutionary trend toward improved homeostasis in both social animals and man, our long-range prediction is that social man will find a solution, but not a perfect solution, ameliorating the destructive effects of overpopulation and international warfare. Social control and regulation of conflict and competition will become homeostatic.

From what I understand about the current philosophy of existentialism, represented by the writings of Jean-Paul Sartre, I think it is incompatible with the order of biological and cultural evolution, the meaning of life, and the destiny of man that I am sketching with broad sweeps of the brush in this essay. The aesthetic impact of existentialism in literature and art is noteworthy and I advocate a philosophy that integrates the sciences and humanities. But I fail to see that existentialism provides a philosophical basis or synthesis for human awareness of order or progress. (See article on "Sartre and Existentialism" in *Life*, vol. 57, no. 19, Nov. 6, 1964, pp. 86-110.)

A number of attempts have been made to find common principles applicable to both biological and cultural evolution. It is well to consider some of the most recent views in the light of the general viewpoint outlined in this paper.

Although the analogous resemblance of the organism to the supraorganism is significant in numerous respects, one must be careful not to assume complete similarity. The logistic curve of growth of an organism and a population of organisms can be demonstrated, but some (Bodenheimer, 1937) have thought that populations of social insects declined after a period of growth and relative stability. This decline was presumed to be due to innate factors within the population. Excessive inbreeding in a small population might result in the fixation of deleterious genes with consequent weakening or extinction of the isolated population. However, we have found no case in nature of an innate intraspecific population trend evolving against the external effects of natural selection (see Allee, *et al.*, 1949, pp. 327, 603, fig. 229D). The decline and extinction of natural populations must be ascribed in very large measure to external or extrinsic factors rather than to innate or intrinsic irreversible sequences producing population or species senescence. Physiological senescence and innate death of the individual organism is a well substantiated, though little understood, phenomenon. We have some data that indicate the adaptive evolution of individual death mechanisms. Rejuvenescence seems to be highly correlated with various forms of reproduction, and thus intraspecies populations are constantly being rejuvenated while the component individuals become senescent and die. In this important characteristic, populations are not wholly analogous to organisms.

About four decades ago, Oswald Spengler proposed a theory of cyclic growth and decline of civilizations, and his ideas of intrinsic social decline influenced the current historical interpretations of Arnold Toynbee, although Toynbee is not rigidly deterministic as was Spengler. Spengler drew many biological analogies to justify his notions of historical decline, but I think that the modern ecologist and population biologist would not find these analogues significant. When I read Spengler's *The Decline of the West* many years ago, I could not help but think that the exponential development of modern science in "western" civilization, and its spread to all other portions of the earth, was difficult to fit into a theory of social decline, and I still think that the cyclic interpretation of history rests upon very inadequate and uncritical information. It is my opinion that the historical and social scientists may learn much from the biologists, and that the reverse is also true, but there are obvious dangers in making superficial extrapolations from one field to the other.

One common denominator for populations of plants, animals, and humans is thought by some to be a thermodynamic trend. Cosmic thermodynamics is sometimes linked with the trend of organic evolution, but I find some recent discussions rather unconvincing. What place organic evolution has in cosmic processes is not apparent at present. Life replicates its systems by means of reproductive mechanisms, and temporarily maintains a dynamic relative equilibrium of matter and energy flux (metabolism and homeostasis) in its organismic systems. Living processes involve chemically complex substances with large molecules, such as DNA and proteins. Both replication and metabolism depend upon protein enzymes that both activate and inhibit physical and chemical processes in a fantastically complex coadapted spatial and temporal organism, including even the simplest and most primitive of living contemporary systems. It has been thought that life may reverse the general increase of entropy or dispersion of energy (Patten, 1959). I do not think that the evidence indicates negentropy in living systems. In my opinion, life may produce a long or short delay in the rate of entropy, but does not change its direction. The confusion seems to be due to the ambiguity of what is meant by organization. The physicist or astronomer may think of the concentration of energy in the sun as equivalent to organization, and entropy as a trend toward diffusion and disorganization. The biologist is aware of a trend toward higher levels of organization during the evolution of life, and this may falsely be termed negentropy. From my point of view, life processes take place within that small part of the linear order of energy diffusion in which temperatures can be maintained close to those of water in a liquid state. Confined to this small temperature span, neither so hot that complex molecules cannot exist or so cold that metabolism cannot occur, life had its origin and evolution. Negentropy would be illustrated by the origin of energy storing atoms in outer space or the concentration of atoms in a radiating body like the sun. The evolution of life seems to play no part whatsoever in any such reversal of the Second Law of Thermodynamics. Life utilizes solar energy without changing the direction of entropy. Human use of atomic energy likewise does not change the direction of entropy.

Lotka (1944, 1945) states that the collective activities and effects of organisms indicate a direction of organic evolution toward maximal energy intake from the sun, and maximal outgo of free energy by dissipative processes in living and in decaying dead organisms. In other words, Lotka suggests that there are evolutionary tendencies toward a high metabolic rate of the biomass of the whole ecosystem. "The net effect is to maximize in this sense the energy flux through the system of organic nature." I think it is questionable whether the "energy flux" has undergone any appreciable increase within the whole ecosystem or biosphere as a result of evolutionary change since, let us say, Cretaceous times. I admit that there is probably some change in energy used by living organisms due to the fluctuations of solar energy reaching the biosphere. I should also guess that the total living energy must have increased when organisms elaborated and improved the efficiency of photosynthesis, and when plants and animals invaded the terrestrial habitat from the sea. It is also possible that the atomic age may usher in a higher degree of energy flux as one of the consequences of the cultural evolution of man. However, the application of the principle of increased energy flux to the evolution of life on the earth seems to be limited and not global or universal. Certainly much evolutionary advance takes place without the necessity of assuming an increase in energy flux through the ecosystem.

Contrasting somewhat to Lotka's principle of increased energy flux through the ecosystem, Zipf (1949) has elaborated a principle of Least Effort. He attempts to order life processes and human social and individual behavior under this principle. Zipf says: "An organism is a movable mathematical point in time-space, in reference to which matter-energy moves in such a way that a physical situation exists in which work is expended in order to preserve a physical system (continual as a whole but not continual as to its parts) from a final gravitational and electromagnetic equilibrium with the rest of the universe. In simple terms, the Principle of Least Effort means, for example, that a person in solving his immediate problems will view these against the background of his probable future problems, *as estimated by himself.* Moreover he will strive to solve his problems in such a way as to minimize the *total work* that he must expend in solving *both* his immediate problems *and* his probable future problems. That in turn means that the person will strive to minimize the *probable average rate of his work-expenditure* (over time). And in so doing he will be minimizing his *effort*, by our definition of effort. Least effort, therefore, is a variant of least work."

An evolutionary trend toward greater efficiency in carrying out the needs and processes of living organisms is evident. I have no doubt that survival of the fittest is often correlated with the survival of the more efficient. But evolutionary progress often necessitates greater, not less, effort. Evolutionary advances of insect and human societies afford examples of increased effort. The rise of scientific and technological civilization in recent centuries has not resulted from a philosophy of reduced work, nor were the great ancient and medieval architectural monuments of Asia and Europe that indicate advanced social organization built with a motivation of least effort. In truth, an increase of efficient coordination and existence among both insects and men is often accompanied by more, not less, effort toward the attainment of higher values. Can the foreign assistance programs of Soviet Russia or the United States (ten times that of Russia), or, for that matter, the enormous build-up of deterent military force against the possibility of aggression, be harmonized with a principle of Least Effort in cultural evolution? It is hoped that an efficiency principle for the welfare of humanity as a whole within a balanced natural environment may ultimately win out over the gross inefficiencies of national warfare and destructive competition. I suspect great effort on the part of large numbers of highly motivated, energetic persons in all nations is necessary to avert destructive disintegration.

A trend toward dominance has also been thought to be a principle or law, both in organic and cultural evolution. In biology, dominance is a term used for a tissue (nervous system or brain) over other tissues, for the male over the female sex, for a parent (usually female) over the off-spring, for the alpha individual in a social hierarchy (flock of hens) over individuals of lower status, for the largest predator (tiger or lion) at the peak of an Eltonian pyramid, for a species in the community that strongly modifies the environment (beaver or reef coral), for a species in a community that is most abundant, for a species that is largest or most conspicuous in a given habitat, or for a successful group in an evolutionary sequence (dominant reptiles in the Mesozoic; dominant mammals in the Tertiary; dominant man in post-glacial times).

In human society we often refer to the dominant father in the family, to the dominant chief of a tribe, to the dominant individual in a hierarchy (pope, military commander, president of a university, king in a monarchy, dictator of a totalitarian state, or a captain of industry), to a dominant language in a polylingual state, or to a dominant social group or class (political party, governing class, or strongest nation in a group of nations).

There are connotations of control and of power in these usages of the term dominant. Sir Julian Huxley goes so far as to say that the emergence of dominant man at the psycho-social cultural level of organization negates further important non-human organic evolution. In some extremes, the concept of dominance in biology and sociology may be used to justify the ruthless use of political, economic, or national power against competitors (*social Darwinism* of the late nineteenth century). Survival of the strong replaces survival of the fit.

The evolution of insect societies and the ecological systems to which they are adjusted seem to show that there is an interdependence of the so-called dominant and subordinate individuals and groups. The food web, the social and community structure, and the organic chemical cycles in ecological communities and the ecosystem indicate a unity of coordinated relations, each individual and each species showing a degree of functional division of labor within a more inclusive entity. The concept of dominance suggests an evolution toward unilateral exploitation of one group by another, and there is much biological evidence that unilateral exploitation and competitive elimination is a factor in natural systems. But an examination of insect social evolution provides rather strong evidence that the emergence of the dominant exploiter, the aggressive predator, or the highly populated society is not the major nor the exclusive direction of biological evolution. The interdependencies in the intricate web of relationships within the individual organism, the intraspecific population, and the interspecific community (Pimental, 1961) point rather clearly to the evolutionary trend toward a balanced integration, toleration, co-existence, and cooperative mutualism between the parts of all coordinated levels of organization, from the smallest gene and enzyme units of life to the largest global ecosystem.

The two ends of the spectrum of relations expressed in the terms exploitation and cooperation should not be considered sharply divided nor mutually exclusive. Not only is every gradation between the two easily observable, but we have reason to think that an optimum balance may have evolved. A certain amount of competition may be beneficial to mutualistic systems and a certain benefit to the exploited species may result from a predator-prey relationship. Incompatibilities certainly occur both within and between organisms, and various types of compromise solutions are apparent. Perfection of optimal adjustments within and between infinitely complex organisms is utterly impossible. Adaptation is never perfect, but there is an evolutionary trend toward improved regulation of optimal conditions of existence and perpetuation (homeostasis) since the dawn of life on this earth.

It seems to me that the homeostatic trend of biological evolution always necessitates compromise solutions of incompatibilities between interdependent parts of living systems at every level of integration. I am of the opinion that evolutionary history provides much substantiation for this broad generalization. To what extent does this principle apply to the cultural evolution of man? We must not extrapolate from one system to the other without substantiating evidence, but such evidence is slowly accumulating. Much further information is necessary before we can say with complete conviction that organic and cultural evolution are based upon similar principles, or that the social life of insects and the social life of humans may be treated as special examples of a more general phenomenon.

I believe the time is ripe, however, when we can make comparisons between convergently evolved insect and human societies and point out significant analogies. Genetic units may be analogized with symbolic units. Hereditary variation and recombination occur in both. Partial isolation produces diversity and pattern consolidation in both. Selection guides both societies toward better adaptive responses. Both conservatism and freedom to change have their roles in progressive evolution. Time dimensions are combined with spatial dimensions in both. Continuation of the past into the future (immortality) is found in both genetic and cultural systems. End-directedness (teleonomy) is discernible and scientifically substantiated in both. Archaicisms and vestiges of past structures and actions occur in both. Behavior and structure are products of physiological processes in both. Cultural heredity (customs, knowledge, aesthetics, ethics, religion) may be analogized with genetic heredity. Both insects and humans incorporate earlier separated units into more inclusive systems. Emergent novelties appear with new associations in both. In evolutionary time both progress toward increased social and ecological homeostasis. The fundamental and measurable component of adaptation is homeostasis in both. False principles based upon authoritarian dogma and superstition may be discarded. Inadequate individual objectives such as "happiness," selfish accumulation of wealth, and luxury consumption can be modified, reoriented, and turned toward socially constructive ends in harmony with fundamental principles of life.

Wisdom attained through the synthesis of science, emotion, and aesthetic appreciation will surely assist us to move progressively forward toward the realistic goals indicated by the evolution of life during the last two thousand million years or more. We may gain perspective and inspiration from a penetrating understanding of insect and human societies. With increasing awareness of our social objectives and responsibilities we can devise techniques to accomplish our purposes more efficiently and rapidly. Abraham Lincoln said, "If we could first know where we are and whither we are tending, we could better judge what to do and how to do it." Francis Bacon, during the childhood of science, said, "Make the time to come the disciple of the time past and not the servant." In ancient times, the advice of Solomon was, "Go to the ant, thou sluggard; consider her ways and be wise; which having no guide, overseer or ruler, provideth her meat in the summer and gathereth her food in the harvest."

Wise pronouncements in any age are only valid when they conform to accumulated experience and assembled data. Science is continuously self-corrective, and other aspects of human thinking and decision should emulate science in this respect. Without minimizing the current dangers to civilization and social progress, I am optimistic that creative discoveries through freedom of inquiry in the natural sciences, social sciences, humanities, and religions will lead man toward better balanced personalities and improved regulation of his society within his modified natural environment. Social man has the capacity and the ethical responsibility to guide his own organic and cultural evolution.

BIBLIOGRAPHY

Allee, W. C., Emerson, A. E., Park, O., Park, T., and Schmidt, K. P. *Principles of Animal Ecology.* Saunders, Philadelphia. 837 pp, 1949.

Anfinsen, C. B. *The Molecular Basis of Evolution.* Wiley, New York. 228 pp, 1959.

Beadle, G. W. *Molecules, Viruses, and Heredity.* Bull. Atomic Scientists, 15:354–360, 1959.

Blum, H. F. *Time's Arrow and Evolution.* Princeton Univ. Press, Princeton, New Jersey. 222 pp, 1951.

Bodenheimer, F. S. *Population Problems of Social Insects.* Biol. Rev., 12:393–430, 1937.

Bodenheimer, F. S. *The Concept of Biotic Organization in Synecology.* Bull. Res. Council Israel, 3:114–121, 1953.

Bonner, J. T. *Cells and Societies.* Princeton Univ. Press, Princeton, New Jersey. 234 pp. 1955.

Booth, E. P. (editor) 1964. *Religion Ponders Science.* Appleton-Century, New York. 302 pp. 1964.

de Chardin, T. *The Phenomenon of Man.* Harper & Bros., New York. 318 pp, 1959.

Dale, A. *An Introduction to Social Biology* (3d edit.). Thomas, Springfield, Illinois. 434 pp, 1959.

Dunbar, M. J. The Evolution of Stability in Marine Environments. *Amer. Nat.*, 94:129–136, 1960.

Emerson, A. E. Termite Nests—A Study of the Phylogeny of Behavior. *Ecol. Monogr.*, 8:247–284, 1938.

Emerson, A. E. Social Coordination and the Superorganism. *Amer. Midl. Nat.,* 21:182–209, 1939a.

Emerson, A. E. Populations of Social Insects. *Ecol. Monogr.,* 9:287–300, 1939b.

Emerson, A. E. Basic Comparisons of Human and Insect Societies. *Biol. Symposia,* 8:163–176, 1942.

Emerson, A. E. Ecology, Evolution and Society. *Amer. Nat.,* 77:97–118, 1943.

Emerson, A. E. Why Termites? *Sci. Monthly,* 64:337–345, 1947.

Emerson, A. E. Dynamic Homeostasis: A Unifying Principle in Organic, Social, and Ethical Evolution. *Sci. Monthly,* 78:67–85, 1954.

Emerson, A. E. Geographical Origins and Dispersions of Termite Genera, Fieldiana: *Zoology,* 37:465–521, 1955.

Emerson, A. E. Regenerative Behavior and Social Homeostasis of Termites. *Ecology,* 37: 248–258, 1956.

Emerson, A. E. Social Insects. *Encyclop. Brit.,* 20:871–878, 1959.

Emerson, A. E. Vestigial Characters of Termites and Processes of Regressive Evolution. *Evolution,* 15:115–131, 1961.

Emerson, A. E. The Impact of Darwin on Biology. *Acta Biotheoretica,* 15:175–216, 1962.

Grassé, P.–P., *et al. Colloques internationaux du Centre national de la Recherche scientifique.* XXXIX: Structure et Physiologie des Sociétés animales. Paris. 359 pp, 1952.

Greenberg, J. H. Language and Evolution. In: Evolution and Anthropology: A Centennial Appraisal. *Anthrop. Soc.* Washington, D. C., pp. 61–75, 1959.

Grinker, R. R. *Toward a Unified Theory of Human Behavior.* Basic Books, New York. 375 pp, 1956.

Hamburgh, M. A Biologist's Reflections on History. *Am. Inst. Biol. Sci. Bull.* (June, 1960), 6 pp, 1960.

Hutchinson, G. E. Homage to Santa Rosalia or Why are there so many kinds of animals. *Amer. Nat.,* 93:145–159, 1959.

Huxley, J. *Man and the Future of Evolution.* Midway, 1:37–49, 1960.

Kluckhohn, C. The Role of Evolutionary Thought in Anthropology. In: Evolution and Anthropology: A Centennial Appraisal. *Anthrop. Soc.* Washington, D. C., pp. 144–157, 1959.

Lindauer, M. *Communication among Social Bees.* Harvard University Press, Cambridge, Mass. 143 pp, 1961.

Lotka, A. J. Evolution and Thermodynamics. *Science and Society,* 8:161–171, 1944.

Lotka, A. J. The Law of Evolution as a Maximal Principle. *Human Biology,* 17:167–194, 1945.

MacNeish, R. S. The Origins of New World Civilization. *Scientific Amer.,* 211(5):29–37, 1964.

Mead, Margaret. Cultural Determinants of Behavior, In: Roe, Anne, and Simpson, G. G. *Behavior and Evolution.* Yale Univ. Press, New Haven, Conn., pp. 480–503, 1958.

Medawar, P. B. *The Future of Man.* Basic Books, New York. 128 pp, 1960.

Medawar, P. B. (Letter in response to criticism by H. J. Muller). *Perspectives in Biol. and Med.,* 4(3): 385–386, 1961.

Muller, H. J. (Review of Medawar, P. B. 1960. The Future of Man). *Perspectives in Biol. and Med.,* 4(3):377–380, 1961.

Murdock, G. P. Evolution in Social Organization. In: Evolution and Anthropology: A Centennial Appraisal. *Anthrop. Soc.* Washington, D. C., pp. 126–143, 1959.

Odum, H. T. Ecological Potential and Analogue Circuits for the Ecosystem. *Amer. Scientist,* 48:1–8, 1960.

Patten, B. C. An Introduction to the Cybernetics of the Ecosystem: The Trophic-Dynamic Aspect. *Ecology,* 40:221–231, 1959.

Pimentel, D. Animal Population Regulation by the Genetic Feed-back Mechanism. *Amer. Nat.,* 95:65–79, 1961.

Roe, Anne, and Simpson, G. G. (editors). *Behavior and Evolution.* Yale Univ. Press., New Haven, Conn. 577 pp, 1958.

Rossiter, C. Adventures of the Mind: Why Marx Failed Here. *Saturday Evening Post,* 233 (No. 8, August 20): 32–33, 78, 80, 1960.

Sahlins, M. D., and Service, E. R. *Evolution and Culture*. Univ. Michigan Press, Ann Arbor, Mich. 131 pp, 1960.

Seevers, C. A. Monograph on the Termitophilous Staphylinidae. Fieldiana: *Zoology*, 40:1–334, 1957.

Shaply, H. (edit.). *Science Ponders Religion*. Appleton-Century-Crofts, New York. 308 pp, 1960.

Simpson, G. G. *The Major Features of Evolution*. Columbia Univ. Press, New York. 434 pp, 1953.

Spencer, R. F. The North Alaska Eskimo—A Study in Ecology and Society. *Smiths. Inst. Bur. Amer. Ethnol. Bull.*, No. 171:1–490, 1959.

Spengler, J. J. Population and World Economic Development. *Science*, 131:1497–1502, 1960.

Tax, S. (edit.). *Evolution After Darwin*, Vol. I. *The Evolution of Life: Its Origin, History, and Future*, 629 pp. Vol. II. *The Evolution of Man: Mind, Culture, and Society*, 473 pp. Vol. III. *Issues in Evolution: The University of Chicago Centennial Discussion*, 310 pp. Univ. Chicago, Press, Chicago, Illinois, 1960.

Vogt, W. *People! Challenge to Survival*. Sloane, New York. 257 pp. 1960.

Waddington, C. H. *The Strategy of the Genes*. Macmillan, New York. 262 pp. 1957.

White, Leslie, A. The Concept of Evolution in Cultural Anthropology. In: Evolution and Anthropology: A Centennial Appraisal. *Anthrop. Soc.* Washington, D. C., pp. 106–125, 1959.

Wolf, S. Disease as a Way of Life: Neural Integration in Systemic Pathology. *Perspectives in Biol. and Med.*, 4(3): 288–305, 1961.

Zipf, G. K. *Human Behaviour and the Principle of Least Effort, An Introduction to Human Ecology*. Addison-Wesley Press, Cambridge, Mass. 573 pp, 1949.

CULTURAL DYNAMICS AND EVOLUTIONARY THEORY

MORRIS E. OPLER

Cornell University

It has been suggested that my contribution to this Conference on Social Science and the Underdeveloped Areas be a consideration from the point of view of a cultural anthropologist of the degree to which current interest in technological, economic, social, and political change in unindustrialized regions reflects a revival of evolutionary theory.

It is true that many anthropologists have been drawn to the study of changes taking place in the underdeveloped parts of the world. It is also true that there is a marked revival of interest in evolutionary theory in anthropology or, at least, a revival of the use of the term. The relationship between these two phenomena is complex and requires considerable background and analysis to unravel.

I have hinted that some of the evolutionary theorizing in anthropology today does not go more than word deep. This in itself is a measure of the fashion or "revival." Apparently a growing number of anthropologists, even when they have no clear evidence of evolutionary progression, feel impelled to use titles or terminology which suggests that they do. For instance, in a recently published book an anthropologist triumphantly characterized as an evolutionary sequence a series of variations in the social organization of a number of related peoples so slight and random that it is absurd to consider them of an evolutionary order.[1] In another paper, entitled "Social Fields and the Evolution of Society," Dr. Alexander Lesser argues eloquently that the complex needs of specific groups can be taken care of by what he terms intercommunal specialization as well as by intracommunal specialization.[2] According to him, too little attention has been paid to the consequences of diffusion, contact, communication,

[1] Meggers, 1960, pp. 312-313.   [2] Lesser, 1961.

68

trade, and the resulting benefits that accrue to all the cooperating and influenced groups within an extended area or broad social field. Instead, he claims, it has been assumed that the fruits of specialization can be enjoyed only by isolated social aggregates in which some technological advance provides a surplus which can then be used to support and encourage specialists of various kinds. Lesser's suggestion that we think about the contributions of interacting groups to one another, rather than confine ourselves to the study of interacting individuals within a particular group, is a stimulating one and deserves consideration. What interests me as much as the idea itself, however, is that it is presented in evolutionary garb. Actually as far as I can see, it is mainly an anti-evolutionary view, for it declares, in substance, that a social group can obtain the benefits of differentiation and specialization by trade and exchange without itself going through an evolutionary development. What Dr. Lesser is really offering is a substitute explanation for effects that have most often been attributed to an evolutionary process.

Even after we have disposed of pseudo-evolutionism and pure verbalism about evolution, there are difficulties in determining what relationship, if any, exists between an interest in change in underdeveloped areas and a revival of evolutionary theory. For there have been not one, but several, significant evolutionary doctrines in anthropology. Which one of them is being revived? Do the concepts of change and development which are being applied to underdeveloped areas stem from a single one, or from more than one of them? Is there a stream of thought about culture change which has little or no tie with evolutionism but which nevertheless has become involved in the study of transitions in underdeveloped areas?

In an effort to answer these questions let us examine the principal doctrines of evolution which have grown up in anthropology, beginning with the formulation of Edward B. Tylor, the noted British anthropologist, who exercised great influence in the discipline from the time of the publication of his first general treatise in 1865 until well after the turn of the century.

Despite the fact that Tylor introduced the definition of culture that most social scientists accept and repeat today and thus paved the way for a sharp distinction between physical inheritance and cultural acquisitions, he himself was not completely emancipated from racism and from notions of the superior cultural attainments and potentialities of "gifted breeds."[3]

Because of the very inclusiveness of his evolutionary doctrine, this type

[3] For instance, in his last general book, the one in which his views were most completely developed, he still could say:

....It cannot be at present made out how far the peculiarities of single ancestors were inherited by their descendants and became stronger by in-breeding; how far, when the weak and dull-witted tribes failed in the struggle for land and life, the stronger, braver, and abler of thinking, with its benevolence toward colonialism and its ethnocentrism, was extremely difficult to avoid, for evolution to Tylor meant concomitant physical, mental, and cultural changes. In the quotation, notice Tylor's strong dependence on Darwinian natural selection as an explanation of the physical differences between groups of men, and the results of the clashes between cultures for "land and life."

Despite these physical differentiations between human groups and the related cultural potentials which he recognized, Tylor saw a much greater gap between man and other primates than between one variety of man and any other. He was therefore inclined, within limits, to consider all mankind as one basic unit; and he tended, in the main, to emphasize the similarities of human physiological response and need, rather than the differences.

Man's biological unity was more than matched, Tylor believed, by his underlying psychic unity. Tylor was impressed by the fact that any human child of sound mind, given the opportunity early enough, could learn any language spoken on earth. It seemed to him that, unless some fundamental unity of the human mind were postulated, similarities in gesture language the world over and the existence of comparable institutions, symbols, and myths in areas widely separated could not easily be explained. Moreover, Tylor saw in man's natural environment a reasonably uniform background of challenge and opportunity. In spite of climatic differences and variations in resources, life could be maintained in most regions into which man penetrated. Everywhere there was need for protection against the elements and foes, human and nonhuman. Throughout most of the world nature provided materials to be used for shelter, dress, and artifacts. In nearly all regions, sufficient animal and vegetable food existed to support human groups. The world and its people appeared to Tylor to be a vast laboratory in which uniform causes operating in similar settings might be expected to yield comparable results, and he felt confident that he had isolated factors sufficiently stable and objective to serve for a science of culture.

It was almost inevitable that Tylor's science of culture should be actively concerned with issues of history and process. Paleontology, geology, and archeology had raised questions concerning the duration and sequence of epochs of the strata of the earth, of plant forms, of animals (including man), and of culture. It was the triumph of Darwinism in biology to offer a generally acceptable explanation of the manner in which life had developed and

tribes survived to leave their types stamped on the nations sprung from them; how far whole migrating tribes underwent bodily alteration through change of climate, food, and habits, so that the peopling of the earth went on together with the growth of fresh races fitted for life in its various regions. (Tylor, 1881, p. 5.)

differentiated over time. Tylor addressed himself to comparable problems with special reference to culture, using most of the same postulates which had proved so helpful in charting inorganic and organic evolution.

One of the postulates of biological evolution which Tylor felt applied as well to cultural evolution was that developments on the whole occurred slowly over immense spans of time. A related postulate was that the changes were minute rather than large and that their effect was cumulative rather than abrupt.[4] In the third place Tylor held that the changes were of significance and that they did not cancel each other out but moved culture in a direction which was, despite minor fluctuations and disruptions, irreversible in principle. In the fourth place, Tylor argued that this movement is prevailingly a progressive one involving more knowledge, greater efficiency, extended control over nature, and higher morality. According to this view, all aspects of culture share in this advance. In successive evolutionary stages family life becomes more secure, thinking more logical, knowledge more detailed, artifacts more efficient, religion more firmly wedded to morality, and abundance more general. Tylor applied this conception of evolutionary progress through stages of savagery, barbarism, and civilization to culture in the first instance; but he also believed that any given group that maintained its existence and vitality for any great length of time could be expected to pass through the defined stages seriatim. He asserted time and again that the ancestors of members of complex civilizations must be presumed to have passed through stages of less exalted practice and must have resembled, at earlier points of history, the barbarians and savages of his day.

One does not have to labor over his writings to winnow out the postulates I have attributed to Tylor or attempt any elaborate analysis to arrive at them. Tylor's works are generously sprinkled with clear summary statements of his premises.[5]

[4] For statements on these points by Tylor in addition to those to be cited below, see Tylor, 1881, p. 144, and Tylor, 1878, p. 122.

[5] In one place he writes:

.... The thesis which I venture to sustain, within limits, is simply this, that the savage state in some measure represents an early condition of mankind, out of which the higher culture has gradually been developed or evolved, by processes still in regular operation as of old, the result showing that, on the whole, progress has far prevailed over relapse .... That the tendency of culture has been similar throughout the existence of human society, and that we may fairly judge from its known historic course what its prehistoric course may have been, is a theory clearly entitled to precedence as a fundamental principle of ethnographic research. (Tylor, 1871, Vol. I, pp. 32–33.)

Another well-known and much quoted passage reads:

On the whole it appears that wherever there are found elaborate arts, abstruse knowledge, complex institutions, these are results of gradual development from an earlier, simpler, and ruder state of life. No stage of civilization comes into existence spontaneously, but grows or

We are not surprised to find that Tylor in one place defined civilization as "the general improvement of mankind by higher organization of the individual and of society, to the end of promoting at once man's goodness, power,

> is developed out of the stage before it. (Tylor, 1881, p. 16.)

Even Tylor's articles and shorter pieces, as the following quotations indicate, seldom fail to provide the evolutionary overview within which he worked:

> The teaching of history, during the three to four thousand years of which contemporary chronicles have been preserved, is that civilization is gradually developed in the course of ages by enlargement and increased precision of knowledge, invention and improvement of arts, and the progression of social and political habits and institutions towards general well-being. . . . Starting from the recorded condition of such barbaric nations [as the older Jews, Greeks, and Germans—M.E.O.] and following the general course of culture into the modern world, all the great processes of mental and social development may be seen at work. Falling back or decay also takes place, but only to a limited extent destroys the results of growth in culture. It is thus a matter of actual record, that the ancestors of civilized nations were barbaric tribes, and the inference seems reasonable that the same process of development had gone on during previous ages outside the domain of direct history, so that barbaric culture itself arose out of an earlier and ruder condition of primitive culture, more or less corresponding with the state of modern savage tribes. (Tylor, 1878, p. 121.)

> . . . . Even the diagrams of this paper may suffice to show that the institutions of man are as distinctly stratified as the earth on which he lives. They succeed each other in series substantially uniform over the globe, independent of what seem the comparatively superficial differences of race and language, but shaped by similar human nature acting through successively changed conditions in savage, barbaric, and civilized life. (Tylor, 1889, p. 269.)

To give the flavor of Tylor's dicta concerning the universal stages and the unilinear progression of human groups through them, we quote two passages from his last general treatise, *Anthropology.*

> . . . . This classification of three great stages of culture is practically convenient, and has the advantage of not describing imaginary states of society, but such as are actually known to exist. So far as the evidence goes, it seems that civilization has actually grown up in the world through these three stages, so that to look at a savage of the Brazilian forests, a barbarous New Zealander or Dahoman, and a civilized European, may be the student's best guide to understanding the progress of civilization, only he must be cautioned that the comparison is but a guide, not a full explanation.

> In this way it is reasonably inferred that even in countries now civilized, savage and low barbaric tribes must have once lived. (Tylor, 1881, p. 19.)

> . . . . As the foregoing chapters have proved, savage and barbarous tribes often more or less fairly represent stages of culture through which our own ancestors passed long ago, and their customs and laws often explain to us, in ways we should otherwise have hardly guessed, the sense and reason of our own. (*Ibid.*, p. 313.)

Even before this, in his first general book, Tylor had delineated his unilinear evolutionary theory:

> . . . . The state of things which is found is not indeed that one race does or knows exactly what another race does or knows, but that similar stages of development recur in different times and places. There is reason to suppose that our ancestors in remote times made fire with a machine much like that of the modern Esquimaux, and at a far later date they used the bow and arrow, as so many savage tribes do still. (Tylor, 1865, p. 371.)

Since we shall be mentioning Darwinism, it is interesting that Tylor, in an encyclopaedia article, refers to his formulation as "the natural development-theory of civilization."

> . . . . It has been especially the evidence of prehistoric archaeology which, within the last

and happiness.'"[6] Yet Tylor was not content merely to indicate the direction of change or to stop at a description of the stages through which he believed culture had passed. He sought to provide an identification of the dynamics—the causative agent or agents—which moved culture from savagery toward civilization.

Tylor found the key to cultural evolution in what I would call "cultural Darwinism," a process of selection of the fittest among artifacts and customs competing for recognition as the most useful and adaptive in their categories. Whether this was a conscious or unconscious use of Darwin's "natural selection" or whether, as some think, it has an independent history, is not central to this analysis.[7] I believe that the appearance of a concept so completely parallel to Darwinism in the work of a scholar so friendly to Darwinism is rather strong presumptive evidence of the influence of Darwin's theories of biological evolution upon this formulation.[8]

Tylor's writings, from first to last, are peppered with expressions of cultural Darwinism of this kind. I should like to make this very explicit, for in some branches of the "revival" of evolutionism there is a tendency to picture Tylor as endorsing a technological, rather than a cultural Darwinian, explanation of developmental dynamics.[9]

few years, has given to the natural development-theory of civilization a predominance hardly disputed on anthropological grounds.... The finding of ancient stone implements buried in the ground in almost every habitable district of the world, including the seats of the great ancient civilizations, such as Egypt, Assyria, India, China, Greece, etc., may be adduced to show that the inhabitants of these regions had at some time belonged to the stone age. This argument goes far to prove that the ancestors of all nations, high and low, were once in that uncultured condition as to knowledge, arts, and manners generally, which within our experience accompanies the use of stone implements and the want of metals. (Tylor, 1878, p. 121.)

[6] Tylor, 1871, Vol. I, p. 27.

[7] White, 1959, p. 107.

[8] Whatever its derivation, Tylor's position is unmistakable, and we can find it summarized pointedly in his own words:

.... It will be seen again and again, by examining such topics as language, mythology, custom, religion, that savage opinion is in a more or less rudimentary state, while the civilized mind still bears vestiges, neither few nor slight, of a past condition from which savages represent the least, and civilized men the greatest advance. Throughout the whole vast range of the history of human thought and habit, while civilization has to contend not only with survival from lower levels, but also with degeneration within its own borders, it yet proves capable of overcoming both and taking its own course. History within its proper field, and ethnography over a wider range, combine to show that the institutions which can best hold their own in the world gradually supersede the less fit ones, and that this incessant conflict determines the general resultant course of culture. (Tylor, 1871, Vol. 1, pp. 68–69.)

[9] Perhaps a few additional excerpts will help us appreciate Tylor's position on this matter:

.... But arts which belong to the daily life of the man or the family and cannot be entirely suppressed by violent interference, do not readily disappear unless superseded by some

Tylor does not merely flourish his doctrine of the survival of the culturally fittest in a general way. He applies it to specific aspects and institutions of culture.[10]

Language, too, according to Tylor, goes through a process of selection and elevation in order to fit it for its modern tasks.[11] Religion is likewise constantly subjected to tests of purpose and fitness, and can maintain itself only by adaptation and improvement.[12] Nor is science exempt from the evolution-

better contrivance, or made unnecessary by a change of life and manners. (Tylor, 1865, p. 185.)

.... On the other hand, though arts which flourish in times of great refinement or luxury, and complex processes which require a combination of skill or labour hard to get together and liable to be easily disarranged, may often degenerate, yet the more homely and useful the art, and the less difficult the conditions for its exercise, the less likely it is to disappear from the world, unless when superseded by some better device. (*Ibid.*, p. 373.)

.... It seems to me that Dr. Klemm, in his dissertation on Implements and Weapons, and Colonel Lane Fox, in his lectures on Primitive Warfare, take a more instructive line in tracing the early development of arts, not to a blind instinct, but to a selection, imitation, and gradual adaptation and improvement of objects and operations which Nature, the instructor of primaeval man, sets before him. (Tylor, 1871., Vol. 1, p. 64.)

.... History, so far as it reaches back, shows arts, sciences, and political institutions beginning in ruder states, and becoming in the course of ages more intelligent, more systematic, more perfectly arranged or organized, to answer their purposes. (Tylor, 1881, p. 11.)

[10] Of legal and political institutions he declares:

.... The history of judicial and administrative institutions may be appealed to for illustrations of the modes in which old social formations are reshaped to meet new requirements, new regulations are made, and new officers are constituted to perform the more complex duties of modern society, while from time to time institutions of past ages, which have lost their original purpose, and become obsolete or hurtful, are swept away. (Tylor, 1878, p. 122.)

[11] .... Ethnography reasonably accounts at once for the immense power and the manifest weakness of language as a means of expressing modern educated thought, by treating it as an original product of low culture, gradually adapted by ages of evolution and selection, to answer more or less sufficiently the requirements of modern civilization. (Tylor, 1871, Vol. 1, p. 239.)

[12] As Tylor puts it:

.... Unless a religion can hold its place in the front of science and of morals, it may only gradually, in the course of ages, lose its place in the nation, but all the power of state-craft and all the wealth of the temples will not save it from eventually yielding to a belief that takes in higher knowledge and teaches better life. (Tylor, 1881, p. 291.)

.... It is the doctrines and rites of the lower races which are, according to their philosophy, results of point-blank natural evidence and acts of straightforward practical purpose. It is the doctrines and rites of the higher races which show survival of the old in the midst of the new, modification of the old to bring it into conformity with the new, abandonment of the old because it is no longer compatible with the new. (Tylor, 1871, Vol. 1, p. 500.)

.... It will aid us to see how much more the fruit of religion belongs to ethical influence than to philosophical dogma, if we consider how the introduction of the moral element separates the religions of the world, united as they are throughout by one animistic principle, into two great classes, those lower systems whose best result is to supply a crude childlike natural philosophy, and those higher faiths which implant on this the law of righteousness and of holiness, the inspiration of duty and of love. (Tylor, 1871, Vol. 2, p. 361.) [Footnote 12 continued next page] ary spiral. Savage conceptions have to give ground and yield to more serviceable knowledge based on careful observation and reasoning.[13]

It must not be supposed that, because Tylor conceived of evolution as a many-sided process, he considered every facet of it to be of equal importance. Actually, he believed that developments in one sphere in particular are of greatest moment, that attainment in this area makes possible a wide range of advance, and that failure here constitutes an effective bar to general evolutionary progress. This was a determinism of sorts, but it was not economic determinism, technological determinism, social determinism, or (if culture be viewed in a holistic sense) cultural determinism. Because it hinges on the importance that Tylor attributes to the evolution of mind and to man's development of a certain level of intellectual achievement as a prelude to his successful control over natural forces and his own destiny, it can perhaps be named "rationalistic determinism."

It is essential to understand the significance and primacy that Tylor attached to the acquisition of rational thought and logic and, in addition, the degree to which he saw in this the gateway to knowledge and to the control of the life forces. Historical materialists and technological determinists subordinate mind to matter and see mental life as the consequence or "superstructure" of the mode of production. In Tylor's view, mental life has an evolution of its own and one that has enormous implications for all the rest of culture and for the further progress of culture. I emphasize this because Tylor's attention to progress in the material arts is sometimes taken to mean that he was a materialist and because his references to man's increasing control over nature are interpreted as evidence of his espousal of technological determinism. Yet Tylor's general position is obviously one of philosophical idealism. It is true that he said that man's first need "is to get his daily food." But he also taught—and this is central to his evolutionism—that man's food quest and all his other endeavors will remain on a humble, brutish level until certain intellectual goals are reached and obstructing mental confusions are eliminated.

> .... Looking at each doctrine by itself and for itself, as in the abstract true or untrue, theologians close their eyes to the instances which history is ever holding up before them, that one phase of a religious belief is the outcome of another, that in all times religion has included within its limits a system of philosophy, expressing its more or less transcendental conceptions in doctrines which form in any age their fittest representatives, but which doctrines are liable to modification in the general course of intellectual change, whether the ancient formulas still hold their authority with altered meaning, or are themselves reformed or replaced. (*Ibid.*, pp. 450–451.)

[13] .... In the evolution of science the new knowledge ever starts from the old, whether its results be to improve, to shift, or to supersede it .... Beginning with this first stage of the science, there lies before us the whole record of the exacter observation and closer reasoning which have gradually replaced these childlike savage conceptions by the most perfect of physical theories. (Tylor, 1878, p. 121.)

Early in his very first general book Tylor gives some indication of the import he attaches to the evolution of mind.[14] Nor does he leave us in doubt about the nature of the "condition of mind which we of the more advanced races have almost outgrown." It is the tendency of man in early stages of mental evolution to confuse an object with the image of it, the word with what it represents, dream with reality.[15]

Philosophy, religion, language, and thought are all vastly affected by the inability to distinguish between the object and its representation during the earlier stages of mental evolution, an evolution which, according to Tylor, is still proceeding.[16] Whatever their appearance and physical characteristics, avers Tylor, those who have not advanced sufficiently far along the path of mental evolution are bound to be childish and ineffective.[17]

[14] . . . . In the following chapter on "Images and Names," an attempt is made to refer a great part of the beliefs and practices included under the general name of magic, to one very simple mental law, as resulting from a condition of mind which we of the more advanced races have almost outgrown, and in doing so have undergone one of the most notable changes which we can trace as having happened to mankind. (Tylor, 1865, p. 3.)

[15] . . . . It needs no very large acquaintance with the life and ways of thought of the savage, to prove that there is to be found all over the world, especially among races at a low mental level, a view as to this matter which is very different from that which a more advanced education has impressed upon us. Man, in a low stage of culture, very commonly believes that between the object and the image of it there is a real connexion, which does not arise from a mere subjective process in the mind of the observer, and that it is accordingly possible to communicate an impression to the original through the copy. (*Ibid.*, pp. 119–120.)

After introducing some examples of the type of thinking among aboriginal peoples which he considers characteristic, Tylor again asserts:

> Such cases as these bring clearly into view the belief in a real connexion existing between an object and its image. By virtue of their resemblance, the two are associated in thought, and being thus brought into connexion in the mind, it comes to be believed that they are also in connexion in the outside world. (*Ibid.*, p. 125.)

[16] It may be said in concluding the subject of Images and Names that the effect of an inability to separate, so clearly as we do, the external object from the mere thought or idea of it in the mind, shows itself very fully and clearly in the superstitious beliefs and practices of the untaught man, but its results are by no means confined to such matters. It is not too much to say that nothing short of a history of Philosophy and Religion would be required to follow them out. The accumulated experience of so many ages has indeed brought to us far clearer views in these matters than the savage has, though after all we soon come to the point where our knowledge stops, and the opinions which ordinary educated men hold, or at least act upon, as to the relation between ideas and things, may come in time to be superseded by others taken from a higher level. But between our clearness of separation of what is in the mind from what is out of it, and the mental confusion of the lowest savages of our own day, there is a vast interval . . . . Lower down in the history of culture, the word and the idea are found sticking together with a tenacity very different from their weak adhesion in our minds, and there is to be seen a tendency to grasp at the word as though it were the object it stands for, and to hold that to be able to speak of a thing gives a sort of possession of it, in a way that we can scarcely realize. (*Ibid.*, pp. 150–151.)

[17] The trite comparison of savages to "grown-up children," is in the main a sound one, though not to be carried out too strictly. In the uncivilized American or Polynesian, the strength of body

Tylor's conviction that a certain level of mental evolution has to be attained by a human group before it can enter creatively into civilization or fully appreciate its benefits leads him to a certain smugness and paternalism concerning native peoples.[18] In fact, Tylor tends to take a rather negative view of the fruits of contact when a marked discrepancy in the evolutionary position of the groups in question exists.[19]

The pre-eminence of mind and its stimulus value for the development of all the other aspects of culture are fundamental premises of Tylor, to which he returns again and again and from which he never strays very far. Of man's "brain-organization" and his ability to use symbols he says: "Man's power of using a word, or even a gesture, as the symbol of a thought and the means of conversing about it, is one of the points where we most plainly see him parting company with all lower species, *and starting on his career of conquest through higher intellectual regions.*"[20] In another place he declares: "Man's power of accommodating himself to the world he lives in, and even of controlling it, *is largely due to his faculty of gaining new knowledge.*"[21] "History," he tells us, "is an agent powerful and becoming more powerful, in shaping men's minds, and *through their minds their actions in the world....*"[22] If anyone still supposes that Tylor was a materialist or a technological determinist,

and force of character of a grown man are combined with a mental development in many respects not beyond that of a young child of a civilized race. It has been already noticed how naturally children can appreciate and understand such direct expressions of thought as the gesture-language and picture-writing. In like manner, the use of dolls or images as an assistance to the operations of the mind, is familiar to all children, though among those who grow up under the influences of civilized society, it is mostly superseded and forgotten in after life. Few educated Europeans ever thoroughly realize the fact, that they have once passed through a condition of mind from which races at a lower state of civilization never fully emerge; but this is certainly the case, and the European child playing with its doll, furnishes the key to several of the mental phenomena which distinguish the more highly cultivated races of mankind from those lower in the scale. (*Ibid.*, p. 108.)

[18] In the comparison of man with other animals the standard should naturally be the lowest man, or savage. But the savage is possessed of human reason and speech, while his brain-power, though it has not of itself raised him to civilization, enables him to receive more or less of the education which transforms him into a civilized man. (Tylor, 1881, p. 42.)

[19] ...It is a general rule that original and independent progress is not found among a people of low civilization in presence of a higher race. It is natural enough that this should be the case, and it does not in the least affect the question whether the lower race was stationary or progressing before the arrival of the more cultivated foreigners. Even when the contact has been but slight and temporary, it either becomes doubtful whether progress made soon afterwards is original, or certain that it is not so. (Tylor, 1865, p. 162.)
For another expression of the "White Man's Burden" see Tylor, 1878, p. 121, where we read: "...indeed, experience shows that independent progress could hardly have taken place among an uncivilized in contact with a civilized race."

[20] Tylor, 1881, p. 42.

[21] *Ibid.*, p. 40.

[22] Tylor, 1871, Vol. II, p. 447.

he can turn to the passage which reads: "Thus man, even while he feeds himself as the lower animals do, by gathering wild fruit and catching game and fish, *is led by his higher intelligence* to more artificial means of getting these. Rising to the next stage, he begins to grow supplies of food for himself."[23] The key to man's achievements, as Tylor saw it, lay in his "power of coordinating the impression of his senses, which enables him to understand the world he lives in, and by understanding, to use, resist, and even, in a measure, rule it."[24]

Moreover, as Tylor viewed it, science and higher developments of culture could not be attained until "one of the most pernicious delusions that ever vexed mankind, the belief in Magic," was surmounted by advanced branches of mankind in the course of mental evolution[25].

In several other passages Tylor describes the evolution of mind from magical associations at one extreme to reasoning, logic, observation, and experiment at the other[26].

In order to demonstrate how magic has been arrested and superseded by rational thought, Tylor traces the history of science. As he pictures it, "progress" in "the various branches of sciences" "has been made in age after age by facts being more fully observed and more carefully reasoned on." Reasoning or logic is now itself a science but "began as an art which man practised without stopping to ask himself why or how." Man thought and talked for untold ages "before it occurred to him to lay down rules how to argue." Reasoning reached a scientific stage when the Greek philosophers, and especially Aristotle, brought argument "into a regular system by the method of syllogisms." By applying exact reasoning to mathematics the Greeks "brought on a general advance in knowledge." The "so-called

---

[23] Tylor, 1881, p. 168.

[24] Tylor, 1878, p. 109. Emphasis in quotations in this paragraph is supplied.

[25] . . . . Looking at Occult Science from this ethnographic point of view, I shall instance some of its branches as illustrating the course of intellectual culture. Its place in history is briefly this. It belongs in its main principle to the lowest known stages of civilization, and the lower races, who have not partaken largely of the education of the world, still maintain it in vigour. From this level it may be traced upward, much of the savage art holding its place substantially unchanged, and many new practices being in course of time developed, while both the older and newer developments have lasted on more or less among modern cultured nations. But during the ages in which progressive races have been learning to submit their opinions to closer and closer experimental tests, occult science has been breaking down into the condition of a survival, in which state we mostly find it among ourselves. (Tylor, 1871, Vol. 1. pp. 112–113.)

[26] The student who wishes to compare the mental habits of rude and ancient peoples with our own, may look into a subject which has now fallen into contempt from its practical uselessness, but which is most instructive in showing how the unscientific mind works. This is magic. In the earlier days of knowledge men relied far more than we moderns do on reasoning by analogy or mere association of ideas. (Tylor, 1881, p. 264.)

scholastic period" was a setback, but "the great movement of modern philosophy with which the name of Bacon is associated as a chief expounder, brought men back to the sound old method of working experience and thought together, only now the experience was more carefully sought and observed, and thought arranged it more systematically." Tylor's survey ends on this optimistic, cultural Darwinian note: "Thus man has but to go on observing and thinking, secure that in time his errors will fall away, while the truth he attains will abide and grow."[27]

In Tylor's opinion, it is not that the savage or barbarian does not reason sensibly about some things but rather that in "matters beyond his limited knowledge, he contents himself with working on resemblances or analogies of thought, which thus become the foundation of magic."[28] When mental evolution has cleared the way for a systematic application of rules of reason to all observed phenomena, the opportunity is at hand for striking and progressive changes.[29]

As one would expect from his preoccupation with rationalism and with the growth and transformation of mind, Tylor was especially impressed by arts and practices which bore upon the accumulation and transformation of knowledge. The written word seemed to him to be such a factor; and whereas he held that agriculture ushers in the stage of Barbarism, it is writing by which he identifies the onset of Civilization, for in his eyes it is this discovery which best preserves the information wrung painfully from experience. On this point he observes: "Lastly, *civilized* life may be taken as beginning with the art of writing, which by recording history, law, knowledge, and religion for the service of ages to come, binds together the past and the future in an unbroken chain of intellectual and moral progress."[30] And in still another place he refers to the same subject in these words: "In the growth of systematic civilization, the art of writing has had an influence so intense, that of all tests to distinguish the barbaric from the civilized state, none is so generally effective as this, whether they have but the failing link with the past which mere memory furnishes, or can have recourse to written records of past

[27] *Ibid.*, pp. 263–267.

[28] *Ibid.*, p. 265.

[29] There have been indeed few more important movements in the course of the history of mankind, than this change of opinion as to the nature and relations of what is in the mind and what is out of it. To say nothing of its vast effects upon Ethics and Religion, the whole course of Science, and of Art, of which Science is a principal element, has been deeply influenced by this mental change. Man's views of the difference between imagination and reality, of the nature of cause and effect, of the connexion between himself and the external world, and of the parts of the external world among themselves, have been entirely altered by it. (Tylor, 1865, pp. 378–379.)

[30] Tylor, 1881, p. 19.

history and written constitutions of present order.'[31]

There is one other dimension of Tylor's thinking which seems pertinent to the present topic, namely, his applied interests. Since he considered civilized man to be much more rational than the savage or the barbarian, Tylor advised that he strive to be even more completely so. He urged his fellow men to assess their opinions and their customs and to cast out or to reform any that were found to be shoddy and burdensome survivals of a past stage of culture. No area of culture, not even religion, should be exempt from this rational scrutiny.[32]

Obviously, anthropology, with its knowledge of the past and its conception of the totality and integration of each stage of culture, should take a leading role in this cultural housecleaning. It is small wonder that Tylor was able to speak of anthropology as "essentially a reformer's science," and as a discipline "active at once in aiding progress and in removing hindrance."[33]

In the distant past, according to Tylor, knowledge was unconsciously acquired, but the garnering, organization, and interpretation of facts has become a science in itself, entered upon deliberately and boldly. Use that knowledge in the interests of progress, and man becomes the architect of his future.[34]

I have presented the views of Tylor at some length because he was the most respected, most creative, and best balanced cultural anthropologist in the classical evolutionary tradition, and also because he enunciated

[31] Tylor, 1878, p. 123.

[32] . . . . Should the doctrine or rite in question appear to have been transmitted from an earlier to a later stage of religious thought, then it should be tested, like any other point of culture, as to its place in development. The question has to be raised, to which of these three categories it belongs;—is it a product of the earlier theology, yet sound enough to maintain a rightful place in the later;—is it derived from a cruder original, yet so modified as to become a proper representative of more advanced views?—is it a survival from a lower stage of thought, imposing on the credit of the higher by virtue not of inherent truth but of ancestral belief? These are queries the very asking of which starts trains of thought which candid minds should be encouraged to pursue, leading as they do toward the attainment of such measure of truth as the intellectual condition of our age fits us to assimilate. (Tylor, 1871, Vol. 2, pp. 451–452.)

[33] *Ibid.*, p. 453; see Lowie, 1937, p. 83.

[34] . . . . Acquainted with events and their consequences far and wide over the world, we are able to direct our own course with more confidence toward improvement. In a word, mankind is passing from the age of unconscious to that of conscious progress. Readers who have come thus far need not be told in many words of what the facts must have already brought to their minds—that the study of man and civilization is not only a matter of scientific interest, but at once passes into the practical business of life. We have in it the means of understanding our own lives and our place in the world, vaguely and imperfectly it is true, but at any rate more clearly than any former generation. The knowledge of man's course of life, from the remote past to the present, will not only help us to forecast the future, but may guide us in our duty of leaving the world better then we found it. (Tylor, 1881, p. 342.)

his interests and principles fully and precisely. Most of the anthropologists who were his contemporaries shared his major premises, so it is quite fitting in the present context to ask how many of these basic ideas are prevalent in the thinking of cultural anthropologists concerned about changes in under-developed areas today.

Some of the postulates of Tylor and the classical evolutionary school are not likely to be applied to the contemporary situation. Most of the peoples of the so-called underdeveloped countries are in what Tylor would have called the cultural stage of "Barbarism," but I do not think we take the position that they are handicapped by mental confusion and childish imaginings. Nor does one hear that their economic and social development must be a long, slow process. Rather, the expectation is that transformation will be rapid. The major apprehension has to do with the political direction in which it will take them. The gradualism and uniformity of the Tylorian evolutionary doctrine are certainly not the anticipations of the present. It is assumed that the breaks with the past will often be sudden and sharp and that there will be as many chasms as there will be gentle transitions between the old and the new. Again, few believe that some inherent, internal unity of a stage of culture will be preserved. Tylor and other classical evolutionists were confident that distinctive forms of family, government, economy, religion, etc., would inevitably coexist. In fact, Tylor developed his concept of "adhesions" and tested it statistically in order to give body to these interdependencies. Though it is predicted that likenesses in technology and new links of communication will stimulate resemblances and parallels, it is becoming apparent that the world is not likely to be made over in any single national or cultural image.

Yet there do seem to be at least two important premises of the evolutionary school which have retained their vitality and which are prevalent in the modern scene. The first is that change is inevitable and that it is, on the whole, desirable and progressive. I think this represents the modern, world-wide temper, despite all the reservations which exist concerning specific situations or programs. The other pronouncement of Tylor which has persisted and gained force is his plea that knowledge and reasoned prediction be employed in charting man's progress and future. If there is any doubt that this has endured, one has only to think of the elaborate plans through which the economic and social resources of underdeveloped countries are harnessed today.

The American counterpart of Tylor, both as a towering figure in anthropology and as an evolutionist, is Lewis H. Morgan, whose views concerning the development of man and culture were best expounded in his book, *Ancient Society*, published in 1877. In 1884, three years after the death of Morgan,

Frederick Engels published *The Origin of the Family, Private Property and the State*, a work which drew handily from Morgan's study. In the preface to his book Engels called attention to the interest of Karl Marx in Morgan's findings, compared Morgan not unfavorably with Marx, and labeled Morgan's formulation "the materialistic conception of history."[35]

This dictum of Engels, that Morgan's evolutionism is set in a materialistic mold, has been accepted without cavil by a long line of commentators of various persuasions from many fields. G. V. Plekhanov, the communist theorist and mentor of Lenin, wrote:[36] "True, Morgan arrived at the viewpoint of economic materialism *independently of Marx and Engels*, but that's all the better for their theory." Harry Elmer Barnes, the historian, finds that[37] "Morgan's emphasis on technological and economic factors in social evolution has made his ideas especially acceptable to Marxians." Stuart Piggott, the British archeologist, refers in a discussion of evolutionary doctrines to[38] "the Morgan-Engels-Marx model," Idus Murphree, the philosopher, after some intellectual shadowboxing, concludes[39] that Morgan "went a long way toward making technology the dynamic force in the evolution of institutions." Morton Fried refers to Morgan's[40] "assumption that key inventions set the stage for major regroupings of cultural life. . . ." Irving Goldman, a cultural anthropologist, speaks of[41] "Morgan's historical materialism." A hint that Morgan was not solidly materialistic in outlook comes from another cultural anthropologist, Leslie A. White, who, after introducing Morgan's point of view as[42] "one of the best as well as one of the earliest" "materialist interpretations of culture," explains that[43] "Morgan had an idealist interpretation of cultural evolution as well as a materialist one. Institutions are expressions of ideas, of germs of thought implanted in the human mind." However, White concludes that Morgan is, in the final analysis, a materialist, for he believes that in Morgan's view",[44] . . . the growth of these ideas, is dependent upon material conditions, specifically upon technological advance."

We shall return to the question whether Morgan is a materialist and technological determinist or is friendly to some other explanation of cultural dynamics. For the moment let us turn to premises it is more certain he

[35] Engels' words, which assure Morgan of a prominent place in socialist annals, are these:
The following chapters are, in a certain sense, executing a bequest. It was no less a man than Karl Marx who had reserved to himself the privilege of displaying the results of Morgan's investigations in connection with his own materialistic conception of history—which I might call ours within certain limits. He wished thus to elucidate the full meaning of this conception. For in America, Morgan had, in a manner, discovered anew the materialistic conception of history, originated by Marx forty years ago. In comparing barbarism and civilization, he had arrived, in the main, at the same results as Marx. (Engels, 1884 (1902), p. 9)

[36] Plekhanov, 1895 (1947), p. 239. The page reference is to the English edition of 1947.

[37] Barnes, 1948, p. 32. [38] Piggott, 1960, p. 95. [39] Murphree, 1961, p. 297. [40] Fried, 1961, p. 419.
[41] Goldman, 1959, p. 61. [42] White, 1949, p. 361. [43] *Ibid.*, p. 363. [44] *Ibid.*, p. 364.

entertained, many of them familiar from our discussion of Tylor. Morgan held that man's course has been one of progress from rude beginnings. In fact, the subtitle of *Ancient Society* is "Researches in the Lines of Human Progress from Savagery through Barbarism to Civilization." The word "progress" appears a hundred times in *Ancient Society* for every use of the word "evolution"; actually the term "evolution" is to be found but three times in the 570 pages of the volume, and it is used each time in the sense of "progress." Like Tylor, Morgan conceived of cultural evolution as a slow and gradual process, taking place by numberless minute advances over an immense period of time. The evolutionary developments can be divided into stages (Savagery, Barbarism, and Civilization), and the stages further divided into Ethnical Periods (Lower, Middle, and Upper). Each stage or period is marked by a cluster of material, social, and moral traits. In respect to the last, Morgan actually believed he could identify the stage and period when such qualities as rectitude and courage began to grace the human scene.[45]

Not only were there sets of stages and periods fixed in relation to one another, but the cultures of human groups evolved through them in inevitable and irreversible order. Particular tribes and peoples need not pass through the stages at the same pace or the same time, and therefore groups can be found at any moment in various conditions of development. Many groups have been eliminated before going very far along the evolutionary road. Others, because of unfavorable environment or oppression, have actually degenerated. Still others may exist for a long time in an arrested state. It is not necessary for a people to invent or personally develop all traits and characteristics which identify them with a higher period or stage; they may acquire these diagnostic elements by contact and borrowing. But such a population must be in a position to appreciate and use these items.[46] The preconditions of the higher stage must have been assured by mastery of the materials of the stage below. On the other hand, there are those who have moved more quickly and independently through the stages and periods and who have aided others to advance by their inventions, proddings, and example. The Semites and Aryans are particularly singled out for praise in this connection, and Morgan is especially ecstatic over the achievements and qualities of the Aryans.[47] In fact, Morgan is guilty of that same confusion of physical and cultural traits which we encountered in Tylor. He seems to think that the size and complexity of the brain, and therefore, the ability to think creatively, can be correlated with different periods and stages of cultural evolution. This, in turn, is involved with rather mystical notions concerning the benefits of a meat diet.

[45] Morgan, 1877, p. 542. Morgan divides Civilization as it has developed so far into two periods, Ancient and Modern (see also p. 12.)

[46] *Ibid.*, p. 540. [47] *Ibid.*, pp. 25; 38–39; 513–514; 562–563.

According to him, the settled peoples of the New World had brains inferior in size and quality to those of the Old World. They progressed more slowly culturally because they gave little attention to animal husbandry and consumed less meat and milk than did the superior Semites and Aryans.[48]

But, whatever the pace, the originality, and the amount of progression of the individual group, the direction and sequence are clear. If a culture does change, unless it is on the way to collapse and extinction, it will move seriatim through the designated periods and stages. Time after time Morgan declares that the ancestors of the civilized peoples of today must have passed through the periods and stages he outlines. The evolutionary framework, as he pictures it, is a fixed, irreversible sequence of stages through which individual peoples progress unilinearly to the point where they are found at the historical moment at which they are studied.[49]

There are other postulates of Morgan that are reminiscent of Tylor. Morgan holds that all living men belong to one species, and, therefore, that all have essentially the same needs. Consequently, similar responses and reactions must be expected of groups of men in like environments and "ethnical periods." Man's brain, too, is basically the same in all periods and environments, and it contains attributes and proclivities which yield comparable results in similar conditions and roughly parallel developments in equally favorable circumstances.[50] The consistency of this notion is somewhat blurred by a view of mental evolution which is, as we have noted, almost Lamarckian in its conception of the consequences of the exercise and lubrication of the brain by experience.[51] In addition, there is an unsettling note of racial or folk "unconscious" with which to conjure. Mormonism, which Morgan abhorred, was an example of "mental atavism," an outcropping of attitudes which properly belonged to "old savagism."[52] But, despite these lapses, Morgan generally accepted and built on the psychic unity of man.

In his explanation of cultural evolution Morgan made use of some of the dynamic factors to which Tylor had appealed. He made no secret of his utilization of what I have termed "cultural Darwinism." In fact, he openly called it "natural selection." He uses the concept primarily in connection with the transition from one unit of social organization to another. In one place he writes: "The organization into classes upon sex, and the subsequent higher organization into gentes upon kin, must be regarded as the results of great social movements worked out unconsciously through natural selection."[53] In another place he explains: "This second form of the family was the final result, through natural selection, of the reduction within narrower limits of a stupendous conjugal system which enfolded savage man

[48] *Ibid.*, pp. 24–25.   [49] *Ibid.*, pp. v-vi; 3; 7–8; 12–13; 16–17; 18; 22; 86; 151–152; 155; 423; 557; 562.
[50] *Ibid.*, pp. vi; 8; 17–18; 562.   [51] *Ibid.*, p. 36.   [52] *Ibid.*, p. 59.   [53] *Ibid.*, p. 48.

and held him with a powerful grasp.[54] But, compared to Tylor, Morgan uses the principle of cultural Darwinism more sparingly.

In respect to philosophic idealism and what I have named "rationalistic determinism," Morgan is much closer to Tylor, though there is an important difference that must be recognized ultimately. Certainly there is little comfort here for those who claim to see in Morgan a philosophical materialist. To begin with, *Ancient Society* is, by definition, a study of mental and moral evolution and of the growth of certain fundamental ideas. The very titles of the four parts into which the book is divided are, respectively: "Growth of *Intelligence* Through Inventions and Discoveries. Growth of the *Idea* of Government. Growth of the *Idea* of the Family. Growth of the *Idea* of Property." [Emphasis supplied—M.E.O.] On the very first page of his text Morgan defines his intentions in these words: "An attempt will be made in the following pages to bring forward additional evidence of the rudeness of the early condition of mankind, of the gradual evolution of their mental and moral powers through experience, and of their protracted struggle with opposing obstacles while winning their way to civilization."[55] "The earliest inventions were the most difficult to accomplish," we are told, "because of the feebleness of the power of abstract reasoning."[56] When Morgan turns to the question of why the Greeks "became, for their numbers, the most distinguished, the most intellectual and the most accomplished race of men the entire human family has yet produced," he does not return the answer expected of a materialist but explains: "It was because the ideas which had been germinating through the previous ethnical period, and which had become interwoven with every fibre of their brains, had found a happy fruition in a democratically constituted state."[57] The decline of Greece and Rome is interpreted as well by rationalistic determinism. "If the Greeks and Romans had learned to respect the equities of monogamy," he tells us, "instead of secluding their wives in the gynaeconitis in one case, and of holding them under power in the other, there is reason to believe that society among them would have presented a very different aspect." He goes on to say: "The premature destruction of the ethnic life of these remarkable races is due in no small measure to their failure to develop and utilize the mental, moral and conservative forces of the female intellect, which were not less essential than their own corresponding forces to their progress and preservation."[58] This is gallantry in abundance, but it is hardly materialism.

There are other statements that are just as difficult to reconcile with materialism. Marxists are forever quoting Morgan's words: "The maintenance of life, through the constant acquisition of food, is the great burden

[54] *Ibid.*, p. 388. (see also pp. 433–434.)   [55] *Ibid.*, p. 3.   [56] *Ibid.*, p. 41.   [57] *Ibid.*, p. 261.
[58] *Ibid.*, p. 487.

imposed upon existence in all species of animals." But they seldom include the material two sentences below which reminds us that, as soon as the human level is reached, "Intelligence from henceforth becomes a more prominent factor"[59] in the pursuit of subsistence. Much is said of Morgan's opinion that property had become "an unmanageable power." We are made less well acquainted with his conviction that "human intelligence will rise to the mastery over property."[60] "The next higher plane of society," as Morgan envisaged it, was to be realized through "experience, intelligence and knowledge."[61] The point need not be labored. One can open *Ancient Society* at almost any page and find evidence of the idealistic and rationalistic outlook to which attention has been called.

Could it be true, as White and Murphree have suggested, that the philosophical idealism I have documented, although present in *Ancient Society*, is subordinated to a materialist tenet, and that Morgan meant to convey to us that the development of the germs of thought is ultimately dependent upon technological advance and augmented subsistence? This is strained reasoning. It seems to me that, because of Engels' book, we have been peering at Morgan so long through the distorting bifocals of materialism and determinism that we have an increasingly vague image of what he really wrote. In a descriptive sense Morgan is an idealist; he emphasizes the basic importance of the idea, of the intellect, and of reason, as the very titles of his sections indicate. Moreover, the very essence of his doctrine is its very lack of any unitary determinism. He is an evolutionist in the literal meaning of the word; his is an account of an unfolding or unrolling of potentialities present from the beginning. To distinguish Morgan's brand of evolution from others, we may perhaps call it a doctrine of "eduction" or "unfoldment."

It has been said that Morgan was a materialist because he identified his periods and stages with material traits and technological advances. Actually this is not the case, as we have demonstrated. Each stage is marked by related congeries of features—material, institutional, and ideological. No stage is complete until the full complement of characteristics is present. No one of these characteristics is the cause and master of the others. Writing is just as diagnostic of the civilized horizon as is the smelting of iron. When Morgan is dealing with the development of inventions and discoveries or when he is discoursing on the growth of methods of subsistence, material and technological features seem central and the key to future progress. But just as surely, when he is tracing the evolution of the germs of thought which give rise to social institutions, a like impression is conveyed; then *they*—the appearance of the gens, for instance—are all important, and further progress waits on *their* maturation and effect. And from his vantage point, Morgan is

[59] *Ibid.*, p. 20.   [60] *Ibid.*, p. 561.   [61] *Ibid.*, p. 562.

correct in both instances. Given a lack of determinism and an emphasis upon parallel development and emanation, there is no feature which is not significant for the unity of a particular stage and the realization of the next.

Technological determinists have seized upon Morgan's statement: "Until iron and its uses were known, civilization was impossible."[62] But Morgan never doubted that iron and its uses *would* ultimately be known. In the same paragraph he asserts of civilization: "Its attainment at some time was certain." All he is willing to grant is that "civilization might as naturally have been delayed for several thousand years in the future, as to have occurred when it did in the good providence of God."[63] In Morgan's hands, the doctrine of cultural evolution was a scroll which he could unroll or retract. In it he could see both the inevitabilities of the past, such as the emergence of successive family forms and the mastery of the technique of smelting, and the outline of the next higher plane of society, an era of "Democracy in government, brotherhood in society, equality in rights and privileges, and universal education."[64] After all, in attempting to decide whether Morgan's theory is one of eduction or technological determinism, we might turn to the words of the man himself, for the very last sentence of his book describes the "labors," "trials," and "successes" of our savage and barbarous ancestors as "a part of the plan of the Supreme Intelligence to develop a barbarian out of a savage, and a civilized man out of this barbarian."[65]

Morgan's view that technological and socio-ideological advances proceed along parallel and coordinate lines and equally contribute to the characteristics and potentialities of a stage is so frequently expressed by him, and so well reinforced by examples, that there should be no question of his stand.[66]

Morgan spends a good deal of time seeking to convince us that it is the coordinate and combined effects of the social and the technological and not the subordination of one to the other which accounts for progress. Too much has been read by Marxists and materialists into Morgan's statement: "The

---

[62] *Ibid.*, p. 563. [63] *Ibid.*, p. 563. [64] *Ibid.*, pp. 561-562. [65] *Ibid.*, p. 563.

[66] In lashing out at the hypothesis of degradation, he explains his double-pronged concept of progress thus:

.... inventions and discoveries would come one by one; the knowledge of a cord must precede the bow and arrow, as the knowledge of gunpowder preceded the musket, and that of the steam-engine preceded the railway and the steamship; so the arts of subsistence followed each other at long intervals of time, and human tools passed through forms of flint and stone before they were formed of iron. In like manner institutions of government are a growth from primitive germs of thought. Growth, development and transmission, must explain their existence among civilized nations. Not less clearly was the monogamian family derived, by experience, through the syndyasmian from the punaluan, and the still more ancient consanguine family, (*Ibid.*, pp. 514–515.)

growth of property would thus keep pace with the progress of inventions and discoveries."[67]

In interpreting the Greek experience, advance in inheritance rules is again made contingent upon a combination of material and intellectual factors.[68]

Other assertions of Morgan on this same problem seem just as explicit. "Inventions and discoveries stand in serial relations along the lines of human progress, and register its successive stages; while social and civil institutions, in virtue of their connection with perpetual human wants, have been developed from a few primary germs of thought. They exhibit a similar register of progress."[69] There is no hint here that the social and the political are the creatures of the technological. The two are obviously treated as coordinate and parallel. Morgan knew the value of words, and he does not choose the language of determinism. Plainly, as he conceives it, technology and social institutions both "register" or afford a clue to the evolutionary level or degree of progress. Neither is the prime mover; both are aspects of a more inclusive process.

Less than a page later, after speaking about inventions and discoveries, the idea of government, the family, and the idea of property, Morgan tells us: "The four classes of facts above indicated, and which extend themselves in parallel lines along the pathways of human progress from savagery to civilization, form the principal subjects of discussion in this volume."[70] Why should there be this stress on "parallel lines" if this is a treatise bristling with notions of subordination and determinism?

Early in his book, in speaking about the evidence that he plans to present, Morgan states: "It will be drawn, in part, from the great sequence of inventions and discoveries which stretches along the entire pathway of human progress; but chiefly from domestic institutions, which express the growth of certain ideas and passions."[71] This wording suggests no patronizing attitude toward "domestic institutions" or their place in Morgan's argument. A few lines later Morgan remarks in the same vein: "Two independent lines of investigation thus invite our attention. The one leads through inventions

[67] They forget that Morgan goes on to say:

> . . . . The customs upon which these rules of proprietary possession and inheritance depend, are determined and modified by the condition and progress of the social organization. The growth of property is thus closely connected with the increase of inventions and discoveries, and with the improvement of social institutions which mark the several ethnical periods of human progress. (*Ibid.*, p. 535)

[68] After houses and lands, flocks and herds, and exchangeable commodities had become so great in quantity, and had come to be held by individual ownership, the question of their inheritance would press upon human attention until the right was placed upon a basis which satisfied the growing intelligence of the Greek mind. Archaic usages would be modified in the direction of later conceptions. (*Ibid.*, pp. 562–563)

[69]*Ibid.*, p. vi.   [70]*Ibid.*, p. vii.   [71]*Ibid.*, pp. 3–4.

and discoveries, and the other through primary institutions. With the knowledge gained therefrom, we may hope to indicate the principal stages of human development."[72]

Because Morgan thought in terms of parallel lines of development and marshalled his evidence of the importance and progress of these lines (inventions, arts of subsistence, idea of government, idea of property, etc.) in separate chapters, his work is extremely vulnerable to selective thinkers and special pleaders. It is easy enough by quoting copiously from any particular chapter to give the impression that Morgan thought *that* subject or institution formative for the rest of culture. Such use has frequently been made of the passage from the chapter on the arts of subsistence which reads: "It is accordingly probable that the great epochs of human progress have been identified, more or less directly, with the enlargement of the sources of subsistence."[73] But note the neutral language. Morgan does not say that human progress *has* been due to increased subsistence; he says it has been "identified" with it. In fact Morgan takes pains to disassociate himself from those who have used technology too exclusively as a criterion of progress. On this point he says: "Some of the ancient poets and philosophers recognized the fact, that mankind commenced in a state of extreme rudeness from which they had risen by slow and successive steps. They also perceived that the course of their development was registered by a progressive series of inventions and discoveries, but without noticing as fully the more conclusive argument from social institutions."[74]

Morgan's practice of treating separately every line of progress and "developing germ of thought" makes it possible, as I have pointed out, to prove the primacy of almost anything by a judicious selection of quotations. On the basis of what he says in his chapter on the organization of society upon the basis of sex, for instance, one could make him out a social determinist of the same type as A. R. Radcliffe-Brown quite as easily as some have made him out a materialist. In his treatment of the marriage classes of an Australian tribe he declares: "The *jura conjugialia*, which appertained to the classes, were the dead weight upon the Kamilaroi, without emancipation from which they would have remained for additional thousands of years in the same condition, substantially, in which they were found."[75] After explaining how the gens arose to save this situation, Morgan declares: "An important inference at once arises, namely, that the institutions of mankind have sprung up in a progressive connected series, each of which represents the result of unconscious reformatory movements to extricate society from existing evils."[76] And he continues: "The arts by which savages maintain their lives are remarkably persistent. They are never lost until superseded by others higher in degree.

[72]*Ibid.*, p. 4.   [73]*Ibid.*, p. 19.   [74]*Ibid.*, p. 37.   [75]*Ibid.*, p. 57.   [76]*Ibid.*, p. 58.

By the practice of these arts, and by the experience gained through social organizations, mankind has advanced under a necessary law of development, although their progress may have been substantially imperceptible for centuries." The touch of cultural Darwinism, the importance of social institutions for all of culture, and the implication in these passages that change in the social order occurs from an inner necessity, rather than to accommodate technological change, should not escape us."[77] Time and again Morgan subordinates both the institutional and the technological to intellect.[78]

[77] Even more revealing is another passage in which Morgan states his doctrine thus:

Out of a few germs of thought, conceived in the early ages, have been evolved all the principal institutions of mankind. Beginning their growth in the period of savagery, fermenting through the period of barbarism, they have continued their advancement through the period of civilization. The evolution of these germs of thought has been guided by a natural logic which formed an essential attribute of the brain itself. So unerringly has this principle performed its functions in all conditions of experience, and in all periods of time, that its results are uniform, coherent and traceable in their courses. These results alone will in time yield convincing proofs of the unity of origin of mankind. The mental history of the human race, which is revealed in institutions, inventions and discoveries, is presumptively the history of a single species, per-petuated through individuals, and developed through experience. Among the original germs of thought, which have exercised the most powerful influence upon the human mind, and upon human destiny, are these which relate to government, to the family, to language, to religion, and to property. They had a definite beginning far back in savagery, and a logical progress, but can have no final consummation, because they are still progressing, and must ever continue to progress. (*Ibid.*, pp. 59–60)

Here, as we see, the "developing germs of thought" are credited with quite as much influence upon human destiny as are inventions and discoveries; and both are treated as clues to "the mental history of the human race."

[78] In one of the strongest of his statements bearing upon these relationships he writes:

The principle of intelligence, although conditioned in its powers within narrow limits of variation, seeks ideal standards invariably the same. Its operations, consequently, have been uniform through all the stages of human progress. No argument for the unity of origin of mankind can be made, which, in its nature, is more satisfactory. A common principle of intelligence meets us in the savage, in the barbarian, and in civilized man. It was in virtue of this that mankind were able to produce in similar conditions the same implements and utensils, the same inventions, and to develop similar institutions from the same original germs of thought. There is something grandly impressive in a principle which has wrought out civilization by assiduous application from small beginnings; from the arrow head, which expresses the thought in the brain of a savage, to the smelting of iron ore, which represents the higher intelligence of the barbarian, and, finally, to the railway train in motion, which may be called the triumph of civilization. (*Ibid.*, p. 562)

The "vast results" wrought by the human mind and the developing germs of thought (quite apart from considerations of technology) are mirrored in still another passage:

. . . . The human mind, specifically the same in all individuals in all the tribes and nations of man-kind, and limited in the range of its powers, works and must work, in the same uniform channels, and within narrow limits of variation. Its results in disconnected regions of space, and in widely separated ages of time, articulate in a logically connected chain of common experiences. In the grand aggregate may still be recognized the few primary germs of thought, working upon primary human necessities, which, through the natural process of development, have produced such vast results. (*Ibid.*, p. 262)

Those who consider Morgan an arch materialist or a technological determinist might ponder what he has to say about the place and importance of the gens and other forms of social organization in the passage that reads:[79] "The real history of mankind is contained in the history of the growth and development of institutions, of which the gens is but one. It is, however, the basis of those which have exercised the most material influence upon human affairs."

It might be well to say a word about Morgan's applied interests. When Morgan, then a youth in his early twenties, joined a secret society of young men of Aurora, New York, and wanted to give the organization a serious purpose, its goals became "the study and perpetuation of Indian lore, the education of the Indian tribes, and the reconciliation of these tribes with the conditions imposed by civilization." His successful defense of the Seneca Indians against the rapacious Ogden Land Company is well known. He constantly sought to portray the American Indian in a sympathetic light and it has more than once been claimed that he overidealized the democratic leanings and other virtues of the Iroquois. Yet he took the supremacy of Western culture for granted and concerned himself with theoretical, rather than with practical, problems. Despite his posthumous association with radicals and revolutionaries, there is little call for militant reform in Morgan's pages. It is Tylor who sees humiliating survivals everywhere in modern civilization and pleads for conscious efforts to rectify these undesirable features. Morgan is more complacent about the present and displays a quiet faith in future progress. This is what one would expect from a knowledge of the theories of evolution of the two men. Tylor emphasizes competition and the increasing role of rational thought; Morgan, in his formulation, stresses unconscious reformatory mechanisms and inevitable fulfilment of potentialities.

To what degree, we may ask, do the postulates with which Morgan worked apply today to the problems of foreign aid and development? Certainly his convictions concerning the physical and psychic unity of man are pertinent. If we are not beings of the same type, capable of the same understandings and motivations, little besides friction and irritation can come of contact and joint undertakings. Morgan's recognition of multiple causation is implicit in the multipurpose development plans being launched today. When planners bend efforts toward accomplishments in respect to health, education, communication, and social and political organization as well as production, they show agreement with Morgan's conception of the unity of a cultural horizon and the creative synthesis of its features. There is no more precarious balance in the world today than the one which exists between ideology and technology.

[79] *Ibid.*, p. 390.

Those who assert in a brisk, doctrinaire manner that technology always determines ideology are not watching events in underdeveloped areas too closely.
Much of the political and social unrest which engulfs some of these regions
has arisen, as I see it, from aspirations and demands that the technological
and economic systems cannot satisfy. The problem often is to keep the
economic and productive system abreast of the changing social and intellectual climate. Morgan understood this dual, delicate relationship much
better than many contemporary materialists, planners, and statesmen. That
change is inevitable, that it follows, in the main, along necessary and
progressive lines, and that its pace is at first slow but accelerates as time
goes on, are ideas widely accepted in principle by planners and development
agencies. There is even a good deal of discussion today about the relevance
of the concept of stages to development theory.[80] Morgan's study of human
progress, dated and naive though it is in parts, battered though it may be by
the tussle of radicals and their opponents over its contents, stiff though its
spine may be with the uncompromising evolutionary fervor of its author, still
contains insight and erudition that students of change cannot afford to ignore.

We have taken Tylor and Morgan as representatives of the evolutionism
of the nineteenth century in cultural anthropology. A twentieth century
cultural anthropologist whose evolutionary views, so forcefully and pungent-
ly expressed in his writings, have attracted considerable attention is Leslie
A. White.

White has written that he[81] "has endeavored to develop the materialist
philosophy introduced into ethnology by Morgan, and at the same time to
rehabilitate the theory of cultural evolution." There is no doubt of White's
materialism, but I have the strong feeling, as I have indicated, that he involves
Morgan in the materialist pedigree, as Engels did, only by making him over
in his own image.

According to White's view, man is an animal whose fundamental needs are
for food and protection. He uses his organic capabilities in coping with the
external world, and he also uses a mechanism which is unique to him alone,
culture. Thanks to articulate speech, man is able to pass culture from one
generation to another and, by diffusion, to neighboring peoples. Culture is
cumulative, continuous, and adjustive. It moves in accordance with its own
principles; the culture process is not biologically or psychologically determined. Man is prerequisite to culture, but culture is not determined by man
and his wishes, will, hopes, or fears. On the other hand, human behavior is
determined by culture. All life is a struggle for free energy. Culture is merely

[80] Morgan taught that progress accelerates at a geometric ratio. See Morgan, 1877, p. 37. See
also Rostow, 1960.

[81] White, 1949, p. 373.

a special form assumed by this life process; it is a mechanism for harnessing energy and putting it to work. Culture has grown as the amount of energy harnessed per capita per year has increased. But the means by which energy is harnessed, the efficiency of tools and machines, has a bearing, too, on the output of goods and the advance of culture. When the efficiency of the tools has reached a limit, only additional energy will move civilization forward again. The progress of a culture thus can be gauged by the increasing amount of energy harnessed per capita per year and the improvement in the efficiency of the means through which this energy is put to work. The nontechnological segments of culture depend on the technological segment; the type of social organization, art, and philosophy of a given cultural system is determined in form and content by the underlying technology.[82]

What are the implications of a theory such as this for an interest in under-developed areas? To a large extent the view is alienated from the problems of development by the premise that culture and the evolution of culture are not influenced by the hopes, plans, and fears of men.[83] Development plans, as I understand them, are much concerned with man's wishes, hopes, and fears. Nor is the implication that, if the energy supply and technology are improved, all else will follow, likely to provide a ground plan for development work. No government or agency can be so single-minded and mechanical, nor would it last a month if it were.

It is obvious that a doctrine with these precepts, which, moreover, makes a basic distinction between impersonal culture (which it is the business of the cultural anthropologist to study) and the member of the culture ("the catalyst that makes the interactive culture process possible[84]" who is *not*, according to White, the concern of the cultural anthropologist) is not likely to arouse enthusiasm for concern over the applied problems of today. In my opinion the growth of this variety of evolutionary thought in anthropology has, and is likely to continue to have, but few links with the study of culture change in the underdeveloped countries.

These are the areas in which technologies will change dramatically, and in which the theorists of this persuasion would be afforded an exceptional opportunity to test their doctrines. But these are programs which have grown up out of regard for people rather than systems, and theorists of this persuasion are sensitized mainly to the study of culture as such.

[82] White, 1949. This statement is a summary of White's exposition of his views on pp. 373–379. For the writer's reservations concerning the mechanical and anti-psychological aspects of this doctrine, see Opler, 1948; 1953; 1964a; 1964b.

[83] This is a theme frequently found in White's writings. See White, 1948.

[84] White, 1949, p. 374.

Thus I have the feeling that, while certain evolutionary premises which have remained a part of our intellectual stock in trade have been applicable and useful, present developments in evolutionary theory have not contributed very substantially to interest in underdeveloped areas or the changes that are in process there. I suggest that the stream of interest that does exist flows, instead, from the large, general body of work and workers in the subfields of acculturation and of culture and personality.

Most Western anthropologists have been obliged, by the canons of the profession, to gain special knowledge about some foreign area. These regions have been, almost by definition, areas of political and social separatism and technological simplicity. It would be an odd social scientist of any brand who would be different to movements and massive programs intended to transform the cultural contours of a region with which he is most familiar. Moreover, anthropologists have long had to cope with problems of change. In the great majority of instances their opportunities to study non-Western groups came after the peoples to whom they addressed themselves had been subjugated or colonized. Often conquest and contact had altered the traditional way of life before the first anthropological note could be written. Even in the attempt to reconstruct older patterns the field worker was forcefully reminded of what had been already transformed. It was not long before a positive emphasis was laid on the study and interpretation of changes attributable to outside contact, and the subfield of acculturation was born. As the "White Man's Burden" became less mountainous in his own eyes and pressures for reform and accommodation began to grow, the anthropologist was increasingly called upon to give advice concerning applied problems. Therefore an interest in culture change and even involvement in policies growing out of problems raised by culture change developed in cultural anthropology long before peasant and tribal cultures were touched by the post-war development plans. In a field-work situation one cannot become concerned with change and acculturation without giving some attention to indivduals who welcome change, who oppose it, who gain by it, and who are left destitute by it. Consequently the personal life history and, indeed, many aspects of the whole field of culture and personality are the by-products of the developing interest in culture change. In turn, it is the group who have been most active in the acculturation and in the culture and personality fields who have so far contributed most to modern theories of cultural dynamics.[85]

Our review has indicated that evolutionary theory, even of the nineteenth

[85] A few of the books and key papers which have grown out of these interests are: Barnett, 1953 and 1954; Beals, 1953; Hallowell, 1952; Herskovits, 1938; Hoselitz, 1952; Keesing, 1952; Linton, 1940; Malinowski, 1945; Opler, 1941; Redfield, Linton, and Herskovits, 1939; Spicer, 1952; Spindler, 1955.

century, was not a unity, but differed in regard to conceptions of cultural dynamics and in respect to the degree of interest in applied problems. The neo-evolutionism of the present departs even more markedly from former evolutionary doctrines in both of these respects[86]. Its anti-psychological tenor and its premise that man cannot control his own destiny have isolated it to date from events taking place in the underdeveloped lands—or anywhere else, for that matter. Whether it will become less remote, less mechanical, and less rigid under the pressures of contemporary world events remains to be seen.

[86] If space permitted, the description and analysis of the views of evolutionists in anthropology could be much extended by giving attention to the doctrines of Henry Maine, J. F. McLennan, John Lubbock, Clark Wissler, A. R. Radcliffe-Brown, Ralph Linton, and Julian Steward, among others.

BIBLIOGRAPHY

Barnes, Harry Elmer, *Historical Sociology: Its Origin and Developments*, New York, Philosophical Library, 1948.

Barnett, H. G., *Innovation: The Basis of Cultural Change,* New York, McGraw-Hill Book Co., Inc., 1953.

Barnett, H. G., Broom, L., Siegel, B. J., Vogt, E. Z., and Watson, J. B., "Acculturation: An Exploratory Formulation," *American Anthropologist*, Vol. 56, No. 6 (1954), pp. 973–1002.

Beals, Ralph, "Acculturation," in Kroeber, A. L., ed., *Anthropology Today*, Chicago, University of Chicago Press, 1953.

Engels, Frederick. *The Origin of the Family, Private Property and the State,* trans. by Ernest Untermann, Chicago, Charles H. Kerr & Co., 1902.

Fried, Morton, Comment on Hoyt, Elizabeth, "Integration of Culture," *Current Anthropology*, Vol. 2, No. 5, (1961), pp. 418–420.

Goldman, Irving, "Evolution and Anthropology," *Victorian Studies*, Vol. III, No. 1, (Sept. 1959), pp. 55–75.

Hallowell, A. Irving, "Ojibwa Personality and Acculturation," in Tax, Sol, ed., *Acculturation in the Americas: Proceedings and Selected Papers of the XXIXth International Congress of Americanists,* Chicago, University of Chicago Press, (1952), pp. 105–112.

Herskovits, Melville J., *Acculturation, the Study of Culture Contact,* New York, J. J. Augustin, 1938.

Hoselitz, Bert F., ed., *The Progress of Underdeveloped Areas,* Chicago, University of Chicago Press, 1952.

Keesing, Felix, *Culture Change*, Stanford, Stanford University Press, 1952.

Lesser, Alexander, "Social Fields and the Evolution of Society," *Southwestern Journal of Anthropology,* Vol. 17, No. 1, (1961), pp. 40–48.

Linton, Ralph, ed., *Acculturation in Seven American Indian Tribes,* New York, Appleton-Century, 1940.

Lowie, Robert H., *The History of Ethnological Theory,* New York, Holt, Rinehart and Winston, Inc., 1937.

Malinowski, Bronislaw, *The Dynamics of Culture Change*, New Haven, Yale University Press, 1945.

Meggers, Betty J., "The Law of Cultural Evolution as a Practical Research Tool," in Dole, Gertrude E. and Carneiro, Robert L., eds., *Essays in the Science of Culture,* New York, Thomas Y. Crowell Co., (1960), pp. 302–316.

Morgan, Lewis H., *Ancient Society or Researches in the Lines of Human Progress from Savagery through Barbarism to Civilization,* New York, H. Holt & Co. 1877.

Murphree, Idus L., "The Evolutionary Anthropologists: The Progress of Mankind. The Concepts of Progress and Culture in the Thought of John Lubbock, Edward B. Tylor, and Lewis H. Morgan," *Proceedings of the American Philosophical Society,* Vol. 105, No. 3, (1961), pp. 265–300.

Opler, Morris E., "Three Types of Variation and Their Relation to Culture Change," in Spier, Leslie, *et al.,* eds., *Language, Culture, and Personality,* Menasha, Wisconsin, George Banta Publishing Co., 1941, pp. 146–157.

Opler, Morris E., "Some Implications of Culture Theory for Anthropology and Psychology," *The American Journal of Orthopsychiatry,* Vol. XVIII, No 4, (1948), pp. 611–621.

Opler, Morris E., "A Current Phase of Separatism in Social Science," in Hulett, J. E., Jr., and Stagner, Ross, eds., *Problems in Social Psychology,* Urbana, Ill., University of Illinois Press, (1953), pp. 205–213.

Opler, Morris E., "The Human Being in Culture Theory," *American Anthropologist,* Vol. 66, No. 3, (1964a.), pp. 507–528.

Opler, Morris E., "Values and Education in Cultural Perspective," in Brameld, Theodore, and Elam, Stanley, eds., *Values in American Education,* Bloomington, Ind., (1964b.), pp. 115–137.

Piggott, Stuart, "Prehistory and Evolutionary Theory," in Tax, Sol, ed., *Evolution After Darwin,* Vol. 2: *The Evolution of Man: Mind, Culture, and Society,* Chicago, University of Chicago Press, (1960), pp. 85–97.

Plekhanov, G. V., *In Defence of Materialism: The Development of the Monist View of History,* trans. by Andrew Rothstein, London, 1947.

Redfield, Robert, Linton, Ralph, and Herskovits, Melville, "Memorandum on the Study of Acculturation," *American Anthropologist,* Vol. 41, No. 1, (1939), pp. 514–517.

Rostow, W. W., *The Stages of Economic Growth: A Non-Communist Manifesto,* New York, Cambridge University Press, 1960.

Spicer, Edward, ed., *Human Problems in Technological Change,* New York, Russell Sage Foundation, 1952.

Spindler, George D., *Sociocultural and Psychological Processes in Menomini Acculturation,* Berkeley, University of California Press, 1955.

Tylor, Edward B., *Researches into the Early History of Mankind and the Development of Civilization,* London, John Murray, 1865.

Tylor, Edward B., *Primitive Culture: Researches into the Development of Mythology, Philosophy, Religion, Language, Art, and Custom,* London, John Murray, 1871.

Tylor, Edward B., "Anthropology," in the *Encyclopaedia Britannica,* Ninth Edition, (1878), Vol. II, pp. 107–123.

Tylor, Edward B., *Anthropology: An Introduction to the Study of Man and Civilization,* London, 1881 (N.Y., J. A. Hill and Co., 1904).

Tylor, Edward B., "On a Method of Investigating the Development of Institutions: Applied to Laws of Marriage and Descent," *Journal of the Royal Anthropological Institute,* Vol. 18, (1889), pp. 245–269.

White, Leslie A., "Man's Control over Civilization: An Anthropocentric Illusion," *The Scientific Monthly,* Vol. LXVI, No. 3, (March, 1948), pp. 235–247.

White, Leslie A., "Ethnological Theory," in Sellars, R. W., *et. al,* eds., *Philosophy for the Future,* New York, Macmillan Co., (1949), pp. 357–384.

White, Leslie A., "The Concept of Evolution in Cultural Anthropology," in Meggers, Betty J., ed., *Evolution and Anthropology: A Centennial Appraisal,* Washington, D.C., The Anthropological Society of Washington, (1959), pp. 106–125.

Part II
STUDIES OF POLITICAL AND SOCIAL CHANGE

INTRODUCTION TO PART II

The papers in this section are primarily data-oriented. Nonetheless, discussion of them continued to focus on the theoretical level set at the opening session of the conference.

Weiner raised the salient question of the conditions which allow traditional political systems to develop into modern political systems. He concluded that "theories of political development, no less than theories of economic development, depend upon the analysis of data which cover a span of time . . . *and a theory of political development must be a theory of causation.*"

Brace's use of evolutionary theory employs a philosophical system approach, as is indicated in his paper. Following Northrop, he was led to an interest in aspects of culture which we might call "cultural epistemologies." Brace indicated, for example, that Algeria is typified by a form of "concreteness" (Northrop's aesthetic orientation). In general, he felt it was a mistake to impute a Western-type evolutionary theory to these people. This of course points up the basic *Verstehen* approach of Brace: his concern with evolutionary theory is in its aspect as a theory of actors and particularly the intellectual elite.

Moskos views his study of Albanian elites as illustrating the possible relevance of a stage conception of societal change. Bell urges us to view the recent changes in Jamaica's social structure "not as startling discontinuities with Jamaica's prior history, but rather as continuations of certain long-term social trends which can conveniently be summarized as *increases in the scale of society.*"

None of the conferees indicated that present studies of underdeveloped areas were based upon explicit, formal theories of evolution. Opler's interest in the theories of Tylor, Morgan, etc., appear to be a possible start in this

97

direction, but if we define evolutionary theory as a formal system of theoretical propositions from which hypotheses are derived and tested, then none of the approaches represented at the conference can be considered formal evolutionary theory. The methods of Spencer and Sumner, for example, appear, in fact, to be dead. Again, and as Snyder pointed out in his summary of the conference, no clear distinction was made between evolutionary or non-evolutionary theory, but if Campbell's or Emerson's presentations are at all near the ideal type of evolutionary theory, it must be concluded that nothing approaching formal evolutionary theory is being employed at present.

The positions of Campbell and Emerson are, as indicated previously, that biological or social evolutionary models may be useful heuristic devices for social-scientific studies of change in underdeveloped areas. However, none of the approaches mentioned by the conferees appeared to have much relationship to these models. Again, we must conclude that at present none of these theories of change in underdeveloped areas employ evolutionary models even as analogies.

Implicit Evolutionary Notions Underlying Explicit Theories

The idea that theories of social change are based upon implicit, perhaps unconscious, evolutionary models is closest to the question posed by Blanksten and Mack. This is also the most difficult question to answer without the aid of a group psychotherapist. However, several relationships which emerged at the conference are of interest. First, the aforementioned exchange between Opler and Rottenberg over technological proficiency indicate that both economists and anthropologists are interested in the adaptation of a system to an environment, though one is technological and the other primarily cultural and physical. The interest of sociologists in adaptations of the social system to the environment is very similar. It could be argued (though not too vigorously) that the evolutionary notion of adaptation to the environment underlies structural-functionalism. This is rather unlikely, for as Opler pointed out, Radcliffe-Brown explicitly disclaimed the utility of evolutionary theory for structural-functional analysis, and looked rather to "universal principles," in the manner of Durkheim.

Again, De Schweinitz indicated a relationship between Campbell's contention that a stable environment is necessary for stable homeostatic devices and the economic principle that some stability is necessary for economic growth. Emerson also pointed to similarities in the development of the scientific method to evolutionary theory. As several of the conferees pointed out, however, the mere fact that similarities exist does not demonstrate an underlying theoretical connection. On the other hand, privately expressed opinions of several conferees that evolutionary theory has absolutely nothing to do with the studies of underdeveloped countries seems unwarranted. Herskovits, at one point, accused sociologists of being "ethnocentric" in their approach to emergent areas. If this charge is true, and if that ethnocentrism contains elements of evolutionary theory, then it would be well to be aware of it. Certainly various opinions expressed concerning the relationship of Western democracy to evolutionary theory (to be discussed subsequently) indicate a possible implicit value position of social scientists.

Evolutionary Theories as Theories of Actors, or "Definitions of the Situation"

As discussed previously, the approaches of Brace and the anthropologists present employ evolutionary theory as theories of actors. In other words, various evolutionary (or revolutionary) theories are imputed to the subjects of investigation or culture in question as explanatory or predictive devices. It would appear that this is the only use of evolutionary theory which can be pointed to as explicit at the present time in the social sciences. Sociologists concerned with definitions of their subjects, particularly the so-called "phenomenologists," might also be led to such an approach, although it did not appear to be of much interest to those attending the conference.

Although the foregoing tentative answers to Blanksten's and Mack's initial question may not satisfy the curiosity of everyone, it did appear that evolutionary theory has very little or no explicit use at present, except in the above sense. However, various suggestions were made for its possible future employment.

The Utility of Evolutionary Theory for Studies of Underdeveloped Areas

In his concluding address, Snyder indicated that social scientists do appear to have thrown out evolutionary theory, but added, "The baby may have been thrown out with the bath." He expressed the opinion that various worthwhile heuristic devices have been ignored as a consequence.

Not all the conferees appeared to agree, however. Both Feldman and Mack preferred to concentrate on universal social processes or laws of social action. Moskos maintained that his own analysis went beyond evolutionary theory, and Greer felt that most evolutionary concepts were too crude to predict changes accurately. The evolutionary theory referred to here, however, was probably that which had been rejected by sociologists previously—social Darwinism. All of the sociologists present indicated a tentative renewal of interest in the theories explicated by Emerson. Bell and Cottrell, as we shall see, discussed the possibility of a relationship between evolutionary theory and Western democracy. Spengler indicated that organic evolutionary theories were sometimes useful for economic analysis, but rejected social evolutionary theories because of poor conceptual definitions. Brace said that Emerson's models of biological evolution convinced him of their utility as formal theoretical devices. Anthropologists, consistent with their methodology, appeared less interested in the formal biological models, possibly because they have not yet become a part of any cultural system. Condit, with his interest in purposeful action, was critical of the anti-intellectual, formal models. Weiner apparently leaned to this view also, maintaining that the reaction of folk societies to change does not appear to fit the evolutionary model very closely. He indicated that the revival of folk concepts, for example, is not selective retention, but rather selective reinterpretation of the past.

Emerson, as indicated previously, championed the modern versions of evolutionary theory as heuristic devices, and possible hypothesis generators for the social sciences. Campbell, while in essential agreement, expressed interest in Darwinian and social evolutionary models in addition to the newer theories. Also he viewed them purely as analogies, or convergences to be explained, rather than as predictive devices themselves. Both Emerson and Campbell maintained that purposeful action, rationality, or cultural factors could be incorporated in these models as mechanisms of the evolutionary process.

Problems with Statics and Dynamics

Related to the preceding discussion was a recurrent difference of opinion concerning the status of "statics" vs. "dynamics." Herskovits felt, for example, that Moskos' use of stages in his paper was essentially static. The same question came up with respect to other sociological categories. However, Emerson and Campbell indicated that it is quite easy to belabor the difference between statics and dynamics. They pointed out that theoretical categories at least imply an underlying continuum, which is essentially dynamic. Feldman agreed, asserting that numerous dimensions of social process underly any social-scientific category. All the conferees agreed that one of the major tasks of social scientists was to make these underlying continua explicit. Snyder cautioned, however, that it is not always easy to decide when is the most advantageous time to forsake discrete categories for continuous variables.

Some Problems from the Point of View of a Philosopher of Science

Herbert Hochberg, in his critique of evolutionary models, suggested some problems of considerable significance. First, in discussing Brace's paper, he warned that Northrop's analysis of evolution leads one to think of evolutionary theory in terms of time only. Hochberg offered the following criteria for the identification of evolutionary theories:

1. If theories cannot be reduced completely to some basic physical model at the microlevel. 2. If theories involve a necessary process of qualitative change (over and above scientific lawfulness). 3. If change is seen in terms

of an hierarchical structure. 4. If ethical notions appear to be mixed with scientific processes.

The most important difference between evolutionary and non-evolutionary thought, however, is that evolutionary theory "talks about properties and laws together." Evolutionary theories employ "various properties which emerge at certain points, and which cannot be reduced to scientific laws." Hence, maintained Hochberg, they do not explain in the scientific sense.

Emerson dissented, indicating that the principal aspects of evolutionary theory, such as the concept of "emergence," are in fact reducible to empirical propositions. However, Hochberg held that "observed differences do not necessarily indicate emergence." In reply to another objection concerning the mixing of values and science, Hochberg reiterated his concern with this problem, labeling it the "value mess." (Referring to the confusion of the "is" with the "ought.") It is interesting to note that this problem with evolutionary theory is one of the principal reasons for its earlier rejection by sociologists and anthropologists.

The question of the utility of evolutionary theory for future studies of underdeveloped areas was answered largely in terms of the disciplines involved. Furthermore, there was some indication that the typical methodologies of these disciplines influenced their representative's attitudes toward evolutionary theory. Anthropologists appeared to favor older, more generally known theories as cultural entities. Economists were mildly favorable to the organic theories. Campbell (social psychology) demonstrated enthusiastic support for evolutionary theory, but only as analogy to process. Political scientists and historians appeared divided (perhaps reflecting recent methodological changes in their respective disciplines), and sociologists exhibited little or no interest in evolutionary theory, choosing rather to seek for "regularities in human behavior." One of the reasons for the negative attitude of sociologists may have been the alleged failure of evolutionary theory to reveal these regularities as universal properties.

POLITICAL MODERNIZATION AND EVOLUTIONARY THEORY

MYRON WEINER

Massachusetts Institute of Technology

Until recently, French colonialists in West Africa have used the term *évolué* to describe the native who had proceeded from "savagery" to "civilization." The French spoke of the "subjects" as children, who must move through stages of social development until they could become *citoyen*. The origins, the stages of development and the end-product were precise. To be an *évolué*, one had to be literate, speak French, dress in European fashion, and in general behave in the manner prescribed by French culture. The test of having achieved modern civilization was thus a particular style of life. And to be modern was, by definition, to be French. In theory (but not in practice) the *évolué* was admissible as an equal into the company of Frenchmen.

Evolutionary theory in the colonies had no Darwin. It was part of a common European heritage which permeated many schools of thought: evangelism, liberalism, utilitarianism, and even the unnamed philosophy which guided McKinley's colonial policy in the Philippines. Each political philosophy had its own notion of the appropriate stages in the evolutionary process, depending on its conception of the end: Christianity, or the Rule of Law, or Democracy, or French Culture. But by the latter part of the nineteenth century, some form of evolutionary theory had influenced all colonial thinking, just as Social Darwinism had infiltrated all American social thought. But although the concepts of "struggle for survival" and "survival of the fittest" became the bedrocks of *laissez-faire* conservatism in the United States, for colonialists these same concepts justified governmental paternalism. For if Western man had evolved further than had the natives of Asia and Africa, they reasoned, it was the "white man's burden" to direct and hasten the process of evolution elsewhere through positive government.[1] In con-

[1] It thus came about that the scope of government in Asia and Africa increased as a result of the

temporary jargon one might say that the colonialists believed that cultural diffusion was the key to inevitable evolution toward modernity.

Other forms of evolutionary theory affected political thinkers in the late 19th and early 20th centuries. Many American publicists and scholars, especially before the First World War, believed that all political systems were evolving towards democracy. This evolution, they believed, was inevitable: the spread of education and the growth of mass media would so diffuse knowledge that ruling elites could no longer deny power to the masses. An awareness of self- and group-interests would develop among the masses, voluntary associations would multiply, and a plural society would emerge as a matter of course, accompanied by a system of representative government and public liberties. In the prevailing democracies, the spirit and substance of equalitarianism would grow. In the lands of Czars and Kaisers, popular revolts would lead to the creation of new democracies. And in Asia and Africa, a new spirit of nationalism would ultimately lead to "self-determination."

Another form of evolutionary theory—the most powerful and persuasive in the contemporary world—is Marxism. According to the Marxist theory, social and political systems have evolved in history from the most primitive state of slavery to feudalism, then to capitalism, and would ultimately evolve into socialism and communism. As with democratic evolutionary theory, Marxists believed that what was inevitable was also progressive.

Thus, in the latter part of the nineteenth and early twentieth centuries there were at least four versions of evolutionary theory held by political thinkers: colonial evolutionary theory, Social Darwinism, democratic evolutionary theory, and Marxism. They all shared the belief that political evolution was unilinear, that it was inevitable, and above all, that it was desirable. In the twentieth century, scientifically-oriented political scientists turned away from these evolutionary theories, and today, we would describe these theories as both culture-bound and value-loaded.

In the past decade there has emerged in the United States a group of younger scholars concerned with theories of political development free from the biases of past evolutionary theories. These scholars, heavily influenced by anthropological and sociological theory, have sought to develop more precise ways of describing and analyzing political change. They have turned to the writings of Maine, Toenies, Durkheim, Weber and Parsons to find more sophisticated tools of analysis. On the assumption that political change is not random but can be described in some patterned fashion, students of political development have sought to develop new classifications for political systems.

preferences of the colonial elite, not as a consequence of internal social, economic and political developments, as was the pattern in the countries of Europe and North America.

The quest is, of course, an ancient one, dating to Aristotle; but Aristotle classified political systems only by their form—autocracies, oligarchies, democracies, etc.—and analyzed the changes from one form to another. A different question is now being raised by contemporary students of political development: how is a given traditional system transformed into a modern system?

The fundamental issue being raised here is whether there is a modern state which is independent of form. Is there a common core of "modernity" shared by the totalitarian and democratic state which distinguishes them from non-modern totalitarian and democratic states? Any classification system which places incompatible political forms in the same category may be unpalatable to the student of politics. For one can accept the notion that the United States and the Soviet Union have similar industrial systems, or that there are similarities in their social organizations; recently Alex Inkeles has even argued that there may be a common social psychology shared by individuals in all industrial societies. But in the realm of politics, efforts to point out similarities have been stoutly resisted, for it is here that one's fundamental values and preferences are involved.

Clearly the range of variation in political systems in the contemporary world is so vast that discrete categories become impossible unless one arbitrarily creates models. I shall not attempt here to spell out any such models,[2] but only to indicate briefly some of the categories commonly used by political scientists in the study of political development. They assume that (1) the scope of government is greater in a "modern" than in a "traditional" model—that there is a wider range of functions performed which affect the individual citizen; (2) the wider range of activities pursued in a modern state requires a highly developed two-way network of communications between the citizen and the government; (3) secondary associations play a more prominent role in the modern state, and personal, primary groupings are predominant in the traditional state; (4) the legitimacy of authority tends to be sacred in a traditional state, but legal in a modern one; (5) the bureaucracy of a modern state is task-oriented, recruits on the basis of skills, and is subservient to a policy-making elite, while in a traditional model the bureaucracy maintains existing structures, recruits on a particularistic basis and draws no line between policy and administration; (6) traditional politics concern office-holding almost exclusively, while in the modern society greater

[2] Suggestive attempts at model construction have been made by F. X. Sutton, "Social Theory and Comparative Politics," an unpublished paper prepared for a conference under the auspices of the Committee on Comparative Politics of the Social Science Research Council, Princeton, June 2-4, 1955, and by Fred Riggs, "Agraria and Industria—Toward a Typology of Comparative Administration," in William J. Siffin, ed., *Toward the Comparative Study of Public Administration* (Indiana University Press, 1957).

attention is paid to public policy; and finally, (7) the citizens of a modern society have a sense of attachment to the nation as a whole, while in traditional societies ties to kin, caste, and tribe predominate.[3]

A fundamental assumption underlying the construction of models is that a social or political system is made up of a range of discrete but interrelated parts. The task of the social scientist is, then, to discover how various *structures*—that is, behavior patterns—are related to the *functions* performed within the social system. It follows that the analyst is not concerned with the history of the system, but with its operation at a given time—the present. The formation and development of the system is an interesting problem, but of no importance in understanding the system as it now functions.[4]

This distinction between social science and history is important because it helps us to understand still further why evolutionary theory, so popular in the developing social sciences of the 19th century, lost its importance when social scientists began to explore the *operations* of social, political and economic systems. Nineteenth century scholars were deeply interested in the origins of man and his institutions, an inquiry given great impetus by Darwin's own work. The beginnings of ethnological studies of primitive peoples, studies of the origins of language, and the growth of archeological research coincided with the development of evolutionary theory in the biological sciences. And students of politics, too, gave great attention to theories of the origin of the state—Sir Henry Maine's *Ancient Law*, and *Village Communities*, Fustel de Coulange's *Ancient Cities* were products of this movement.

While the search for origins resulted in some impressive scholarly accomplishments, it also led to reconstructions on the basis of inadequate evidence. As a result, new myths replaced the old; the doctrine of social contract was rejected in favor of a host of specious, undocumented theories concerning the origin of the state. After the First World War, American political scientists turned their attention to the systematic analysis of contemporary political behavior, and 19th century evolutionary theory

[3] I have suggested characteristics commonly referred to in the contemporary literature of political science. This usage might be compared with the tighter but narrower definition of the modern state given by Max Weber. "According to Weber," writes Reinhard Bendix, "a modern state exists where a political community possesses the following characteristics: (1) an administrative and legal order that is subject to change by legislation; (2) an administrative apparatus that conducts official business in accordance with legislative regulation; (3) binding authority over all persons—who usually obtain their citizenship by birth—and over more actions taking place in the area of its jurisdiction; (4) the legitimation to use force within this area if coercion is either permitted or prescribed by the legally constituted government, i.e., if it is in accordance with enacted statute." Reinhard Bendix, *Max Weber: An Intellectual Portrait* (Doubleday, 1960), p. 413. Weber's conception, therefore, is based upon the notion of legal authority.

[4] The psychoanalyst shares a similar attitude. What *really* happened in the patient's past is not so important as what the patient *believes* happened. History is relevant only insofar as it is part of the present.

became irrelevant. Social Darwinism, with its paradoxical belief in inevitable progress while firmly convinced of the sanctity of the existing order, lost its hold on a new generation of scholars. Legal and institutional analysis was put aside, as was the study of origins, and attention was turned to the precise study of contemporary behavior. Theories from the developing fields of sociology and psychology were adopted by political analysts and empirical research was soon the bedrock of political science. In the famous words of a Young Turk in the movement, Harold Lasswell, political science became the study of "conditions, not preferences."[5] A self-conscious science of politics was emerging.

While political scientists moved closer to the sociologists and psychologists, they moved away from anthropologists and historians. Anthropologists were too concerned with the study of primitive societies to appear helpful to political scientists studying modern political systems. And the historian was too tied to the particulars of history—to events rather than to processes—to be of help to the science-oriented student of politics. Furthermore, the new questions posed by the political scientists did not require historic data for their answers: why do men vote as they do, what is the relationship between interest groups and government, how are psychological types related to political roles, how do administrative structures operate, and how are political decisions made? Behavioral studies and historical studies soon became bifurcated; evolutionary theory, with its concern for origins and with long-term processes of change was cast aside in favor of the behavioral approach, and the study of short-term changes in the contemporary world. Political Science, as Peter Odegard wrote, was "no longer a hostage of history."[6]

The achievement of independence by Asian and African nations in the post-war era had a profound effect on the social sciences. Anthropologists added to their study of primitive societies the study of small communities within the new nations. Economists began to devote greater attention to theories of economic growth. And political scientists turned again to the problem of political development; the overriding question was now, how to analyze the transformation of a traditional society into a modern state. Theories of political change were obviously needed. But political science could only offer the student of political development propositions about relations within

[5] Harold D. Lasswell, *Politics: Who Gets What, When, How* (1936).

[6] Quoted approvingly by Heinz Eulau in *A Reader's Guide to the Social Sciences*, Bert Hoselitz, ed. (Free Press, 1959), p. 126. One finds a similar bifurcation between theory and history in economics. The line has been so sharply drawn in economics that scholars of economic history are more likely to find an academic home in departments of history than of economics. In recent years, however, economic historians have come to assume a more honorable place in the social sciences, as they have increasingly applied economic theory to their historical analysis.

industrial societies, and analyses of short-term changes. It is not surprising, therefore, that the scholars of political development turned for their categories of analysis to the writings of Maine, Durkheim, Weber and Parsons rather than to the writings of political scientists of the '30s and '40s. These social theorists had been concerned with understanding fundamental *changes* in systems, while the political scientists had been preoccupied with the functioning of these systems. The former had built their analysis on comparative and historical data, while the latter had tended to study only the contemporary American or European scene.

The fundamental question was this: *under what conditions do traditional political systems develop into modern political systems?* In other words, how and why does the pattern of legitimacy change?[7] How and why does the communication network change, and what effects do these changes have upon political orientations?[8] What are the differences between traditional and modern bureaucracies and what brings about changes from one to the other?[9] How and why do voluntary groupings arise?[10] Studies of these questions have just begun. The most comprehensive and systematic attempt to analyze the political process in systems which are neither traditional nor modern, but which have been characterized as "modernizing," "developing," or "emerging" has been offered in a six-man study edited by Gabriel Almond and James Coleman, *Politics of the Developing Areas*.[11] This study is of great interest because it used a functional analysis of political development and is, at present, the most ambitious systematic attempt to use cross-cultural comparative data for the analysis of political change. It is particularly instructive, therefore, to analyze this attempt briefly, for an analysis of the study's limitations calls attention to some of the problems of developing a theory of political development.[12]

The authors of *Developing Areas* were torn by two objectives: to find a rigorous method for describing and analyzing the operation of politics in the emerging societies; and secondly, to try to explain the changes that have been occurring, why these are occurring and what are the consequences of these changes for the functioning of the system. To answer the first question, the

[7] See David Apter, *Gold Coast in Transition*, (Princeton Univ. Press, 1956).

[8] See Daniel Lerner, *The Passing of Traditional Society* (Free Press, 1958).

[9] See Fred Riggs, *loc. cit.*

[10] See Myron Weiner, *Politics of Scarcity* (Univ. of Chicago Press, 1961), especially chapter III, "Community Associations."

[11] (Princeton Univ. Press, 1960). Other members of the group were George Blanksten, Dankwart Rustow, Lucian Pye and Myron Weiner.

[12] Lest the reader mistakenly assume that any criticisms here represent a dissenting note by one of the authors, let it be understood that these thoughts have occurred only since the study was completed.

group turned toward the literature of social theory. Gabriel Almond, in his introductory chapter to the study, describes the intellectual parentage of the study and stresses the group's indebtedness to the social theorists who developed functional analysis. He then defines and interrelates the various functional categories employed in the analysis: political communication, political recruitment and socialization, articulation and aggregation of interests, rule making, rule administering and rule adjudication. It was soon apparent to the group that while functional categories were useful in analyzing the operation of emerging societies, and even in illuminating the existing factors which were causing the systems to change, these analytical categories contributed little to explaining the origin or cause of particular social and political forms. It was assumed that the sources of political change lay in the social and economic system, and each of the authors therefore spelled out the processes of social change in the society and the effects of these changes on politics.[13] The impact of modern technology and commerce, population growth, the introduction of new patterns of education, and changes in social stratification were all explored. Brief attention was also given to the character of the traditional societies and the pattern of the Western impact which had set these processes of change in motion.

Functional analysis of contemporary data thus proved to be just as inadequate to a theory of political change as were the concepts produced by students of political behavior in the '30s and '40s. Although nonhistorical functional analysis may contribute to, and indeed should provide, specific and limited predictive hypotheses, it tells us virtually nothing about the general development of an existing system—how it came to operate as it now does. An exploration of current economic data may permit the economist to predict whether a rise in production will occur, but such an analysis can contribute little to a general theory of economic growth. Similarly, an analysis of the functions performed by organized groups in the political system may provide us with predictions of the content of public policy, but such an analysis contributes little to a theory which will explain the conditions under which voluntary associations develop. Theories of political development, no less than theories of economic development, depend upon the analysis of data which covers a span of time. *The study of functions is not a study of causes, and a theory of political development must be a theory of causation.*

If this criticism of functional theory is interpreted as an argument for historical analysis, let it not be interpreted as an argument for historians. Political history, as now written by historians, can no more offer the basis for a theory of political development than has the history of economies or the

[13]Each of the area studies in *Developing Areas* contains *separate* sections on "processes of change" and "political functions."

history of customs contributed to a theory of economic development or of cultural change. Let me illustrate briefly this argument that theories of political development must pay closer attention to new types of historical data.

It is widely agreed that voluntary associations, political parties and interest groups, are modern phenomena. At least four characteristics separate these modern political associations from traditional political groups. First, they are voluntary; unlike the caste or tribe to which one may be born, the modern political association is a group which men voluntarily choose to enter. Secondly, the modern political association is not ordinarily a primary group and is usually too large for all members to know one another. Thirdly, the modern political association operates in the public sphere, that is, it is organized to enter into relationships with an external political authority. It may also have internal rules to regulate the behavior of its membership, but these are largely to increase its effectiveness in dealing with external authority. Moreover, its coercive powers are ordinarily limited—it may expel, but it cannot arrest. Fourthly, it has durability, indicated both by the presence of an internal bureaucracy and by the longevity of its existence. These characteristics thus exclude from the notion of modern political organizations castes and tribes (but not political organizations formed by members of a given caste or tribe), mob outbursts and peasant rebellions (but not peasant associations), the military (but not veterans associations), the church, cabals, and estates of the realm. Although these latter groupings may be found in modern as well as traditional societies, they are not characteristically modern political organizations.

Modern societies produce many different types of voluntary associations. Societies whose social organization has historically been based upon caste, tribe, or religious sects are likely to develop voluntary associations based upon communal loyalties. Societies in which stratification has centered around occupational rankings are more likely to produce associations based upon class loyalties. The conditions under which modern political associations develop appear to be many, but thus far we have no systematic theory. Most explanations focus on the "collapse" of the old economic, political and social order under the "impact" of a new, modern order: the "breakup" of traditional political and social structures (e.g. "detribalization"), urbanization, the rise of western education, commercialization, social mobility, the growth of a new middle class, the emergence of a money economy to replace barter arrangements, the rise of an industrial labor force, the impact of Christian missions, and the creation of new political structures by colonial powers. Which of these variables are critical and which are not, why some are accompanied by the growth of modern associations in some circumstances but not in others, and most importantly, what characteristics of the traditional societies themselves facilitate or retard the development of voluntary associations are questions which must be answered if a theory of the development of modern political associations is to be produced.

The answers to these questions will not be forthcoming from a perusal of the conventional histories of political organizations, for these focus largely on national developments and pay undue attention to the ideological issues which precipitated their organization. How these associations developed at the local level, what kinds of incentives were provided to those who joined, what their relationship was to traditional social and political groupings within the community and to traditional notions about the conduct of politics are matters we are just beginning to explore in field studies of voluntary associations in the developing areas. And to answer these questions with respect to 18th and 19th century Europe will require a different kind of historical literature than is, as far as I know, now available.

Conclusion

In the nineteenth century, cultural evolutionists argued that all cultures pass through parallel, unilinear stages of development. Historical scholarship and the development of cultural relativism led to the conviction that, on the contrary, cultural development is divergent, except as differences are reconciled through cultural diffusion. Out of this rejection of unilinear evolutionary theory came two twentieth century modifications: the thinking of those who saw a universal evolution of man (as distinct from individual cultures), and the theories such as that of the anthropologist Julian Steward, which hypothesize multilinear evolution. Steward argues that the cultural evolutionist must search for parallels of limited occurrence rather than universal laws. There are, he argues, recurrent forms, processes and functions, and he wisely warns that the choice is not between world-embracing universal laws and endless historical and cultural particularisms. "It is," Steward writes, "our basic premise that the crucial methodological feature of evolution is the determination of recurrent causal relationships in independent cultural traditions."[14]

What in evolutionary theory, then, is appropriate to contemporary political scientists studying political development? The notion that evolution, political as well as biological, is a natural process, and that change, in human affairs as well as in the organic and inorganic world, involves regularities, is an acceptable notion to political scientists. The notion of unilinear political development is not appropriate, however, for clearly there are divergent patterns of political development—both in the process through which change occurs, and

---

[14] Julian H. Steward, "Evolution and Process" in *Anthropology Today*, A. L. Kroeber, ed. (University of Chicago Press, 1953), p. 324.

in the forms which emerge. In the study of the evolution of functions, on the other hand, there may be a strong case for a unilinear concept; the scope of government, the character of the communication process, the spread of associations, the nature of legitimacy, the character of the bureaucracy, and the public sense of "civicness" may differ fundamentally between non-modern and modern societies, whether the modern state is democratic, authoritarian or totalitarian, and even if the process of achieving modernity has varied considerably between the states.

The evolutionary notion that processes of change can be understood by examining the history of an organism's development has profoundly affected the study of human culture, and is now affecting the study of political development. But in place of an historian's study of *events*, we can look forward to the study of *processes*—of the patterned interrelationships which make up political evolution. By linking historic studies of political development with the systematic study of existing political systems, we may yet be able to develop a satisfactory theory of political development.

EVOLUTIONARY THEORY IN INTELLECTUAL HISTORY AND ITS MEANING IN ALGERIA

RICHARD M. BRACE

Oakland University

If we can conceive that the goal of the intellectual historian is to relate the ideas of the big minds to the masses of thoughtful people who "carry the tasks of civilization," we have at least a direction to follow in our task of tracing evolutionary thought in the Western world. In a real sense, the intellectual historian is a parasite. He is not a philosopher trained to evaluate esoteric systems of thought or to build a system of his own. He must also accept the astounding achievements of science from authority since he lacks the special competence to repeat the experiments and to test the conclusions he accepts. In the study of ideas he often deals with noncumulative knowledge: He is thus forced at the end to make choices, to set values, which are personal, unscientific, and are scarcely more than a collection of opinions.

Intellectual history, as some of us play it, is a game whose rules are scarcely codified, but it is nevertheless serious. At its best, it tries to focus on such relevant problems as man's control of, or adaptation to, his total environment. It certainly does not come up with pat answers. But in its study of past basic issues in human relationships, it becomes a survey of social scientific success and failure. It still resembles Condorcet's "social physics," but has come far from that point.

Evolutionary theory, both natural and social, has a long, involved, and distinguished history in the human quest. Darwin and his friends hold it together at midpoint, but they had much to build upon, and since 1859 there have been countless re-applications, most of which have added positive and vital contributions to the possibility of increasing human control over environment. The early adaptation of evolutionary theory to society too facilely assumed "that the universe was designed to produce man and civilization, that cultural evolution everywhere must be governed by the same principles and follow the same line, and that all mankind would progress toward a civilization like that of Europe."[1] Buried under the assault of Boas and Lowie, this mound led social scientists into new diggings from which cultural development was separated from biological evolution—an idea with deep philosophical implications. New relationships discovered by investigations of this kind, and obviously this is simply an example and possibly a poorly chosen one, could be exceedingly fruitful in orienting our approach to the underdeveloped world.

F. S. C. Northrop has written an incisive and thoughtful study of the concept of evolution in Western thought from Aristotelian philosophy of the Middle Ages through the nineteenth century, that child of the Age of Perfectibility, which, under the influence of Darwinian thought, brought evolutionary concepts to their broadest social projection.[2] He points out that the primary postulate of all evolutionary occurrence is concerned with time: that is, all matter, inorganic or organic, any species of a natural order, man, and even ideas, are what they are now, or at any given time in the past or future, because of the interaction between time in its moving, not periodic, sense, (its sense of "becoming") and the universe. The second major concept of evolutionary thought is one of change, or development in the direction of increasing complexity. This change has been described most generally by a theory of gradualism—a simple survival of the organism, by means of heredity, which was able best to adapt itself to its environment. Darwin, in the beginning, unlike his predecessor Lamarck, was a confirmed gradualist. He rejected the idea that a revolutionary or radical change in species by means of a mutation was normally possible. Of course, he believed that one species developed from another by means of small variations which were inherited. The older Lamarckian idea, to be revived in our time with the famous controversy over the work of the biologist Lysenko, gave more importance to environment that did a gradualistic theory of development. It claimed, for example, that use and need were the fathers of drastic change in the characteristics of a given species. The idea of revolutionary change, while not Darwinian, has always been a sub-corollary, or at least an active possibility, in evolutionary thought. If biologically difficult to prove, it was philosophically most productive. It can be traced throughout the philosophies of Kant, Fichte, Hegel and Marx and it took form in such block-world states as the Communist and Fascist states of the twentieth century.

[1] Julian H. Stewart, "Cultural Evolution," *Scientific American* (May, 1956), p. 70.

[2] Persons, Stow, ed., *Evolutionary Thought in America*, (F.S.C. Northrop, "Evolution in its Relation to the Philosophy of Nature and the Philosophy of Culture.") Yale Univ. Press. (New Haven, 1950), pp. 44–84.

The next postulate of evolutionary thought is actually an intellectual addenda to biological Darwinianism. If natural selection was a continual weeding out of the unfit biological specimens, a development toward the best specimens (if the idea of best can be related to the "strongest" or the most apt to survive), then could it not be argued that the evolutionary development of man must be in the direction of his greater good? Of course such an application of biological theory to the progress of man—inevitably in the direction of strength, that is, goodness, must be made by a speculative or philosophical person who believes that the general laws of the universe are susceptible to a synthesis of reason. One must also accept the point of view that complexity itself is synonymous with greater good. And here Mr. Northrop carries the matter much too far for the cautious and empirical historian by postulating the idea that the "True" for natural science must have its corollary in a dominant philosophy of the "Good" for culture. He believes that Western civilization is disintegrating because of a pluralistic belief in the good for culture which is, for Western Man, more dangerous than the problem of the atom bomb.[3]

Whether or not a social scientist can accept the block-world concept of such thinking, there is no doubt that evolutionary doctrine as it ascends from the natural sciences into philosophy, through social, economic, and political thought, is extremely lively and controversial at the present time. As evolutionary thinking can be said to have influenced Western monist philosophies, it can be traced in the formation of such block states as the Communist and Fascist have built. The Hegelian line of evolutionary thought as it appeared in the work of such giants as Malthus and Marx has

[3] In his conclusion he says:

It is exceedingly important, therefore, that we seek out as quickly as possible the error occurring at the very beginning of the modern world which led us, in our passage from its philosophy of science to the attendant philosophy of culture, into the relativistic ideological impasse in which we now find ourselves. Elsewhere this error and its eradication have been indicated. The result seems to be a philosophy of science [the now questioned "steady-state theory of the universe"] verified by the methods of science in a manner which makes it valid for everyone, which at the same time provides a unique and apparently globally adequate philosophy of culture. Thus the classical identification of the philosophy of the good for culture with the philosophy of nature as derived by formal analysis (i.e. dialectic) from the publicly verifiable hypotheses of science as specified first by Socrates and Plato, is restored.

In any event, this identification of the philosophical criterion of the good for culture with the scientifically verified philosophy of the true for nature enables us to understand why not merely the evolution of cultural institutions but also the evolution of the natural scientists' experimentally verified theories concerning nature undergo the abrupt revolutionary changes in time as specified by the Hegelian dialectic of negation. If one's correct ideology of the good for culture is in part at least defined in terms of one's scientific theory of the experimentally verified for nature, it follows that when in time new scientific evidence forces scientists to negate the postulates of their traditional theory then one's idea of the good for culture must undergo a similar revolution. (*Ibid.*, pp. 78–79.)

enormous importance in contemporary ideology. One can even postulate that the Democratic ideal of a state fits the Hegelian pattern of a pre-conceived and immutable goal, while Democracy in action constantly fluctuates between a more or less authoritarian concept of the Democratic ideal. We will try later to examine both the block-world and the pluralistic versions of Darwinian thought as they still ripple through the undeveloped world of the *Maghrib*.

The three major concepts of evolutionary thought as they have developed over the centuries in the Western world are, briefly, the Aristotelian synthesis, the Fichtean, Kantean, Hegelian dialectic, and the Anglo-American (not to exclude French) philosophies of evolution associated with the names of Comte, Spencer and Darwin. Going into the twentieth century the pre-dominantly block-world quality of these systems fell apart to some extent under the assault of such philosophers as Bergson, James, Dewey and the Existentialists.

Aristotle conceived that the reality of temporal changes in nature could not be understood apart from the metaphysical and physical or scientific realities of the world. For Aristotle, who rejected the Democritean and Platonic atomic theory of matter, and therefore, the epistemological distinction between nature as sensed and nature as conceived, natural matter was the simple equivalent of sensed matter. And sensed matter was presented as being in continuous change, not fixed and immutable. Aristotle, then, did not endow matter with absolute qualities. He regarded generation as real and "the principle of becoming" as metaphysically basic. Time was regarded as part of the essence of actual existent things. Since Aristotle believed that a living organism was a growing, changing, and developing thing (so also a living species) the idea of generation (time plus change) was implicitly established in his philosophy. Here we see an early application of evolutionary thought. The previous Democritean philosophy of living creatures held that all change that seemed an alteration of property was merely an alteration of position, due to motion rather than time. It was a philosophy of fixed and immutable properties and completely alien to the temporal nature of Aristotle's more flexible theory. Aristotle's thesis that the real natural object is the sensed natural object gave the idea of change due to generation a real status in scientific knowledge, and in this respect was a forerunner of later versions of scientific philosophy.

But Aristotle added another postulate to his physics, from his metaphysics, which changed the free direction of his thinking. He posited a theory of the object's ideal form which was derived from the sensed plus the cognitive qualities of the object, that is, hot, cold, wet and dry, their combinations and their opposites, which were derived from sensory experiences and then elevated by a philosophy of potentialities and a doctrine of negation called "privation." This form or sensuous quality is logically or cognitively present in experience as the opposite of the positive form which is sensed. This theory is responsible for the monistic and absolute basis which Aristotelian thought continually takes, even though its beginnings were rooted in empirical observation. It is an establishment of the importance of the essence over the existential, or the actual, being, for Aristotle declared that "no form can be exemplified actually in time in a given substance as positive form if that form was not in that substance logically and initially in the status of form by privation." Therefore, the Aristotelian conception of evolution is a teleological one, and its ultimate goal is determined from the beginning as one absolute predetermined goal, defined by a form which is non-temporal and immortal, even though forms for new species can originate at any instant in time, as Darwin later was to claim.

Aristotelian science had one other quality in common with Darwin's study of origin of species. Aristotle arranged all natural creatures in hierarchies following a process of observation, description, and classification, into genera and species.[4] The fact that Aristotle's science is quickly whipped up into a cosmology becomes plain. It is also plain that two important elements of evolutionary thought have crept by him into the Western world.

The Aristotelian philosophy of science was given a rude jar by the new physics of Galileo and Newton's science of mechanics. Each time there is a revolutionary change in physics, there seems to be a corollary change in philosophy. Galileo repudiated Aristotle's final forms and causes in favor of a new concept of force. He also separated the object's intrinsic properties from the object's sense-perceived properties, thus setting clearly apart the known and the knower. The mechanistic theory of Newton defined the state of an object by its position and energy. A living or natural organism began to be defined by its physical and chemical structure. It was apparent that organisms were adaptable with nothing of the immutable or eternal about them. So one cosmogony went out the window, and Darwin was left with a problem to explore—the adaptations of the living organism to its natural environment. This evolutionary concept seems to me to remain one of the most valid social applications of Darwinian natural theory.

[4] Any given species is defined by specifying its nearest genus in the system of classification and the differentiating quality which distinguishes it from other species in that genus. This means that any creature in nature is in its very essence, or in other words as designated by its scientific definition, a part of a hierarchical order. Thus there is not merely the organization of formal cause of a given organism, but also there is an organic relationship between the final causes of all natural objects. In fact, the temporal process is the result of the embodiment of the hierarchical order of the organic relations of all species in otherwise formless matter. Northrop, "Evolution in its Relation to the Philosophy of Nature," p. 53.

When Darwin went to work on his biological material, he was fortified by Aristotelian methods of observation and Newtonian concepts of the adaptability of matter. For a half dozen years he observed, described, and classified, then cautiously came up with the central evolutionary theme that species are not immutable. Here was the first positive concept of evolution not to be applied in a teleological manner. By careful study, he ascertained that minute variations of the species existed in close geographical locations. He also classified them by geological time. In 1838 he found a synthesizing thought in Malthus, who declared that "many more individuals of each species are born than can possibly survive." This statement gave him an hypothesis from which to work. And also an hypothesis that could be spread out to embrace a rationale of war, imperialism, and even racism, as it did in the thought of Spencer.

The idea of time was central to Darwin's thesis, just as the idea of eternal form was central to Aristotle's. Darwin said at the end of the *Origin of the Species* that a natural arrangement must be genealogical, and that both the origin and the actualization or eventuation of form were temporal events. Different species were therefore joined by a temporal relation involving descent, not only within the species, but between the species by means of mutations. In fact, the origin of diverse species was said to come from "incipient species" or varieties of the original species, brought forth by the "force of inheritance."

It is not far from this concept to "Natural Selection" nor from there to Spencer's concept of the inevitable progress of man, blind and over-optimistic as his social philosophy might seem now.[5] In this concept, any organization with a variation which permits it to survive in the struggle for existence will perpetuate itself and grow stronger, either within the species or by means of a new variant. It is a theory which holds nothing to be immutable, but progress is possible, even though brought about by a wasteful, variable, and imperfect process. There is no monistic world necessarily deducible from this theory. No final end, only a continuum of development. However, social scientists, and even Theodore Roosevelt, were to find in it "Manifest Destiny" and "Anglo-Saxon" superiority.

Although Darwin was forced later to admit the existence of abrupt genetic changes (mutations which are unpredictable and yet inheritable), the philosophical drift of his thoughts was most readily reducible to the idea of gradual

[5] The ultimate development of the ideal man is logically certain—as certain as any conclusion in which we place the most implicit faith; for instance that all men die. . . . Progress, therefore is not an accident, but a necessity. Instead of civilization being artificial, it is a part of nature; all of a piece with the development of the embryo or the unfolding of a flower. Quoted by Richard Hofstadter, *Social Darwinism in American Thought* (Rev. ed., Boston: Beacon Press, 1955), p. 40, and from *Social Statics*. pp. 79–80.

change, a progression due to an accumulation of innumerable slight variations. "If we allowed long enough intervals of time, geology plainly declares that species have all changed in the manner required by the theory, for they have changed slowly and in a graduated manner." It was in this direction that the Anglo-American-French schools have taken Darwinian thought into philosophy and social science. Not so the German Hegelians and later Marxists.

When Herbert Spencer, Haeckel, Bergson and others took over evolutionary thought and tried to develop it into a cosmology of progress, they made the mistake of raising certain laws of natural phenomena into general principle. Man's development in society was equated, in a very simple manner, with biological development. This type of belief or inquiry has proved neither plausible nor useful. Anthropological investigations, beginning with an attempt to discover a single line of evolution from a primitive condition to its present-day descendant have failed to reveal a very satisfactory conclusion, and this failure led to other points of departure which may be more fruitful because any social organization is "at least partly invented by human intelligence to meet particular conditions. In the highly developed cultures, rational selection plays a far more influential role than natural selection." Although the negative and conservative interpretation that Spencer and Huxley gave to evolutionary thought in the social and moral field is not useful to today's vital synthesis, this fact does not at all deprive them of the recognition that in transferring evolution into the large world they opened a field fertile in possibilities for coming social development.

Just as Darwin was intrigued with Newtonian ideas of mechanism, Kant earlier became interested in the new science. He set about discovering a world philosophy to fit the new physics and the new mathematics, for he did not believe that the philosophies of Locke or Hume were sufficiently explicit in concepts of space, time, and causality. In his *Critique of Pure Reason* he demonstrated that nature was purely mechanistic and deterministic in character, that strict causality existed—as strict as Darwinian necessity. He translated these ideas from the object, or the known, to the subjective or the knower and he gave his categories the attributes of universality and necessity. He had no belief, therefore, in human freedom or free will. This left him with a dichotomy between the physical sciences and moral philosophy which he reconciled by saying that the immediate grounds for practical action held the key to man's moral dilemma. Therefore, for the first time in Western philosophy there was a gulf between natural philosophy and morality or religion. He believed that moral life had no meaning unless it involved a freedom of choice, so his natural laws of necessity were not acceptable in that field.

It remained for Fichte to rationalize once more the dichotomy with his concept of the primacy of practical reason. He declared that natural science's theories of life, even nature itself, are consequences of the demands of the morally free ego. Like Kant, Fichte believed that morality which existed without opposition was meaningless. Therefore he pre-supposed the non-ego or self-negation which became ultimately identified with nature. So once more, by one of those intellectual stunts of dialectic the Germans loved, the moral and natural world became one—the world was a closed reality formed by the opposing relations of the moral agent and the natural agent—between a thesis and its anti-thesis.

Fichte thus produced the synthesis, which he posits in an Absolute ego to which man's free will is enslaved. We have once again come full circle from Kant's original doctrine of man's free choice. And we have posited a new kind of evolutionary causation—or rather revolutionary evolution—from which changes were made by means of sharp negations, complete reverses and new syntheses. Hegel took it from there, accepting the idea of divine determinism. He was therefore obliged to posit the ideal in culture in the evolution of historical reality, and we follow him, balking all the way, to the logical conclusion that the ideal is the real and the real is the ideal.

Whether one examines Marxian materialistic philosophy arising from this basis, or Hegelian idealism, in both systems reality is basically evolutionary (really revolutionary), monistic, and historical in character. These doctrines are much closer to Lamarckian mutation than to Darwinian gradualism. Such a concept can be recognized in the Russian Revolution, where the gradualist Mensheviks lost out to the radical Bolsheviks who believed in a socialist state. Lenin, for example, believed that the Hegelian evolutionary line was more important for new or underdeveloped states than Darwinian gradual-ism, which showed a predisposition toward a revolution of the bourgeoisie rather than one of the proletariat. A few years ago, during the French-Algerian war, de Gaulle's attempt to tie Algeria to French methods of evolution might be considered Darwinian in concept, whereas the Provisional Algerian Republic's plan was one of revolution by and for the people—a much more Hegelian evolutionary form.

In each of the main lines of Western evolutionary thought, then, there has been established the idea that the evolution of cultural institutions is identical with, or shares important relations to the laws governing natural evolution, and also a belief in historical (in evolutionary terms we might say 'temporal') determinism. Examples can be found in England, France, the United States, and later in Russia, China, Mexico and in the states of the *Maghrib*, particularly Algeria. Each of these states has had a revolutionary goal, and then an evolutionary one. These means have not always been philosophically unified even if they have been teleological. In fact, the pluralism of evolutionary thought, as it has become a social phenomena, is probably one of the most significant of its recent developments.

Certainly it would appear that the revolutionary ideas of both the Hegelian idealism and Marxian dialectic, the ideas of development by opposing negatives (such as, for example, the contradictory cultural ideas to be found in ex-colonial states now trying to fuse indigenous ideas of culture with the applied ideas of the colonial powers to form a new synthesis) and the gradualism inherent in Western Democracies long past their original revolutionary stage, are all valid sources for the growth of the underdeveloped state. The Aristotelian philosophy of one final, timeless cause, which perhaps one might equate with Communist or Fascist philosophy, does not seem sufficiently flexible to embrace the diversity of social evolutionary procedures in new or old states. Nor is there necessarily an identical temporal development or "becoming" in different states at the same moment or at different moments. Certain phases of development may perhaps be traced, however. Neither of these ideas is sufficient to explain the modern evolutionary idea which seems perhaps of most interest and most importance—that is, the belief that each new product of the evolutionary process *might* introduce a new primitive assumption—a new and unique verity, having to do with free will.

In this direction, Bergsonian idealism adds still another evolutionary concept to the Western basket—or at least alters an old one. His philosophy is something of a revival of the ideas of Schelling and Schopenhauer, but important in its own right. From the more or less mechanistic evolutionary thought of the nineteenth-century—the block-world concepts—Bergson emerged with an idea of time that was at once novel and active.[6] Time was no longer a static or eternal element in which a species changed or progressed or mutated because of its own inherent quality of movement. It was itself the author of evolution having a causal relationship with the person or organism reacting "temporally," doing something in time. Bergson's theory held that man is continuously evolving intuitively as a result of past actions in time, and, above all, memory (including organic or racial memory which acted in a subliminal fashion) and is therefore altering himself and his actions at each possible moment. In this condition, the quality of intuition is much more important than the quality of reason—a higher faculty. Because of man's evolution in time and his corresponding intuition, he was never exactly the same from one moment to the next. His experience, though it might be to some extent patterned, could always be a unique evocation of the past and the temporal present—a "becoming" always creative and never entirely repetitious.

[6] Arthur O. Lovejoy, "Bergson and Romantic Evolutionism," *University of California Chronicle.* (Berkeley, 1913), pp. 429–487, *passim.*

This particular spirit of evolution Bergson called *élan vital*, a free creative life force from which any new evolution might be expected. Described once by an American in dire need of an English equivalent as "oompf," this new and exciting element added an open-world view to the block-world or mechanistically determined monism of the nineteenth century and gave a great positive bound to the possibilities of evolutionary thought. It was a buoyant and hopeful philosophy which predicated infinite possible advance and new creation. It is such a reference, romantic and over-idealistic though it might be, in which it would be interesting to place the best aspects of the Algerian state.

In some of Existential philosophy's further destruction of the block-man in favor of the individual—of the destruction of man formed by generalities in favor of man isolated by the human condition—and evolving most fully because he is aware that only in developing his potential as a human being can his history be meaningful in the face of the absurdity of the world, can we place the action of some of the new revolutionaries whom we have met in the *Maghrib*. In many of them we can see reflected the vision of "Kierkegaard's lonely existential revolt against systematic thought in general and his leap into faith on the wings of absurdity.[7]" Is there anything more absurd than Ben Bella's robbing of a post office to find the first substantial funds for the Algerian Revolution? Is there anything more absurd and more lonely than to be a Frenchman with the Algerians today, like the young people of the *Reseau Jeanson*, with ten years' imprisonment on their head because they believe in a France that has almost ceased to exist? This kind of personal and heroic evolution in the face of rational and systematic block repression is one of the great triumphs of human evolution outside a system.

The pragmatism of James, which added free will, the action of man upon his environment, and a belief in a pluralistic world, has also helped widen the possibility of evolutionary thought and action. It seems to me that it is precisely as evolutionary thought becomes less highly intellectualized, less systemized and more pluralistic that it becomes most helpful in the Social Sciences. The larger the free swing of Western ideas from the block-world to an open system, the greater are the resources open to the Third World states. They borrow what they need from evolutionary thought depending upon their own period of progress. They need dialectic and *dirigisme* for their revolution and for the insufficiently "encadred" state. They need an active belief in progress of a gradual nature, yet they are acutely aware of the need to move in a revolutionary sense, to develop against galloping populations. They need a belief in the possibility of ethical progress, of a non-materialistic

[7] Hans Meyerhoff, ed., *The Philosophy of History in our Time*. (New York: Doubleday Anchor Original, 1959), p. 15.

development, and they need understanding of the enormous possibility inherent in the individual, or the state, to modify environment. It would seem that as the highly intellectualized background of evolutionary thought becomes more dilute, less pure, and more controversial, it has more meaning for the underdeveloped areas. Development in time—they call it the direction of history—of the institutions and the individuals of a state, we might call it progress (progress being more related to the eighteenth century idea of human perfectibility than to the survival of the fittest)—to a degree of greater complexity, i.e. efficacy for life in a modern world, all these goals have counterparts in general Darwinian theory.

The scientists, the block-world men who believe in the conservation of energy in the universe (the steady-state theory of Fred Hoyle) and the open universe advocates summarized by George Gamow, are still formally carrying on the old story of the "true for nature and the good for culture" ideas, as are the philosophic systems and those who make our theologies. But the people in the underdeveloped world are pirating all things from all people. Perhaps they will be able to prove the strength of the free and pluralistic world, whose proofs, strangely enough, can be found hiding beneath Darwinian evolutionary causality.

When we apply evolutionary thought in its purest scientific state, and even in its popular conception, to the "third world" of our time, we are obliged to make a difficult transition. For one thing, the behavioral sciences are certainly less predictable than the natural sciences and the problem of social control looms formidable. The importance of human volition and freedom have been added to the inevitability of the evolutionary picture, and, are extremely potent, if difficult, to analyze. Man's[8] "profound sense of individuation is clearly of great importance, and makes it quite hard to analyze him in quite the same way the physicist does the atom or even the biologist does the lesser animals." Yet we should be the last to retreat before this challenge.

The "third world," no matter how one defines it, is an exceedingly large area inhabited by possibly two billion human beings of great diversity, and from all observations "there'll be more tomorrow." Therefore, let us choose a definite target. The ensuing thought tries to place observed facts, feelings and hopes sensed in a limited part of this "third world," the *Maghrib,* particularly Algeria, against some of the general views on evolution considered earlier in this discussion.

Throughout the *Maghrib,* whether one refers to the young leaders in the independent states of Morocco and Tunisia, or to their equivalent in the Algerian National Liberation Front, there exists a common article of faith.

[8] Robert E. Larsen, "Education and Ethics," *Saturday Review* (April 15, 1961), pp. 65–67.

The leaders believe that their states and people will evolve toward a happier, more productive future than was possible under colonial rule. Sekou Touré illustrated his feeling about the past and future of Guinea in an informal analogy he drew while speaking at Northwestern University in 1959. "If I place a peanut on this table, it does not sprout; if I plant it in the soil, it germinates, grows, and yields. The table represents the old colonial order; the soil represents the new independent environment." This faith is shared by the common man in Africa. Often it is disputed by the remaining Europeans, and, in Algeria, by a few Muslims who for one reason or another feel their future, as was their past, to be linked with France.

In Algeria the vast majority accept first a course which comes close to the Hegelian dialectic of revolution and second, an idealistic belief in perfectibility—faith in the possible. In acting upon this second conviction, the leadership in Morocco and Tunisia, for example, has surely embraced the view that the future must be planned as scientifically as possible. Starting with whatever surveys and plans the French protectorate left—here a note of gradualism creeps in—the new governors altered objectives from colonial to national, made new surveys, and set forth upon what they hope will be a voyage of progress.[9] It is a voyage taken under heavy time pressure. Untried leaders face a crucial challenge without adequately trained Muslim cadres. They must succeed in order to prove themselves and to justify their view that Moroccans know better than Europeans what is good for themselves and are capable of achieving that good. They are, then, whether or not they are aware of it, deeply involved in a time and necessity rationale—the time is ripe for an independent nation-state; history is working for them.

They thus set about training human resources faster than Lyautey, the most forward-looking French administrator, ever dreamed possible, and developing natural resources. If their people are to benefit from the much desired status of independence, they must first be equipped to evolve toward a practically and philosophically better future. That the leaders feel the pressure of time is clearly demonstrated by the crash educational program for young and old alike. The Moroccans are proud of the statistical fact that in 1961 they had 700,000 people in school, whereas in 1956, under the protectorate, 150,000 attended. If educational opportunities are undoubtedly greater, we have poor means of comparing the quality of instruction and the standards of the two systems.

In Tunis and Algeria today, this progression is thought to be inevitable.

[9] For transitional planning see, Ministère de l'Economie Nationale, *L'évolution économique du Maroc dans le cadre du deuxième plan quadriennal (1954–1957)* (Casablanca, 1958); for a scholarly study of political change 1955–1959 see, Douglas E. Ashford, *Political Change in Morocco* (Princeton, 1961).

Ministers in Tunis and Algeria all agree that their movement flows with history's tide. They note that since 1954 they have grown, consolidated, and developed more complexity. Nor are they unaware of the growth of their relative strength as they witness the death of the Fourth French Republic and the civil and military *putsches* which have plagued the Fifth Republic.

Algerian political and military leaders seemed to be highly pragmatic about their revolution and the state's future evolution. Their first objective was liberation; the second phase is reconstruction and development. They see the state as reflecting the national need and desire. And, unlike the case of Morocco and Tunisia, states whose independence the Algerian rebellion made possible without serious struggle on their own part, the Algerians stand ready to see that peace is secure and that the second phase of the revolution reflects the people's will.

All the elements of evolutionary thinking are present in today's Algerian state, with an ideology, structure, and the overwhelming support of the nation. As we have said, the Algerians believe in their freedom. Algeria is trying to move by carefully planned steps from a primitive economy toward a more complex society. Finally, under independence, all—European, Jew, Muslim—who accept citizenship are welcome to work, develop, and improve. In this view the best of the old reinforces the best of the new.

This optimism is general. One comes upon it at all levels, among ministers, trade union leaders, editors, teachers and social workers, soldiers, and even the orphaned children from the recent rebellion. Yet while it is easy enough to show that these leaders adopt the basic assumptions of various evolutionary social theories, they do so rather *unconsciously*. These people are not holding a conference discussing "Social Science and the Underdeveloped Areas: A Revival of Evolutionary Theory?" They fought a revolution and planned a future. It would be a serious error, in my opinion, to attribute to them a direct consciousness of our reflexions on the niceties, the sophisticated nuances of evolutionary thought in today's intellectual clime. These were matters they may have read about in French schools. Ridha Malek, the editor of *El Moudjahid* (*The Freedom Fighter*), published in Arabic and French editions twice each month, expressed the point. "Some people say we are communists, others say we are *dirigiste*; we are practical men, . . . with all the influence that power can muster. We are accused of being communists because we have had help from Yugoslavia or because some Eastern countries recognize us. Do you seriously think we care about the nuances of Marxism? What do I care about deviationism or Titoism? We are Algerian nationalists and we will adopt any institutions we can use from anywhere to fit the needs of our nation. We don't care about theory."

Aït Chalal, a graduate of the University of Paris in medicine, the President of the *Union Générale des Etudiants Musulmans Algériens* (U.G.E.M.A.), gave this answer in 1961 to a question which asked, "How do you expect Algeria's future to evolve?" "In the field of education, we must abide by the experience in our own country, we must exploit our own people's genius. We must examine the experience of advanced countries and make a synthesis. There will obviously be state action but it must make concessions to all national forces. In all areas of our development there should be rationalization consistent with North African values and abilities." Such a prognosis could be interpreted as a synthesis of block-world philosophy, with gradualism, and pragmatism.

To explain the "third world" to the Western world we require a new vocabulary, a different reference frame than either communist or modified capitalist; East or West, "good guys or bad guys" as seen in Washington or the American press. They seek an original synthesis—this is the overwhelming impression one gains from the Algerians after reading about them, talking to them, and watching them construct their state. They defy being categorized into any single school of thought. In the fact that they fought for seven years for independence and accepted a million dead in the process, one might crudely say they followed an Hegelian-Marxist pattern. Thesis (nationalism) opposed antithesis (colonialism) to yield synthesis (independence) after a firm assist from Lenin's thought on imperialism or Hobson's, with no attention being given to the analyses of Moon, Schumpeter, or Winslow. Algeria of today is certainly revolutionary, but it might be a colossal error to expect such neat dialectical formulae to govern the future. From all sides comes the firm objection to any future tinkering with the Muslim family. This is one page which will not be taken from the Soviet notebook. Nor will the Algerian *fellah*, peasant (and the nation is overwhelmingly peasant in composition) wish to accept less than land of his own. Algerians cite the difficulties Stalin had trying to collectivize the Muslim peasantry in Turkestan. Again, on the other side, they anticipate the necessity of agrarian reform including redivision of the large estates.

Despite certain Algerian antipathy to any overpowering ideology and block-world practice, there is the conviction that the new state must reflect the people's will. Political and military leaders know that if they fail the people, the people will throw them out.

A good deal was made, particularly in the American press and in French information releases, of communist influence in the F.L.N. movement, and the inference was drawn that independent Algeria would menace the West from the southern flank. Lenin is even quoted "to prove" this. Anyone familiar with the failure of the French and Algerian Communist Parties to play any active role in the revolution would find it hard to accept this view.

The communists tried, stupidly, very late, in 1956, to join the nationalist cause, to infiltrate and obtain command position, but they failed dismally and ended up on missions in which they were expended. An acrimonious correspondence between the F.L.N. and communists was published. From the exterior, via Moscow-Peking, one sees a different approach. Recognition was extended to the Provisional Government of the Algerian Republic; Algerian delegations made trips to Moscow and Peking; there are representatives of the Government of the Algerian Republic in those cities, as there are in New York. The Algerians explain their conduct this way. "When a man is lost in the desert without water, he does not ask a stranger who offers water what his political affiliations are." The major aid from the East has been moral recognition, a lever to show de Gaulle that just as he could draw upon NATO arsenals and American financial aid, the P.G.A.R., too, had a reservoir. But the Algerians said they had no intention of compromising an independent position won after a seven year struggle against bombers, helicopters, napalm, concentration camps, and torture chambers. What the Algerians wanted was independence and freedom to make their own future. They appreciate the Swiss house for orphaned children established in Tunis as they do the 10,000 packages of clothes from "the children of Yugoslavia to the children of Algeria", and as they do the wheat from the United States distributed through the United Nations. "Foreign ideology no, foreign aid from the heart and without strings, yes."

Nothing has greater importance in the minds of Algerian leaders than education, the heart of any future development and the hope of the nation. In the academic year 1960-1961, 1,070 Algerians studied in foreign universities, excluding those in France. At home much thought is given the problem of illiteracy, measured at 94 per cent among Muslim Algerians in 1950. This concern and the early action provides an insight into the ways of the new state. Arabic and French are the languages of instruction. These languages are being taught to the Algerian refugee and orphaned children in Tunisia and Morocco. In the refugee camps on the Tunisian frontier, Arabic is the language of instruction, and where the camps are close to Tunisian or Moroccan schools, the Algerian children attend those schools. French is the key to unlock the modern technological world's door; Arabic will preserve Islamic culture. A trained engineer evaluated instruction in French this way. "All things being equal, ... we ... prefer to work with the French in developing Algeria. We know their methods and language. But, if all things are not equal, if, for example, the Americans offer 60 per cent where the French offer 50, then we will take the American offer and learn English." You can substitute Russians, Canadians, or any other name for "Americans."

The seven year Algerian war of independence has not simply built a state.

It has changed the long standing sheltered position of the Muslim woman. Madame Mania Chantouf, President of *L'Association des Femmes Algériennes,* whose husband, a lawyer, worked in Ben Tobbal's ministry of interior, claims that the revolution forced the emancipation of the Algerian women. The veil and feminine withdrawal from the world of affairs disappeared when the women took their places as nurses, communications workers, and porters of weapons. In this position of liaison they suffered the worst repression and torture if they were captured.

It is practically impossible for a western-oriented reader to appreciate the dimension of this change. What one must remember is not simply twelve centuries of Muslim tradition, but also that for twenty years French policy, acting on the instruction of the Arab Bureaus, pressed the formula, *"Ayons les femmes et le reste suivra."*[10] French sociologists specializing in the study of Algerian society thought the essence of the structure was "matrimonial." They portrayed Muslim society as one of exteriors, of formalism and important personalities. The Algerian woman, as an intermediary between the obscure forces and the group appeared to possess great importance. The society at its base was a matriarchy. To keep Algeria French, these sociological findings were applied, or perhaps more correctly, were misapplied. French administrators and French ladies' aid societies were going to emancipate Muslim womanhood, modernize them, forever win their gratitude, and in so doing, keep Algeria.

Immediately the French authorities adopted a policy advocating the unveiling of the Muslim female, of modernizing her, hoping she would drag her man and children after her, tricolor in hand, in the process. "With each pound of semolina distributed to the Muslim women a corresponding dose of indignation against the veil and the sheltered life was administered."[11]

When the rebellion began in 1954, the Muslim women played no role, often not even being aware of the activities of their husbands and sons. By 1956 they were engaged to do work which the men could no longer do efficiently under French surveillance. Unmarried girls who had never been outside their homes without their mothers began to travel all over the country with messages and money for the cause. With or without veil, depending upon French surveillance techniques at the moment, these women served the revolution. "Emancipated" Muslim women went back to the veil and the long-flowing gown. This reversal was related directly to the fact that the French thought unmodernized Muslim women were apolitical and, besides, the flowing gown could easily hide an automatic weapon carried to a point selected for violence. With a proper attaching device Muslim women could

[10] Frantz Fanon, *L'an V de la révolution algérienne* (Paris, 1960), p. 15.

[11] Ibid., p. 17.

show their empty hands to police and military searching parties. In the villages the women fed, nursed, and gave refuge to Freedom Fighters they had never before seen, often keeping them in their homes during the absence of their husbands. The male reaction to this was one of unrestrained pride; before the revolution it would have been one of outrage.

The wearing of a black veil has no particular meaning in Muslim custom in Morocco. Yet, when the sultan was ousted by the French in 1953, Moroccan women adopted this western symbol of mourning to impress the Europeans—an interesting and telling example of cultural sniping or adaptation, at the same time a telling demonstration of political consciousness.

In Algeria since the revolution the role of the woman has undergone the sharpest change—an historian not too well versed in the scientific vocabulary might be forgiven for calling it a cultural mutation. The French failed abjectly to win the Muslim woman by trying to "emancipate" her. Instead, this policy of "counter-acculturation"—a meaningless formula in a colonized society in the twentieth century—backfired with a devastating noise. It is highly improbable that the Muslim women of the new Algeria, particularly those directly involved in the struggle, will return to the sheltered life. Inevitably, they will be in the foreground of the infinitely more difficult second phase, that of development.

This development has its own evolutionary pattern. An immediate issue, which Libya, Tunisia, and Morocco, neighboring states in the Arabic West never faced, stems directly from the independence struggle. One million dead leaves many orphans. Over two million Algerians lived in French Regroupment Camps in 1961, often likened to German concentration camps. In them, death came annually to 150,000 of the campers, no occupation was possible; for the inmates, food and shelter were inadequate, and disease ran rife. Then, another 200,000 lived in *camps d'hébergement*, those camps instituted to brainwash Algerians who were arrested for revolutionary activity and later released for "reeducation." Finally, there were 300,000 refugees living inside the Tunisian and Moroccan borders. Some three million people, 30 per cent of the Muslims, had to be kept alive, then salvaged for future useful work. When we remember that "pauperization" was the classification given by Germaine Tillion to the vast majority in 1955, the problem becomes more complex.[12]

Problems of this dimension called for an enormous planned ameliorative effort. This small segment of the "third world" was forced by its condition and goals to utilize every means at its command—mobilization of its own resources, aid from all quarters. It is an informed guess that no single theory will dominate, but most likely gradualism, pragmatism and some block-state

[12] Germaine Tillion, *Algeria, The Realities* (New York, 1958), p. 16.

practices (land division, redivision of wealth), will be employed consistent with Islamic-Arabic cultural demands. However, powerfully influencing the future, will be the bitter experience of the revolution, and the circumstances under which independence was attained. Western ideas will only continue to be influential in the *Maghrib* and in Algeria as long as the West has practical meaning for these people. Those who are educated seem to prefer the openness of our ideas. If by helping in their long fight for independence, sharing the burden of their education and technical training, we have shown the vitality of Western thought, of evolution within Democracy, these people will not forget that *Maghrib* means "The West."

It is worth noting that since independence in July, 1962, Algeria adopted what its leaders call "scientific socialism *without materialism.*" The latter ingredient cannot be accepted by an Islamic community which refuses the view that "religion is the opium of the masses." Block-state policies have governed the new state's agrarian reform, in which the *fellah* with ten hectares or less has kept his land but been encouraged to become more efficient by joining co-operatives and obtaining agricultural education, and nationalization of some industrial and commercial elements. Since much of the nationalized property was held by French owners, who, in many cases, just left their crops in the fields and ran, out of fear or out of shame at being associated too closely with the Secret Army terrorist organization, it is rather difficult to distinguish between a nationalist-inspired act on the part of the Algerian leadership and a deep conviction in scientific socialism. *Comités de gestion* operate these nationalized properties.

A one-party system, the Party of the Masses (new name for the F.L.N., *Front de Libération Nationale*) allows no opposition outside the party framework, thus forcing vocal opponents like Khider and Aït Ahmed underground or into exile. The Algerian Communist Party found itself, at least formally, dissolved and its members make cooperative noises with the leadership of the regime—after all "scientific socialism" even without materialism is far along the road which they travel.

Official Algeria decried vigorously and organized demonstrations against the Belgian-American parachute operation into the Congo in November, 1964. The venture was called colonialist-imperialist and a violation of African independence. The Algerian press made scant mention of the European hostages, interpreting their presence as bait for the military operation in support of Tshombe.

The new state has not entirely closed its eyes to the West. The French language and administrative techniques are in far greater use than Arabic equivalents; French teachers numbering 10,000 serve in the educational system, which is still quite French in nature; French financial aid reached nearly one billion dollars per year in the first two years of independence. American food in the same period fed approximately three million Algerians daily. These aids receive less attention than smaller contributions from the iron curtain countries. New socialist countries can do no wrong, colonialism and capitalism are bad things in the official mind, and propaganda, which pushes slogans like "Forward under the Socialist Revolution of the Masses" and "The Army Will Insure the Socialist Revolution" is given out by the Government. Even the bland Bourguiba in Tunisia has taken to nationalizing European-held land and inserting the word "Socialist" before Neo-Destour in the party name. How deeply these tendencies run will remain to be seen, but in Algeria they appear to be the foundation of the new independent state.

RACE, CLASS, AND POWER IN BARBADOS:

A Study of Stratification as an Integrating Force in a Democratic Revolution

RAYMOND W. MACK

Northwestern University

In reply to a question, asked in Barbados, as to whether a man is a Negro, we might get an answer, "No, Graham's not Negro. His mother was, but he's pass-as-white."

In Barbados, the existence of this hyphenated phrase is evidence of a sophistication as yet foreign to the United States: the admission that a man known to have a Negro ancestor can achieve the social status of a white person. We shall return to Barbados as an illustrative case; but first, let us look at the general theoretical question of the boundaries of human groups.

RACE AND THE BOUNDARIES OF GROUPS

Would you want your daughter to marry a Negro? If a man abandons the Judaism of his forefathers and becomes a convert to Roman Catholicism, is he still a Jew? What about English-speaking Jamaicans, born in the West Indies, descendants of African slaves: are they English? Jamaican? West Indian? African?

Every one of these questions (and many other similar ones) poses an issue about which many people care deeply. The first is considered by many white people the most telling stroke in a discussion of voting rights in Alabama, housing in Detroit, or immigration to England. The judiciary of Israel has had to address the question of who is a Jew in the same year that the Parliament of Great Britain has debated the status of Jamaicans.

These are questions about the boundaries of groups, questions of central concern to sociologists. When is race relevant to the boundaries of groups? Under what circumstances is it irrelevant? People are willing to lay down their lives for their group. But which group? During World War II, Italian-

American soldiers fought Italian soldiers in Italy. In Italy, too, Japanese-American soldiers killed and were killed by white Christian enemies of their white Christian fellow Americans, at the same time that relatives of those Japanese-Americans were imprisoned in the United States because of their race. An American Indian (who at least escaped the onus of being a recent immigrant) was honored as a war hero, then refused burial in his home town cemetery because he was not white.

Obviously, race is often at the center of group identification. When are racial characteristics used to establish and maintain the boundaries of human groups? Why are they not always used? Since our goal in sociological theory is to explain as much of the behavior of human groups as possible in the most parsimonious terms, we want to start at the most general level. The first question, then, is: What creates and maintains the boundaries of any group, regardless of whether or not race comes into play? If we can answer this question, we can then turn our attention to why race is sometimes, but only sometimes, relevant, and under what circumstances race is brought to bear in bounding a group.

What will account for the existence of a delimited group with its policies of inclusiveness and exclusiveness? What creates and maintains group boundaries? Sanctions do; so do social rewards and social punishments. People want to affiliate themselves with those groups in which membership promises them rewards: business associations which will increase their profits, unions which will increase their wages, parties which will promote their platforms, the denomination which seems to have the inside track to salvation, clubs in which they will find friends, congeniality groups in which they may find love, colleges which will educate them, fraternities which will help them get jobs, families which will improve their power, neighborhoods which will convey prestige.

Just as people seek rewarding associations, they avoid punishing ones.[1] They decline the invitation to the dull tea, the square congeniality group, the ineffectual commerce association, the low prestige country club. A man may date, but not marry, the girl from the wrong side of the tracks; he may study, but reject, the erroneous theology. In the same way, he will try to protect the prestige of his reward system by keeping the wrong people out. Indeed, excluding them is itself a reward. My wife claims to

---

[1] As always in dealing with analyses of voluntaristic action, we must remember that the objective fact is the sociologist's, but that one of his objective facts is the actor's definition of the situation. The sociologist may watch an individual join the wrong fraternity and still recognize that his motives were pure—he believed it to be the right one. Or we may note that he seeks what we would objectively define as punishment rather than reward, but that is because punishment is rewarding to him. He is a datum for our colleague in the department of psychology; his perverse behavior does not undermine our theory.

have been vice-president, at the age of five, of a three-person organization which had as its stated purpose: "To keep Bob Kingsley out." Neighborhoods band together to exclude those who would lower property values; sororities blackball candidates with foreign names; colleges discriminate against applicants with low CEB scores; churches excommunicate heretics; debutantes who marry inappropriate spouses are dropped from the Social Register.

Rejection in turn creates walls of defense. Discrimination creates a reaction to itself. Institutionalized exclusion spawns a culture of anti-discrimination. The formation of Jewish clubs which exclude Christians is a function of the same process whereby minorities retaliate against rejection by inventing epithets for the dominant population. If a man must bear hearing himself referred to as a "spade" or "coon" or "nigger," he can at least enjoy the luxury of jeering about "ghosts" and "ofays."

Thus are group boundaries born and guarded. Men seek rewards, avoid punishments, and band together for both purposes.

When, then, is race relevant in creating and maintaining group boundaries? Race becomes socially meaningful when the social organization associates racial status with another status or structural characteristic which is sanction-conveying. Race becomes socially meaningful when biologically inherited characteristics are correlated, or tend to match up with, social characteristics which are considered especially desirable, such as a lot of education, or especially undesirable, such as low income. When a condition which is rewarding or punishing, such as social class with its concomitant life chances, is highly correlated with race, then race is a convenient shorthand for specifying the boundaries of groups enjoying or suffering that condition.

RACE IN EMERGING SOCIETIES

The emergence of new nations—twenty-two in Africa since 1950—gives new significance to the old question of who is a Negro when and where. For over three hundred years, the white portion of the world's population has dominated the colored portion, politically and economically. Suddenly, largely since World War II, the rules of the game have been altered. The political and economic maze has been restructured. The performers in the rat race have had to redefine roles and learn new paths of social organization. Farmers in Kenya, civil servants in Nigeria, shopkeepers in Indonesia, camel drivers in Pakistan, scholars at the University College of the West Indies—all have felt the impact of rapid social change. In most such cases, a colored majority, historically disenfranchised under colonialism, finds itself in charge of the political machinery, or at least, for a change, governed by a non-Caucasoid oligarchy. What does this mean for the involvement of whites in the economic order? In some cases, independence may foment a black nationalism which expropriates the property of native-born whites suddenly defined as foreigners. On the other hand, it may result in a colored government dedicated to representing the interests of a propertied class which remains largely white.

White people have provided a three-centuries old tradition of exploiting race as a critical variable in defining the boundaries of groups. Colored people have learned, literally at the feet of white people, that race can be used as an excuse for political dominance, economic power, educational opportunity, and differential access to life chances. As Sherif says: "The most elaborate 'race' superiority doctrines are products of already existing organizations of superiority-inferiority relationships and exploitations. The superiority doctrines have been the deliberate or unconscious standardizations of the powerful and prosperous groups at the top and not the ideas of the frustrated and deprived majority at the bottom."[2]

Is it possible, then, for a black proletariat suddenly granted political autonomy to resist the temptation to define privilege in racial terms? I think so, if some integrating force, crucial to the social order, cuts across racial lines instead of emphasizing racial differences.

We know, of course, that the emphasis of racial differences need not be a cultural tradition; both Hawaii and Brazil serve as examples. In Hawaii, the earliest contacts between whites and non-whites introduced neither master-slave relationships nor the hierarchy of foreign exploiter and colonial native. On the contrary, race relations were characterized by cordiality and relative social equality. For example, the king of Hawaii, to express his pleasure and gratitude to some of the white men who had served as his advisors, honored them by granting them permission to marry ladies of the royal court. Since, for many white Hawaiian families, it was a sign of honor, recognition, and achievement to have intermarried with a non-white group, it became meaningless in Hawaii to employ race as a definer of group boundary lines. This established a tradition of ignoring race as a factor in social status in Hawaii; the consequences of this tradition are still evident today.[3]

The history of Brazil, too, demonstrates that circumstances different from those of the slavery or colonial patterns of the United States, Africa, and much of Asia can minimize the significance of race as a boundary mechanism. The Portuguese, who colonized Brazil, had a long history of contact with the Moors. This background included an extensive period of

[2] Muzafer Sherif, *An Outline of Social Psychology*, New York: Harper & Brothers, 1948, p. 343.

[3] Otto Klineberg, *Tensions Affecting International Understanding*, New York: Social Science Research Council, 1950, p. 192.

Moorish supremacy and a considerable amount of acculturation. The early Portuguese migration to Brazil was typically by unattached males with less race prejudice than they would have learned had they been Northern Europeans. Slavery was abolished without the emotional scars which a war of emancipation left in the United States, and the freeing of slaves was a custom aided by backing from the Church. The status of freedmen was clearly defined and protected legally. Therefore, it was possible to evolve an ideology which approved the blending of diverse racial stocks in "Brazilians."

"Today one finds at Bahia a freely competitive order in which individuals compete for position largely on the basis of personal merit and favorable family circumstances. Individual competence tends to overbalance ethnic origin as a determinant of social status.[4]

"However, the darker portion of the population . . . have had to contend with the serious handicap that their parents or grandparents or other immediate ancestors began on the bottom as propertyless slaves of the white ruling class and now bear constantly with them, by reason of color and other physical characteristics, indelible badges of this slave ancestry, ineradicable symbols of low status. It is not surprising, therefore, to find that the relatively unmixed blacks are still concentrated in the low-pay, low-status employments and that they gradually disappear as one ascends the occupational scale, until in the upper levels they are seldom to be found . . .

"But it is just these few individuals who indicate most clearly the actual racial situation in Bahia. The Negroes began at the bottom. The acceptance, then, of an occasional black, a few dark mulattoes as well as numerous light mixed-bloods into the upper circles points conclusively to the fact that if a person has ability and general competence, the handicap of color can be, and is constantly being, overcome."

But in most of the underdeveloped areas now emerging as new nations, race has been socially defined as an important part of a colonial pattern of culture, and the utility of physical differences as boundary mechanisms is reinforced by economic and educational inequalities highly correlated with race. The possibility of minimizing the meaning of race, then, rests upon the existence of elements in the social order which are highly rewarding or very punishing, and which cut across racial lines. Cricket may be as important to the West Indies as baseball and football have been to the United States in weakening the acceptability of race as an acknowledged boundary criterion. The New York Giants' distinguished Mississippi alumnus, Charlie Conerley, finds Roosevelt Grier an acceptable teammate because Conerley would rather keep his health than his regional prejudices—and thousands of fans apparently share his conclusions. Similarly, when a white Barbadian speaks

[4] Donald Pierson, *Negroes in Brazil,* Chicago: University of Chicago Press, 1942, pp. 177, 204.

of "our cricket team," he means a predominantly Negro West Indian team, not a bunch of white foreigners.

One obvious example of the establishment of group boundaries is the structuring of groups around occupational specialties. Each situs, or family of related occupations, builds up a set of norms peculiar to it. These occupational subcultures insulate their participants from the members of another situs. Doctors and nurses have values not shared by railroaders or truck drivers; the occupational norms of the longshoreman are not those of the laboratory worker.

Societies with elaborate occupational differentiation, therefore, while bound together by a common culture, are at the same time fragmented by occupational subcultures. People who share an occupational history develop norms, enforce an in-group ideology, and come to serve as a reference group for each other. We see this at its extreme when physicists from the Soviet Union and from the United States have more to talk about with each other than either group has with the farmers from their own county.

Craft knowledge, then, creates group boundaries. Any specialized learning is quasi-magic; it gives one power over others who do not have the information. Thus, from the earliest days of priesthood and laity until very recently, a basic variable in most class systems has been literacy. But race comes to bear in such a system only if physical attributes are correlated with style of life and life chances. If race is associated with the opportunity for apprenticeship or entry into an occupation, or if race helps or hinders one's performance, then occupational groups may become racial castes. But if race is neither an aid nor a block to access or success, it remains irrelevant to the process of bounding the occupational group.

Race is used to demarcate an out-group when it is rewarding to use it. If the stratification system flaunts enough exceptions to racial stereotypes, it is no longer useful to use race as a synonym for class. Hence the Barbadian withering of racial boundaries, epitomized in the category "pass-as-white."

INTELLECTUAL STRATEGY AND RESEARCH TACTICS

My involvement with Barbados grew out of my interest in social organization and stratification. As a student of class structure, I have found myself drawn increasingly during the past decade into research on, and analyses of, the role of race in the social structure of the United States. One can hardly pretend to any significant comprehension of the American stratification system without addressing the peculiar definition of race in the United States, where institutionalized color-caste mars the democratic ideal.

Having studied and written about race relations in the United States, I thought that I could broaden my perspective and might deepen my insight into the American situation by observing the meaning of race in another society. Reading about Caribbean societies led me to the conclusion that Barbados had experienced enough historical parallels to the American situation to make comparison meaningful, and was sufficiently different to make contrast enlightening.

Like the American South, Barbados had imported slaves from Africa and built a plantation system on fields worked by Negroes and owned and operated by Anglo-Saxons. Like American Negroes, Barbadian Negroes saw a century elapse between formal emancipation and significant participation in political power. Unlike American Negroes, Barbadian Negroes are a mathematical majority. While social definitions of who is a Negro differ somewhat between the two societies, it can be said that the American distribution of ninety per cent white and ten per cent Negro is roughly reversed in Barbados.

During the two years between my first look at Barbados and the writing of this manuscript, I was able to spend only about six months living in Barbados. If one is going to try, as I did, to achieve some understanding in such a brief period of how a total society is structured, then he must seize every available tool to help accomplish the mission. My work, therefore, cannot be described as library research, nor as participant observation, nor as an interview study. I was shamelessly opportunistic in data gathering.

I read seventeenth century history, eighteenth century political science, twentieth century travel guides, and both daily newspapers in Barbados, the *News* and the *Advocate*. I studied census bulletins, government economic reports, civil lists, and gossip columns. I was a participant observer at dinner parties, at picnics, on the beach, in bars and restaurants, at dances, and at cricket matches and horse races. I attended House of Assembly meetings and Town Council welfare hearings. I interviewed cane cutters, planters, taxi drivers, refinery owners, cooks, insurance brokers, maids, automobile salesmen, housewives, newspapermen, storekeepers, waiters, real estate speculators, government ministers, schoolteachers, clergymen, hotel owners, airline employees, leisured expatriates, students, radio announcers, civil servants, one shoeshine boy, and the American Vice-Consul. My interviewees included white Barbadians from the "Big Six" families of the island's power structure, Negro Oxford graduates who have achieved enough political power to make the "Big Six" nervous, mulattoes whom an observer accustomed to the rules in the United States would call "Negro," but who are pass-as-white, old-family whites chronically in debt after the fashion of Southern "genteel poverty," working class Negroes, and poor whites viewed with contempt by everyone else regardless of race, color, or creed. My conclusions are based upon data from no specifiable sample of the universe of Barbadians, but if total immersion is the way to salvation, I have tried to demonstrate good faith.

Since my goal was to learn about race and class and their interrelationship, my strategy led me to start at the bottom of the class structure. The tactic of avoiding early contact with members of the power structure was based on the assumption that I could present scholarly credentials late in the game which would explain lower class associations to upper class people, but if I became identified early with the occupants of seats of power, it would be extremely difficult later to achieve rapport with workers dependent upon the moguls or with middle class people resentful of their exclusion from the inner circle.

So I talked first with taxi drivers, bus conductors, waiters, the yard man next door, and gradually became involved in a network of informants as the baby sitter expressed an opinion, the baby sitter's boyfriend disagreed, the baby sitter's boy friend suggested that I meet and talk with his friend who worked on the docks, and so on. I used to work as a dance musician before retiring into social science; this provided useful entree into the night world of the island. Many of the musicians working in hotels and night clubs had listened to records and become greatly interested in jazz, and I was able to play with them and talk with them after working hours. My pre-school children spent hours on the beach, and were good enough to introduce me to the parents of their friends, who spanned the color spectrum and the power pyramid.

Gradually, my network of middle class acquaintances widened. My landlord introduced me to the extension officer of the University College of the West Indies. He in turn introduced me to a school principal, a newspaper columnist, and a government officer. The newsman took me to a welfare hearing; the school principal introduced me to a police officer.

I learned to capitalize on the Barbadian's enthusiasm for his island as a probing open-ended question. When new acquaintances asked what I was doing there, I answered truthfully that it was a delightful place for my wife and children to vacation, and that I was writing a book on race relations and social class in the United States. Almost invariably, a Barbadian would respond to this information with the observation that "If you're interested in race relations and social class, you ought to study Barbados." However the Barbadian phrased this sentiment, I replied with questions. Barbados is pretty similar to the United States, isn't it? Yes, I write about social class and race—why? What's unusual about Barbados? Yes, politics has a good deal to do with race relations in the United States; does it here, too?

Such an informal approach to a design for data-gathering has its obvious disadvantages. But I came to the task of analysis and writing feeling that the shuttling from library to observation to interview and back to library had not only equipped me with reliability checks, but had given me insights I might have missed with a more limited armamentarium.

THE SETTING

Barbados is the easternmost of the Lesser Antilles and the largest island, since the departure of Jamaica and Trinidad, in what used to be the British West Indies Federation. It has the approximately triangular shape of a pork chop; its greatest length is 21 miles and it is 14 miles across at its greatest width, with a total land area of 166 square miles. There are a few hills, but the highest point, near the center of the island, is only 1100 feet above sea level, and most of the terrain is flat or gently rolling.

Barbados lies almost outside the hurricane belt; it has experienced only two severe hurricanes within the past century. But as in other trade-wind islands, the breeze is a constant part of the environment. The average wind velocity is 11.2 miles per hour, and velocities of less than 3 miles per hour are extremely rare. There are no great variations in temperature: the annual mean Fahrenheit reading is 75° on the windward side of the island, 79° on the leeward side. Temperatures range from a low of 61° to a high of 91°. The average annual rainfall varies from 40 to 80 inches.

Bridgetown, the chief port and capital city, and Speightstown, on the northwest coast, have populations of 18,650 and 2,600, respectively. But the population density in the suburbs of these urban parishes ranges from 10,000 to 20,000 per square mile. In the 166 square miles of Barbados, the 1960 census counted 232,100 people, a density of 1400 persons per square mile. The population density of Barbados is nearly twice that of Rhode Island, the most densely populated state in the United States. The entire island is as densely settled as the suburbs of London, a statistic more astonishing when one realizes that 83 per cent of the island is devoted to farmland. A capsule description of the paradox of such population density in an agricultural economy is the saying that "Barbados is a city where sugar grows in the suburbs."

Of the 106,470 acres of land in Barbados, approximately 83,000 are arable. Nearly 85 per cent of this farmland is in estates of 100 or more acres. Agriculture in Barbados is not highly diversified; sugar cane is the principal cash crop, and the sugar industry dominates the economy. Some 46,000 acres are planted in sugar cane: about 10,000 acres of sugar cane are distributed among 30,000-odd peasant holdings, while the remaining 36,000 are owned by 260 sugar estates.[5] The 1960 crop yielded 153, 668 long tons of sugar, of which 11,775 tons were consumed locally and the rest exported. Almost 90 per cent of Barbadian exports are destined for the United Kingdom and the Commonwealth. The extent to which Barbados can be characterized as a one-crop economy is evident from its export figures. Domestic commodity exports in 1960 totalled 35 million dollars;[6] of this, 26.8 million was sugar, 3.2 million was molasses, and 2.4 million was rum: 93 per cent of the total domestic commodity exports were sugar and sugar products. This is well over one-fourth of the total 1960 gross national product of 120 million dollars. The Labor Department's estimate of the distribution of labor during March 1960, when employment was at its peak, emphasizes the dominance of the sugar industry (see Table 1).

Table 1. DISTRIBUTION OF EMPLOYED WORKERS IN BARBADIAN LABOR FORCE, MARCH 1960*

Industry	Number of Full-Time Employees	Per Cent of Total
Sugar Estates	19,445	27.7
Sugar Factories	2,646	3.7
Hotel, Guest Houses, Clubs	210	0.3
Retail Clerks	719	1.0
Manufacturing	517	0.7
Repairing	298	0.4
Minor Industries	2,047	2.9
Construction	1,128	1.6
Domestics in Private Homes	15,000	21.3
Agricultural Workers in U.S.A.	1,274	1.8
Other Trades and Professions	26,726	38.2
TOTAL	70,010	100.0†

†(percentages do not total 100 because of rounding)

*Computed from Barbados Department of Labour, *Special Report*, 1961.

[5] Detailed statistical tables on land use, percentage of farmland in mature sugar cane, percentage of land in cane reaped, average tons of cane cut per acre, and so on, appear in David Lowenthal, "The Population of Barbados," *Social and Economic Studies,* 6 (December, 1957), pp. 455-501. Most of the data in this paragraph are from quarterly publications of the Barbados Statistical Service: the Statement of Imports and Exports, the Overseas Trade Report, and the Digest of Statistics. Also useful to the social scientist are the monthly reports of the Department of Agriculture, the annual reports of the Department of Labour and of the Barbados Development Board.

[6] All figures in this paper are in West Indian dollars. One West Indian dollar equals about sixty U.S. cents; one U.S. dollar equals about $1.67 in West Indian currency.

Even leaving aside the extent to which workers in repairing, construction, or domestic service, for example, may derive their incomes through the sugar industry, sugar estates and factories alone employ nearly one-third of the labor force.

Readers should note that estimates of the number of people unemployed during most of the year run as high as 30,000. As in most underdeveloped areas, unemployment and underemployment are endemic. Both have been aggravated, at least temporarily, by progress: at a cost of 28 million dollars, the government has built a deep-water harbor which permits direct bulk loading of sugar. What it also does, of course, is throw out of work all the men who used to put sugar in bags at the sugar factories, load the bags onto trucks, unload the bags at the wharves and place them in small boats called "lighters," row the boats out to the ships waiting in deep water, and transfer the bags of sugar from lighters to cargo ships.

Another facet of the story is that, since the deep-water harbor opened in 1961, large cruise ships, which used to bypass Barbados, find it easier to stop there, thus contributing to the island's second most important industry: tourism. In 1960, in addition to the 35,535 tourists who visited Barbados, 24,172 cruise ship passengers visited the island for less than a day. The Barbados Development Board estimates that, at the present rate of expansion, the tourist industry may provide as much income for Barbados as sugar by 1965.

But the deep-water harbor is only a first tentative step toward industrialization, and no other important moves seem imminent. Sugar cane is reaped by hand. It is planted in depressions approximately three feet in diameter, called "cane holes." A mechanical reaper would cut the cane above ground level, leaving a considerable part of the stalk still in the hole. The Sugar Association contends that mechanical reaping would be uneconomical. At the moment, it is not industrialization but rapid political change that seems to provide the catalyst for restructuring the racial and social fabric of Barbados.

A BRIEF ETHNIC AND POLITICAL HISTORY OF BARBADOS[7]

During my first visit to Barbados, I was given a succinct synopsis of its racial and cultural history by a Negro taxi driver. Since we had disposed of the weather, which, while relatively invariable, is lovely enough to merit

[7] My most important sources for this section were Morley Ayearst, *The British West Indies: The Search for Self-Government*, London: George Allen & Unwin, Ltd., 1960; Alan Burns, *History of the British West Indies*, London: George Allen & Unwin, Ltd., 1954; G. E. Cumper, "Employment in Barbados," *Social and Economic Studies*, No. 8, (June, 1959), pp. 105–178; Great

a daily tribute, I sought to continue the conversation by remarking that I found in Barbados no evidence of the Indian, French, Spanish, East Indian, Dutch, and other influences which one associates with other Caribbean islands. My black informant replied in clipped British accents: "Oh, no! We've always been English, you know."

And so they have. Early histories suggest that the bearded fig trees led Spanish or Portuguese mariners who first visited the island about 1600 to call it "Los Barbados." Archeological evidence—weapons and sea shell implements—indicate the presence of Caribs or Arawaks as late as the sixteenth century. But the English, when they came, found neither Iberian nor Indian. Various reports place the first British contact with Barbados from 1605 to 1625. At any rate, the first English settlers—80 of them—came to the island in 1627; by the end of 1628 there were 1,850 persons there. The early social structure was one of small freeholders who raised tobacco with the help of indentured servants and a few slaves. Thirteen years after it was settled, the island had become divided into 11,000 small holdings, most of them poor because they were unable to compete successfully with the tobacco grown in the North American colonies.

Then, in 1640, the introduction of sugar cane to Barbados sparked a social and economic revolution which set the pattern of life on the island for almost two centuries. The cultivation of sugar necessitated large plots of land and a much larger labor force. As tobacco prices fell, small landholders were forced out, the tobacco acreage was converted to sugar, and Barbados became a land of estates. Many of the small proprietors emigrated to the French islands or the mainland, or joined the cadre of settlers of Jamaica. There had been 11,000 holdings in 1640; by 1665 the number of proprietors was reduced to slightly more than 700.

Faced with the enormous need for labor, the planters resorted to purchasing slaves from the Dutch. Thus, the Negro population began to increase as the white population was decreasing through emigration. Historians' esti-

Britain Colonial Office, *The Colonial Office List, 1958,* London: H. M. Stationery Office, 1958; Great Britain Colonial Office, *Annual Report on Barbados, 1956–1957,* London: H. M. Stationery Office, 1959; J. H. Parry and P. M. Sherlock, *A Short History of the West Indies,* London: Macmillan & Co., 1957; and Ronald V. Sires, "Government in the British West Indies: An Historical Outline," *Social and Economic Studies,* No. 6, (June, 1957), pp. 109–132. Also useful are E. H. Carter, G. W. Digby, and R. N. Murray, *History of the West Indian People–Book IV,* London: Thomas Nelson and Sons, 1953; Annette Baker Fox, *Freedom and Welfare in the Caribbean,* New York: Harcourt, Brace & Co., 1949; Richard Ligon, "A True and Exact History of the Island of Barbados, 1647–1650," *Caribbean Affairs,* 1957 (abridged); Frank Wesley Pitman, *The Development of the British West Indies: 1700–1793,* New Haven: Yale University Press, 1917; John Poyer, *The History of Barbados,* London: J. Mawman, 1808; Agnes M. Whitson and Lucy F. Horsfall, *Britain and the West Indies,* London: Longmans, Green & Co., 1948; and Hume Wrong, *Government of the West Indies,* Oxford: Clarendon Press, 1923.

mates vary widely, but the white population seems to have reached an all-time high of between 23,000 and 40,000 in the period between 1640 and 1655. Since then, whites have declined slowly and steadily in number to their present population of less than 10,000. As a proportion of the total population, the white decline was swift and drastic. The ratio of Negroes to whites in Barbados was about 1 to 35 in 1629, 1 to 1 by 1658, 2 to 1 a decade later,[8] 4 to 1 a century later, and by now whites constitute only about 5 per cent of the population.

The original English settlers of Barbados came as a company under proprietary letters patent from the King's Court, and Barbados has been under English law ever since. Representative government dates from the Royal Charter granted by the Crown in 1627 and confirmed by Parliament in 1652. An elected legislative body, the House of Assembly, was established in 1639.

In 1807, an act of Parliament made it illegal for any British subject to trade in slaves. This worked no hardship on Barbadian planters, since the rate of natural increase among the slaves assured an adequate labor force. Suspicions of a continuing illicit trade in slaves spawned a Bill in Parliament in 1815 requiring the registration of slaves in all the colonies. This Registry Bill is credited with inspiring the slave uprising which took place in Barbados in 1816; the Bill supposedly led the slaves to believe that emancipation was imminent.

Parliament in 1831 abolished all civil and military distinctions between free British subjects regardless of color. This, with the Reform Bill of 1832, prepared the ground for the abolition of slavery in 1833. On August 1, 1834, the Abolition of Slavery Act, passed by Parliament a year earlier, became effective throughout the Empire.

In many British colonies, including Barbados, the social structure was altered little by emancipation; true freedom is more realistically dated from the abolition of the apprenticeship system in 1938. The apprenticeships were intended to provide a transitional status for the ex-slaves, who would gradually emerge as an independent peasantry. Actually, since they were in an open labor market where there was virtually no free land available, most ex-slaves were forced by economic necessity to remain as wage-earning laborers on the estates. During this post-emancipation period, therefore,

[8] Estimates of the Negro-white population ratio for the period between 1665 and 1685 range from 2 to 1 to 10 to 1. On the basis of what we know about rapid social change and the visibility of a minority population, I incline to favor the conservative estimates. Consider, for example, the implications of the data in William M. Kephart, "Negro Visibility," *American Sociological Review*, No. 19, (1954), pp. 462–467, reprinted in Kimball Young and Raymond W. Mack, *Principles of Sociology: A Reader in Theory and Research*, Second Edition, New York: American Book Co., 1962, pp. 161–165.

Barbados did not experience the labor shortage suffered by some of the other West Indian islands, and hence did not draw the waves of indentured servants and East Indian immigrants who poured into neighboring islands ("We've always been English, you know").

Indeed, not immigration but emigration has for years been a basic fact of the social and economic life of Barbados. Immediately after emancipation, fear of a labor shortage led the House of Assembly to try to restrict emigration. But with the fall of sugar prices, a long period of drought, and the ensuing economic crisis, the government began, early in the 1860's, to foster emigration as its economic policy. Conservative estimates place emigration during the next 60 years at over 100,000 (see Table 2). No systematic records

Table 2.   NET EMIGRATION FROM BARBADOS, 1861–1921*

Period	Male	Female	Total	Percentage Migrating to Neighboring Colonies
1861–1871	7,500	2,600	10,100	90
1871–1881	7,600	3,400	11,000	85
1881–1891	6,700	1,600	8,300	85
1891–1911	33,500	16,200	49,700	35†
1911–1921	13,700	10,700	24,400	30†
TOTAL	69,000	34,500	103,500	

*Adapted from data-presented on pp. 275–276 in G. W. Roberts, "Emigration from Barbados," *Social and Economic Studies*, No. 4, (September, 1955), pp. 245–288.

†The reason for the sharp drop in the percentage emigrating to neighboring colonies between 1891 and 1921 is that the bulk of those leaving during this period went to work on the Panama Canal. After the Canal was complete, many of the workers went to the United States.

of migration were kept prior to 1903; some estimates place the emigration total between 1861 and 1921 as high as 150,000. The importance of emigration as an instrument of social policy is obvious when these figures are compared with the census report of a total Barbadian population in 1921 of 156,774.

There have been only two periods in recent history when immigration to Barbados has exceeded emigration from it: from 1923 through 1933, when Barbadians who had worked in Panama were being repatriated, and from 1947 through 1949, when people returned from war work and from the Armed Forces. During the 1950's, emigration again exceeded immigration, with thousands of workers moving to the United Kingdom.

Since the emigrants have been predominantly young males, their departure has resulted in a skewed age distribution and a low sex ratio: in 1956 there were only 4 men to 5 women in the 15-64 age group.

Despite the dwindling for three centuries of the white population, both in numbers and as a proportion of the total population, Barbados remained in 1940 a plantocracy, governed politically, economically, and socially by whites. Executive power was in the hands of an Executive Committee consisting of the Governor, the Colonial Secretary, and the Attorney General (all ex-officio and all appointed by the Crown), plus such other persons as the Governor chose to appoint. The nine Superior Courts are presided over by the Chief Justice, who is also a Crown appointee. The legislature was, and is, bicameral, consisting of a Legislative Council appointed by the Crown and of the House of Assembly, composed of 24 members: two members from each of the eleven parishes and two from the city of Bridgetown. Before 1940, a candidate would often be elected in his constituency without opposition. Because of severely restricted suffrage, the mass of the population took little interest in politics.

But a young colored barrister, Grantley Adams, was elected to the House of Assembly in 1934 and gained celebrity when he defended Clement Payne, the leader of the 1937 riots. Then Hope Stevens, a Barbadian returned from the United States, founded the Progressive League in 1938, and in 1939, Adams became its president. The League stood for moderate socialism, social welfare and an extension of the franchise. It attracted a high proportion of the few qualified black and colored voters, and when it ran its first slate, in 1940, elected five of its six candidates. Thus began the marked change in the Barbadian power structure, which was to see political power used to bring about alterations in the boundaries of groups.

RACE AND CLASS: THE STRATIFICATION STRUCTURE OF BARBADOS

Another colored Barbadian, Hugh Springer, returned from Oxford, was instrumental in the founding of the Barbados Workers' Union in October 1941; Adams became its first president. The Progressive League became the Barbados Labour Party. Adams and his supporters achieved two crucial political successes: he was appointed to the Executive Committee, and a bill was passed reducing property requirements for voting by almost one-half and extending the franchise to women. The bulk of the black population was still excluded from the polls, for even with the reduced property requirement, voters were still required to have an annual income of 30 or more pounds, and most canefield workers earned about 25 per annum. Nonetheless, the voting reform bill spelled the end of automatic white political dominance, as can be seen from Table 3, for it increased the electorate from about 6,000 to nearly 30,000.

Table 3.   POPULATION OF BARBADOS BY RACE, 1946*

White	9,839
Black	148,923
East Indian	100
Syrian & Asiatic, not shown elsewhere	7
Chinese	29
Mixed or Colored	33,828
Not specified	74
TOTAL	192,800

*Great Britain Colonial Office, *Digest of Colonial Statistics*, No. 36 (January-March, 1958), London: H. M. Stationery Office, 1958, p. 67.

With this expansion of the non-white electorate, Adams, as president of both the Barbados Labour Party and the Barbados Workers' Union, was able to dominate the political scene, picking his candidates and throwing the power of the union behind them. In 1944, the B.L.P. increased its House representation to eight, and Springer joined Adams on the Executive Committee. By forming a coalition with another socialist group, the National Congress Party, which had also won eight seats, the B.L.P. gained a two-to-one majority over the conservative Electors' Association.

Now that the whites could no longer politically validate their economic and social dominance, subsequent changes came swiftly. In September, 1949, the House of Assembly requested the establishment of a full ministerial system. The next year, property qualifications for membership in the House were abolished, the life of the House was extended to three years, and—most important from the point of view of changing the significance of racial status in the social structure—universal adult suffrage was introduced. In the December, 1951 elections, the B.L.P. won 16 seats in a House of 24. Five salaried ministerial posts were established and, on February 1, 1954, Grantley Adams became the first Premier of Barbados.

The correlation between race and class was starkly evident during the debate in the Legislative Council on the eve of the introduction of the ministerial system. Legislative Councillors have been chosen generally on the basis of their representation of private economic interests—notably sugar, of course. The Crown-appointed Legislative Council has been almost exclusively white in membership; in 1954, only two Councillors were colored. At the same time only three members of the elected House of Assembly were white, and one of those was a maverick, a left-wing member of the B.L.P. The Councillors attacked the proposed ministerial system "mainly upon the cost involved, with about half of the Labour Party's elected members now due to receive ministerial salaries. Die-hard conservative members in the Legislative Council asserted that universal suffrage had been granted prematurely and predicted grimly the financial collapse of the government, the breakdown of popular government and an eventual dictatorship."[9] The Honourable Ronald G. Mapp, one of the new ministers, retaliated in the House of Assembly: "A lot of people are disappointed that Barbados isn't like BG. . . . They want to see ministerial status collapse. . . They want to say that the coloured boys cannot run anything. The Malans do not want to see the Nkrumahs come up by their side."[10]

Mapp's remarks reflect accurately the traditionally rigid stratification structure of Barbados. The criteria of class differentiation have been chromatic and economic, with considerable congruity between racial and occupational status. The importance of money and skin color are, if anything, magnified by the absence of other differentiation among the population on other characteristics which might serve as criteria of class status in a less homogeneous society. In Barbados, for example, unlike Jamaica, literacy is virtually universal: as long ago as 1946, the percentage of illiteracy in the population over 10 years of age was only 7.3, the lowest in the British Caribbean. Similarly, religion hardly counts as a class indicator where there is an Established Church of such influence, and despite the fact that the religious attitudes of the populace seem fundamentally evangelical, the Anglican Church claims two-thirds of the population as members. Basically, then, neither religious nor educational status has, in the past, been sufficient to override economic and racial status, and property position and race have been highly correlated. The island has been accustomed to a social structure composed of a white upper class of plantation and sugar factory owners, appointed high government officials, and top professionals, a colored middle class of lower professionals, shopkeepers, middle range government employees, and clerical and kindred workers, and a black lower class of craftsmen, peasant farmers, canefield hands, and other laborers.

Here, then, was a population in which, as recently as the Census of 1946, occupations classified as professional, public service, clerical, trade, and finance accounted together for about one-eighth of the labor force. Over 85 per cent of the labor force consisted of poor or landless peasants and

[9] Ayearst, *op. cit.*, p. 93.
[10] *Ibid.*

laborers. Average weekly household income was about ten U.S. dollars a week. In this social structure, race was so closely associated with class position that they could usually be used as synonyms. There were a few poor whites; there were some educated, relatively prosperous Negroes. But in general, black meant that one was a peasant or laborer, while white could be taken to refer to both the color and the collar.

Barbados has long had the reputation among West Indians of being the most prejudice-ridden island in the British West Indies. Yet in only a few years, racial boundaries have lost much of their significance to Barbadians.

Fermor summarizes his impressions of the Barbadian way of life, gained during a visit to the island in the late 1940's, as follows: "Looking backwards we could almost see, suspended with the most delicate equipoise above the little flat island, the ghostly shapes of those twin orbs of the Empire, the cricket ball and the blackball."[11]

Yet, less than 15 years later, the widely institutionalized discrimination which offended Fermor has all but disappeared. During a total of over six months which I spent on the island in three separate visits during 1961 and 1962, I interviewed, observed, and investigated various areas of discrimination reported by Fermor: in restaurants, bars, government meetings, business discussions, and social gatherings in private homes. The world he observed has changed in a remarkably short time.

SOCIAL CHANGE AND INSTABILITIES IN STATUS

Barbadians are notorious among West Indians for their local pride, ethnocentrism, and insularity. I have long ago lost count of the number of times I have been assured that Barbados is a better place to live than Trinidad, or than St. Lucia, or than Jamaica, and many Barbadians simply state that there is no other place as nice to live as Barbados. Some of the people who told me of the virtues of Barbados as contrasted with less desirable lands were adults who had never been to "the other side of the island"—14 miles away. In such a tight little island society, we might expect to find well-defined status groups, relatively few status aggregates of ambiguous rank in the class hierarchy, and a minimum number of status dilemmas and contradictions.

And so it was until the seizure of political power by non-whites. To understand the rapidity and extent of change in the past 20 years, one must remember its racial and demographic context. As in Jamaica,[12] the gradual

---

[11] Patrick Leigh Fermor, *The Traveller's Tree,* London: John Murray, Ltd., 1950, p. 108.

[12] See Leonard Broom, "The Social Structure of Jamaica," *American Sociological Review,* No. 19, (1954), pp. 115–125, reprinted in Young and Mack, *op. cit.,* pp. 165–173.

dwindling of white population coupled with the growth of a sizable mulatto population helped to define the relevance of race to the boundaries of status groups. The lack of an adequate supply of whites to staff the middle-class positions, and the presence of a mulatto population over three times as numerous as the white segment, afforded the colored population the opportunity to differentiate themselves from the blacks.

Hence, when the whites lost absolute political power, an educated, ambitious elite of non-whites stood ready to exploit their opportunities.

Furthermore, despite recognized social differences between colored and black Barbadians, the political ideology of the new leadership tended to ignore these distinctions; the principal notice taken of race was a sentiment not of contempt for the blacks at the bottom of the hierarchy, but of resentment toward the whites above, who had long blocked the road to mobility.

The whites, who had run the society politically, economically, and socially, no longer exercise political dominance. Once this is true, it is no longer rewarding—indeed, it could be severely punishing—for them to try to maintain their social dominance through institutionalized segregation. The only way in which the whites can protect their economic power is to accommodate to black political power, which means the weakening of social distinctions associated with race.

Universal suffrage has resulted in a black Premier, a Negro cabinet, and a House of Assembly where only two of 24 legislators are white. But more important, racial distinctions have been blurred by an increasingly open stratification system. Where there are some poor, uneducated whites and an increasing number of powerful, educated Negroes, the old automatic interpretation of skin color becomes untrustworthy. The status of mulattoes becomes increasingly ambiguous, and race is used less as a group boundary line. If the formerly all-white club is to boast the Premier among its members, it cannot remain an all-white club. (This is not a hypothetical illustration; the Premier's invitation to membership broke the color barrier of one of the last white clubs in Barbados in 1961.)

Barbados, of course, is not a unique case. Emily Hahn's report of the coming of independence in Tanganyika[13] provides another illustration of how swiftly and drastically change occurs where political power can be translated into increased social acceptance.

"The sight of Africans and Europeans dining together amicably at the Twiga Hotel pointed up for me the contrast between Dar es Salaam today and the city I ·vaguely remembered from the thirties. It was a smug little

[13] Emily Hahn, "Changeover in Tanganyika," *The New Yorker*, XXXIX (April 27, 1963), pp. 110, 113, 114, 116, 118, 121, 122, 124, 127, 128, 130, 132, 134, 136, 137. Quoted material from p. 124.

place then—as socially ingrown a community as I have ever seen. In those days, its hotels were, of course, segregated, and any European out shopping would have been haughtily incredulous if it had been suggested to him that he wait his turn while an African was being served. Now Europeans wait their turn quite pleasantly, and Africans go where they like, if they can afford it. . .

"British girls in Dar were working placidly away as secretaries for new, African bosses, though I have no doubt that up to very recent times they had felt this to be one thing they would never, never do. Africans were to be seen dancing in public with the wives of British dignitaries. And at a beach that stretches its spreading shallows just north of the city anyone who wanted to go swimming—African, Asian, or European—was free to do so."

What has occurred in Barbados is the emergence of status aggregates which cut across racial boundaries, although they are aggregates of persons similar in income, education, occupation, religion, and amount of social power. One such aggregate might include a white Canadian investor and a university-educated Negro cabinet minister. Neither was an integral part of the old status structure, but, as Stone and Form point out,[14] their presence is vital to explain the mechanisms of change. For, because of the similarities in life style of the members, these status aggregates are gradually becoming status groups. As they do so, the emerging class structure obliterates the old meaning of race.

In these circumstances, people of an ambiguous class status are placed according to color, while people of ambiguous racial ancestry are placed according to class status. That is, a small store proprietor who has ten years of education and a slightly above average income is white if he looks white, and black if he looks black. But a person who in the United States would be called light mulatto is white if he is an educated, prosperous, business or professional man, but black if he is a poor laborer.

In Bridgetown, a shoe-shine man of ambiguous racial ancestry uses as his opening conversational gambit the observation that he is in business for himself because he "wouldn't work for any of those niggers"—a fairly bold attempt to reap social rewards and avoid punishments by drawing boundaries around the privileged group so that he is included. The existence of the hyphenated phrase "pass-as-white" indicates an awareness among Barbadians that class position can override genetic history.

The extent to which group boundaries can be socially defined in the process of seeking rewards through association is illustrated by a Barbadian brother and sister, one of whom has run for public office as a Negro, while the other

---

[14] Gregory P. Stone and William H. Form, "Instabilities in Status: The Problem of Hierarchy in the Community Study of Status Arrangements," *American Sociological Review*, No. 18, (1953), pp. 149–162, reprinted in Young and Mack, *op. cit.,* pp. 136–145.

is a member of an exclusively white club! Their mother was mulatto; their father white. Both the brother and sister have relatively Caucasoid features. One has chosen to be white. The other prefers to be colored for the political advantages this offers in a predominantly colored society. People there are aware of their background, and respond to them on the basis of the choices they have made. Obviously, an "exclusively white" club there is working on a different set of social definitions than it would in the United States. But they are social definitions, and clear examples of bounding groups to maximize social rewards.

In Barbados, race is used less as a group boundary line than it used to be because it is less meaningful as it fails to correlate with other criteria of class status. A peasant or laborer can still sponsor a social hop (a juke box dance in a hired hall with drinks and a modest admission charge) with confidence that all his guests will be black, but a businessman can no longer extend invitations for cocktails to the ten most influential Barbadians and have a party that is all white. A meeting of the Town Council of Bridgetown, or of school principals, or of Barbadian writers, or of the Barbados Flying Club—any such gathering based upon shared education or mutual interests will be an interracial affair. A well-educated pass-as-white girl may prefer the attentions of an educated mulatto suitor to those of a poor white man— and furthermore, she is considerably more likely to have met socially a mulatto or Negro of a class status comparable to hers than a white man who is beneath her in the stratification system. A pass-as-white girl's dating a Negro man is, of course, less startling in Barbados than it would be in the United States; as a white Barbadian man said to me: "No sensible person whose family has been here for over two hundred years would claim that he's all white—for sure."

CONCLUSION

We have addressed one of what Wendell Bell has called "the big decisions of nationhood:" what kind of social structure should the new nation have?[15] Leaders of new nations do not usually take the answer to this question as pre-ordained or historically determined; they talk as if there were a possibility of man making himself. I heard Prime Minister Barrow address the white businessmen of the Barbados Hoteliers Association in 1962; speaker and audience seemed caught up in an image of the future calculated to force a change in the realities of racial discrimination in Barbados. "We," said

[15] Wendell Bell, "The Big Decisions of Nationhood: Some Examples from the West Indies," paper presented to the University of Denver seminar on The Emerging Nations: The Problems of Modernization and the Role of U. S. Foreign Aid, Aspen, Colorado, September 1963, p. 42.

Barrow, "are all Barbadians, and we must learn to trust one another and to work together to achieve the best society for us all." The two proprietors I was sitting with had come to the meeting filled with suspicion and hostility; they left reassuring one another, "I think he's right;" "I think we can do it."

The self-conscious decision to try to create a certain kind of social structure will itself, of course, have enormous impact on Bell's other "big decisions of nationhood:"[16] What should the new nation's global alignments be? What form of government should the new nation have? How large a role should the government play in the affairs of the society? What should the new nation's social and cultural history be? What kind of people should the new nation have?

But most critically, this paper has addressed the last of Bell's questions for the new nations: what is real?[17] Beliefs about reality affect images of the future, and nowhere more drastically than where race is defined as coterminous with class, and where perceived racial differences are used to reinforce group boundaries.

In Barbados, we have seen how class differences can create and maintain group boundaries. When the division of a population according to race is almost the same as the division according to property or income or some other important criterion of social power, race is highly relevant to the boundaries of groups.

The recent history of Barbados also suggests that, when class boundaries shift rapidly, the boundaries of races also become fluid. The acquisition of political power by non-whites allowed them to use that power for rocking the rest of the social system.

But this diminishing of the importance of racial distinctions in Barbados was able to occur because there were many non-whites eager and able to fill statuses previously held by whites. Too, the insularity and intimacy of the society made it difficult to pretend that these ambitious, educated, powerful Negroes were not there. In the United States, on the other hand, it is possible for many white people to have little or no contact with Negroes except as their social inferiors: bellboys, bootblacks, cleaning women, janitors, parking lot attendants, steel mill laborers, and field hands. Ambitious, educated, wealthy, powerful Negroes live and prosper in America, but the United States is not a small island like Barbados, and most white Americans can remain conveniently unaware of the existence of Negroes whom they might have to reckon with as their intellectual or economic equals.

Where an efficient segregation system minimizes one's exposure to members of a minority who do not conform to the stereotype of what they

[16] *Ibid.,* pp. 19, 26, 32, 36, 46.

[17] *Ibid.,* p. 48.

should be like, a culture of discrimination can flourish. Since many white Americans deal most of the time with Negroes who conform to their stereotype of Negroes—that is, Negroes who are poor and ignorant and subservient —it is easy for white Americans to think of the term Negro as a synonym for poor, ignorant, and subservient. If one is as isolated from the mainstream of society as many white Southerners are, this culture of discrimination can become a norm in itself, further isolating them from "outsiders" who do not share their belief in Negro inferiority, or do not share it with the same intensity and conviction. When discrimination is basic to the culture, is part of "our way of life," it is easy to think of it as a natural, even an inborn, trait. Thus people may justify racial discrimination as a consequence of the "natural human aversion" to differentness, rather than the learned behavior which it is.

When psychologists want, for experimental purposes, to turn a normal little white rat into a neurotic one (and that's the kind of people some psychologists are), they change the rules of everyday life on him. They teach the rat that, if he finds his way through a maze and trips a lever with his paw, he will be rewarded with a piece of cheese. Then they block one of the passages he has learned to expect, changing the path of the maze. When the rat takes what used to be the correct turn to reach the lever and the cheese, he bumps into a wall. Suppose the little chap has sufficient emotional strength to sustain this frustration and learn the path of the new maze. When he finally arrives at the lever and presses it with his paw, the psychologists have fixed it so that, instead of his cheese, he gets an electric shock. Even a well-balanced, secure little rat from a happy home environment will take only so much of this before he goes all to pieces. An abrupt change in the rules he has learned to live with puts a strain on one's emotional balance, whether one is a rat or a man. A sudden alteration in the path of the maze causes the cheese to seem hard to get at or even unattainable, and the rat will become irritable and perhaps quit trying. A sudden alteration by a new dean in the promotion policy of a university causes salary increases to seem hard to come by, and the psychologist may also become surly or even quit trying. When the rules are changed, the game of life seems difficult or incomprehensible. Ambiguity and uncertainty about what is expected may lead either rats or people to abandon their goals. Instead of using their energy to achieve what used to be ends which were well understood, they are likely either to withdraw or lash out at the environment, using up their resources in random aggression and expressing their hostility toward an unfair world.

New political and economic situations are unsettling, but they may for that very reason be destructive of traditional patterns of racial prejudice and discrimination. It becomes increasingly obvious that the caste system of India will not be able to withstand the assault of urbanization and industrialization. Despite the tenacity of cultural norms, it is difficult to maintain patterns of prejudice and discrimination against a group as it loses its identifying sociological characteristics—and especially difficult if the group loses its physical stigmata.

The new nations offer fertile breeding grounds for political upheaval, economic chaos, social unrest, and the exacerbation of racism. But where stratification is an integrating variable which cuts across racial lines, they also offer fertile breeding grounds for revolutions in attitudes of racial prejudice and in the practice of racial discrimination as concomitants of revolution in the political and economic structure.

I should like to express my thanks to the Program of Comparative Politics of Northwestern University, which financed part of my field work in Barbados, and to the Social Science Research Council. The paper was written during my tenure as a Faculty Research Fellow of the Council.

SOCIAL CHANGE AND ELITES IN AN EMERGENT NATION*

WENDELL BELL

Yale University

The emergence of politically new and economically developing nations has been one of the major features of change since World War II. Among former colonies, increasing internal self-government has culminated in political independence, and the creation of large-scale programs, often government-sponsored and government-encouraged is resulting in economic and social development. In these emergent nations, elites of various kinds are in relative short supply; there are comparatively few persons possessing highly differentiated technical and professional skills and often there are few indigenous "entrepreneurs" who think and act in terms of large-scale innovative operations, either in or out of government.

Of course, the elites in any society have an importance for the society far exceeding their numbers. In a preface to the Stanford University comparative study of elites, it was stated that:[1]

"The ways of a society are largely fixed by the myths and doctrines of a ruling few. Democracy differs from oligarchy not in the presence or absence of an elite who wield most influence, but in the closed or open, representative or unrepresentative, responsible or irresponsible character of the elite. Who these elites are, how they live, what training they get, how they circulate, are among the most significant facts of the history of a society."

In the new and developing nation-states, elites may assume even more

*I wish to thank the Social Science Research Council, New York, N. Y. for a Faculty Research Fellowship during the tenure of which the data reported here were collected and analyzed, and the Penrose Fund, American Philosophical Society, Philadelphia, Pa. for a grant-in-aid. Also, the assistance of Lora-Lee Bell, Charles C. Moskos, Jr., and Emily Smith Reed is gratefully acknowledged.

[1] Harold D. Lasswell, Daniel Lerner, and C. Easton Rothwell, *The Comparative Study of Elites*, Stanford: Stanford University Press, 1952.

importance by their sheer scarcity than in the older and more developed countries. Even though few in numbers it is they who lead and facilitate change, or oppose and hinder new developments. Their talents and initiative are crucial in getting new ideas accepted in the society, yet their function is also to maintain a continuity with the past and to preserve social integration. They are mediators and communicators, interest articulators and aggregators, creators and disseminators of culture, preservers of values, change leaders, and standard makers for the general population. Thus, with the transformation of former political dependencies into new states, the development of indigenous leaders having adequate training and experience becomes of great importance. Political change formally transfers political power from an old colonial elite, often intertwined with an indigenous traditional elite, to an emergent national elite, and at the same time, planned economic and social changes place a premium on new skills and talents, and demand new personnel possessing them.[2]

Of course, the social composition of elites is inextricably linked to political, economic, and social developments in the emerging nations. Increased governmental functions, the development of responsible self-government, new patterns of elite recruitment and socialization, the changing modes of interest articulation and aggregation, economic advancement, increased social welfare and educational opportunities, the spread of national citizenship, and other developments are changing the social characteristics of elites as well as changing the nature of elite positions themselves, and their interrelationships. In turn, the changes in elites affect the direction, tempo, and content of future political, economic, and social changes.

One purpose of this paper is to understand some of the changes in the social composition of elites during a country's transition from colonial status to political independence, and to describe the social backgrounds of the elites who are leading a country into independence. We know a good deal about the polity and economy of the new states, but we know considerably less about related social changes within them. Thus, this paper is addressed to the following questions: As progress toward political independence and economic advancement has been made, how have the elites changed? What are the social characteristics of the emergent elites when compared to the elites of the late colonial period? What distinctions have developed between the occupants of different types of elite positions? Is the social base from which elites are recruited changing? If so, in what way? Have shifts in the locus of political power changed the superordinate-subordinate relationships between different types of elites? What positions are held by the most influential persons in an emerging nation?

[2] See S. F. Nadel, "The Concept of Social Elites," *International Social Science Bulletin*, Vol. 8, (No. 3, 1956), pp. 413–424.

A second purpose of this paper is to understand the recent changes in elites and the present social characteristics of elites by relating them to the context of social change in which they have occurred. Certain long-term social trends that summarize an aspect of the entire history of the new nation under consideration are discussed. Thus, the facts and figures given on elites are not simply descriptions, but they also represent an underlying theory of social change. This theory derives most directly from the work of Godfrey and Monica Wilson[3] and uses, as its key concept, the notion of "scale." My thesis is that social change in the emergent nation under consideration can be understood as a long-term trend toward an increase in the scale of society, that is an increase in the range of relations, an increase in the scope of social interaction and dependency. Space does not permit a full exposition of this thesis here, but one aspect of it, the increase in the internal inclusiveness of society, or more particularly, the evolution of human rights, is discussed in some detail.

JAMAICA: A NATION EMERGENT

Jamaica is a country of over 1.6 million people, a mountainous island about 146 miles long and 50 miles across at its widest part, located just 90 miles south of Cuba in the Caribbean Sea. Discovered by Columbus in 1494 during the explorer's second voyage to America, Jamaica was first settled by the Spanish in 1509. However, the British captured Jamaica in 1655 and have held the island for three centuries, until the present political transition to independence. The original inhabitants of Jamaica at the time of discovery, a branch of the Arawaks known as the Tainos, have contributed practically nothing to the present population. Little remains today of the 146 years of Spanish rule. A few sites and decaying buildings are left, place names of headlands, bays, rivers, mountains, etc. have remained, and there still are a few everyday terms which are left from the Spanish period.[4]

Oversimplifying, one can say that the people of Jamaica were imported from Africa while the dominant ideas and institutions of Jamaica were imported from England. For example, between 1655 and the end of the British slave trade in 1808 between 736,000 and 759,000 slaves from the west coast of Africa were brought to Jamaica in excess of those exported.[5]

[3] Godfrey and Monica Wilson, *The Analysis of Social Change*, Cambridge: Cambridge University Press, 1945. Also see the discussion of Albanian elites by Charles C. Moskos, Jr., in this volume, Chapter 7.

[4] Most of the Spanish terms in present day use have been brought back from Cuba and Panama by migrant laborers during the last eighty years. See R. B. Le Page and David De Camp, *Jamaican Creole*, London: MacMillan and Co. Ltd., 1960.

[5] Le Page and De Camp, *ibid*, p. 74.

Throughout most of the history of Jamaica since "Discovery," black men and women have been numerically superior while being socially inferior. In 1943, 78 per cent of the population was classified as black, 17.5 per cent colored, about one per cent white, one per cent Chinese, two per cent East Indian, and less than one per cent was classified as "other races[6]." Very small, but socially significant, numbers of Jews and Syrians were also ethnically differentiated.[7]

Although "Africanisms" are still apparent in one form or another in some aspects of lower class life in Jamaica, especially in religion and magic, dancing and singing, folklore and women's hair styles, the dominant institutions of the society are generally English in form and content. African-style political institutions, systems of justice, economic organization, and family life did not survive the plantation system of slavery, although slavery itself has left its mark in more or less subtle ways on modern Jamaican life, especially among members of the lower classes. In addition to the black lower classes, there is a small, predominantly white, upper class which[8] "... represents the culture of mid-twentieth-century West European society." and a brown intermediate section which "... is culturally and biologically the most variable, and practices a general mixture of patterns from the higher and lower groups." Also, there have emerged distinctive Jamaican (or West Indian) cultural forms which are often mixtures or combinations of past forms from all classes and which, with the coming of independence and the stirring of national pride, are achieving a new unity.[9]

Modern political changes may conveniently be viewed as beginning during 1937-38. During that time strikes, riots, and other disturbances, and the Royal Commission report which resulted, called attention to the political, economic, and social deprivations of the vast majority of Jamaicans and

[6] George W. Roberts, *The Population of Jamaica*, Cambridge: Cambridge University Press, 1957, p. 65.

[7] Leonard Broom, "The Social Differentiation of Jamaica," *American Sociological Review*, Vol. 19, (April, 1954), pp. 115–125.

[8] M. G. Smith, "The Plural Framework of Jamaican Society," *The British Journal of Sociology*, Vol. 12, (September, 1961), p. 250.

[9] *Cf.* M. G. Smith, "West Indian Culture," *Caribbean Quarterly*, Vol. 7, (December, 1961), pp. 112–119. In this discussion, Smith stresses the divisive effects of the duality of the West Indian culture complex. His partitioning of West Indian culture into a dominant European-Creole component and a subordinate African-Creole component is based upon historical and sociological facts, but it slights other facts: both components are shared to some degree by members of every social class at the present time and the trends in emergent West Indian culture increasingly transcend the dominance of the old European tradition, the subordination of the African tradition, and the gulf between the two. The cultural duality certainly exists, but it should be considered along with the fact that there is emerging a distinctive combination of elements in a new unity, although in Jamaica, this new unity is likely to be more "Jamaican" than "West Indian" and yet it is likely to be increasingly universalistic, that is, a part of the modern world culture.

helped to set in motion changes toward increasing self-government, representative democracy, economic development, and social reform.[10] World War II stalled political developments in Jamaica temporarily, but universal adult suffrage was first introduced, along with limited self-government, in November, 1944. Since then, there has been steady constitutional advance during a period which can be described as "tutelary democracy"—with less tutelage and more democracy having come in 1949, 1953, 1956, 1957, and 1959. During 1958, Jamaica became part of the West Indies Federation, along with other British territories in the Caribbean. However, a referendum held September 19, 1961 resulted in a Jamaican decision to "go it alone." Today, a new constitution has come into effect, and on August 6, 1962 Jamaica shook off the last remnants of colonial dependence and donned the new garb of a politically independent nation-state within the British Commonwealth of nations.

Although it is too early to tell for certain, there is much evidence to indicate that sometime during the mid-1950's Jamaica entered the stage of economic growth which W. W. Rostow calls the take-off into self-sustained growth.[11] Recent economic changes have transformed Jamaica from an underdeveloped to a partially developed country, although by comparison with developed economies Jamaica remains a relatively poor country. Agriculture is of great importance to the Jamaican economy, with almost half of the gainfully employed persons being engaged in agricultural work, but manufacturing has increased in recent years and now rivals agriculture in size of its contribution to the domestic product. Furthermore, Jamaica suffers from unemployment and poverty; its land is often wasted or poorly used; it has a growing population; it lacks capital, although capital resources have increased; it has relatively low, although increasing, per capita productivity; it contains a relatively large, though diminishing, proportion of illiterates compared to developed countries; and its people are poorly, but increasingly better, educated.[12] Thus, Jamaica is moving out of a past not only of political dependence, but also of economic deprivation, into the modern world.

THE INCREASING SCALE OF SOCIETY

The changes that have taken place in Jamaica during the last two

[10] *West India Royal Commission Report*, London: His Majesty's Stationery Office, Cmd. 6607, July 1945.

[11] W. W. Rostow, *The Stages of Economic Growth*, Cambridge: Cambridge University Press, 1960.

[12] *The Economic Development of Jamaica*, by a Mission of the International Bank for Reconstruction and Development, Baltimore, Md., 1952; *Economic Survey, Jamaica, 1960,* prepared by the

decades are striking, but they are further extensions of events that can be traced back as far as the discovery of the island by Columbus. There are certain continuities and trends which suggest developmental changes. These can be conveniently summarized as *increases in the scale of society*. The idea of increasing scale is not suggested as a cosmic principle; but as a theory that can usefully be applied to different times and places. Jamaica represents since discovery, and perhaps even before that, a society which is expanding in people, in degree of organization, in total power, in internal inclusiveness, in space, and in time. This is not to say that there have never been contractions in scale in the course of Jamaican history, but the long-term non-repetitive movements of the time series—the *trends* not the cycles nor apparently random fluctuations—have been toward the increase in the scale of society.

At least from the time of discovery Jamaica has increasingly been drawn into a network of relations that have been expanding territorially. At first, interaction and interdependence involved parts of Europe, Africa, and other places in the "new world." Although the densities of communication vary with different parts of the world, Jamaica has become part of global society. With independence, the links of economics and government necessarily binding Jamaica to a metropolitan power are no longer enforced by colonial domination. Jamaica is now free to establish wider territorial ties, both economically and politically through agreements, treaties, and alliances.

Jamaican society has expanded through time by the spread of literacy, increasing education, and most recently an increasing emphasis upon a Jamaican (or West Indian) perspective to Jamaican history. Not only are more contemporary Jamaicans "in touch" with more of their own past, but their thoughts and actions are increasingly informed by the accumulated knowledge of Western civilization and by other civilizations as well.

As Jamaican society has increased in scale, it has increased in complexity and has become organized into manifold hierarchical levels of skill, income, and prestige. The organization of human effort has become more intricate, and managerial and supervisory personnel both in and out of government, occupying positions of co-ordination, control, and direction, have increased in importance. Differentiation of function, specialization, rationality and impersonality have increased.[13]

Jamaican society has increased in total power. I am not referring here to technological advance, although it is related, but to *social power*. The ability of the Jamaican people to achieve their collective goals has increased

Central Planning Unit, the Government of Jamaica, 1961.

[13] Some of the generalizations given here closely follow Wilson and Wilson, *op. cit.*, or Eshref Shevky and Wendell Bell, *Social Area Analysis*, Stanford: Stanford University Press, 1955.

immeasurably. This is partly due to technological advance, but it is also due to increasing differentiation of function, increasingly complex organization of effort, and increasing social mobilization. The application of a zero-sum concept of power—the notion that power is limited and a scarce commodity— is simply inadequate to describe the *changing* total power of Jamaican society—and probably other developing societies as well. However useful the zero-sum concept of power may be to describe the competition over the distribution of power *at any given time*, it is more accurate to view power as a resource which can be developed when describing *changes in total power through time*.

Belief in ancestors and local spirits, in magic and witchcraft has declined greatly, and is now of little practical importance. There has been a spread of universal religions with membership in world organizations. The aboriginal culture has been wiped out; although *obeah* men still exist, their influence and their clientele have declined greatly.

An increasing consciousness of the widening relations and dependence on past and contemporaneous groups among more and more Jamaicans has followed the increase in the scale of society.

Although social stratification increased as Jamaican society increased in scale, there has been a reduction of hereditary privilege. As will be pointed out in detail later, the circulation of elites has increased, and the elite has expanded in relative size and has become less exclusive. Elites are recruited from a wider range of social origins than before—although they may eventually be more homogeneous in origin with respect to one characteristic, country of birth—and recruitment of elites is increasingly based upon universalistic criteria of achieved skills. Elites have become more accessible to the masses, and the masses have become more accessible to the elites.

As Jamaican society increased in scale, an increasing diversity occurred with the resulting isolation of subgroups which were functionally significant for the total society. Jamaican society was a heterogeneous aggregation of individuals of diverse origins resulting from migration, by choice and by force. However, the contacts between diverse groups were pre-conditions for the reduction of heterogeneity, for an increase in the *internal inclusiveness of the society*. This process has not yet run its course, but the trend is in the direction of the reduction of ascriptive barriers which have in the past prevented the association of some persons with other persons in the society and the institutionalization of equal opportunities for the mutual access to facilities and services. It is the process of repeated redefinitions of society to include more and more people within it on a more equal basis in some respects with the formerly more favored members of the society. In part, this is an aspect of increasing mobility, in that the size of the group within which any Jamaican may move freely has increased in social as well as in geographical distance.[14]

The trends toward increasing mobility and circulation, more equal opportunities, and the reduction of ascriptive barriers have occurred *pari passu* with the trends toward increasing social stratification. The spread of equality and increased stratification are sometimes viewed by writers, when they don't simply ignore one or the other, as a dilemma in that the two trends seem opposed to one another. However, they both can contribute to an increase in the ability of members of a society to achieve their collective and individual goals and in this sense, at a higher level of abstraction than before, they appear, not opposed, but alike in their consequences. Increased stratification can contribute added power, more effective organization of effort, and higher levels of social mobilization. And the trend toward equality can result in more people in the society being more committed to it, in more people being more highly motivated to achieve, in a greater overall development of human resources, and in a more effective distribution of talent and skills in the most important positions in the society.

THE EVOLUTION OF HUMAN RIGHTS

The trend toward the increasing internal inclusiveness of Jamaican society can be identified by the extension of rising minimums of human rights, universally applied to an increasing proportion of persons in Jamaica. Following the United Nations' usage, I include civil, political, economic, and social rights[15] by the term, human rights, as defined as follows:

Civil rights—freedoms from torture and slavery; freedoms of religion, expression and assembly; the right to security of person, equality before courts and tribunals, a fair and public hearing by competent and impartial tribunals established by law, presumption of innocence until proved guilty, and the right of everyone to be considered a person before the law, among other such rights.

[14] Of course, in one sense this trend seems to be contradicted by the dismantlement of empires and the creation of new nations. The resulting new "nationality" becomes a new ascriptive barrier, sometimes where little national identification existed before, between the peoples of the different new states and the peoples of other states, both old and new. However, the rise of the new nationalism has served to reduce many ascriptive barriers that used to stand between various social groups *within* the territory of the new states, and has provided a basis for a new and more thorough-going internal unity. Also, the transfer of highest loyalty and allegiance from traditional or primordial groups to the state may set the stage, as others have pointed out, for a further step in which political and other organizations may be developed, which transcend the nation-state in the priority of its claim on the individual and which are larger in geographical scale than presently existing nation-states. Among the older nations of Europe, this trend is already apparent. There, the growth of supra-national organizations and the consequent decline of some degree and aspects of national sovereignty can be clearly seen today.

[15] I have included cultural with social rights.

Political rights—freedom to take part in the conduct of public affairs, voting, and equal access to public service as well as others which define the people's rights to participate in the political system on the basis of equality.

Economic rights—the right to fair wages and equal remuneration for work of equal value, safe and healthy working conditions, equal opportunity to be promoted subject only to considerations of seniority and competence, rest and leisure, reasonable limitation of working hours and periodic holidays with pay, ownership of property either alone or in association with others, the right to form and join a trade union for the promotion and protection of one's economic interests, and the right to strike, among others.

Social rights—the right to marry and establish a family, to the free choice of a marriage partner, to enjoy the highest attainable standard of physical and mental health, to free primary education and equal access to secondary and higher education, to an adequate standard of living including adequate food, clothing, and housing, and the right to take part in the cultural life of the nation, among others.

From the point of view of the historical extension of these rights, it is accurate to describe much of the social history of Jamaica in terms of the changing, that is *rising* status of the lower classes be they white, brown, or black or be they slaves, indentured bond servants, agricultural laborers, urban workers or unemployed poor people. The Jamaican lower classes have emerged as participants in the society on the basis of more equality than they have enjoyed in the past. The gradual extension of civil, political, economic, and social rights—*rights* which are embedded in law not simply benefits deriving from benevolent paternalism that may be granted in exchange for personal subservience and submissive gratitude—to the lower classes in Jamaica can be easily documented. Unfortunately, no Jamaican has as yet come forward to do the necessary research and to tell the story with the relevance to present aspirations, and with the vigor and vision that the story deserves.

This is not to say that gross inequalities of status and opportunities do not exist in Jamaica today. Although it is true that there is equality of civil and political rights, as these are expressed in law, such equality is partly irrelevant and partly nominal when actual practice is considered. The laws against *obeah* and the use of *ganja*, for example, apply *equally* to the upper and middle classes, who generally consider these practices to be foreign, and to the lower classes, for whom such practices have been part of accepted cultural patterns. Furthermore, the high costs of legal advice, differential unfamiliarity with the law, and differential participation in legal administration reduce the power of the lower classes to implement and realize their civil rights.

Since 1944, equality of political rights has been more fully achieved than equality of civil rights. However, the inequalities of social and economic stratification in Jamaica result in some reduction of real equality in the political arena. Money buys election propaganda and thus may influence the election outcome, the conferral of prestige coopts some elected political leaders to some degree, and the differential distribution of skills by classes tends to restrict the formulation and administration of governmental policies to members of the middle and upper classes.

Economic and social inequalities in Jamaica are even greater than civil and political inequalities. As social facts rather than as legal statements, economic and social equality and equality of opportunity do not exist. In his analysis of Jamaican social structure, M. G. Smith[16] accurately highlights the present inequalities in Jamaica. The white upper classes, the brown middle classes, and the black lower classes are grossly unequal with economic and social advantages accruing most to the upper and least to the lower classes.

The present inequalities with respect to civil, political, economic, and social rights, however, have a past during which the inequalities were far greater; and the long-term trends in these rights have been toward increasing equality, toward rising minimums applied to more and more people. The new constitution of Jamaica entrenches a comprehensive set of human rights to apply equally to all Jamaicans.[17]

Also, as the internal inclusiveness of Jamaican society has increased, there has been a decreasing reliance on brute force for the maintenance of social cohesion and an increase in social integration based on consensus. This process has not yet run its course either. In fact, serious problems of the creation of more social unity now face Jamaica, but the trends are clear.[18] Consent has increased and naked power has decreased in importance.

There is interaction between scale in space, in time, and in internal

[16] Smith, "The Plural Framework of Jamaican Society," *op. cit.*, pp. 249–262.

[17] Materials on human rights in Jamaica can be found in the following sources: W. L. Burn, *Emancipation and Apprenticeship in the British West Indies*, London: Jonathan Cape, 1937; W. J. Gardner, *A History of Jamaica*, London: Elliot Stock, 1873; Douglas Hall, *Free Jamaica 1838–1865: An Economic History*, New Haven: Yale University Press, 1959; William Law Mathieson, *British Slave Emancipation 1838–1849*, London: Longmans, Green and Co., 1932; William Law Mathieson, *The Sugar Colonies and Governor Eyre 1849–1866*, London: Longmans, Green and Co., 1936; Mary Proudfoot, *Britain and the United States in the Caribbean*, New York: Frederick A. Praeger, 1953; Robert Worthington Smith, "The Conflict between Planter and Parliament over the Slave Laws of Jamaica," unpublished Ph.D. dissertation, University of California, Los Angeles, 1942; H. A. Wyndham, *Problems of Imperial Trusteeship: The Atlantic and Emancipation*, London: Oxford University Press, 1937.

[18] A detailed investigation of change in relation to social unity in Jamaica is available in James A. Mau, "Social Change and Belief in Progress: A Study of Images of the Future in Jamaica," unpublished Ph.D. dissertation, University of California, Los Angeles, 1963.

inclusiveness. One type can occur without the others, and instability may result. For example, increase in territorial scale can occur with very little internal inclusiveness such as may occur with the emergence of empires. As a result, the integrative institutions may be inadequate to maintain the geographical scope of the society and contraction in territorial scale may take place. Such scale contraction has occurred, usually in connection with other discontinuities, several times in the history of Jamaica.

Finally, there is interaction between demand for and achievement of civil, political, economic, and social rights. Although the long-term trends show that the direction of change is toward the application of an equal set of rights to all adults in the society, at any given time there may be a substitution rate of one type of right for others. That is, certain rights can be gained at the expense of others. For example, with emancipation, new civil rights were obtained, but certain traditional economic rights were lost. The former masters of the former slaves no longer were obligated to prevent economic deprivation among their workers, although today new and more thorough-going economic rights are enjoyed by all Jamaicans.

Of course the identification of a long-term trend toward equality, toward the rising minimums of civil, political, economic, and social rights to an increasingly large number of persons, does not mean that the continuation of the trend is inevitable, nor that it will continue automatically without definite actions being taken. Also, mathematically speaking, one can write a number of formulas which would each adequately fit the known past trend but which each extrapolate the trend in a different direction; that is, each would predict a different future from the same past. In addition, the trend has not always occurred without agitation and violence, and it may not continue without further disorder. Thus, the future of human rights in Jamaica may be problematical, but the analysis of social trends suggests that the trend toward equality of rights has been no accident and may reflect some underlying principle of change.

A DYNAMIC MECHANISM OF CHANGE

How has the trend toward equality of rights come about? What has been the dynamic mechanism underlying the changes in the nature and application of civil, political, economic, and social rights in Jamaica? Tentatively, the answer seems to be the resolution of problems of legitimacy. Changes in human rights have occurred as a result of resolutions of anomalies between structures and practices on the one hand, and ideas about what is legitimate on the other. There has been a demonstrable interplay between ideas and institutions throughout the history of Jamaica. Institutions fostered certain ideas about what is right or wrong, what should or should not be; and ideas, often exogenous to Jamaica itself originally, have led to organized social action which often resulted in changing, eliminating, or creating institutions. For example, ideas about the social inferiority of Negroes were fostered in and diffused from Jamaica and elsewhere in the West Indies during one period of history when a justification of an important institution, slavery, was needed. The currency and spread of these ideas were in some sense "caused" by the institution, and validated it. On the other hand, ideas emerging in Europe raised questions of legitimacy concerning slavery, and social action based on these ideas eventually resulted in the disappearance of an institution: the slave trade was abolished and the slaves were freed.[19] From this viewpoint, social change in Jamaica, to be understood more fully, should be set against the background of developments which have taken place in Europe and in the United States since the breakdown of feudalism. The rise of the modern state in Europe, the formation of a national citizenry (which implied equality for all adults in some respects), the American and French revolutions, the industrial revolution in England, the trade union movement, the formulation of new ideologies—political, economic, and social, the spread of mass education, and the growth of the welfare state are each relevant to political, economic, and social changes in Jamaica. Available evidence supports the contention that ideas, usually imported from Europe and to some extent from the United States, have, over the course of Jamaican history, led to social action which has resulted in the reduction of anomalies between such ideas and institutions. Usually, the result has been structural change toward more equality, and what might be considered "progress"; that is, more equality was created by giving more people more rights. (But not always. One of the more interesting examples occurred in 1865 when the white ruling oligarchs created more equality by giving away some of their own political rights because it was no longer, after emancipation, legitimate for one section of the citizenry to have such rights without the newly-created citizens, the former slaves, having the same rights too.)

Ideas regarding human rights of various kinds often have been expressed in lower-class demands, discontents, disaffection, and alienation. Before 1944, when universal adult suffrage was begun, lower-class collective protests took the form, as Reinhard Bendix says of Europe before the formation of the modern political community, "... of millenarian movements, social banditry, and direct outbursts of violence, which ranged from an inchoate venting of accumulated grievances to a cunning or righteous insistence

---

[19] Some of these points are documented in Elsa V. Goveia, *A Study on the Historiography of the British West Indies*, Mexico: Instituto Panamericano de Geografia e Historia, 1956.

upon the customary rights even of the most subordinate groups."[20] Such patterns of protest remain in Jamaica today, but their frequency and significance are greatly diminished because in recent years major protests have been expressed by participation of the lower classes in the new national political community. Legitimate political action and legal trade union activity account for the expression of many modern demands.

The elites, of course, have played a crucial role throughout the whole process of circular causation between ideas and institutions. Their actions or inactions, their ideologies, attitudes and beliefs have contributed toward expansion or contraction of internal inclusiveness or helped maintain existing barriers of exclusiveness. Upon occasion, they have boldly led scale-increasing change, and on others they have, as Tawney points out in a similar connection, walked reluctantly backwards into the future, as other European governments did after the levelling doctrines of France, doing from above what is sometimes accomplished by revolution in spite of their contrary ideologies and attitudes, but because of their belief that, if they didn't, something far worse than a change toward equality might befall them.[21]

There is ample evidence of lower-class discontents, disaffection, and alienation today. Many lower-class persons say that their interests are not being served. They raise questions about the civil service ("a middle-class preserve"), the new office buildings for the Ministries ("why not more housing?"; "The brown men take care of themselves!"), they see new factories and a new air terminal, but they see their own circumstance improved less than they expect. Some members of the new Jamaican elite realize that, although Jamaica has experienced considerable economic growth on the basis of conventional criteria, not enough of Jamaica's increased wealth has yet trickled down to the mass of the population. They hope to spread available resources wider than in the recent past. But some of them also realize that the lower-class Jamaican can be a recalcitrant tool of action, usually uneducated and perhaps illiterate, suspicious of change, often actively resisting efforts of field workers to change his ways, short-tempered in his expectations for government to do something for him, being only half a citizen in that his duties and obligations are not clear to him, while his rights are increasingly in his consciousness, and increasingly alienated if his expectations are not met and if his obligations are pointed out to him.[22]

[20] Reinhard Bendix, "National Citizenship of the Lower Classes: A Comparative Perspective," unpublished paper, pp. 2–3. I am greatly indebted to Professor Bendix for the conception of social change as being constituted in part by changes in human rights. See his "Social Stratification and the Political Community," *Archives Européennes de Sociologie*, Vol. 1, (1960), pp. 181–210; and "The Lower Classes and the 'Democratic Revolution'," *Industrial Relations*, Vol. 1, (October, 1961), pp. 91–116.

[21] R. H. Tawney, *Equality*, London: George Allen and Unwin, Ltd., 1952, pp. 97–98.

[22] Lower-class conceptions of their duties and obligations are the subject of detailed research

Jamaica today may have reached another stage where a new anomaly has emerged between the current ideas concerning human rights and the elites' ability or willingness to provide for them. New problems of legitimacy have arisen; new solutions are being sought. The formulation and implementation of such solutions is an important part of elite functions. With the political developments which led to an independent Jamaica, the social composition of elites has been changing, a new leadership group has been forming—especially since 1938. The decisions that will mold future social change in Jamaica are in the hands of this new Jamaican elite.

TOP GOVERNMENTAL ELITES, 1939–1954

In 1939, Jamaica had a modified Crown Colony government little changed since 1884 and faced five more years before the beginning of tutelary democracy. Although there were elected members in the Legislative Council, the electorate was limited and generally uninterested in politics. For the most part, the elected members played the role of an irresponsible opposition, and they had special powers over finance that often made governance difficult. The Governor had great powers which included the reserved right to override the elected members in case of necessity. In addition to the Governor, the Legislative Council contained a number of *ex officio* and nominated members equal to the number of elected members.[23]

In contrast, Jamaica had been ten years on the road to self-government by 1954, the most recent political change at the time being the introduction of the ministerial system in 1953. The Legislative Council then was composed of only official and nominated members and its powers had been reduced with a few exceptions to the consideration of legislation passed by the new House of Representatives. The latter body consisted of 32 members elected on the basis of universal adult suffrage from the 32 constituencies into which Jamaica had been divided. At the general election in 1949, "...477,107 votes were polled out of a total of 732,217 persons eligible to vote, or 65.2%."[24] The Executive Council was the principal policy-making

in Andrew P. Phillips, "The Development of a Modern Labor Force in Antigua," unpublished Ph.D. dissertation, University of California, Los Angeles, 1963.

[23] Morley Ayearst, *The British West Indies, The Search for Self Government*, Washington Square: New York University Press, 1960; Charles Henry Kunsman, Jr., "Recent Developments in Representative Government in Jamaica, 1938–1953," unpublished M.A. thesis, University of California, Berkeley, 1955; C. M. MacInnes, "Constitutional Developments of the British West Indies," in *Developments Towards Self-Government in the Caribbean*, The Hague, Bandun: W. van Hoeve Ltd., 1955; Hume Wrong, Government of the West Indies, Oxford: Clarendon Press, 1923.

[24] *The Handbook of Jamaica for 1954*, Kingston, Jamaica: The Government Printing Office, 1954, p. 37.

body and had become a kind of quasi-Cabinet (and a schoolroom for full-fledged Cabinet members-to-be). Thus, it included eight elected members from the House of Representatives, who were Ministers with responsibility over the work of the government departments, in addition to the official and nominated members. Although the element of tutelage was still present in the Governor's reserved legislative power, which could be exercised without the consent of the Executive Council, there was considerable responsible self-government regarding internal affairs under the 1953 Order in Council. In fact, political power had shifted significantly, although not completely, into the hands of the elected representatives of the Jamaican people.[25]

Table 1 shows some of the changes in the social characteristics of the top governmental elites during this transition period. Included among "top governmental elites" for each year are members of the executive and legislative branches of the government, the directors, permanent secretaries, and other important civil servants of all governmental departments (and in 1954 of the new Ministries as well), and the *custos* (a nominated person) of each parish. In other words, elected political leaders, higher civil servants, top officials, and occupants of certain nominated positions are included among the top governmental elites. As far as possible, persons occupying functionally equivalent positions were selected for both times, although this was not a simple thing to determine because of the proliferation and change in governmental positions between 1939 and 1954. The data are based upon information on such persons available in the *Handbook of Jamaica* and in *Who's Who, Jamaica* for 1939 and 1954.[26]

From Table 1, note that about half of the top governmental leaders were Jamaican-born in 1939, but by 1954 the percentage had increased to 75. Thus, from the point of view of Jamaicans, the top governmental leadership

---

[25] It should be noted that Jamaica has moved slower and more carefully toward independence than many other new nations. There is no question but that this has been beneficial in many ways. A large cadre of Jamaicans have been trained for leadership in politics and the civil service and to a lesser extent in commerce and industry. However, one negative effect may be that the average person in Jamaica faced full independence in 1962 with less thrill and challenge than if independence had come rapidly rather than in gradual increments from 1944 to 1962. The drama of the political transformation was somewhat diffused by many little excitements rather than a single climax. Some members of the Jamaican masses felt that they had been told they were getting freedom from colonialism so many times since 1944 that they were a bit cynical when independence finally fully came. As a result, the psychological impact of independence may have been less than it might have been.

[26] *The Handbook of Jamaica for 1939*, Kingston, Jamaica: The Government Printing Office, 1939; *The Handbook of Jamaica for 1954*, Kingston, Jamaica: The Government Printing Office, 1954; *Who's Who and Why in Jamaica 1939–40*, Second Edition, compiled and published by L. A. Thoywell Henry, Kingston, Jamaica: The Gleaner Co., Ltd.; *Who's Who, Jamaica 1954*, edited by Clifton Neita, Kingston, Jamaica: The Gleaner Co., Ltd., 1954.

positions were less exclusive in 1954 than they were in 1939, with Jamaicans having a greater chance of occupying such positions in 1954.[27] There was a relative reduction of non-Jamaicans (mostly English) in these roles. During the period under consideration, this was accomplished in part by the replacement of Englishmen by Jamaicans in given leadership roles, and also by the creation of new roles (e.g. an increase in elected political leaders from 14 to 32) which were filled by Jamaicans for the most part. This process of increasing the total number of leadership roles in government has continued as the functions and services of government have expanded, and the replacement of foreign personnel in existing roles since 1954 has increasingly contributed to an increased access to such leadership positions on the part of Jamaicans. Still more new roles for Jamaicans have been created in defense and foreign affairs with the coming of independence.

The top governmental elites are subdivided further in Table 2. For each type of elite the trend is the same—an increase in the percentage of Jamaican-born persons from 1939 to 1954. The smallest increase was for the elected political leaders, but for 1954 the percentage of Jamaicans among them was 93 per cent. The largest increase was in the case of the higher civil servants, yet in 1954 about a third of such persons were still non-Jamaicans. This large increase for the civil servants reflects the results of a deliberate policy to "West Indianize" the civil service[28] and the steps which had been taken to promote opportunities for Jamaicans (and some other West Indians) to receive formal, technical, administrative, professional and other specialized training. They also reflect the facts that comparatively few Jamaicans possessed the necessary skills and experience to perform top civil service roles expertly in 1939 and that, although the increase in Jamaicans in these positions has continued since 1954, Jamaica, as other new nations, may be in part dependent for some years on the distribution of specialized and

[27] Of course from the point of view of non-Jamaicans, one can say that the top governmental elites are now more exclusive rather than less so in one way, since Jamaican nationality status, although in a sense being achieved by Jamaicans through political change, was emergent as an ascriptive criterion for membership in the governmental elite group. At the same time, the need for persons possessing certain specialized and differentiated skills in connection with economic and social development (e.g. in the bauxite industry and the University of the West Indies) increased the number of non-Jamaicans among some types of elite groups.

[28] The facts are somewhat more complicated than this statement suggests in that for about two decades it was believed that Jamaica might become independent as part of a nation larger in geographical scale than the boundaries of Jamaica itself. An independent West Indies Federation was to include nine other British territories in the Caribbean as well. Thus, a few non-Jamaican West Indians also moved into elite roles in Jamaica as part of the transition to independence. Now that Jamaica has reached independence on its own, we can expect such roles to be further "Jamaicanized" rather than "West Indianized." However, this may be accomplished in part by some non-Jamaican West Indians opting to become Jamaican citizens under the new Constitution.

differentiated skills available in technologically more advanced societies. Officials and nominated persons (for convenience designated "appointees") increased from 54 to 70 per cent Jamaican-born.

Table 1. **PERCENTAGE OF TOP GOVERNMENTAL ELITES HAVING SELECTED SOCIAL CHARACTERISTICS, 1939 and 1954**

	Elites Having Selected Characteristic in:	
Selected Social Characteristics	*1939 (N = 63)* Per Cent*	*1954 (N = 126)* Per Cent*
Jamaican-born	53	75
Urban-born (Jamaican-born only)*	29	34
Holds at least one non-governmental elite position	62	41
Elementary education or less	20	12
Secondary school education	44	54
Some university or more	36	34
Upwardly mobile	70	71
Age 55 or older	40	34

Source: 1939 and 1954, *Who's Who, Jamaica.*

*The number of cases are only approximate because of a few cases in which no information was available for some of the variables. The percentages of urban-born persons are based upon the Jamaican-born elites only and is 31 for 1939 and 90 for 1954.

Of the persons born in Jamaica, 29 per cent were urban-born (in Kingston, Spanish Town, or Montego Bay) in 1939 compared with 34 per cent in 1954 (see Table 1). Thus, the 1954 top governmental elites were slightly more urban with respect to place of birth than the 1939 elites. The elites were more likely to be urban-born than the entire Jamaican-born population. In 1943 about 12 to 14 per cent of the population was urban-born.[29]

However, the general comparison on urban birth is somewhat misleading, since the different types of elites did not change in the same way. The elected political leaders increased in percentage of urban-born from 0 to 20 per cent, while the appointees and the higher civil servants had reductions in the percentage of urban-born (from Table 2). In 1939, the differences between the three types of elites were greater than in 1954 with the civil servants most urban, the appointees next, and the elected political leaders least

[29] The 1943 percentages for the entire population are estimates based on data given in *The Eighth Census of Jamaica, 1943, ibid.*, Table 10, p. 6. Unfortunately, comparable data for the entire population in 1960 are not available.

urban. The rank order was the same in 1954, but the differential changes resulted in the different types of elites being more alike in 1954 than in 1939 in this respect.

The study of governmental elites becomes increasingly meaningful as the relationships between such elites and other institutional sectors of the society are specified. One such relationship is revealed by an examination of the relative number of top governmental elites concurrently holding elite positions in other social institutions. The simultaneous occupancy of elite positions in different institutions creates networks or circles of communication and influence that transcend particular institutional structures, and the number of non-governmental elite positions held by top governmental elites is one indicator of the range of their influence in the larger society. For example, top governmental elites who also occupy an elite position in the private economic sector are able to extend their influence into the economic life of the nation in ways that would be impossible if they occupied only their governmental roles. Also, governmental elites who are simultaneously economic elites may have their performance in their governmental roles affected by economic interests in ways that would otherwise be impossible.

The percentage of top governmental elites who hold at least one elite position in an institution other than government (mostly economic) is given in Table 1. From 1939 to 1954, the percentage of top governmental elites holding at least one non-governmental elite position declined from 62 to 41 per cent.

However, from Table 2 it can be seen that the different types of elites did not change in the same way. Consistent with the general trend, the higher civil servants were less likely to hold non-governmental elite positions in 1954 than in 1939, the percentage decreasing from 36 to 20. At both time periods, the civil servants were most likely, compared to elected political leaders and appointees, to have their authority confined to their governmental roles. This finding is consistent with the fact that the civil service has been increasingly professionalized while the governmental bureaucracy has increased in size and functions.

Also consistent with the general trend is the change in elected political leaders. Changing more than any other type of top governmental elite, the elected political leaders had 100 per cent who occupied at least one non-governmental elite position in 1939 but only 45 per cent in 1954. Thus, although the elected political leaders had much more formal responsibility and authority in 1954 than in 1939 as a result of constitutional changes which redefined their duties, their authority was more confined to purely *governmental and political* roles at the later time.

A bifurcation—or at least a partial bifurcation—of power is reflected in this

Table 2. PERCENTAGE OF TOP GOVERNMENTAL ELITES HAVING SELECTED SOCIAL CHARACTERISTICS BY TYPE OF ELITE POSITION, 1939 and 1954

Selected Social Characteristics	*Type of Elite Position**					
	Elected Political Leaders		*Appointees*		*Higher Civil Servants*	
	1939 (N = 14)†	*1954* (N = 32)†	*1939* (N = 27)†	*1954* (N = 29)†	*1939* (N = 22)†	*1954* (N = 64)†
	Per Cent	*Per Cent*	*Per Cent*	*Per Cent*	*Per Cent*	*Per Cent*
Jamaican-born	85	93	54	70	32	68
Urban-born (Jamaican-born only)	0	20	38	26	57	48
Holds at least one non-governmental elite position	100	45	63	83	36	20
Elementary education or less	29	36	13	3	23	3
Secondary school education	57	46	35	54	46	58
Some university or more	14	18	52	43	31	39
Upwardly mobile	83	93	58	35	79	76
Age 55 or older	27	23	63	63	23	26

Source: 1939 and 1954, *Who's Who, Jamaica.*

*The percentages represent the relative number of persons in each type of elite position having a particular social characteristic.

†The number of cases on which the percentages are based is given for each type of elite. It is approximate for some variables since a few cases did not have full information. The urban-born percentages are based upon the sub-universe of Jamaican-born only. These N's are: elected political leaders 11 (1939) and 29 (1954); appointed officials 13 (1939) and 19 (1954); and higher civil servants 7 (1939) and 42 (1954).

trend. As the economic and social elites lost direct control over the elected political positions, representatives and spokesmen of the laboring classes gained. Both major political parties in Jamaica—the People's National Party (PNP) and the Jamaica Labour Party (JLP)—are in a sense labor parties. Each is linked to a particular trade union, and although each has middle and upper class supporters, both must depend upon the lower socio-economic groups for the bulk of their support at the polls. Increasingly committed to economic and social development, the new Jamaican popular government has taken an increasingly larger part in economic and social life. Thus, whatever decline in the total power of the elected political leaders may be indicated by the confinement of their authority to purely governmental and political roles may be somewhat offset by the increase in the authority of such roles themselves over certain aspects of the Jamaican economy and society.

Contrary to the general trend is the change in appointees. The dual occupancy of governmental and non-governmental roles increased among them from 63 to 83 per cent from 1939 to 1954. Thus, while constitutional changes reduced the formal responsibilities and authority of the role of the appointees, the occupants of these roles in fact were more likely to be persons who had a wide range of influence due to interlocking elite positions in governmental and other institutional sectors. In other words, the established economic and social elites grasped more firmly the diminishing powers of the nominated positions.

Returning to Table 1, fewer of the 1954 elites had only an elementary school education than the 1939 elites, and more of them had a secondary school education. However, there was little difference between the two groups with respect to the percentage who had university education. The elected political leaders were the least educated of all the top governmental elites both in 1939 and 1954 (from Table 2). Also, unlike both the appointees and the higher civil servants, they had a larger percentage of their number who had received no more than an elementary school education in 1954 than in 1939. Since educational levels are rising generally in Jamaica, one cannot expect this particular change to reflect a trend. Also, many educated persons were somewhat reluctant to risk their positions in society by standing for elected office before a generally black, lower-class, and poorly-educated electorate—especially in the years of limited self-government when the element of tutelage still restricted to some extent both the authority and prestige of elected positions, and when many members of the highly educated groups were still suspicious and uncertain about domination by what they thought of as "mob-rule." With full self-government and complete independence and with the chance of becoming an honorable member of the recently created Cabinet, elected political office should be somewhat more enticing to members of the educated groups.[30]

Even though the elected political leaders, with 36 per cent of their number

[30] Also, membership in the two major parties had become more acceptable to many educated people since at this time the PNP had deemphasized its early socialism and since the demogogic rule of the charismatic leader of the JLP had given ground to a more bureaucratic and democratic party organization. See C. Paul Bradley, "Mass Parties in Jamaica: Structure and Organization," *Social and Economic Studies*, Vol. 9. (December, 1960), pp. 375–416.

having no more than an elementary school education in 1954, were more like the general population than they were in 1939, and even though they were more like the general population than either the appointees or the higher civil servants with respect to education, they were still considerably better educated than the average person in Jamaica. In 1943, 95 per cent of the Jamaican population over age 25 had received no more than an elementary school education, and in 1960 the Provisional figure was 92.5 per cent.[31]

The higher civil servants were more highly educated in 1954 than in 1939, and they were more highly educated on the average than the elected political leaders at both times, especially in 1954. After the ministerial system was introduced in 1953, this fact (and correlated differences in outlook and behavior) apparently resulted in friction between some members of the two types of elites in their day-to-day working relationships, the higher civil servants sometimes chafing under the rule of a less-educated politician and a politician in turn sometimes overly asserting himself in an effort to validate himself in his new role as head of a ministry. Of this problem, one informant told me the following:

"The political leader is looked upon as a real leader of the country. At public functions he is the top man. He has dominated the scene from a power point of view in the public mind. At the same time, the civil servants in the governmental bureaucracy in some senses have become the real rulers and they have assumed too much importance in the actual making of policy. Take a politician who has power that derives from the formal position that he occupies, but he is surrounded by high powered civil servants who have benefited from higher education, special courses of various kinds, etc. This government has, by the way, done a great deal, has invested a great deal, in giving civil servants and others the opportunity to receive high powered technical training. The politician represents the will of the people since he was elected by them. And yet, the high powered technical advice he gets tends somehow to submerge the will of the people. As you know, high powered technical people can do great damage in the policy-making process. Policies may have no relation to the ordinary conditions of the life of people of the country if the technical people play too much of a role in either formulating a policy or in a non-supervised implementation of it . . . Sometimes a Minister is so intimidated by his civil servants, by what he assumes is their superior technical skill and higher education, that he may seek refuge in Cabinet to turn down his own recommendation. That is, he was afraid to tell his civil servants that he didn't want to recommend something because he couldn't think of the definitive reasons for his action. But he could go back to the civil servants in his ministry and say that Cabinet had turned it down and that was that."

Of course, as the same informant pointed out later in the interview, the civil servants have legitimate complaints too. What appear to be correct policies

[31] *Eighth Census of Jamaica and its Dependencies, 1943, op. cit.*, Table 70, p. 127; and *West Indies Population Census, 1960* (provisional), Bulletin No. 20 (Jamaica), Kingston, Jamaica: Department of Statistics, 1962, Table 6, p. 70, and Table 7, p. 86.

to them in terms of the economic and social development of Jamaica are sometimes not adopted by the politicians for "political reasons," that is because the politicians must be concerned with the public reaction to their policy. Perhaps this would be acceptable if the "public reaction" involved were the responses of the general public, but it is often some special group, especially some articulate and already favored minority.

This conflict between politicians and civil servants, however, should not be overemphasized, and few other new nations are in as enviable a position as Jamaica. One of the distinctive features of Jamaica's transition to independence has been early and sustained efforts to develop a governmental bureaucracy containing an increasing number of qualified Jamaicans at all levels. A competent and experienced bureaucracy composed of Jamaicans gives Jamaica considerable advantage over some of the other new nations in achieving stability and effectiveness in efforts to attain the national goals of a newly independent country. England has been, perhaps, the most enlightened of the colonial powers during the dismantlement of its empire, and Jamaica may be the best example of adequate preparation for independence among the former British colonies, although the Colonial Office bungling which led to the collapse of the West Indies Federation has had deleterious consequences for the smaller islands.

As expected, the appointees were the most highly educated type of governmental elites at both time periods, although the higher civil servants were almost as well educated on the average in 1954. Although the percentage of appointees having no more than an elementary school education decreased from 1939 to 1954, so did the percentage having a university education.

One might expect the governmental elites to be more upwardly mobile in 1954 than in 1939, since the constitutional changes opened up new routes to power and influence, and included the participation of the lower socioeconomic classes in the political process. However, no such trend is apparent from Table 1. Both in 1939 and in 1954, the elites were highly mobile with respect to upward occupational mobility, 70 and 71 per cent respectively were upwardly mobile.[32]

However, the percentages for upward mobility in Table 1 are averages of

---

[32] An intergenerational measure was used, if possible, which was based upon the relationship between an elite's occupation and his father's occupation. If the father's occupation was not given, a measure of career mobility was used based upon the relationship between an elite's first reported job and his present job. Where possible, both measures were examined in order to increase the validity of the measure. The occupational rating scale used was a modified version of that given in W. Lloyd Warner, Marchia Meeks, and Kenneth Eels, *Social Class in America*, Chicago: Science Research Associates, Inc., 1949, pp. 140–141; and in Carson McGuire, "Social Status, Peer Status, and Social Mobility," a mimeographed memorandum for research workers, Committee on Human Development, University of Chicago, Chicago, Ill., 1948.

differential changes for the different types of elite groups. As one would expect, the elected political elites were more upwardly mobile in 1954 than in 1939, and they were the most upwardly mobile of the three types of elites (from Table 2). The higher civil servants had about the same rate of upward mobility at both times. However, the appointees were the least upwardly mobile group both in 1939 and 1954, and contrary to the change for elected political leaders, they were considerably less likely to be upwardly mobile in 1954 than in 1939. Considering the fact that these persons are elites, one can assume that about 65 per cent of the appointees (the non-mobile persons) had elite backgrounds.

Thus, while the predominantly black lower-classes were obtaining representation through their elected leaders and the elected political positions were becoming somewhat more accessible to the "average Jamaican," the predominantly light or white persons representing the established interests were increasing their hold over the nominated positions. This is consistent with the findings concerning joint occupancy of governmental and non-governmental positions discussed earlier. However, since 1954, changes increasing the participation of the leaders of the political parties, while decreasing the discretion of the Governor in making nominations to these offices, have resulted in a decrease in the exclusiveness of this group. In the new constitution for an independent Jamaica, the Legislative Council is replaced by a Senate, all members of which will be political appointees. Thus, the appointees can be expected increasingly to approximate the social characteristics of the elected political elites, although differential campaign contributions and other favors to the political parties and the differential distribution of skills by social classes may still result in the representation of some members of the highest socio-economic groups among the appointees.

In Table 1, note that the 1954 elites were slightly younger than the 1939 elites, 34 and 40 per cent respectively being 55 or older. However, none of the types of elites actually changed in age even as much as six per cent. Rather, this average reduction of six per cent was due to changes in the differential proportions each type of elite represented at the two times. That is, at both time periods the elected political leaders and the higher civil servants were much younger on the average than the appointees (see Table 2), and there were relatively more of them compared to the appointees in 1954 than in 1939. In fact, none of the three types of elites changed much in the percentage of those 55 or over. The appointees were exactly the same, with 63 per cent.

The appointees were much older than the average adult in Jamaican society, but the elected political leaders and higher civil servants were much nearer in age to the general population. Of all Jamaicans age 25 and over, 20 per cent were age 55 and over in 1943. In 1960 the percentage was 23 per cent.[33]

COMPARISON OF DIFFERENT TYPES OF ELITES, 1958

A more complete description and analysis of the social composition of Jamaican elites requires a more inclusive definition of elites than that so far employed. Persons occupying the "command posts" in institutions other than government need to be considered. Leaders in business, religion, education, law, medicine, and other institutional sectors also exert influence on public affairs in Jamaica and perform a variety of elite functions. Additionally, the transition to independence continued beyond 1954, with the introduction of more self-government and less tutelage in 1956 and again in 1957. By the summer of 1958, Jamaica had nearly achieved full internal self-government.

A sample of all Jamaican elites was selected and their social characteristics determined by reference to *Who's Who, Jamaica*. A description of this sample is given in Appendix I. These characteristics are given by type of elite position in Table 3. The categories of "elected political leaders," "appointees," and "civil servants" are not strictly comparable to those same categories in Tables 1 and 2, but are somewhat more inclusive. Elected members of the then-new Federal Parliament, mayors and some parish councilors were added to the elected political leaders. Also, the then-newly-appointed Senators to the federal government were included among the appointees. And the civil servants in Table 3, although excluding judges, doctors, and teachers who are categorized separately, include some fairly low ranks in the civil service, in addition to the higher civil servants considered earlier. Thus, one must be cautious about attributing trends to these data in comparison with the 1939 and 1954 top governmental elites. However, by logical elimination of alternatives, one will note that most trends noted earlier are borne out by the 1958 data.

Since many elites hold more than one elite position simultaneously, it would be possible to categorize them more than once in Table 3. However, a given individual has been classified only once, as before. Arbitrarily, governmental elites who held other elite positions were classified only by their governmental positions. That is, governmental positions were given priority over other types of elite positions, the only exceptions being among civil

---

[33]*Eighth Census of Jamaica and its Dependencies, 1943, op. cit.*, Table 21, p. 22; and *West Indies Population Census, 1960*, Bulletin No. 18, Table 1, p. 1. For a more detailed discussion of the data given in Tables 1 and 2, see Emily Roberta Smith (Reed), "Self-Government and the Political Elite in Jamaica, 1939 and 1954," unpublished M.A. thesis, Northwestern University, Evanston, Ill., 1957.

Table 3. PERCENTAGE OF JAMAICAN ELITES HAVING SELECTED SOCIAL CHARACTERISTICS BY TYPE OF ELITE POSITION, 1958

Selected Social Characteristic	Elected Political Leaders (N = 52)*	Appointees (N = 34)*	Civil Servants (N = 185)*	Economic Elites (N = 269)*	Religious Leaders (N = 33)	Educational Leaders (N = 35)	Judges (N = 9)	Medical Elites (N = 71)	Barristers and Solicitors (N = 36)	Social Welfare Elites (N = 7)
Per cent Jamaican-born	98	91	82	69	28	71	63	76	94	43
Per cent residing in metropolitan Kingston-St. Andrew	23	47	87	66	64	63	78	75	81	71
Per cent with highest occupational rating	94	100	45	73	94	29	100	93	100	57
Per cent upwardly mobile	83	31	79	62	57	51	56	35	52	57
Per cent male	100	94	96	96	100	66	100	87	97	43
Median age in years	50	61	46	49	50	48	53	46	46	50
Per cent Anglican	38	73	58	47	25	55	57	53	57	29
Per cent Protestant	49	19	30	23	44	34	29	25	17	72
Per cent Roman Catholic	9	8	9	20	28	3	14	18	13	0
Per cent Jewish	0	0	1	8	3	0	0	2	3	0
Per cent atheist, agnostic, or independent	4	0	2	1	0	7	0	3	3	0
Per cent elementary education or less	27	0	2	13	0	0	0	0	0	0
Per cent secondary school education	42	61	52	64	6	31	22	0	58	43
Per cent some university or more	31	39	47	23	94	69	78	100	42	57
‡Of those with some university or more† the percentage whose university was located in:										
Jamaica	7	0	4	0	3	4	0	3	0	0
British Isles	53	92	69	40	53	78	86	59	93	75
Canada	0	0	12	23	3	13	14	11	0	0
United States	40	8	11	30	40	4	0	20	0	25

Source: *Who's Who, Jamaica,* 1957.

* Except where indicated (‡), the approximate number of cases on which the percentages are based is given in parentheses.
† Does not always add up to 100 per cent, because of a few elites educated in countries other than those shown.

servants who were professionals. For non-governmental elites, an attempt to determine their major activity was made.

Country of birth. There was a wide range of differences between the various types of elites with respect to country of birth in 1958. Nearly three-fourths of the religious leaders were foreign-born. They continued in the tradition of the missionaries of the nineteenth century, who did much to spread humanitarian values in Jamaica, and throughout the world. Their relative role in Jamaica today has been greatly reduced in many ways, and is far less militant compared to the role that their predecessors played in spreading ideas of equality and freedom. They have been in part displaced by change-leading, national elites, especially elected political leaders and higher civil servants who man the policy-making and administrative positions of a growing welfare state. Also, they have had to make room for a growing number of other professionals and voluntary workers who are promoting economic and social development through secular organizations.

Social welfare elites (workers and administrators) were more likely to be Jamaican-born than religious leaders, but over half were still foreign-born in 1958. The foreign-born originated from technologically more advances societies—in this case primarily from England and the United States.

Sixty-three per cent of the judges were born in Jamaica, and fully 94 per cent of the barristers and solicitors were. Of course, the foreign-born among the judges were mainly English. Related to this is the fact that one of the highest percentages of foreign-born among any type of civil servant was among the higher officers of the police. Also, in 1958 there were only a few top military officers in Jamaica, but expatriates controlled the top ranks with minor exceptions. Of course, the position of the military reflects the constitutional situation at the time which still left the defense of Jamaica to the former imperial power. However, the interpretation of the law and especially the legal use of force within Jamaica was more controlled by expatriates than might have been expected considering the constitutional developments. This reflects in part a preoccupation of the established economic and social elites with the problems of order as self-government increased and complete independence came nearer. They considered the black lower-classes increasingly to be a threat to order as the British withdrew and the Jamaican government, with more limited resources for controlling civil disorder and with fewer commitments to the old established elites, took over. With independence, a new commanding officer, born in the Bahamas, but identified as a "local" has been appointed to the new Jamaica Regiment.

Almost a third of the Jamaican economic elites, including commercial, agricultural, and others, are foreign-born. This seems relatively high, but may be accounted for in part by a colonial attitude toward commerce. For example, Broom says:[34]

"It is ironic that British colonialism, which historically has been so heavily influenced by commercial interests, should have implanted a disdain of commerce among many colonial peoples. This may be in part because a colonial may seek recognition in two places, in the colony and in the metropolitan 'home.' The dual striving is apparently achieved without conflict of ends most readily in the public service and, of course, some immediate status is acquired by the very identification with official functions."

However, it may be less ironic in this way than Broom thinks. Like so many things in Jamaica today that are identified as being colonially-induced backwardness and debilities, "a disdain of commerce" may be not so much a result of colonialism *per se* but more a British trait, a transplanted English tradition. As David Granick has recently pointed out, businessmen in England, in contrast to those in other European countries and the United States, are regarded more or less as second-string civil servants.[35]

However, the nature of enterprise in Jamaica, the problems of capital formation and investment, and the scope of economic development, have each contributed to maintaining, in some instances increasing, expatriates among the economic elites.

Education and health are two important areas in which expansion is necessary to bring about change in Jamaica as directed by the emergent national elites, thus an increasing need for skills in these areas has developed since 1944. It is not surprising, then, to find that Jamaicans constitute only about three-fourths of the educational and medical elites. For example, the founding of the University College of the West Indies (now University of the West Indies) in Jamaica in 1948 and the development of the medical school and a university hospital have contributed to the number of (non-West Indian) expatriates among these elites. However, at the rate Jamaicans and other West Indians are being trained in these areas, the relative number of expatriates will probably be reduced within a decade even though educational and health facilities will continue to expand.[36]

---

[34] Leonard Broom, *op. cit.*, p. 125.

[35] David Granick, *The European Executive.* New York: Doubleday, 1962.

[36] Since the University of the West Indies (U.W.I.) has been a cooperative service including not only Jamaica but each of the former territories of the West Indies Federation and British Guiana and British Honduras as well, "West Indianization" rather than "Jamaicanization" gives the appropriate frame of reference in this example. As of 1957, only 38 per cent of the entire University staff and even less, 26 per cent, of the University teaching staff were West Indians. Only in the non-teaching, administrative roles did West Indians outnumber non-West Indians where the former occupied 71 per cent of the positions, according to a mimeographed University report.

The rank order of the governmental elites with respect to Jamaican birth, as shown in Table 3, is the same as shown earlier for the top governmental elites in 1954. However, in each case the percentage for 1958 is even larger than that for 1954. This may show a continuation of the trend for the reduction of foreign-born persons among these groups, but the categories for 1958, as earlier stated, are defined somewhat differently than in 1954. However, it is interesting to note that the elected political leaders in 1958 were nearly as likely to be Jamaican-born, with 98 per cent so classified, as was the general population of Jamaica, 98.6 per cent of whom were Jamaican-born in 1960.

Metropolitan residence. The percentages of different types of elites residing in the metropolitan Kingston-St. Andrew area serve to illustrate the concentration of elite functions in Jamaica's major city. About half or more of the different types of elites, with the exception of the elected political leaders, live in the metropolitan area. These percentages range from 47 per cent for appointees to 87 per cent for civil servants, and compare with about 24 per cent of the general population of Jamaica who live in the Kingston-St. Andrew metropolitan area as of 1960. Only the elected political leaders, with 23 per cent residing in the urban area, approximate the distribution of the general population. Mayors and chairmen of the parish councils, of course, were located in the areas in which they held office. Also, members of the House of Representatives (MHR's) had to stand for election in the constituencies into which Jamaica was divided geographically, and their official residences were generally retained in them.[37] However, the House meets in Kingston and the MHR's spend a considerable amount of their time in the city. A few MHR's listed two addresses in *Who's Who*, one in the parish in which their constituency is located and one in the Kingston-St. Andrew metropolitan area.

Occupational rating and mobility. The occupational ratings of the different types of elites are shown in Table 3. The rating scale used is the same as that used earlier. The largest percentages having the highest occupational ratings are appointees, judges, barristers and solicitors. Each of these groups have 100 per cent of their members in the highest occupational rank. Next are elected political leaders (94 per cent), religious leaders (94 per cent), and medical elites (93 per cent). Seventy-three per cent of the economic elites are in the highest occupational rank, followed by the social welfare elites with 57 per cent. Then come the civil servants with 45 per cent in the highest occupational ranks. Finally, the educational leaders have the fewest in the highest occupational rank with only 29 per cent so classified.

[37] A summary of the qualifications of MHR's in *The Handbook of Jamaica for 1958* (p. 40) says that an MHR had to reside in the parish which contained the constituency in which he stood for election; however, the relevant clause in the constitution (p. 60 of *The Handbook*) states only

With respect to upward mobility, the most mobile group were the elected political leaders, 83 per cent of whom were upwardly mobile. They are closely followed, however, by the civil servants 79 per cent of whom were upwardly mobile. Thus, although over half of the civil servants were not of the highest occupational rank, they are a group with one of the highest rates of upward occupational mobility. Appointees are the least likely of any elite group to be upwardly mobile with only 31 per cent so classified. This lends support to the discussion of the findings reported earlier for the 1954 top governmental elites, and shows further that elected political office and the civil service comprised new routes of access to the achievement of higher socio-economic positions for Jamaicans of relatively humble socio-economic origins, while the *ex officio* and nominated positions tended to go increasingly, until 1958, to the already entrenched higher socio-economic classes.

With the exception of the appointees and medical elites, each of the other types of elites have over 50 per cent of their number who are upwardly mobile. This shows little about new channels of upward mobility for Jamaicans in the case of religious leaders, since so few religious leaders are Jamaican-born. But it shows that the upper classes, although greatly over-represented, do not have a monopoly over the high positions in the economy, education, the judiciary, law, and social welfare.

Sex. With the exception of two types of elite groups, 87 to 100 per cent of each type of elite is composed of men (see Table 3). The dominance of men over the important roles in public affairs and business is so well known as to require little further comment here.[38] The two exceptions are educational leaders 66 per cent of whom are men, and social welfare elites, 43 per cent of whom are men.

Age. Supporting the conclusions for the 1954 elites given earlier, the appointees are older on the average than either the elected political leaders or the civil servants. Also, they are older than any other elite group, their median age being 61. The youngest groups are the civil servants, medical elites, and barristers and solicitors who have median ages of 46. The other groups are as follows: educational leaders, 48; economic elites, 49; elected political leaders, religious leaders, and social welfare elites, 50; and judges, 53.

Religion. In 1960, 19.8 per cent of the general population of Jamaica were Anglicans. Yet among the different types of elites, the percentage of Anglicans was much larger (see Table 3). Seventy-three per cent of the appointees were

that residence in the island of Jamaica is necessary.

[38] For example, see Wendell Bell, Richard J. Hill, and Charles R. Wright, *Public Leadership*, San Francisco: Chandler Publishing Co., 1961, Chapter Three. "Male Dominance in Public Leadership," pp. 34–55.

Anglican, another reflection of the high social status and the centrality to the "established interests" in Jamaica of this type of elite at this time. The percentage of Anglicans in other groups is: civil servants, 58; judges and barristers and solicitors, 57; educational leaders, 55; medical elites, 53; economic elites, 47; and elected political leaders, 38. Closer to the general population are social welfare elites of whom 29 per cent are Anglican and religious leaders themselves, of whom 25 per cent are Anglican.

Roman Catholics are a larger proportion (28 per cent) of the religious leaders than they are of any other elite group. In descending order, according to the proportion of Catholics, are the economic elites (20 per cent), medical elites (18 per cent), judges (14 per cent), barristers and solicitors (13 per cent), elected political leaders and civil servants (9 per cent each), appointed officials (8 per cent), educational leaders (3 per cent), and social welfare elites (none). With the exception of educational and social welfare elites all of the elites contain a larger proportion of Catholics than would be expected by chance alone since only 7.2 per cent of the general population of Jamaica is Catholic.[39] One reason for this is that the Catholic Church has offered secondary school educational opportunities which have been a route to the attainment of elite positions for some persons.

Jews, who are only about 0.04 per cent of the general population, are most overrepresented among the economic elites of whom they constitute 8 per cent. They are also overrepresented among barristers and solicitors and religious leaders themselves (3 per cent). Although they constitute only 2 per cent of the medical elites and 1 per cent of the civil servants, the Jews are somewhat overrepresented among these groups as well.[40]

Educational leaders have the largest percentage, 7.0, of atheists, agnostics, and independents, followed by elected political leaders, 4 per cent, medical elites and barristers and solicitors, 3 per cent each, and civil servants, 2 per cent. However, atheists, agnostics, and independents are underrepresented even among these elites, since they constitute 11.4 per cent of the general population.

[39] *West Indies Population Census, 1960*, Bulletin No. 14, Table 4, p. 27.

[40] There appears to be a discrepancy between the data given here showing the percentage of lawyers who are Jewish in 1958 as 3 per cent and data given by Broom for 1951 which shows 7.1 per cent of the lawyers as being Jews. It is likely that the apparent discrepancy is accounted for in part by the differences in the methods used to sample the lawyers at the two time periods. For 1951, Broom selected a sample from all barristers and solicitors in residence and in practice, listed in the Handbook of Jamaica, and then used informants to determine ethnicity. For 1958, I tried to select only those barristers and solicitors who were among the more powerful or prominent ones, and used *Who's Who* information to determine religion. Also, another difference is that I classified them by their major activity. Thus, some solicitors were not classified as solicitors but as economic elites since their major activity was in the economic sphere. In my data, Jews are overrepresented among people who are qualified solicitors whose major activity is

There are some types of religions adhered to by members of the general population of Jamaica which are not present among the elites shown in Table 3 to any extent, if at all. Some of these are Hindu, Moravian, Pocomanian, and Ras Tafari brethren, among others.

Education. As can be seen from Table 3, by 1958 the elected political leaders were still less educated than the appointees and the civil servants, but they were more educated than they had been in 1954. Comparison of this variable between 1958 and 1954 can lead to a reliable conclusion since the 1958 group, being more inclusive of the lower rungs of the various hierarchies in the cases of elected political leaders and civil servants, should show a lesser educated group than the 1954 group unless there had been some real changes toward higher education. Also, the civil servants appear to be better educated in 1958 than they were in 1954; and in 1958 they were more likely to have attended a university than were the appointees.

The different types of elites ranked with respect to percentages, who have had some university education (from high to low), are: medical elites, religious leaders, judges, educational leaders, social welfare elites, civil servants, barristers and solicitors, appointees, elected political leaders and economic elites. However, the elected political leaders were the least educated group when the entire educational distribution is considered, having 27 per cent who had no more than an elementary education. Thus, the politicians were most like the general Jamaican public in this regard.

Table 3 also shows the percentage of persons with at least some university education who received their university training in a given country. The dependence of Jamaica for higher education on external areas is clearly seen in the very small percentages of persons who had received university training in Jamaica. Of course, the University College of the West Indies had just begun ten years before, so its effects in providing trained elites had not yet really begun to be felt. Britain is the place where many Jamaican elites received their higher educations. Three-fourths or more of the barristers and solicitors, appointees, judges, and social welfare elites went to universities in the United Kingdom. However, of those who attended a university, 40 per cent of the elected political leaders did so in the United States; and 53 per cent of the economic elites, 31 per cent of the medical elites, and 23 per cent of the civil servants did so in Canada and the United States combined. With the predominance of imported English laws in Jamaica, barristers, solicitors, and judges will probably continue to be educated in Britain for some time, but for the other types of elites it is safe to predict a considerable decrease in the proportions attending universities in Britain. Not only the University of the West Indies, but also American universities

not practicing law but engaging in commercial activities. *Cf.* Broom, *op. cit.*, p. 124.

will make inroads. In the case of UWI, the reasons are obvious; and in the case of American universities, they are closer, the education they offer is increasingly recognized as being more practical and useful, given the needs of a developing nation, and an increase in educational grants from sources in the United States seems likely now that Jamaica is independent.

One of the more interesting and important developments in future years will be the impact of the University of the West Indies. Aside from the obvious academic implications and the advantages of having classroom examples and illustrations selected for a West Indian student body with greater emphasis on West Indian events and conditions by West Indian instructors, there are other consequences. What will be the effects of UWI in instilling general attitudes toward government and the political system, toward Jamaica, Trinidad, and other new nations in Africa and elsewhere, toward the world situation, toward alternative modes of political organization, etc.? The intellectual climate of Jamaica—and the West Indies generally—may change as more and more of the future elites are trained at UWI and as Jamaican and other West Indian intellectuals become a larger, more locally trained and less European-oriented group.[41]

It is difficult to overemphasize the importance of the growth of a West Indianizing West Indian university. In addition to the obvious skills that it can impart, it can contribute importantly to the resolution of certain ambivalences and dilemmas which are characteristic of many Jamaican and other West Indian intellectuals. For example, among UWI students today there is considerable effort, deliberate and self-conscious and often quite sophisticated, to achieve intellectual freedom. However, this may be more difficult to attain than political independence. Despite the emergence of Jamaican and West Indian cultural forms and unities, the West Indies represent a particular cultural hybrid which has developed under the cultural hegemony of England. England—the great power—hangs over intellectual life like a spectre. As Scott Greer has said,[42] Jamaica is "... not only itself, it's a shadow of England, but not England, the Empire, but not the Empire—high noon, Victorian time." When searching for their own identity, West Indian intellectuals often appear to be a mixed bag of contradictions, all neatly internalized to maximize agonizing self-recriminations. Alternately, they denounce England, defend England, and pounce on each other with accusations of having a "colonial mentality." They write poems, stories, and plays celebrating Jamaica's awakening and nationhood, but at the same time give

---

[41] James T. Duke has completed a study of students at UWI, "Equalitarianism Among Emergent Elites in a New Nation," unpublished Ph.D. dissertation, University of California, Los Angeles, 1963.

[42] Personal communication.

voice to words which are reminiscent of England's modern "angry young men" and which are more appropriate to the sorrows of a declining nation with a golden past than to the joys of a former colony facing a new and better future. Some are finding intellectual freedom, but some still turn to England, denying part of themselves and aspiring to be a shadowy substance of what they never could have been, never can be, and to what few Englishmen are anymore. The University of the West Indies can help to create new alternatives, Jamaican and West Indian models.

ELITES AND INFLUENCE, 1958

Objective indicators of scope of influence. Table 4 shows the percentage of the different types of Jamaican elites having certain amounts of influence in addition to their major elite positions. Two objective indicators of the scope of influence were used. The first is the percentage who occupy elite positions in three or more different institutional sectors simultaneously, the interpretation of which was discussed earlier. According to this indicator, the different types of elites rank as follows with respect to the scope of their total influence from highest to lowest: appointees, elected political leaders, barristers and solicitors, economic elites, medical elites, educational leaders, civil servants, and finally religious leaders, judges, and social welfare elites, who were tied for last place.

Note that the rank order of the three types of governmental elites is the same as that given for 1954, the appointees having the most, and the civil servants the least scope of influence. In addition to the appointees and elected political leaders, only the barristers and solicitors and the economic elites had more than one-fifth of their numbers with wide influence according to this indicator.

The second objective indicator is membership and office-holding in formal associations (excluding business concerns and government and including mostly voluntary associations ranging from social and recreational clubs to professional organizations).[43] The three indicators used (membership in at least one association, holding at least one office in an association, and membership in six or more associations) were averaged in order to construct an index of participation in the organizational membership structure. Such an index shows the relative access to organizational networks of influence and communication, and are taken as a further indication of the scope of a leader's influence.

From most to least influence, as measured by participation in the organiza-

[43] For a discussion of the social participation approach to the study of influence see Bell, Hill and Wright, *op. cit.*

Table 4. PERCENTAGE OF JAMAICAN ELITES HAVING CERTAIN AMOUNTS OF INFLUENCE BY TYPE OF ELITE POSITION, 1958.

Objective Indicators of Scope of Influence	Type of Elite Position									
	Elected Political Leaders (52)*	Appointees (34)	Civil Servants (185)	Economic Elites (269)	Religious Leaders (33)	Educational Leaders (35)	Judges (9)	Medical Elites (71)	Barristers and Solicitors (36)	Social Welfare Elites (7)
% with three or more elite positions	37	56	1	22	0	3	0	10	25	0
Average % based on formal association indicators which are given below:	51	73	31	35	33	42	19	26	41	48
% with at least one membership in formal associations	87	94	69	71	61	77	56	65	81	100
% who hold at least one office	46	71	19	20	24	40	0	10	22	29
% with membership in six or more formal associations	19	53	6	13	15	9	0	3	19	14

*The approximate number of cases on which the percentages are based is given in parentheses.

tional membership structure, were the following types of elites: appointees, elected political leaders, social welfare elites, educational leaders, barristers and solicitors, economic elites, religious leaders, civil servants, medical elites, and judges. The rank order is fairly similar to that given for simultaneous occupancy of three or more different elite positions with appointees heading the list, followed by elected political leaders. Civil servants ranked considerably below the politicians, thus the governmental elites retained their relative rankings as shown earlier. However, social welfare elites and educational leaders rank much higher by the formal association indicator than they do by the indicator of simultaneous occupancy of elite positions in different institutional structures.

The nominations to appointive office in part have shown the accomodation of the new representative government to the economic and social elites of Jamaica by giving them a voice in government which most of them could not have obtained by running for elective office. Also, a position in the top circles of influence in Jamaica, while not a pre-condition to appointment, was certainly a consideration of importance in the selection of appointees. However, judging from the appointments made in 1958, political considerations and the racial characteristics of members of the Legislative Council were also taken into account. Three appointments made at that time included an influential man of high reputation[44] from the economic-commercial sector who was ethnically identified as a Syrian, a second-echelon reputational influential man from the economic-commercial sector who was ethnically identified as being light to medium brown, and a retired educator and civil servant who was not among the reputational influentials at all (although he occupied several elite positions simultaneously and belonged to several formal associations) who was ethnically identified as dark brown or black. Appointments made since 1958 further show the increasing importance of political considerations in these appointments.

It was reported earlier that the elected political leaders had their power increasingly confined to the governmental structure from 1939 to 1954. Yet in 1958 they still rank higher by two objective measures of scope of influence than any other elite except for appointees. By 1958 the participation of the elected political leaders in the organizational membership structure and to some extent their interlocking occupancy of elite positions in different institutional structures had increased and was more the result of their governmental position than a cause of it—to the extent to which these can be unentwined in this context. That is, the elected political elites were in part being coopted by the pre-existing and established social and economic

[44] See the discussion of the methodology used to identify reputational influentials which is given in Appendix II.

elites. This should not be overemphasized in that it has been a two-way flow of communication and influence—the old established elites recognizing the new power of the elected political leaders by including them in some of their associations, both formal and informal, and being subsequently affected by their membership. In turn, the elected political leaders have become somewhat circumscribed in new and unanticipated ways by their new associations. For example, a few social and recreational clubs had a near monopoly on the validation of certain kinds of prestige. Accommodating to the shifts in political power, they have included a few elected political leaders who would not have been acceptable before their rise to political power. This accommodation constitutes a change in the system of social stratification by altering the criteria of differential evaluation—by reducing the relative importance of family background and other ascriptive variables while increasing the relative importance of achieved characteristics. Also, some control over the new additions to the power elite—the politicians—may be exerted in return for this conferral of prestige. The elected political leaders are far from fully coopted, but there is some indication that some to a certain degree have been. Cooptation of the new political leaders contributes to social stability in that it reduces cleavages and antagonisms, while promoting cooperation, between different types of elites. But it produces potential instability to the extent to which it leaves inarticulate or unattended the discontents of the lower-classes.

Institutional sectors and reputational influence. During the late spring and summer of 1958, the basic sample of 803 Jamaican elites, whose selection has been described in Appendix I, were sent mail questionnaires. (See Appendix II.) One of the questions asked was as follows:

Considering all aspects of Jamaican life, who would you say are the most influential *individuals* on the entire island? That is, who are the people who can really get things done and who are really most important in influencing major economic and political decisions which affect all of Jamaica? In each case, does the person usually stay behind the scenes or is he in the forefront of affairs?
(Please list 10 individuals in order of their importance)

One hundred-twenty-five persons were nominated as being among the top ten influentials of Jamaica. However, 41 of them were nominated by only one respondent each and 12 of them were nominated by only two respondents each. These were removed from the analysis and the remainder of 72—persons nominated by three or more respondents—are shown in Table 5 according to various social characteristics.[45]

[45] The validity of this list of top influentials was tested by going over the list with a few key informants who were themselves among the top 72 influentials. With two or three exceptions, there was general agreement that this list was an accurate ranking. Also, during

Table 5. SELECTED CHARACTERISTICS FOR EACH REPUTATIONAL LEADER WHO WAS NOMINATED FOR INCLUSION AMONG THE 10 MOST INFLUENTIAL PERSONS IN JAMAICA, 1958*

No. of Times Nominated	Rank Order	Institutional Sector of Major Elite Position	No. of Elite Positions	No. of Memberships in Formal Associations	Percentage of Nominations Reputed to Work Behind the Scenes
194	1	Majority Party*	2	5	2
150	2	Minority Party	3	6	2
132	3	Economic – commerce†	7	8	42
122	4	Majority party	2	9	19
117	5	Economic – agriculture†	3	8	29
107	6	Majority party	1	0	1
73	7	Economic – commerce (federal Senator)	7	11	42
59	8	Economic – agriculture†	4	7	18
57	9	Majority party	1	1	4
48	10	Economic – agriculture	7	0	64
45	11	Economic – commerce	7	5	91
41	12	Religion†	2	0	48
31	13.5	Economic – commerce	7	0	77
31	13.5	Economic – commerce†	7	6	36
30	16	Economic – commerce	7	5	85
30	16	Economic – commerce	2	8	89
30	16	Economic – commerce	5	3	86
28	18	Education†	2	2	57
26	19.5	Minority party	2	1	5
26	19.5	H.E., The Governor	1	12	58
25	21.5	Economic – agriculture	3	10	57
25	21.5	Mass media	1	2	48
24	23	Labor	1	6	13
21	24	Economic – commerce†	6	10	53
20	25	Religion	1	2	75
19	26.5	Professions†	2	12	67
19	26.5	Civil Service	2	0	88
18	28	Majority party	2	7	27
17	29	Economic – commerce	7	8	93
16	30	Civil service	1	2	100
12	31.5	Minority party (federal elected pol. leader)	3	2	27
12	31.5	Minority party	2	6	8
11	34	Economic – commerce (Privy Council)	7	2	100
11	34	Economic – agriculture (Custos)	4	3	73
11	34	Majority party	1	7	10
10	36.5	Economic – agriculture	5	2	100
10	36.5	Minority party	3	3	38
8	38	Arts	1	1	100
7	42	Economic – commerce	7	8	100
7	42	Economic – commerce	4	9	83

Table 5—*continued*

No. of Times Nominated	Rank Order	Institutional Sector of Major Elite Position	No. of Elite Positions	No. of Membership in Formal Associations	Percentage of Nominations Reputed to Work Behind the Scenes
7	42	Minority party (party officer)	2	0	33
7	42	Economic – commerce	2	8	43
7.	42	Majority party	2	1	0
7	42	Religion	1	1	83
7	42	Religion	1	2	86
6	48.5	Economic – commerce	2	7	100
6	48.5	Social welfare†	1	1	67
6	48.5	Economic – commerce	7	10	75
6	48.5	Minority party (party officer)	1	6	17
6	48.5	Economic – commerce†	2	8	75
6	48.5	Economic – agriculture	2	6	60
5	53	Civil Service	2	1	80
5	53	Mass media	2	5	0
5	53	Education	1	6	100
4	56.5	Majority party (party officer)	2	3	100
4	56.5	Majority party (party officer)	1	3	100
4	56.5	Social welfare†	1	7	25
4	56.5	Majority party (mayor)	‡	‡	67
3	65.5	Majority party (party officer)	2	1	100
3	65.5	Economic – agriculture	3	1	67
3	65.5	Economic – agriculture	3	10	33
3	65.5	Majority party (party officer)	1	1	100
3	65.5	Professions†	2	9	50
3	65.5	Economic – commerce	7	5	100
3	65.5	Economic – agriculture	7	9	50
3	65.5	Professions†	2	12	50
3	65.5	Majority party	1	1	0
3	65.5	Economic – agriculture	3	7	33
3	65.5	Economic – commerce	7	5	100
3	65.5	Economic – commerce	6	3	100
3	65.5	Economic – commerce†	7	7	100
3	65.5	Economic – commerce†	7	3	33

*All persons who are shown to be part of the majority or minority parties are members of the House of Representatives except where otherwise indicated.

†These persons were also members of the Legislative Council.

‡This person was not listed in *Who's Who* for 1957 owing to an oversight in the preparation, thus these data are unknown.

From Table 5, note that the two most highly ranked reputational leaders were elected politicians. Their high rankings in reputational influence are themselves significant indicators of the transfer of power and the shift in influence toward greater representation and participation of the mass of Jamaicans. For example, the first person is Norman W. Manley, then Chief Minister of Jamaica and Minister of Development, founder and president of the People's National Party, and founder of Jamaica Welfare, Ltd. The second person is Sir William Alexander Bustamante, then Leader of the Opposition, former Chief Minister of Jamaica, present Premier, founder and president of the Bustamante Industrial Trade Union (BITU), and founder and leader of the Jamaica Labour Party. These men are the two great Jamaican leaders who emerged from the riots, strikes, and disturbances of 1937–38 as spokesmen of the people. More than any other Jamaican leaders they have been associated with these significant events, and their efforts for 25 years have identified them with the trends toward the economic betterment of the general population, civil and political equality (including self-government), and equal access to facilities, services, and social institutions. The rankings of Manley and Bustamante can be compared to the ranking of the Governor of Jamaica who was tied for 19th place in reputational influence in 1958. Considering how much the Governor's formal powers had been reduced by 1958, one may wonder that the Governor was ranked as highly as he was. However, compared to the paramount importance of the Governor before 1944 under the Crown Colony form of government, his ranking in reputational influence in 1958 was relatively low. Since 1958, the formal powers of the Governor have continued to dwindle, and so has his reputational influence.

Because of the predominance of political and economic elites among the 72 top reputational leaders, a somewhat different classification of institutional sectors was used than was used earlier. The leaders of the then-majority political party (PNP) have been differentiated from the leaders of the then-minority party (JLP), and economic elites in agriculture have been separated from economic elites in other spheres (mostly in commerce). Also, members of the Legislative Council and other nominated persons were classified according to their major activity, and a few other changes have been made for convenience.

the winter of 1961–1962, another list of reputational leaders was compiled relying solely on interviewing and working with the entire list of names when a respondent was ranking influentials. If one makes allowances for deaths between 1958 and 1962 and for the rise of a few new influentials in 1962 who were not on the scene in 1958, the lists are quite similar. See Charles C. Moskos, Jr., "The Sociology of Political Independence: A Study of Influence, Social Structure, and Ideology in the British West Indies," unpublished Ph. D. dissertation, University of California, Los Angeles, 1963.

According to the percentage of top reputational leaders contained within them, the sectors rank as follows: (1) economic-commerce, 30.4 per cent; (2) majority party, 18.1 per cent; (3) economic-agriculture, 15.3 per cent; (4) minority party, 9.8 per cent; (5, 6) civil service (including the Governor) and religion, 5.6 per cent each; (7) professions, 4.2 per cent; (8, 9, 10) mass media, education, and social welfare, 2.8 per cent each; and (11, 12) labor and arts, 1.3 per cent each.

However, a better indicator of the relative reputational influence of each sector may be the percentage of total nominations contained within the sectors. Thus, a sector that had fewer persons who were frequently nominated might rank above a sector that had more persons who were infrequently nominated. Such does occur with respect to the relative ranking of majority political party leaders and the economic-commercial elites, as can be seen by the following ranking based upon the percentage of nominations contained in each sector: (1) majority party, 29.5 per cent; (2) economic–commerce, 27.7 per cent; (3) economic–agriculture, 15.8 per cent; (4) minority party, 12.3 per cent; (5) religion, 4.1 per cent; (6) civil service, 3.6 per cent; (7) education, 1.8 per cent; (8) mass media, 1.6 per cent; (9) professions, 1.4 per cent; (10) labor, 1.3 per cent; (11) social welfare, 0.5 per cent; and (12) arts, 0.4 per cent.

Clearly, the most influential sectors by this measure are the four political and economic groups. Combined, they account for 73.6 per cent of the 72 reputational leaders and 85.3 per cent of the total nominations. Again the reader should be reminded that the low ranking of labor should not be interpreted as indicating little influence for this sector. Rather, labor is represented by the political parties. As indicated, the leader of the JLP was also president of a trade union and a son of the Chief Minister was first Vice-president of the National Workers Union (NWU). For many purposes the parties and unions line up: PNP–NWU and JLP–BITU.

The importance of the political and economic sectors is not entirely due to the use of the terms "economic and political" in the question which was used to elicit the identities of influentials. Key informants agreed that these sectors were the most important ones which affect all of Jamaican life, and the study done in 1961–62 by Charles C. Moskos, Jr. shows the same four sectors to be most important compared to other sectors, according to his respondents, even though "political and economic" were not specified in the question used by him to locate reputational leaders.[46]

In 1958, the economic elites in agriculture were not "playing politics" nearly as much as the economic elites in commerce, an exception being in the rather narrow case of negotiations between management and labor in

[46] Moskos, *ibid.*

sugar where the implications of the PNP–NWU and JLP–BITU alignments have not been irrelevant. Sugar was the dominant industry in agriculture, and its importance to the economy was so well recognized that both political parties would see to it that the sugar industry survived. At the same time, although the economic-agricultural elites were powerful, they were confronted with a heavily unionized labor force and their influence could be counterbalanced by trade union activity. Also, the agricultural sector was already being squeezed by wage increases. On the other hand, the mercantile class had considerably more freedom within which to exercise influence. The labor force in the commercial sector was less organized than in the agricultural sector and the imposition of controls on the commercial elites had to be carried out more by the use of governmental authority rather than by labor-management negotiations. Also, the expansion of commercial and industrial activities, the angling for markets, and the importance of governmental policies for economic development spurred the commercial elites' interest in politics and government. In this situation, it is understandable that the economic-commercial elites were very active behind the scenes trying to protect their interest.

The economic-commercial elites shown in Table 5 were most influential according to the average number of elite positions which they simultaneously occupied ($\overline{X} = 5.8$) and they were higher than any sector, except for the professions, in average number of formal association memberships ($\overline{X} = 6.3$). The economic elites discussed earlier in connection with Table 4 did not show up as being so influential because they included quite a number of relatively small and middle-sized operators and because the appointees among them were given a separate category. The reputational economic-commercial elites as shown in Table 5, however, contain only the largest operators, and, as noted, they were very high on each of the three indicators of influence employed. Also, the then-chairman of the Board of Directors of The Gleaner Company, which owns the only two daily newspapers in Jamaica, is an economic-commercial elite as is every other member of the Board. Finally, of the 17 appointees shown in Table 5, eight are economic-commercial elites.

These economic elites generally preferred the JLP to the PNP. It is true that each of the major political parties draws heavily on laboring-class and small-independent-farmer support with an edge perhaps to the PNP among the former and an edge to the JLP among the latter. Also, each party draws some support from among the members of every social class, notably so with respect to a few well-known top economic elites, but differentially so with respect to the proportion of support received from the different social classes. But the PNP has been known for having a good deal of support among middle-class intellectuals and professionals, and the 1958 mail questionnaire survey confirmed this, showing much more support for the PNP than for the JLP among lawyers, civil servants, educational leaders, social welfare elites, doctors, and religious leaders. However, among the economic elites (including both small and large operators) the PNP received little support. Only 21 per cent of the economic-commercial elites and 7 per cent of the economic-agricultural elites preferred the PNP compared to 48 and 50 per cent respectively of the same groups who preferred the JLP.

Also from Table 5, note that the economic-commercial elites were generally reputed to work more behind the scenes than in the forefront of affairs, the average of such designations being 77.4 per cent. Civil servants, religious leaders, and educational leaders shown in Table 5 were also much more likely to work behind the scenes than in the forefront of affairs. Of the remaining large sectors, economic-agricultural elites were about as likely to work in the forefront of affairs as behind the scenes, and of course, elected political leaders worked almost entirely in the forefront of affairs. However, the party officers of the PNP were "back-room boys" who worked mostly behind the scenes.

ELITES AND ETHNICITY

Historically, ethnic differences have been of considerable importance in differentiating Jamaican society into segments of persons having differential rights and duties. Color, of course, differentiated slaves from free persons at one period, and nationality background and religion have been important differentiating factors also. Ascription on the basis of ethnicity has been reduced as has ascription on the basis of other criteria, but ethnicity has not yet become completely irrelevant to the distribution of elite functions in Jamaica.

Table 6 contains distributions of the Members of the House of Representatives and the Legislative Council by color for 1951 and 1958. Both in 1951 and in 1958 the members of the House were much less likely to be white or light than were the members of the Legislative Council. Conversely, they were much more likely to be dark brown or black. As Broom points out in his discussion of the 1951 data, the House of Representatives[47] "... is more representative of the color characteristics of Jamaica than is any other high-status group. Even so, the darker elements are under-represented, if one's sole criterion is proportionality." This was still true in 1958.

For the House of Representatives in 1951 the color of four members was unknown, so the differences between 1951 and 1958 can not be accepted

[47] Broom, *op. cit.,* p. 125.

Table 6. PERCENTAGE OF MEMBERS OF THE HOUSE OF REPRESENTATIVES AND THE LEGISLATIVE COUNCIL ACCORDING TO COLOR, 1951 and 1958

| | House of Representatives | | Legislative Council | |
| | 1951 | 1958 | 1951 | 1958 |
Color	(Per Cent)	(Per Cent)	(Per Cent)	(Per Cent)
White and light	11	9	86	47
Olive and light brown	36	41	7	29
Dark brown	42	28	7	18
Black	11	22	0	6
Total	100	100	100	100
Number of cases	(28)	(32)	(15)	(17)

Source: 1951 data adapted from Leonard Broom, "The Social Differentiation of Jamaica," *American Sociological Review*, 19 (April, 1954), p. 125. Unfortunately, Broom has data for only 28 of the 32 members of the House in 1951, thus the percentage distribution is approximate and has been computed here under the assumption that the "unknowns" were distributed with respect to color just as the "knowns." All members of the Legislative Council are classified.

1958 data from personal observation or from informants or both. All members of both the House and the Legislative Council are classified.

without caution. However, it appears from Table 6 that the relative number of black MHR's increased while the relative number of dark brown MHR's decreased. But for both 1951 and 1958, the percentage of dark brown and black persons combined was about the same, about 50 per cent. Also, the percentage of white, light, olive and light brown MHR's combined stayed about the same.

There was a decrease in the percentage of white and light persons in the Legislative Council from 1951 to 1958, from 86 to 47 per cent. The largest increase was in the percentage of olive and light brown persons, from 7 to 29 per cent; but there were also increases in the percentage of dark brown persons, from 7 to 18, and an increase in the percentage who were black, from 0 to 6 per cent. The latter appears to be accounted for by the addition of one person who was nominated to the Legislative Council in 1951 just after Broom had completed his classification of members by color. In the sense of proportionality, the Legislative Council members were somewhat more representative of the general population of Jamaica in 1958 with respect to color than they were in 1951, but they were still grossly dissimilar—and much more dissimilar to the general population than were the members of the House. However, as indicated earlier, trends detected in such appointments probably will make the members of the Legislative Council in the future still more similar in color and other social characteristics to the members of the House.

The distribution of the top reputational leaders by sector and color is given in Table 7. No Chinese were among the reputed influentials despite the fact that they were differentiated in the larger society. Also, none of Jamaica's East Indians were nominated. For all 72 influentials the distribution by color was as follows: 11 per cent white (foreign-born), 40 per cent Jamaican white and practically white, 28 per cent light and medium brown, and 21 per cent dark brown and black. Thus, the observation must be made again that the dark brown and black segments were underrepresented.

In addition, color distributions by sector were quite dissimilar. For example, comparing the four most influential groups, one can see that the political elites of both parties were most like the general population with respect to color as was the case with other social characteristics. None of them were foreign-born whites, only four were Jamaican whites or near-whites, eight were light or medium brown, and eight were dark brown or black. Thus, the constitutional changes increasing the number of elected offices, enhancing the power of the elected positions, and permitting the introduction of mass political parties, has meant a shift in power to the colored and black segments of the population.

The economic elites were quite different. Although three economic-agricultural elites were dark brown or black, seven of the others were Jamaican whites or near-whites and one was foreign-born white. The economic-commercial leaders were even more unlike the general Jamaican population than the economic-agricultural elites. None of them were dark brown or black, only four were light or medium brown, fourteen were Jamaican whites or near whites, and four were foreign-born whites. Thus, economic power largely remained directly in the hands of whites or near-whites, although it was limited, as discussed earlier, by the power of trade unions, political parties, and government which was in large part directly in the hands of brown-skinned leaders.

Additionally, the economic-commercial influentials were ethnically differentiated from the other types of influentials further in that two of them were Syrian, eight were Jews, and three had Jewish backgrounds. (These persons are classified as Jamaican whites or near-whites in Table 7). Unlike the Chinese, who were also overrepresented in commercial activity (but more concentrated in retail trade—especially the retail grocery trade), the Syrians and Jews tended not to be ethnically exclusive in their associations, they performed many elite functions, and they were not isolated from the blacks, colored, and the other ethnics of similar social-class levels. Also, their rise

Table 7. THE NUMBER OF TOP–72 REPUTATIONAL LEADERS BY SECTOR AND COLOR

Sector	White* (Foreign-born)	Jamaican White and Practically White	Light and Medium Brown	Dark Brown and Black	Total
Majority political party	0	2	6	5	13
Economic–commerce	4	14	4	0	22
Economic–agriculture	1	7	0	3	11
Minority political party	0	2	2	3	7
Religion	1	0	1	2	4
Civil service	2	0	1	1	4
Education	0	0	2	0	2
Mass media	0	0	1	1	2
Professions	0	2	1	0	3
Labor	0	0	1	0	1
Social welfare	0	1	1	0	2
Arts	0	1	0	0	1
Total	8	29	20	15	72

*Excludes a few foreign-born whites and near-whites who are known to have Jamaican parentage. Such persons are included with the Jamaican white and practically white.

to economic prominence is itself a measure of increasing internal inclusiveness in that the Jews have been legally discriminated against in the past. As Broom points out:[48]

"Like the Chinese, the Syrians are concentrated in commercial activity. Unlike the Chinese, at the turn of the century they entered into competition with the relatively well established dry goods and wholesale firms run by creole whites and colored. In large part through the skill of a single family, the Syrians have become a major economic force, tightly integrated and with close ties to the Syrian community in North America and throughout the Caribbean.

"...the Jews of Jamaica...have never exceeded a few hundred. They were originally of Spanish and Portuguese origin and were important in the entrepot trade with the Spanish Caribbean. Along with the Scots, they dealt in plantation stores, a large scale business in which sales were made in bulk. In the 17th and early 18th centuries Jews suffered from discriminatory taxation and civil disabilities. The

[48] Broom, *ibid.,* pp. 123–124.

special taxes were rescinded first, and then, early in the 19th century they were relieved of the remaining impediments. As the colored population became urbanized and achieved some vertical mobility, intermarriage and concubinage with Jews, as well as with other whites, took place.

"...the group is the most fully integrated of all the ethnic minorities into Jamaican society. Like the colored, many of their number perform elite functions."

Two of the persons classified in Table 7 as civil servants were foreign-born whites. One was the Governor and one was a special UN economic and social advisor to the Chief Minister. The latter person has now left the island, and with independence, a new Governor has been appointed who is a dark-skinned Jamaican.

CONCLUSION

I have described and analyzed the social composition of elites in a new nation, the former British colony of Jamaica. Recent political developments, economic transformations, and social changes have altered the leadership structure, and a new Jamaican elite has arisen. However, such recent changes have been viewed here, not as startling discontinuities with Jamaica's prior history, but rather as continuations of certain long-term social trends which can conveniently be summarized as increases in the scale of society.

Oversimplifying, one can say that Jamaicans have moved from slaves, to become citizens and leaders. The increasing internal inclusiveness of Jamaican society, one aspect of increasing scale, has resulted in the reduction of ascriptive barriers and the institutionalization of more equal opportunities. It has meant the extension of rising minimums of civil, political, economic, and social rights for every Jamaican. One manifestation of this, of course, has been the creation of a national citizenry on the basis of political equality, and another has been the transcendence of past economic deprivations and social limitations.

Another aspect of the increase in the scale of society has been the increase in the size and inclusiveness of the elite. Circulation of elites has increased as elites have become less exclusive. The recruitment of elites has been increasingly based upon universalistic criteria and achievement, resulting in a wider range of social origins than before. A new national elite has developed which is more aware and concerned about the welfare of the lower-classes. Elites have become more accessible to the masses, and the masses have become more accessible to the elites. Today, the descendants of the former slaves not only are fullfledged citizens of their own country but also are prominent among its national leaders.

Whether the trend toward equality of opportunities will continue now that

Jamaica is independent is problematical. Independence itself has been a spur to the further rise of the lower-classes and the further spread of equality in that it has dramatized the past struggle for equality and affirmed the present aspiration for more equality in the future as a national goal. Also, from data reported elsewhere,[49] one can conclude that the new elites of Jamaica are fairly equalitarian in their attitudes. The overall level of equalitarianism is relatively high and variations by elite subgroups generally support the contention that equalitarianism among the elites may increase in future years. However, it is not simply a matter of sitting back and letting an inevitable trend unfold. Policies must be formulated and effective actions must be taken. Although much progress toward it has been made, the ideal of equality has not yet been achieved.

[49] Wendell Bell, "Equality and Attitudes of Elites in Jamaica," *Social and Economic Studies*, Vol. 11, (December, 1962), pp. 409–432; and Wendell Bell, *Jamaican Leaders: Political Attitudes in a New Nation*, Berkeley and Los Angeles: University of California Press, 1964.

APPENDIX I

DESCRIPTION OF 1958 SAMPLE OF JAMAICAN ELITES

The first step in constructing a basic list of names to constitute a sample of 1958 Jamaican elites was to select a 25 per cent sample of names from *Who's Who, Jamaica, 1957*, Kingston, Jamaica: The Gleaner Co., Ltd., no date. This was done in May, 1958 by selecting every fourth name after a random start from 1 to 4 using page proofs from *Who's Who*, which was then in press. In this manner, 598 persons were selected. Of these, seven persons were eliminated from the analysis, because it was later learned that they had died, were critically ill, or had left the island permanently. Because the 1957 *Who's Who* was still being compiled and revised in 1958, these data are accepted as 1958 information and have been so designated throughout this paper.

The second step was to add to the 591 persons selected as part of the random sample from the *Who's Who*. New names were selected from the King's House Invitation List, which is a ranking of persons in Jamaica according to their official status, be they elected politicians, civil servants, religious leaders, bank officials, foreign trade commissioners, or what. Also, other lists were used to check the up-to-dateness of the Invitation List, such as the Civil Service Seniority List; the list of members in the House of Representatives and the Legislative Council; and the list of Chairmen of Parish Councils and Mayors. However, the King's House Invitation List was the basic frame of reference for the supplementary sample. Thus, for some groups (appointees and higher civil servants) the sample selected equalled the universe from which it was drawn. However, lesser civil servants were sampled by means of the *Who's Who* random sample. For elected political leaders, the sample approached the universe, but parish councilors were included only if they occupied the office of Chairman or fell into the random sample. In this manner, 212 additional names were added to the basic sample of 591 Jamaican leaders drawn from *Who's Who*, making a total of 803 persons who comprised the basic list. The King's House Invitation List was used to obtain a complete list of top leaders and to compensate for any omissions of top leaders in the *Who's Who*.

Finally, of the 212 persons selected from the King's House Invitation List, 59 were not listed in *Who's Who*. Thus, the data shown in Table 3 are based upon 744 out of the 803 persons who constituted the basic sample of 1958 Jamaican elites, or the equivalent of a 93 per cent response rate.

APPENDIX II

BRIEF DESCRIPTION OF THE 1958 MAIL QUESTIONNAIRE SURVEY

Mail questionnaires were sent to the basic sample of 803 Jamaican elites whose selection is described in Appendix I. They were posted in Jamaica on May 27th through June 1st, 1958. After one follow-up letter, a second wave of questionnaires, and a follow-up by telegrams, 238 properly filled-out questionnaires were returned by December 22, 1958, for a response rate of 30 per cent. However, all but five of the returned questionnaires were received before October 25, 1958.

The linkage between the selection of the sample for the *Who's Who* analysis and the mail questionnaire survey permits an evaluation of· the response bias. Of the 238 respondents to the questionnaire survey, 218 were listed in *Who's Who*. Of the 565 non-respondents, 526 were listed. These 218 respondents were compared with these 526 non-respondents with respect to thirteen variables: type of elite position, nature of the sample, age, sex, country of birth, urban-rural residence, occupational rating, education, occupational mobility, marital status, religion, total number of memberships in formal associations, and total number of officerships in formal associations. On eleven comparisons the respondents were the same as the non-respondents. However, two comparisons revealed significant differences between the respondents and non-respondents. These were education, with the more educated persons more likely to respond than the less educated persons, and occupational mobility, with the upwardly mobile persons somewhat more likely to respond than the stable one.

However, in addition to the systematically collected questionnaire data reported in Table 5, I have had repeated discussions with informants and lengthy interviews with many persons including Jamaican leaders (both with respondents and non-respondents to the mail questionnaires). These took place in 1956, 1958, 1960, 1961, and 1962, and in the more recent years sometimes included a discussion of the results of the mail questionnaire survey itself. Thus, I am confident that the reputational leaders resulting from the mail questionnaire survey represent a generally accurate picture of the distribution of reputational power in Jamaica. Also, my comments about Table 5 and elsewhere in the text have been informed by additional information acquired more informally than by the questionnaire data themselves.

For other reports containing additional data from the 1958 mail questionnaire survey in Jamaica, see Wendell Bell, "Attitudes of Jamaican Elites Toward the West Indies Federation," *Annals of the New York Academy of Sciences*, 83 (January, 1960), pp. 225–248; "Equality and Attitudes of Elites in Jamaica," *Social and Economic Studies*, 11 (December 1962), pp. 409–432 *Jamaican Leaders: Political Attitudes in a New Nation*, Berkeley and Los Angeles, University of California Press, 1964; "Attitudes of Elites Toward Independence in a New Nation," unpublished paper; and James A. Mau, Richard J. Hill and Wendell Bell, "Scale Analyses of Status Perception and Status Attitude in Jamaica and the United States," *Pacific Sociological Review*, 4 (Spring, 1961), pp. 33-40. Acknowledgment is gratefully made for permission given by the University of California Press to use materials from *Jamaican leaders: Political Attitudes in a New Nation.*

FROM MONARCHY TO COMMUNISM: THE SOCIAL TRANSFORMATION OF THE ALBANIAN ELITE

CHARLES C. MOSKOS, JR.

University of Michigan

The question of whether or not there is any long-term direction in social change has recently been raised in the growing body of literature dealing with developing societies and newly independent nations. Yet, with regard to one important facet of a changing social system—its ruling group—one may note two contrasting views having antecedents in previous centuries. One interpretation associated with the writings of Gaetano Mosca, Vilfredo Pareto, and Robert Michels sees real political power always remaining in the hands of a small elite. Such elite theorists hold, that, even when the social composition of rulers change, the basic distribution of power persists with the role of the masses being largely impotent. Even the very movements which are explicitly committed to broadly socially inclusive programs are themselves gripped by an iron law of oligarchy. In many respects, elitist sociology is conducive to a cyclical view of social change.

Another view sees social change as the progressive emancipation of humanity. Whether in a halting, dialectic, or unilinear fashion, there is through history a reduction of traditional barriers which impede popular access to the sources of power. Exponents of this essentially evolutionary viewpoint include, diversely, the *philosophes* of the Enlightenment, Marxists and their revisionists, and the bulk of European and American liberal thinkers.

This study approaches an aspect of the question of the direction of social change by examining the transformation of the elite structure of one nation— Albania—before and after a major revolution. By placing these findings in an historical and conceptual framework, we are alerted not only to continuities and discontinuities in Albanian ruling groups, but to some of the basic changes in the structure of Albanian society as well. At the same time, this is an essay in social science, an effort through the use of empirical data to suggest propositions which may be relevant in other societies also undergoing social upheavals.

Owing to the highly authoritarian character of the previous Albanian regime and the totalitarian nature of the present government, the role of the political elite has consistently been paramount. Institutions such as a free press, legitimate opposition groups, an independent judiciary, and viable local governments have always been weak or absent. Coupled with the absence of democratic forms, the emergence of non-political elite groups has been handicapped by Albania's low level of economic development and isolation from the metropolitan world. Thus, domination of the national political structures has meant decisive control over the major decision-making processes in Albanian society.

HISTORICAL AND SOCIAL BACKGROUND[1]

Albania, whose current population is approximately 1,700,000, began its modern awakening in the latter part of the 19th century. At that time it had been part of the Ottoman Empire for over 400 years and the basic social structure which emerged during the Ottoman era persisted to a large degree up to the Second World War. The most advanced and cosmopolitan section of the country, a large number of whose inhabitants were Orthodox Christians under strong Hellenic influence, was in the south. What little existed of an entreprenurial class in Albania was found in the southern cities, and these urban centers were focal points of Western thought. The central and most populous region of Albania, heavily Moslem, was characterized by a feudal system dominated by the land-owning beys who were strong supporters of Ottoman rule. The northern and highland areas were inhabited by Moslem

[1] This capsule account of Albania's modern history has been synthesized from several accounts. The best discussion of the early development of the Albanian state is probably Joseph Swire, *Albania: The Rise of a Kingdom*, London: Williams and Northgate, 1929. The definitive work on the territorial dispute between Greece and Albania is Edith Piepoint Stickney, *Southern Albania or Northern Epirus in European International Affairs*, 1912–1923, Stanford, Calif: Stanford University Press, 1926. A readable and enlightening account of the partisan movement is Julian Amery, *Sons of the Eagle: A Study in Guerrilla War*, London: Macmillan and Co., 1948. Stavro Skendi, editor, *Albania*, New York: Frederick A. Praeger, 1958, offers the casual reader and serious student highlights of Albanian development along with a collection of statistical information. Excellent accounts of Albanian history from the Ottoman era to modern times are found in relevant parts of L. S. Stavrianos, *The Balkans Since 1453*, New York: Rinehart and Co., 1958; and Robert Lee Wolf, *The Balkans in Our Time*, Cambridge, Mass.: Harvard University Press, 1956. The immediate post-World War II period is comprehensively covered in Hugh Seton-Watson, *The East European Revolution*, New York: Frederick A. Prager, 1961. For recent developments see William E. Griffith, *Albania and the Sino-Soviet Rift*, Cambridge, Mass.: M.I.T. Press, 1963.

(and some Roman Catholic) pastoral tribesmen. These tribesmen, most of whom were armed, remained largely unaffected by the old Ottoman order or the subsequent tribulations of the new state.

Starting in the 1870's, Albanian emigres began to agitate for Albanian independence. The decline of the Ottoman Empire in Europe after the First Balkan War coupled with the conflicting ambitions of the major powers resulted in the creation of an independent Albanian state in 1912. A German prince was selected by the major powers to rule the country, but he remained in Albania only a short time. A period of turbulence followed, and during World War I various parts of the country were seized by the Italians, Greeks, Serbs, Austrians, and French. After the armistice, Albania became a virtual protectorate of Italy and it was not until 1920, after objections by the major powers including the United States, that Italy evacuated the country.

A regency was set up in 1920 to rule in the absence of a monarch. This provisional government, headed by an American-educated Orthodox bishop, Fan Noli, sought to initiate economic reforms while laying the groundwork for representative political institutions. The leadership in the provisional government was largely Western-educated, and a middle class group with a disproportionate number of Orthodox Christians. The economic policies of the provisional government centering around land reform never overcame the opposition of the beys. As Noli later wrote, "By insisting on the agrarian reforms I aroused the wrath of the landed aristocracy; by failing to carry them out I lost the support of the peasant masses . . .".[2]

Failing to establish either its effectiveness or its legitimacy, the provisional government fell in 1925. In that year a *coup d'état* let by Ahmed bey Zogu, a chieftain of one of the most important tribes, abolished the provisional government and declared a republic with Zogu as president. In 1928, with the support of the landed interests, a monarchy was proclaimed with Zogu I as king. Toward the end of his rule, Zogu took tentative steps toward laying an economic base for a modern state. This required foreign capital which was furnished by Italy. Through financial subsidies, military missions and other means, Italy attained a dominant position in Albanian affairs by the close of the 1930's. Efforts by Zogu to halt Italian penetration brought quick reprisal, and in 1939 he was forced into exile; Emmanuel of Italy became king of Albania. From his Albanian base, Mussolini launched an invasion of Greece in 1941 and after suffering major reversals, it was necessary for German troops to come to his assistance. World War II saw Albania a satellite under German and Italian auspices. The fascist puppet government was staffed largely from the same groups who had always occupied the privileged positions in Albanian society.

[2] Swire, *op. cit.*, p. 444.

During the war, Albanian guerilla troops steadily increased in numbers, the most effective unit being the communist-dominated National Liberation Movement. Because of their worsening position on other fronts, the Germans were forced to withdraw from Albania in late 1944. The evacuation of the German troops was followed by the establishment of a provisional government with Enver Hoxha as premier, the leader of the National Liberation Movement. In 1946, at Tirana, the capital, a new Constituent Assembly, all seats of which had been gained by Hoxha's party in a one-slate election, proclaimed the "People's Republic of Albania". Hoxha, who resigned as head of the provisional government, was installed as prime minister. During the immediate post-World War II years, Albania was within the Yugoslavian sphere of influence. But following Tito's break with the Kremlin in 1948, the Albanian communist party underwent a period of crisis. The execution of Koci Xoxe signified the victory of the anti-Titoists, and Albania shifted its allegiance to the Soviet Union. In 1954, Mehmet Shehu replaced Hoxha as prime minister, while Hoxha retained his position as head of the communist party. The past decade has seen Albania remain a stalwart communist country with little indication of serious internal dissension.

In recent years, however, Albania's role on the international scene has undergone a significant change. It has again shifted its allegiance, becoming an outspoken ally of China. Although ideological and personality clashes with the Soviets have contributed to the Tirana-Peking alliance, the major reason for the new policy has been, in this writer's opinion, the traditional Albanian fear of the territorial ambitions of its neighbors. In 1960, before the Albania-Soviet break, Khruschev intimated to a Greek political leader that he sympathized with the Hellenic sentiments of the Greek population residing in southern Albania or "Northern Epirus". From the north, there was the threat of Albania becoming a "republic" within a greater Yugoslavia.

Despite Albania's hectic military and political history, its social structure changed very little for at least a century preceding the end of World War II. The last decade and a half, however, have witnessed many changes initiated by government development programs. The scope of these changes may be partially adduced from the following statistics. Before World War II, 58,000 Albanians were enrolled in school, by the early 1960's the figure was 200,000. Six radio broadcasting stations now exist as compared to one in 1940. Coal output has increased from 4,000 tons in 1938, to 116,000 tons in 1954, to 300,000 tons in 1961. Where there were no tractors in the country in 1939, twenty years later there were 1,800. Despite the progress indicated by the official statistics, it must be stressed that Albania still remains an underdeveloped country. Although the rates of increase are high, the bases on which they are computed are extremely low.

Perhaps the single best indicator of the changes which are occurring in Albania is to be found in the occupational movement of the population. Rough estimates of the occupational distribution in Albania for the years 1935 and 1955 based on a compilation of available statistical information and informed opinions are reported in Table 1. Even though these figures cannot come close to an exact specification of the occupational distribution, they do suggest a general trend. There has been some shift away from agricultural to industrial labor. The percentage of "bureaucratic" workers, such as military, government, and educational personnel, has increased. At the same time, there has been a rather sharp decline in the number of economic independents, e.g. self-employed businessmen, artisans, free professionals.

Table 1. ESTIMATED OCCUPATIONAL DISTRIBUTION OF ALBANIAN POPULATION OVER 15 YEARS OF AGE FOR THE YEARS 1935 AND 1955

Occupation	*1935*		*1955*	
Agriculture	512,000	80.0%	676,000	70.0%
Industrial or Manual Labor	40,000	6.3	145,000	15.0
Government Workers	25,000	3.9	55,000	5.7
Education (includes secondary school and university students)	8,000	1.2	30,000	3.1
Military (army, police, frontier guard)	15,000	2.3	45,000	4.7
Independents (self-employed, artisans, free professionals)	40,000	6.3	15,000	1.5
Total	640,000	100.0	966,000	100.0

Sources: S. Skendi, *Albania; United Nations Demographic Yearbook, 1952; United Nations Demographic Yearbook, 1958; Anuari Statistikor i Republikes Popullore te Shqiperise, 1959; Annuario Statistico Italiano, 1943*; miscellaneous travellers' accounts.

BASIC DATA

Most of the tabular data reported in this study were derived from two sources. Information pertaining to the 1935 monarchist elite was obtained from the 1937 edition of *Who's Who in Central and East Europe.*[3] From the

[3] Zurich, 1937.

156 Albanian personages listed in this volume, 35 were identified as the top political elite. This group consisted of: the monarch (one), heads of all the various ministries (eleven), secretary-generals of the major ministries and heads of departments within ministries (eleven), official royal advisors (seven), highest ranking military personnel (three), and the presidents of the parliament and supreme court (two). Owing to the time interval involved between obtaining the required information and its publication, the data derived from the 1937 *Who's Who* represents the composition of the Albanian elite in the year 1935.

Data pertaining to the 1955 communist elite were obtained from a series of biographical sketches of the leading figures in Albania. This information is found in the appendix of "Albania" edited by Stavro Skendi, part of a larger study of communist Europe being conducted by the Mid-European Studies Center.[4] The 1955 group, totaling 27 persons, consisted of: the premier and vice-premiers (seven), heads of all the various ministries and commissions (eleven), leading communist party members not holding government positions (six), president and vice-president of the parliament (two), and the ambassador to Moscow (one).

Because the conclusions of this report are essentially based upon an examination of the social characteristics of these two elite groups, their degree of comparability must be specified. The most important fact is that both groups are closer to being "universes" rather than "samples" of the Albanian elites. For both time periods, the elite groups are regarded as the top 35 and 27 influentials in Albania for the years 1935 and 1955 respectively. Although the two groups possessed similar opportunity to affect national decision-making, there were obviously several points of disparity between the formal structure of power under the monarchists compared to that under the communists. For example, the 1935 monarchist elite included royal advisors and a monarch not found in the later communist elite, while the 1955 elite included persons who did not occupy formal positions in the government, but who held senior positions in the communist party hierarchy. Needless to add, the findings to be reported are limited to the kinds of information available in "who's who" sources.

DIFFERENCES IN SOCIAL CHARACTERISTICS

Sex. As indicated in Table 2, one difference between communist Albanian society and the *ancien régime* is reflected in the appearance of female elites in the current regime. Three of the 27 communist elites were females contrasted to none among the 35 monarchist elites. Although it is

[4] Skendi, *op. cit.,* pp. 323–345.

true that even in the 1955 elite, 89 per cent of the top leaders were men, the presence of women in the communist regime suggests a change in the social values of Albania when viewed in historical context. Though never occupying a position as abjectly subservient as was the situation in the more orthodox Moslem societies of the Middle East, women in traditional Albanian life had little or no education and were subject to exclusion from areas outside the home. While this pattern was most characteristic of the feudal region, it also extended to the highland areas and the Christian community in the south. The upsetting conditions of World War II with the concomitant growth of the communist partisan movement made it possible for women to take advantage of a new order officially committed to egalitarian standards, and thereby vacate the subordinate status formerly held by virtually all Albanian females.

Age. The communists, as reported in Table 2, tended to be younger than the

Table 2.   PERCENTAGES OF 1935 MONARCHIST AND 1955 COMMUNIST ALBANIAN ELITES BY SELECTED SOCIAL CHARACTERISTICS

Social Characteristics	*1935 Monarchist Elites (35 cases)*	*1955 Communist Elites (27 cases)*
Sex		
Male	100%	89%
Female	0	11
Total	100%	100%
Age		
51 and over	34	0
40 to 49	34	41
39 and under	32	59
Total	100%	100%
Education		
Some college or more	51	48
Secondary school or less	49	52
Total	100%	100%
First Gainful Job		
Government service	60	0
Professional	20	12
Military	13	12
Teacher	7	16
Laborer, clerk	0	28
Political agitation*	0	32
Total	100%	100%

*Engaged in political or revolutionary activity directly upon leaving school.

monarchists, all being under 50 years of age. The comparative youthfulness of the communist elite cannot be accounted for in terms of tenure alone, inasmuch as both the monarchists and communist groups were in power for about a decade in 1935 and 1955, respectively. It must be noted, however, that even the monarchist elite had a relatively youthful cast, two-thirds being under 50 years of age.

Education. One important trait which does not distinguish the communist from the monarchist elites is their level of education. Approximately one-half of each group had more than a secondary-school education. Also for both elite groups, virtually all of the college-educated were products of Western and Central European countries, there being no advanced educational institutions in Albania until very recent years. Of those few college-educated Albanian elites who did not receive their higher education in Western Europe, the monarchists attended schools in Turkey, and the communists received their advanced education in the Soviet Union.

Occupational Background. The first gainful jobs of the Albanian elites are given in Table 2. A majority of the monarchists, 60 per cent, started their careers as government officials, the remainder having been military personnel, professionals or teachers. Among the communist elites, on the other hand, three-quarters were initially laborers, clerks, teachers or persons who engaged in political or revolutionary activity directly upon leaving school. Thus, despite the similarity in the educational levels of the two elite groups, they differed markedly in their initial position in the Albanian social system. That is, where the majority of the monarchists started their careers in relatively high prestige positions, the communists tended to come from low prestige occupations. Higher education, then, appears to be associated with the emergence of a radical revolutionary outlook among Albanian elites only when accompanied by an initially disadvantageous position within the traditional social structure.

The picture of a quasi-inherited elite structure for the monarchist period, a characteristic of a highly stratified society, is supported by an examination of the occupations of the fathers of the monarchists. Among the 28 monarchists for which this information is known, ten were sons of large land-owners, seven of high government officials, seven of merchants or professionals, and only four had fathers who were artisans, workers or clerks. (Unfortunately, comparable information on the generational mobility of the communist elites is not available.)

DIFFERENCES IN RELIGIOUS BACKGROUND AND ETHNICITY

Religious Background. As reported in Table 3, Orthodox Christians comprised only 11 per cent of the monarchist elites, about half the ratio of Orthodox Christians in the total Albanian population. Among the 1955 elite, on the other hand, the number of Orthodox Christians increased to 29 per cent, a proportion exceeding that found in the general population. The number of Roman Catholics dropped in the 1955 elite, while the percentage of Moslems in both the monarchist and communist groups remained constant. Although nominally a Christian group, Albanian Roman Catholics were typically mountaineers who differed little in either cultural values or social structure from their Moslem counterparts in the highlands. Hence, the cleavage between Orthodox Christians and non-Orthodox Christians has had more social significance than the distinction between Christian and Moslem elements. It is, of course, to be realized that classifying the Albanian elites by religious characteristics refers to their familial backgrounds and not to their adult religious beliefs or practices.

Table 3. PERCENTAGES OF 1935 MONARCHIST AND 1955 COMMUNIST ALBANIAN ELITES AND TOTAL ALBANIAN POPULATION BY RELIGIOUS AND ETHNIC BACKGROUND

Religious and Ethnic Background	1935 Monarchist Elites	1955 Communist Elites	Total Albanian Population*
Religious Background			
Roman Catholic	22%	4%	10%
Moslem	67	67	70
Orthodox Christian	11	29	20
Total	100%	100%	100%
Number of Cases	(35)	(27)	
Ethnicity			
Gheg	69	40	50
Tosk	31	60	50
Total	100%	100%	100%
Number of Cases	(35)	(27)	
Ethnicity of Moslems Only			
Gheg	70	39	70
Tosk	30	61	30
Total	100%	100%	100%
Number of Cases	(23)	(18)	

*Based on *Annuario Statistico Italiano,* 1943.
Number of cases on which percentages are computed (given in parentheses).

Ethnicity. In addition to the religious divisions of Albanian society, there exists another ethnic cleavage. North of the Shkumbi River, which flows west across Albania's central region, live the Ghegs, to the south are found the Tosks. These two groups differ from each other in minor physical and linguistic traits. The ratio of Ghegs to Tosks within the Albanian state is approximately equal, but the Ghegs outnumber the Tosks if one includes the 700,000 Gheg Albanians living in Yugoslavia. The Gheg-Tosk cleavage cuts across religious lines with Moslems comprising 80 per cent of the Ghegs and 60 per cent of the Tosks. The Tosks have typically been oriented to Italy, Greece, and to the Western world in general. The Ghegs, on the other hand, among whom were the tribal leaders and beys, have remained outside the general mainstream of European thought.

In Table 3, we find 69 per cent of the monarchist elite consisted of Ghegs, while the situation is almost reversed among the communists. That is, the Tosks were underrepresented in the elite structure of 1935, with regard to their proportion in the total society, and overrepresented in the later, communist, elite.

Because Orthodox Christians are Tosks and Catholics are Ghegs, the Tosk increase among the communists may be another indicator of the previously noted religion correlations. When the religious factor is held constant, however, by dealing only with Moslems, the findings continue to show a large rise in the number of Tosks in the communist elite. Thirty per cent of the Moslem monarchists were Tosks as contrasted with 61 per cent of the communists.

The presence of a disproportionate number of Orthodox Christians and Moslem Tosks in positions of power within the communist regime might be seen as a resurgence of the same elements whose attempt at modernizing Albania after the end of the First World War was aborted. It appears probable that had the early Albania state acceded to the territorial claims of Greece for its southern area, or "Northern Epirus," the likelihood of a communist state in present-day Albania would have been greatly reduced. In historical terms, the success of the communist movement in Albania can be interpreted as the alternate triumph of those groups which were unable to establish a liberal-capitalist Albanian society in the early 1920's.

MARGINALITY AND AGE

Persons may be marginal when they belong to distinct and minority religious groups. In a rural and isolated society, ethnic groups with relatively greater exposure to the metropolitan world community tend to be marginal. In a society largely illiterate, advanced education can be a marginal trait. In Albanian society, then, three indicators of social marginality were an Orthodox Christian religious background, Tosk ethnicity, and a college education. The distribution of these marginal traits among the Albanian elite by two age groups, 40 years and over versus 39 years and younger, is given in Table 4.

The overriding finding is that marginal traits were most characteristic of the younger monarchists and the older communists. The older monarchists and the younger communists, on the other hand, tended to be more alike in their shared heartland traits or non-marginality. This tendency toward a mirror distribution gains import when we note that marginality among Albanian elites was reaching a maximum within a near contemporary age group—the younger monarchists and the older communists.

The trend away from marginality among the younger communist elites corresponds with some of the observations noted in other revolutionary societies. A hypothesis put forth by Harold Lasswell holds that an initial radical revolutionary elite is characterized by a membership which is intellectual, Western exposed, and marginal in its ethnicity; and that the second generation of the radical revolutionary elite witnesses a rise in heartland-born, less educated and non-Western exposed individuals.[5]

Also noteworthy is the increased marginality of the younger monarchists. In light of Albanian history, we suggest that as the pressures for coping with internal and external difficulties increased in the period between the two World Wars, a greater need arose for persons with administrative and diplomatic skills. And it may be that traditional obstacles in the way of attaining top political positions could be bypassed by those individuals who possessed the needed skills acquired by higher education in a Western European nation. In other words, Western education for the marginal ethnic

[5] Harold D. Lasswell, Daniel Lerner, and C. Easton Rothwell, *The Comparative Study of Elites*, Stanford, Calif.: Stanford University Press, 1954, pp. 29-36.

Table 4. PERCENTAGES OF 1935 MONARCHIST AND 1955 COMMUNIST ALBANIAN ELITES BY AGE GROUPS AND THREE INDICATORS OF MARGINALITY

Indicators of Marginality	1935 Monarchist Elites		1955 Communist Elites	
	40 years and over (24 cases)	39 years and under (11 cases)	40 years and over (11 cases)	39 years and under (16 cases)
College education	42	73	55	45
Orthodox religious background	4	27	45	19
Tosk ethnicity	21	55	82	44

and religious elites of the monarchist regime was the mobility equivalent of participation in the partisan movement for the communist elites. In either fashion, it became possible to circumvent traditional structures of stratification.

ELITE GENERATIONS

The different age patterns of marginal traits among both the monarchists and the communists suggests the utility of conceiving generations of elites within both ruling groups. Provisionally, we specify four analytically distinct elite generations: (1) the early traditional elite, (2) the later traditional elite, (3) the early revolutionary elite, and (4) the later revolutionary elite. Although these distinctions within the traditional 1935 and revolutionary 1955 elite groups can be made conceptually, there is in fact no sharp point of demarcation between early and later elite generations. Rather, there is an ongoing process of replacement. As summarized in Table 5, the notion of Albanian elite generations is used as a point of departure to indicate certain historical, social, and conceptual correlates.

The early traditional elite was typical of the leadership of Albania from a period originating in the late Ottoman era to sometime in the 1930's. This stage was marked by an establishment of an Albanian state and an increase in awareness by its inhabitants of their shared nationality. The later traditional elite began its rise in the early 1930's and was beginning to predominate by the time of the outbreak of the Second World War. This period saw a growing · interaction of the Albanian nation with the metropolitan world through commercial intercourse and the education of more of its youth in Western nations. The later traditional elite, however, never fully came to prevail in Albania as the Second World War intervened before a transfer of power could come about within the *ancien régime*. (The succeeding puppet fascist government represented a reversal in the general historical trend as it was a throwback to the social types of the early traditional elite.) The early revolutionary elite came to power in 1945 and is now being replaced by the later revolutionary elite. The early revolutionary elite initiated a program of agricultural and industrial development through a state-centered bureaucracy, a policy which the later revolutionary elite may be expected to continue.

Social Characteristics. The early traditional elite, that category based on the older monarchists, was relatively low in educational level and came mostly from the predominant religious and ethnic groups of Albanian society. That is, heartland characteristics were most typical of this group. The later traditional elite, the younger monarchists, possessed a high level of education

Table 5. CORRELATES OF ALBANIAN ELITE GENERATIONS

Elite Generations	Albanian Elite Types	Historical Period
early traditional	older monarchists	establishment of Albanian nation
later traditional	younger monarchists	increased contact with metro-politan world
early revolutionary	older communists	establishment of communist state
later revolutionary	younger communists	internal development and isolation from metropolitan world

Elite Generations	Religious and Ethnic Background	Education Level
early traditional	majority	low
later traditional	minority	high
early revolutionary	minority	high
later revolutionary	majority	low

Elite Generations	Pareto's Typology	Lasswell's Typology
early traditional	lions	non-applicable
later traditional	foxes	non-applicable
early revolutionary	non-applicable	marginal
later revolutionary	non-applicable	heartland

Elite Generations	Rostow's Economic Stages	Sources of Legitimacy
early traditional	traditional	ascribed status
later traditional	traditional	achieved status
early revolutionary	preconditions for take-off	achieved ascription
later revolutionary	take-off(?)	ascribed achievement

and tended to be marginal in religious background and ethnicity. The social composition of the early revolutionary elite was more similar to that of the preceding later traditional elite than of any other elite generation. Among the later revolutionary elite, the younger communists, there was a swing back to heartland characteristics and a somewhat lower educational level.

Rostow's Economic Stages. Though not couched formally in evolutionary terms, W. W. Rostow has delineated five stages which societies undergoing economic growth will sequentially experience: (1) traditional economy, (2) preconditions for take-off, (3) take-off, (4) drive to maturity, and (5) high mass consumption.[6] Certain structural and cultural features necessarily accompany each of the economic stages and in the final phases there is an opening up of the class system and a greater participation of the masses in the material benefits of a society.

Albania has experienced the first two stages of economic growth and may enter the third stage sometime in the near future. During the period of monarchist domination, the Albanian economy was a traditional one. Before the Second World War, despite the investment of some Italian capital, nearly all Albanians were engaged in primitive agricultural and pastoral activity. In the past decade and a half, the revolutionary elite has brought Albania into the second stage of economic growth, the preconditions for take-off. Government programs have started rudimentary industrialization and have laid the groundwork for an effective transportation and communication network.

Pareto's Typology. Different from an evolutionary viewpoint of social change is Pareto's classic statement on the circulation of classes within the elite structure of a society.[7] According to Pareto, elites alternate between those possessing traits, in the metaphor of Machiavelli, of "lions and foxes." Simply put, lions represent "persistent aggregates" or heartland social characteristics, and rely on force and abjure compromise in their relations with the masses. Foxes, on the other hand, represent "instincts for combinations" and typically use guile and accommodation in their dealings. Whichever group is in control, however, there is little change in the participation of the masses in national decision-making.

The designation of lions to the early traditional elite is appropriate not only because they represented heartland social characteristics, but also because they used force or the threat of force to insure compliance with their demands. The later traditional elite, on the other hand, seems close to the foxes of Pareto. The younger monarchists appear to have relied on cunning rather than force in their attainment of elite status. Also, there was toward the end of Zogu's rule some concern with setting up at least the forms of parliamentary democracy.

Although the early revolutionary elite was ruthless in its manner of governing and had seized power by force, to designate them as lions in the meaning of

[6] W. W. Rostow, *The Stages of Economic Growth*, London and New York: Cambridge University Press, 1960, pp. 4-72.

[7] Vilfredo Pareto, "Elites, Force and Governments", in C. Wright Mills, editor, *Images of Man*, New York: George Braziller, 1960, pp. 262-291.

Pareto seems unwarranted. The older communists represented a high degree of social marginality rather than "persistent aggregates." Nor is it appropriate to call the generation of the later revolutionary elite foxes owing to the predominance of heartland social characteristics among the younger communists. In brief, Pareto's typology of alternating elites makes sense in the *ancien régime* case, but is inapplicable and misleading in a revolutionary situation. Rather, revolutionary elite generations are better conceived in terms of Lasswell's marginal early revolutionaries and heartland later revolutionaries.

Sources of Legitimacy. The effectiveness of both the traditional and revolutionary governments lay in their control of the means of physical coercion in Albanian society. But this does not mean that the Albanian elite generations possessed the same sources of legitimacy, i.e., the capacity to engender belief that their occupancy of top political positions was appropriate.[8] Although it is debatable if any of the Albanian elite generations were viewed as legitimate by the majority of the population, we can nevertheless distinguish the sources of what amount of legitimacy they did possess.

The legitimacy of the early traditional elite was based primarily upon ascribed criteria. That is, Albanian leaders traditionally came from certain tribes or landowning families. The later traditional elite's occupancy of their high status was based instead upon their attainment of administrative and diplomatic skills. In other words, their source of legitimacy rested on their personal expertise or achieved criteria. We seem to find in the younger monarchists a "coopted" group, a social phenomenon whose generality has been widely observed in many other contexts.

For the early revolutionary elite, legitimacy was based on their overthrow of the old order, coupled with a radical ideology formally committed to egalitarian ends. Although this form of legitimacy might be regarded as "achieved" in one meaning, it differs fundamentally from that of the preceding later traditional elite. We must distinguish between achievement within a system and the setting up of an entirely different system. In other words, participation in the revolution itself becomes the standard by which authority can be legitimized. For persons who did not take part in the revolution, the credentials of elite status are not available. For these reasons, we call the legitimacy of the early revolutionary elite "achieved ascription." In a sense, they achieved what developed into an ascribed status.

With respect to the source of legitimacy of the later revolutionary elite, the following seems to be taking place. Younger communist elites are typically recruited from quasi-governmental organizations such as the communist party, labor unions, and youth groups. Once placed within these organizations,

[8] Seymour M. Lipset, *Political Man*, Garden City: Doubleday and Co., 1960, pp. 77-83.

a rise to a leadership position rests largely on competent performance of duties. Albanian communist elites too young to have participated in the revolution will graduate from leadership in such quasi-governmental institutions to top positions within the formal political structure in a sort of "escalator" mobility process. Because this source of legitimacy has aspects of both personal merit and social exclusivism, it is termed "ascribed achievement." Achievement criteria, that is, operates only for those fortunate, idealistic, or shrewd enough to be included early in their lives in what approximates an ascribed group.

CONCLUSION

To close this brief account of the transformation of the Albanian elite, we return to the issue posed at the start of the discussion. Is there any long-term direction in social change? From the Albanian case, there is contradictory evidence. Certainly there has been little increase in the participation of the general population on national decision-making. In addition, the social composition of the Albanian ruling group has not reflected a single direction. Rather, we found that the earliest and latest elite groups, the older monarchists and the younger communists, tended to display many of the same social characteristics. Further, it may be that membership in quasi-governmental organizations in a totalitarian society such as contemporary Albania has parallels with the recruitment of elites from kinship-based groups in a traditional society. In both situations, segments of the population are precluded from entering avenues leading to top positions by their initial location outside of an exclusivist elite pool.

Yet, it is equally true that the absolute and relative size of the communist elite pool greatly exceeds that of the monarchist regime. Perhaps more fundamentally, the discernment of elite generations with their own distinct characteristics is an indicator of broad changes occurring in the basic structure of Albanian society. Albania has experienced an increase in the range and interaction of its inhabitants with each other and to some degree even with the larger world community. The early attempts at economic modernization, the participation of large numbers in the partisan movement, the development of an independent foreign policy, the spread of educational facilities and the induced industrialization in recent years, have all been involved in expanding the social scale of Albania.[9]

[9]The notion of scale of society is introduced in Godfrey and Monica Wilson, *The Analysis of Social Change*, London: Cambridge University Press, 1945. See also Eshref Shevky and Wendell Bell, *Social Area Analysis*, Stanford, Calif.: Stanford University Press, 1955, pp. 3–19.

The increase in the scale of Albanian society through its engendering of structural changes may set in motion forces leading to an eventual allievation of the deprevations of the Albanian people. And such an eventuality would imply qualitative as well as quantitative changes in the institutional order, the true measure of a social evolutionary scheme. From this perspective, the dynamics underlying the Albanian experience may not be entirely dissimilar from the processes of social change we are currently witnessing throughout much of the non-Western world. In fine, the empirically derived and provisional formulation of distinct Albanian elite generations may have some conceptual relevance to an understanding of the nature and direction of change occurring in other developing societies.

Part III

ECONOMIC DEVELOPMENT, TECHNOLOGICAL CHANGE, AND EVOLUTIONARY THEORY

INTRODUCTION TO PART III

Spengler, Feldman, and Cottrell all took quite a broad-gauged approach to the general topic of the conference. Each really addressed the large issue of a theory of social change.

The question of reification of stage concepts was stressed repeatedly during the conference, particularly by anthropologists. As Feldman indicated, and Emerson verified for the biological sciences, "stages" are purely theoretical constructs. In addition, both anthropologists and economists were concerned about the possibility of these concepts blinding the observer to pertinent data. Emerson was negatively inclined toward the notion of "cyclic stages," noting that they can easily lead the observer to ignore subtle changes in apparent recurrences. The same point was made on several occasions with respect to "linear" or "non-linear" models of change. Conferees agreed that stage concepts are useful heuristic devices, but Bohannan, particularly, objected to the use of "deductively constructed stages."

Another possible use of evolutionary theory emerged from discussion, that of a theory of democracy. Although the subject was not discussed expressly as a normative theory, discussion shifted back and forth from scientific analysis to normative evaluations, in a manner reminiscent of Marxist theoreticians. Substantively, however, the proposal was anti-Marxian, with a suggestion that Western forms of democracy are more advanced forms of government than totalitarian regimes. Specifically, the subject arose from Cottrell's pessimism with respect to the decision-making efficacy of democratic processes in a rapidly changing environment. Cottrell contended that Americans "consented" to the 1961 Cuban invasion after the fact. Bell objected, maintaining that the decision to invade Cuba was made with the

223

implicit consent of Americans. Nevertheless, Cottrell retained his position, arguing that the complexity of the modern world has rendered democratic processes almost useless.

It was suggested that selective retention systems should form a complex, segmented (as opposed to monolithic) power system in a society operating in a complex environment. For this reason, both Campbell and Spengler expected Communist systems to become more "democratic" as time passed. However, Campbell did indicate agreement with Cottrell that rapid changes in the environment might not let the selective retention systems operate properly. During another discussion, Bell picked up this same point, suggesting that in underdeveloped areas, the greatest development may be taking place in democracies, because their flexibility allows them to adjust better to the rapid change and complexity of the international scene. Weiner disagreed, challenging anyone to produce data indicating that democracies were any more successful in rate of growth than totalitarian systems. Studies of Coleman and Lipset were cited as evidence for Bell's point, but Weiner indicated that these studies showed levels of income, which is quite another thing from national progress. At several points, Emerson indicated tentative agreement with the contention that democracy was a more adaptive form than totalitarianism. However, no general agreement was reached on the question.

Feldman especially was concerned with the danger of "taking a managerial view of society," a problem which plagued industrial sociology for many years. Since evolutionary theory points up adaptation of systems to environments, they felt that observers could be led to ignore other useful perspectives. However, both Bell and Emerson suggested that modern social-organizational theories take this into account with the notion of subsystems.

MODERNIZATION AND REVOLUTION IN LATIN AMERICA*

GEORGE I. BLANKSTEN

Northwestern University

I shall attempt to identify and analyze the conditions which make for sustained political and economic modernization in Latin America. So far as many of the American Republics are concerned, this may be translated as the question of whether or not revolution is a species of precondition of sustained development, and I propose, in the following pages, to treat the problem in those terms.

I

I believe it necessary to define at the outset two concepts central to the problem before us. These are the concepts of "modernization" and of "revolution."

Social scientists have done much in recent years to create a body of literature on the concept of modernization. As it is employed in this paper, the concept refers to the change process by means of which a traditional non-Western system acquires characteristics usually associated with more developed or less traditional societies. These characteristics include[1] "a comparatively high degree of urbanization, widespread literacy, comparatively high per-capita income, extensive geographical and social mobility, a relatively high degree of commercialization and industrialization of the economy, an extensive and penetrative network of mass communication media, and, in general, . . . widespread participation and involvement by members of the

* This paper grew out of a larger inquiry into the interplay between economic development and political change in the underdeveloped areas. During the academic year 1959—1960, this project was supported by a fellowship of the Ford Foundation, whose assistance is gratefully acknowledged.

[1] Gabriel A. Almond and James S. Coleman, *The Politics of the Developing Areas* (Princeton: Princeton University Press, 1960), p. 532.

society in modern social and economic processes." Max Weber has suggested that the specifically political characteristics of such a modern society involve:[2] "(1) an administrative and legal order that is subject to change by legislation; (2) an administrative apparatus that conducts official business in accordance with legislative regulation; (3) binding authority over all persons—who usually obtain their citizenship by birth—and over more actions taking place in the area of its jurisdiction; (4) the legitimation to use force within this area if coercion is either permitted or prescribed by the legally constituted government, i.e., if it is in accordance with enacted statute." In another place, I have raised the question of whether or not our current interest in developmental theories of modernization—the passing of traditional society—might represent a revival of a variety of evolutionary theory in social science.[3] While I think that question significant, given the nature of our current interest in social, economic, and political change in underdeveloped areas, I regard it as lying outside the scope of this paper.

No doubt, the concept of revolution is easier to define than that of modernization. Nevertheless, two types of special problems beset the analysis of revolution in Latin America. The first is a question of terminology and the second is a matter of perspective.

The terminological problem arises from the circumstance that few words are more loosely and promiscuously used in Latin America than the word "revolution." An amazing array of dissimilar and unrelated occurrences go by this name in the Americas. The Wars of Independence have been so dubbed, as well as minor changes in government, the promulgation of new constitutions, political violence of almost any variety—in Latin America, even revolutions are called "revolutions." This tendency to use the word almost at the drop of a hat is one of the factors underlying the popular belief that revolutions are particularly frequent and numerous in the Americas. The celebrated Brazilian Emperor Dom Pedro II is said to have remarked, when he visited the Philadelphia Exposition in 1876, that many of the Latin-American countries had more revolutions per minute than the machines he saw on display at the exposition. A recent student of the area has written that thus far in the twentieth century[4] "the governments of the nations to the south have been overthrown . . . seventy-six times . . . . Revolutions are still

---

[2] Reinhard Bendix, Max Weber: *An Intellectual Portrait* (New York: Doubleday and Co., Inc., 1960), p. 413.

[3] George I. Blanksten, "The Aspiration for Economic Development," *Annals of the American Academy of Political and Social Science*, Vol. 334 (March, 1961), pp. 12–15. See also Myron Weiner, "Political Modernization and Evolutionary Theory" (unpublished manuscript, 1961).

[4] Austin F. Macdonald, *Latin-American Politics and Government* (New York: Thomas Y. Crowell Co., Second Edition, 1954), pp. 11–12.

the order of the day . . . . Bolivia, for example, has had violent changes of government in 1920, 1930, 1934, 1936, 1937, 1943, 1946, and 1952." In most of these cases the violence did not bring with it fundamental changes in the social, economic, or political order, and the pre-revolutionary structure of the systems involved remained essentially intact. Indeed, there is an old Ecuadoran saying to the effect that Independence Day is observed as the anniversary[5] of "the last day of despotism and the first day of the same thing." Although Latin Americans seldom hesitate to call all violent changes in government, even if unaccompanied by more fundamental changes in the systems involved, "revolutions," my own preference is to reserve the use of the term for less superficial phenomena.

True revolution—a basic change in the political system, a recasting of the social order—is surprisingly infrequent in Latin America. Revolution as a vast and impersonal movement affecting the entire social order, bringing far-reaching changes in it, is not common in the Americas. It has happened, to be sure. "The Revolution is like a hurricane," the celebrated novelist Manuel Azuela has said of the Mexican Revolution.[6] "If you're in it, you're not a man . . . you're a leaf, a dead leaf blown by the wind." Fundamental revolutions in which[7] "wealth is gradually redistributed, social relations are materially altered and new groups acquire a dominant position in matters of state" are quite rare in Latin America. They have occurred in the area, and the Mexican and Cuban cases are discussed at a later point in this paper.[8]

The problem of perspective is not easy to solve in the analysis of revolution in Latin America. On the assumption that it might be possible to distinguish a superficial change in government from a fundamental revolution on the conceptual or theoretical level, it remains difficult to assess a given revolution— especially while it is occurring—in terms of the superficiality or profundity of its influence on the economic, social, and political order. I have already suggested that I regard the Mexican Revolution which began in 1910 as one of the few true revolutions of twentieth-century Latin America. Yet, during much of the decade after 1910, the United States Department of State insisted on regarding the Mexican upheaval as a superficial if vexatious affair, seeing in it primarily the antics of variously ambitious military and revolutionary leaders chasing each other out of public office. With the hindsight of the

[5] Pio Jaramillo Alvarado, *El régimen totalitario en América* (Guayaquil: Editora Noticia, 1940), p. 71.

[6] Quoted in Russell H. Fitzgibbon, "Revolutions: Western Hemisphere," *South Atlantic Quarterly*, Vol. LV, (July 1956), p. 263.

[7] Robert Hunter, *Revolution: Why, How, When?* (New York: Harper & Brothers, 1940), p. 10.

[8] See pp. 229–235, below.

1960's we can decry that lack of vision on Washington's part. Yet it is not necessary to be a member of the Government of the United States to fail to see a Latin-American revolution with the proper perspective.

Not long ago, I took part in a discussion among Latin America scholars who were attempting to distinguish the superficial from the "real" revolutions of the area. It soon became apparent that, for many of us, there was little doubt that the true and thoroughgoing revolutions were the ones we had witnessed ourselves. To be an eyewitness to political violence is, after all, a traumatic experience, and it is difficult, even for the most rigorously trained of social scientists, to preserve an accurate perspective on such a personal experience. Consider, for example, this eyewitness account of events at Quito during the Ecuadoran revolution of 1944:[9]

> Citizens in general, when they learned that the revolutionary movement had triumphed in the port of Guayaquil . . . , organized delirious demonstrations in which they cheered Dr. Velasco Ibarra, sang the national anthem, and carried the national tricolor and portraits of Dr. Velasco Ibarra.[10] Some of these demonstrations, after moving through their respective neighborhoods, advanced on the Plaza de la Independencia and in front of the statue to Liberty sang the national anthem with great emotion. Various orators spoke in the Plaza de la Independencia, cheering the triumphant revolution at Guayaquil and expressing their satisfaction . . . . The heated speeches of the orators . . . raised the fervor of the enormous throng congregated in the Plaza to the point of delirium . . . . It can be affirmed that by about ten o'clock at night, close to half the population of the city was milling through the streets shouting cries of satisfaction . . . .

The test of time, if no other, has shown, I think, that the Revolution of 1944 did not bring fundamental alterations in the Ecuadoran political system. Yet eyewitnesses to the events at Guayaquil and Quito during the last week of May, 1944, can perhaps be forgiven for their conviction at the time that they were watching a major revolution in the process of unfolding.

Faulty perspective may occasionally have the opposite manifestation. That is, what may seem to the eyewitness to be of little consequence may be, in reality, of great significance. I have already mentioned the early stages of the Mexican Revolution of 1910 as an instance of this. The Argentine Revolution of 1930 is also a case in point.[11] "My personal impression was that the so-called revolution consisted of a twelve-hour parade of cadets from the

[9] *El Comercio*, Quito, May 30th, 1944.

[10] Dr. José María Velasco Ibarra was the political leader in whose name the revolution was launched. He assumed the Presidency of Ecuador in June of 1944, remaining in office until 1947. He also served as president on two subsequent occasions, 1952–1956, and 1960–1961.

[11] Enrique Dickmann, *Recuerdos de un militante socialista* (Buenos Aires: La Vanguardia, 1949), p. 288.

Military School," an eyewitness—and a perceptive one, at that—recorded. "With the exception of a bloody incident at the *Plaza de Mayo*,[12] where two cadets and a civilian lost their lives, the parade met with no resistance. The troops at the *Campo de Mayo* (garrison) did not move; the regiments stationed in the capital declared themselves neutral; and the police remained passive." Yet the parade on September 6, 1930, of General José F. Uriburu's secondary-school cadets has left a staggering political legacy to Argentina. It includes the introduction of European-style Fascism into the country's government; the *Concordancia*, a political coalition joining the landowning "Oligarchy" with political cliques within the Argentine Army; the disruption of some eighty years of stable constitutional government, and its replacement with a condition—euphemistically called "constitutional abnormality"—from which the country has not yet recovered; and the supplanting of civilian government with military regimes.[13] The overthrow in 1962 of the government of President Arturo Frondizi by the Argentine Army offers ample evidence, I think, that the Revolution of 1930 has left its long-range mark on the country's political system.[14]

Serious problems thus beset the analysis of the concepts of both modernization and revolution, particularly as they are manifested in the Latin-American area. These difficulties should be borne in mind in any attempt to assess the interrelationship between the two processes as they occur in the Americas.

II

It may be useful at this point to examine specific instances of revolution in contemporary Latin America in the hope that they might shed light on the problem at hand. I should like to look at the Mexican and Cuban revolutions for the purposes of, first, assessing their relationship to modernization in the two countries involved, and, second, determining the extent to which they might suggest general propositions on the overall question of the interplay between revolution and modernization.

In 1910 Francisco Ignacio Madero, a curiously quixotic lawyer, launched a rebellion that in the following year brought down the government of General Porfirio Díaz, who had ruled Mexico since the 1870's. Madero's action inaugurated a generation of turmoil and reconstruction. This Revolution—

[12] This is the huge open square at Buenos Aires faced by the *Casa Rosada* (literally, "Pink House"), Argentina's White House.

[13] See George I. Blanksten, *Perón's Argentina* (Chicago: University of Chicago Press, 1953), *passim.*, especially pp. 35–44.

[14] See Crane Brinton *et al., Today's Revolutions* (Chapel Hill: University of North Carolina Press, 1962), *passim.*, especially pp. 71–79.

the celebrated "wind that swept Mexico"—has been as profound a revolution as that which struck France in the eighteenth century or Russia less than a decade after the fall of Díaz. Although its initial objectives were more limited, the Mexican Revolution came to constitute a frontal attack upon fundamental problems—such as land tenure, the temporal position of the Roman Catholic Church, the situation of the lower classes, and foreign economic influences in the country—that have historically troubled not only Mexico but also much of the rest of Latin America.

Land tenure has, of course, been a historic political problem in Mexico. It has been estimated that in 1910, on the eve of the Revolution, about one per cent of the population owned approximately seventy per cent of the arable land of Mexico. The Revolution was committed to, and has achieved, a substantial change in the pattern of land ownership. Determined that the large landed estates should be reduced, the Revolution has introduced two other land systems which are held to be mutually compatible. The first of these is designed to create a large group of individual owners of small parcels of land. The second is the *ejido* system, intended to deliver collectively owned lands to rural communities. Particularly in the early years of the Revolution, Mexico sought a solution to its historic land problem through these devices, notably the *ejido* system.

The Revolution has also altered the traditionally dominant role of the Roman Catholic Church in the temporal life of Mexico. Against an historic background of frequent unions of Church and State, the Church had become a major pre-revolutionary social, economic, and political as well as religious force in the predominantly Catholic country. In the wake of the Revolution, the Church has been disestablished and placed in a weakened position. It has been deprived of much of the land it had acquired before the Revolution, and Church officials are forbidden to vote or to present themselves as candidates for public office. In short, much of the Revolution is distinctively anticlerical in nature.

Some redefinition of the place of the lower classes in national life has, further, been achieved by the Revolution. The small upper class, variously known as creoles or "whites," had long dominated the political and economic life of the nation, excluding the two lower groups, the *mestizos*, "mixtures", and the Indians, from effective participation. The Revolution has sought a new national role for these lower classes. This has been attempted partly through the *ejido* system, partially in educational programs designed to combat illiteracy, and in part through a somewhat engineered renaissance of Indian culture. An attempt has been made with some success to destroy the older class system with a view to multiplying the opportunities available to the lower classes of the country.

The Revolution has also challenged the role of foreign capital in Mexico's economy. Especially during the regime of General Díaz (1876-1911), capital, particularly from the United States, was encouraged to enter Mexico on a large scale to develop and exploit natural resources. Especially affected were oil, communications, transportation, and electrical energy. Endeavoring to reduce outside economic influences, the Revolution has placed restrictions and limitations upon the ability of foreigners to acquire most types of property in Mexico. Expropriation and related steps have deprived foreigners of many of their prerevolutionary holdings, particularly in oil, land, and transportation. Outsiders attempting to do business in Revolutionary Mexico frequently find themselves discriminated against by the pattern of the laws.

To pinpoint the date of the beginning of the Mexican Revolution is a far simpler task than to assign the movement a terminal date. Indeed, many writers believe that the Mexican Revolution is still in process.[15] And some scholars, of course, have maintained that all major revolutions undergo a common long-run set of steps and stages during the course of unfolding.[16] This is probably not the place to examine the strengths and weaknesses of such formulations. Nevertheless, it appears to be true that, since the late 1940's and early 1950's, Mexican development has demonstrated strikingly rapid economic growth and modernization.

During this period the nature and rate of social, economic, and political change in Mexico has exhibited remarkable characteristics. For one thing, the country's economic growth bears many of the manifestations of what has been called "take-off." This is the phase in which economic change is particularly rapid. With the coming of "take-off," change appears to be irresistible. Indeed, change at this point seems to be the chief characteristic and the main preoccupation of the society. The "take-off" has been defined as "the interval during which the rate of investment increases in such a way that the real output per capita rises and this initial increase carries with it radical changes in production techniques and the disposition of income flows which perpetuate the new scale of investment and perpetuate thereby the rising trend in per capita output."[17] "Take-off" may thus be regarded as a phase, largely economic in character, of decisive transformation. Change appears to be more rapid at this time than at others. It can be affirmed that mid-twentieth-century Mexico has been experiencing "take-off," thus defined.

[15] See, for example, Howard F. Cline, *Mexico and the United States* (Cambridge: Harvard University Press, 1953), *passim.*; and Robert E. Scott, *Mexican Government in Transition* (Urbana: University of Illinois Press, 1959), *passim.*

[16] See Brinton, *op. cit., passim.*, and Brinton, *The Anatomy of Revolution* (New York: W. W. Norton, 1938), *passim.*

[17] W. W. Rostow, "The Take-off into Self-Sustained Growth," *The Economic Journal* (March

Countries in the process of rapid change tend to have what have been called "dominant non-dictatorial" political parties. These, usually comprehensive and nationalist, resemble one-party systems in that the dominant parties are not seriously challenged by rival political organizations, but differ from dictatorial systems in that other political parties may and do exist legally in addition to the "dominant" ones.[18] Mexico's governing Party of Revolutionary Institutions (PRI),[19] which was formed in the 1920's, is such a "dominant non-dictatorial" party. Although other Mexican parties exist, only the PRI wins most elections and controls the overwhelming majority of the officials of the executive and legislative branches of the country's national government.

As a "dominant non-dictatorial" party, the PRI is, of course, a governing elite. Typically, conventional elite analysis argues that governing groups usually are opposed to change likely to remove them from their controlling positions. Yet the ruling elite of "take-off" is dedicated to change and encourages it. The clear, and at times, passionate devotion of the PRI leadership to change is inescapable. The traditional conception of a ruling elite struggling to preserve the status quo is curiously irrelevant to the governing groups of Revolutionary Mexico. Deeply and even intolerantly committed to economic development and political modernization, the PRI is devoted to an impressive drive toward the industrialization of Mexico.[20] Thus oriented, this "dominant non-dictatorial" party has come to represent those political groups which gain in strength as the country's economic development proceeds. Especially important among these interest groups are the Confederation of Mexican Workers (CTM),[21] the urbanized "middle sectors"—identified as "politically ambitious middle groups" active in commerce and developing industry[22]—and other newly emerging industrializing and entrepreneurial groups. Revolutionary Mexico thus remains committed to change, with an emphasis in more contemporary times upon sufficiently orderly change to promote the country's continued rapid economic development.

A second specific Latin-American instance of revolution is provided by Cuba. On January 1, 1959, after two years of bitter guerilla warfare which had, on occasion, approached the proportions of civil war, the government of

1956), p. 25.

[18] See Almond and Coleman, *op. cit.,* pp. 40–41, 114, 188, 286–94, 295, 397–98, 479–81.

[19] After the initial letters of *Partido Revolucionario Institucional.*

[20] See Robert E. Scott, *Mexican Government in Transition* (Urbana: University of Illinois Press, 1959).

[21] After the initial letters of *Confederación de Trabajadores Mexicanos.*

[22] John J. Johnson, *Political Change in Latin America: The Emergence of the Middle Sectors* (Stanford: Stanford University Press, 1958), p. vii and *passim.*

General Fulgencio Batista y Zaldivar was at length overthrown by a rebel movement led by Dr. Fidel Castro Ruz. Castro had been engaged in revolutionary activity in Cuba since July 26, 1953, when he led an unsuccessful attack against a military post at Santiago, located in the eastern part of the island. Imprisoned for this act, Castro remained incarcerated until he was freed through an amnesty in 1955. He then left Cuba to spend almost two years in exile, principally in Mexico, preparing for his major contest with Batista. In December of 1956, Castro and a small band of guerilla invaders landed in eastern Cuba. In the following two years he acquired legendary status as a revolutionary leader. His movement, which came to power early in 1959, might be analyzed, for the present purposes, in terms of four of its aspects—its function as a manifestation of the island's historic political instability, its place in the severe rural-urban conflict between metropolitan Havana and the remainder of the island, social and economic changes in Cuba, and the international effect of the revolution upon the island's relationship to the Cold War, particularly as reflected in the pattern of Cuba's changing orientations toward the United States and the Soviet Union.

The country's historic political instability is certainly one aspect of the background against which the Castro revolution should be evaluated. Since the achievement of national independence at the end of the nineteenth century, Cuba has developed more than the average Latin-American predilection for "revolutions." Indeed, since the formalization of political independence in 1901, the island's governments had been violently overthrown in 1906, 1925, 1928, twice in 1933, and again in 1952 before the Castro upheaval. Thus, his use of political violence was in keeping with, if not a part of, the Cuban political tradition. The same can be said of the authoritarian and dictatorial nature of the government established by Castro. The *fidelista* regime has been but one more strong government in a culture historically given to political authoritarianism, especially when viewed against the background of the earlier dictatorships presided over by General Gerardo Machado (1925–1933) and Fulgencio Batista (1933–1944 and, more importantly, 1952–1959). Indeed, with the sole exception of the eight-year period from 1944 to 1952, when attempts at civilian constitutional government were made during the presidencies of Dr. Ramón Grau San Martín (1944–1948) and Carlos Prío Socarrás (1948–1952), the history of Cuba has largely been a story of military dictatorship. As another regime of force, the Castro government has nevertheless encouraged a species of democratization of militarism insofar as a popular militia has emerged from the ruins of more upper-class-directed Machado- and Batista-style armies. The place of political instability in *fidelismo* is further attested to in the lack of institutionalization which has characterized the movement. This has been reflected in the absence of constitutionalism, in the inability of civilian political parties to relate to the Castro regime, and in the heavily charismatic, rather than institutional, leadership which has given *fidelismo* much of its course and character.

A second significant aspect of the revolution is to be found in the striking political contrast—and conflict—between metropolitan Havana and the rest of Cuba. The island well illustrates the problem, common to a number of Latin-American countries, known as *la cabeza de Goliat* (Goliath's head), to be found in a country where a giant urban head rests upon a dwarflike rural body. Historically, Havana has stood in a position of political opposition to the rest of the island; and it should be remembered that *fidelismo* took shape in the Sierra Maestra as a somewhat agrarian-populistic rural move-ment at war against Havana interests. Thus, in a sense, Castro's rise to power was the triumph of rural Cuba over Havana. The imprisoned metropolis has seen its interests crushed by *fidelismo*. The industrializing "middle sectors" appear to have fallen prey to the back country. Seen as a rural victory over the metropolis, *fidelismo* is curiously reminiscent of the regime of General Juan Manuel Rosas, who had ruled Argentina more than a century before. It, too, was a triumph of the "interior" over the urban capital, of the intensely indigenous over the secular.

Other Cuban domestic political, social, and economic conditions consti-tute a third aspect. These include the role of *fidelismo*, especially in its early years, as a crusade for public morality in a Cuba grown callous and cynical toward expectations and charges of graft, corruption, and fraud on the part of its public officials. In the days of Machado, Grau, Prío, and Batista, such accusations against chief executives had become commonplace, and exiled ex-presidents were reported as living handsomely thanks to self-enrichment at public expense while in office. Indeed, ex-President Grau was formally charged, three years after the expiration of his term, with having misap-propriated one hundred seventy-four million dollars; the ultimate indictment was for forty million, "mainly because valuable evidence was apparently stolen by gunmen from a public office."[23] As a crusade for public morality, *fidelismo* has borne with it a variety of political puritanism, curiously Spartan-like in character, initially directed toward the purging of graft, corruption, and fraud from Cuban public life. The Castro regime has also been character-ized by agrarian-populistic attempts to improve literacy, housing, medical, and land tenure conditions in the rural areas. In mid-1959, during the course of Castro's agrarian reform program, a government agency, the National Institute of Agrarian Reform (INRA),[24] was established to administer the

[23] Rosendo A. Gómez, *Government and Politics in Latin America* (New York: Random House, 1960), p. 67.

[24] After the initial letters of *Instituto Nacional de Reforma Agraria.*

land-tenure policies of the revolutionary regime. Three years later, INRA, then a gigantic administrative entity, held title to more than one-half the land surface of Cuba.[25] It thus seemed clear that substantial land reform was to be counted among the facets of the revolution.

Finally, the place of the Castro revolution in the Cold War, particularly Cuba's changing relations toward the United States and the Soviet Union, provides a fourth element of the revolution. Under "North American" tutelage from the earliest days of their national independence, Cubans have long protested against the Platt Amendment, which governed their relations with the "Colossus of the North" from 1902 until 1934. This instrument formalized the United States practice of overseeing the conduct of Cuba's foreign and financial affairs, provided for North American military intervention in the island to maintain order there, and authorized the maintenance by the North Americans of a number of naval bases in Cuba. As an early step in the development of President Franklin D. Roosevelt's "Good Neighbor" policy, the Platt Amendment was abrogated in 1934.

Yet the continuation, in the years after the passing of the "Good Neighbor," of North American economic, cultural, and social influence in Cuba gave rise on the island to a phenomenon referred to as "Plattism." This is the circumstance that, despite the abrogation of the Platt Amendment more than a generation before the rise of Fidel Castro, Cuba has "continued to experience a significant degree, probably, of economic and, certainly, of psychological subordination to the United States."[26] The heavy economic and other influences of the "Yanquis," and the retention of the United States naval base at Guantánamo Bay, are, for most Cubans, more than ample evidence that the Platt Amendment still lives. Legally and technically, it was put to rest in 1934; psychologically, it continues to dominate Cubans. This discrepancy is the soul of "Plattism." Much of the interplay between *fidelismo*, Communism, the Soviet Union, and Communist China has derived its peculiar course and character from "Plattism." Initially more negative than positive, that is motivated more by rejection of the United States than by acceptance of the Soviet System, Castro's posture toward Communism has been marked by increased dependence of the Cuban regime upon the Soviet and Chinese Communist governments for political and economic assistance against the common "Yanqui" enemy.

III

A number of points of contrast between the Mexican and Cuban revolutions

[25] See Russell H. Fitzgibbon, "The Revolution Next Door: Cuba," *Annals of the American Academy of Political and Social Science*, vol. 334 (March, 1961), p. 115.

[26] *Ibid.*, p. 114.

emerge from the foregoing paragraphs. The most significant of these points, from the standpoint of the purpose of this paper, has to do with modernization and economic development. The impressively rapid economic development of Revolutionary Mexico has already been noted. However, the Cuban case does not follow a similar pattern.

On the eve of the fall of Batista, Cuba's standard of living, expressed in terms of gross national product per capita, was the third highest in Latin America.[27] To be sure, a degree of perhaps inevitable bias is built into the gross national product figures. For one thing, international economic comparisons are never easy to make, as a number of significant factors are often difficult to reduce to quantitatively comparable terms. Moreover, translation of gross national product figures into United States dollars catches aspects of trade relations and foreign exchange rates not entirely relevant to economic development and standards of living. Finally, Cuban national figures are distorted by the problem of *la cabeza de Goliat*—the pre-Castro standard of living in metropolitan Havana was substantially higher than in the rest of the country. For example, eighty-seven per cent of the dwelling units in the urban center had electricity whereas only nine per cent of Cuba's rural units were so equipped.[28]

Even after due regard is paid to these statistical pitfalls, pre-Castro Cuba's standard of living remained among the highest in Latin America. It did not seem likely, in 1962, that national living standards might rise under *fidelismo*. Indeed, such statistical changes as were in the making seemed headed in the other direction. A number of propositions flow from this situation. In the first place, while revolutions and other political phenomena appear to flow from economic growth in the underdeveloped areas,[29] it is not easy to make a reasonable case for regarding the Castro revolution as contributing to Cuba's economic development. In Latin America, economic development has depended heavily upon emerging industrializing and entrepreneurial groups. These groups—the so-called "middle sectors"— have in general developed in the urban centers of the Americas.

Pre-Castro Cuba had largely followed this pattern, with economic development essentially centered in the metropolitan area of Havana. Insofar as it has been an agrarian-populistic movement directed against Havana interests, *fidelismo* has warred against the urban "middle sectors," seriously paralyzing their ability to continue functioning. In this sense, the Castro regime appeared to be opposing the country's economic development, particularly if

[27] See Table 1, p. 237, below.

[28] Leo Huberman and Paul Sweezy, *Cuba: Anatomy of a Revolution* (New York: Monthly Review Press, 1960), p. 4.

[29] See Almond and Coleman, *op. cit., passim.*

Table 1. ECONOMIC DEVELOPMENT IN LATIN AMERICA*
(Rank Order of Countries Based on Gross National Product per Capita)

Rank	Country	Gross National Product per Capita (in U.S. Dollars)
1	Argentina	$ 688
2	Venezuela	457
3	*Cuba*	*454*
4	Uruguay	382
5	Panama	382
6	Chile	335
7	Brazil	278
8	Colombia	231
9	Costa Rica	203
10	*Mexico*	*199*
11	Dominican Republic	189
12	Guatemala	182
13	Nicaragua	168
14	El Salvador	167
15	Paraguay	166
16	Honduras	134
17	Peru	118
18	Bolivia	109
19	Ecuador	93
20	Haiti	62
For Comparison United States		*2,200*

*See Harold E. Davis (ed.), *Government and Politics in Latin America* (New York: The Ronald Press, 1958, pp. 50–93, especially 60–71; Gabriel A. Almond and James S. Coleman (eds.), *The Politics of the Developing Areas* (Princeton: Princeton University Press, 1960), pp. 455–531; and Blanksten, "The Aspiration for Economic Development," *The Annals of the American Academy of Political and Social Science*, Vol. 334 (March, 1961), pp. 10–19, especially p. 11.

industrialization and technological innovation are regarded as basic to the growth process and modernization.[30]

Students of economic development have argued that certain political prerequisites are necessary for the achievement of economic growth and modernization in the underdeveloped areas. When attempts are made to identify these political prerequisites, revolution is frequently included among

[30] See Johnson, *op. cit., passim.;* and Johnson, "The Political Role of the Latin-American Middle Sectors," *Annals of the American Academy of Political and Social Science*, vol. 334 (March, 1961), pp. 20–29, especially pp. 28–29.

them. Revolutionary regimes are often dedicated to change and usually encourage it, identifying their own interests with it. A recent study has pointed out that in India, Pakistan, and Ceylon[31] "Westernized intelligentsia ... dominate the governments of all three countries and ... dominate the policies of these governments. ... In general the leaderships of all of them are dedicated to 'modernization' in some form or other. ... " Again,[32] "segments of the leadership in Jamaica ... are particularly committed to rapid social, economic, and political change. They feel that they have a mission to perform for their country. They push for ordered, rationalistic plans of economic development. ... They are deeply dedicated. ... " Indeed, one general characterization of revolutionary regimes has it that[33] "all show a passion for technology. ... They are concerned with efficiency and rapid change."

In attempting to identify the interrelationships between revolution and modernization in contemporary Latin America, it should be noted that Revolutionary Mexico conforms to the economic-development-and-rapid-change syndrome while contemporary Cuba does not. Four basic considerations underlie this striking contrast between the two revolutionary situations. These considerations include the nature of revolution, the time contexts in which the two revolutions occurred, their effects upon industrialization and technological change, and the location of the two revolutions in the pattern of international relations.

With respect to the nature of revolution in Latin America, it will be remembered that perspective poses a difficult problem in analysis. It is not easy to assess a given revolution, while it is in the process of unfolding, in terms of the superficiality or profundity of its influence on the economic, social, and political order. With the hindsight of the 1960's it is possible to evaluate the Mexican Revolution, which began in 1910, as one of the few true revolutions the Americas have experienced during the twentieth century. But what of the Castro revolution in Cuba, so close in both time and space that it must be analyzed without benefit of the luxury of the hindsight of a generation? It is easy to mistake the here-and-now immediacy of a revolution for its profundity, just as the opposite error—a true revolution may be thought, because of its immediacy, to be of little consequence—may be made.[34] In these times this perspective problem poses a major difficulty in the assessment of contemporary Cuban affairs.

[31] Almond and Coleman, *op. cit.*, p. 212.

[32] Wendell Bell, "Images of the United States and the Soviet Union Held by Jamaican Elite Groups," *World Politics*, vol. XII, no. 2 (January, 1960), pp. 237–238.

[33] David E. Apter, "Steps Toward a Theory of Political Development," (Chicago: unpublished manuscript, 1959), p. 8.

[34] See pp. 227–229, above.

Certainly both errors have been made in attempts to understand the Castro revolution—some writers have regarded it as displacing the Mexican Revolution as the major Latin-American upheaval of the twentieth century, while others have seen it as one more *coup d'état* in a country plagued by chronic political instability. Analysis of the Cuban revolution with the benefit of accurate perspective would appear to be indispensable to any attempt to relate it to the modernization of the island.

In the second place, the time contexts in which the Mexican and Cuban revolutions are being compared differ from each other in at least two significant respects. For one thing, Mexico was in a vastly different stage of economic development in 1910 than Cuba was a half century later. Industrialization in the contemporary sense had hardly begun in Mexico when the Díaz regime fell, and revolution came to what was in many ways a primitive economy.[35] Fifty years and two world wars later, revolution in Cuba gripped a perhaps inevitably more advanced economy which, despite *la cabeza de Goliat* and other problems, boasted the third highest standard of living in Latin America. In short, the Castro revolution does not appear to have either sprung from or contributed to modernization, which was already well under way in Cuba before the fall of the second Batista regime.

A second aspect of the time problem is also significant. Students of the process of revolution have often argued that all major revolutions, during the course of their development, pass through a more or less uniform set of steps or stages. The first of these, in most formulations, is a period of social unrest, frequently attributed to economic causes. From this initial stage emerges what is sometimes called the desertion or the defection of the intellectuals, a phase in which the writers, artists, teachers, and preachers of the affected society set up a running attack against the existing order. In the third stage it is held that the output of the intellectuals takes on a more positive quality, and the social myth or ideology of the revolution then emerges. Next, the established armed forces, for one reason or another are unable to defend the tottering old regime. Moderates then rise briefly to power. This is followed by the violent physical change in government, after which the revolution enters upon a stage variously called the accession of the extremists, the reign of terror,[36] the era of revolutionary virtue, or the period of dictatorship. Finally, the stage of Thermidor arrives, when the extremists are displaced by new moderates under whose leadership com-

---

[35] See Sanford A. Mosk, *Industrial Revolution in Mexico* (Berkeley: University of California Press, 1950), *passim.*

[36] This period, from roughly 1911 to about 1920, in the Mexican Revolution is generally known as *la tormenta,* often freely translated as "the time of trouble."

promises are made as the social myth of the revolution is reinterpreted.[37]

If some such formulation is accepted, the Mexican and Cuban cases differed vastly from each other in the early 1960's. Mexico's spectacularly rapid economic development and modernization are largely characteristic of the Thermidorean stage, which had set in at about the time of World War II. If the Cuban case turned out in perspective to be a profound revolution, in the early 1960's it was still in early stages, with Thermidor not yet in sight. If revolution is indeed to assume the qualities of a prerequisite of economic development and modernization, it was not yet possible, at the time this paper was written, to examine the Mexican and Cuban cases at comparable stages in the unfolding of their respective revolutions.

Technological considerations also account for some of the differences between the two cases. Essentially, economic development may be viewed as the process of technological innovation, resulting in greater efficiency on the part of the productive arts. A more effective technology draws a higher level of production—that is, a greater gross national product per capita—from a fixed input into an economy. In the first decade of the twentieth century, when revolution struck Mexico, that country's major cities had not yet become the great centers of technological innovation and beginnings of industrialization that the urban centers were noted for a generation or two later. In Fulgencio Batista's Cuba, however, the industrializing "middle sectors" were centered in the metropolitan area of Havana. It has already been noted that the Castro revolution has warred against these sectors, seriously crippling their ability to continue functioning.

The flight of great numbers of Cuban refugees into foreign exile is, no doubt, another facet of the technological problem. Available data on the anti-Castro refugees are sketchy in the absence of systematic studies of the exile groups. Nevertheless, it appears to be true that these groups embrace significantly large percentages of Cuba's technically trained personnel. The flight of skilled personnel left sufficiently acute shortages of trained workers

---

[37] There is, of course, a voluminous literature on revolution, both in general and in Latin America in particular. From the standpoint of the present discussion, the reader may be interested in the following particularly relevant works: Crane Brinton, *op. cit.*; Brinton, *The Anatomy of Revolution* (New York: W. W. Norton and Co., 1938); Lyford P. Edwards, *The Natural History of Revolution* (Chicago: University of Chicago Press, 1927); Robert Hunter, *Revolution: Why, How, When?* (New York: Harper & Brothers, 1940); Harold E. Davis (ed.), *Government and Politics in Latin America* (New York, The Ronald Press, 1958), especially pp. 119–146; Kalman H. Silvert, *The Conflict Society: Reaction and Revolution in Latin America* (New Orleans: Hauser Press, 1961); Russell H. Fitzgibbon, "Revolutions: Western Hemisphere," *The South Atlantic Quarterly*, vol. LV (July, 1956), pp. 263–279; Alfred Meusel, "Revolution and Counter-Revolution," *Encyclopaedia of the Social Sciences* (New York: The Macmillan Co., 1937), vol. IV, pp. 259–262; and Robert N. Burr (ed.), "Latin America's Nationalistic Revolutions," *Annals of the American Academy of Political and Social Science*, vol. 334 (March 1961).

on the island to inspire Prime Minister Castro to complain about this technological crisis in a number of speeches early in 1962.

Location of the Mexican and Cuban revolutions in the pattern of international relations uncovers additional differences between the two situations. There is, for one thing, the overriding question of the relationship of the revolutions to the Soviet Union and the Communist movement. Here the time context is crucial. In the Mexican case, the revolution began a full seven years before revolution came to Russia. Those seven years were decisive. During that hectic period between the rise of Francisco Ignacio Madero and the fall of Alexander Kerensky, the Mexican Revolution acquired its own course, character, and definition—its own identity as a major social and political movement. Although certain similarities can easily be identified between the Mexican and Russian revolutions, especially in the ideological field, the two movements were out of gear, in their timing with respect to each other. The two ships passed in the night. It was a close brush, but the essential point is that they *did* pass each other, to go in different directions. Not so in the Cuban case. Born in—and, in some cases, of—the Cold War, the Castro revolution has been, perhaps inevitably, influenced by the Soviet Union. Cuba's relations with the Soviets and with Communist China have been redefined, sometimes under sensational circumstances. Formal diplomatic relations with these countries have become remarkably cordial, and Cuba has become increasingly dependent upon the Communist states.

An additional consideration in the field of international politics is perhaps more directly relevant to the process of modernization. This has to do with participation in foreign aid programs designed to stimulate economic growth through technical assistance. Mexico has participated in these programs, virtually without interruption, since their inception on the eve of World War II. The assessment of the extent to which Mexico's economic development can be attributed to participation in foreign aid programs is a major feat of economic analysis lying outside the scope of this paper. To the extent that Mexican development and modernization have benefited at all from these programs of technical cooperation, another point of contrast with the Cuban case becomes apparent. Excluded, from the early days of the Castro revolution, from programs of technical cooperation and from participation in the Alliance for Progress, the Cuban regime has been cut off from additional potential stimuli to economic development and modernization. A similar effect is no doubt exercised by the trade embargoes imposed against Cuba by the United States and other American republics. While the Soviet Union, Communist China, and a number of the states of eastern Europe have made gestures of economic assistance to Cuba, these have not been sufficient to fill the gaps left by the American nations and other states of the West.

Thus, while revolution is often regarded as a political prerequisite of modernization in underdeveloped areas, the circumstances under which revolution functions as such a stimulus remain to be formulated with greater precision than has yet been achieved. The Mexican Revolution appears to be a fertile field for research on the interrelationship between revolution and modernization in Latin America. The Cuban case raises serious problems in research on this question. What may be learned in Mexico about the interplay between the two processes cannot be applied to Cuba in the absence of the development of research techniques capable of coping with the comparability problems posed by imprecision in the use of the term "revolution," time differentials, the study of technological change, and differing roles in international politics.

SOCIAL EVOLUTION AND THE THEORY OF ECONOMIC DEVELOPMENT

JOSEPH SPENGLER
Duke University

My main concern will be some of the ways in which the theory of economic development resembles, as well as differs from, the theory of social evolution. Accordingly, I shall outline economic-developmental theory in Part I, though essentially in a manner suited to permit comparisons between it and social-evolutionary theory. Part II continues Part I and is devoted more specifically to certain problems of change; Part III is about earlier evolutionary approaches to the study of economic development, and Part IV concerns a number of illustrative developmental processes which economic researchers believe they have found to be operative in the post-1800 period. Part V is devoted to elements in social-evolutionary theory of possible concern to the student of economic development. Part VI is devoted to assessments and conclusions and to consideration of whether the theory of social evolution is of use to the policy-maker, to the extent that it illuminates the past course of economic development.[1]

---

[1] I have made use, respecting organic evolution, of G. G. Simpson, *The Meaning of Evolution*, New Haven, 1960; Sol Tax, ed., *Evolution after Darwin* (3 vols.), Chicago, 1960; L. Hogben, *An Introduction to Mathematical Genetics*, New York, 1946; and Theodosius Dobzhansky, "Evolution at Work," *Science*, CXXVII, May 9, 1958, pp. 1091-98. Respecting social evolution, I have made use principally of Tax, *op. cit.*; Julian H. Steward, *The Theory of Culture Change*, Urbana, 1955; Leslie A. White, *The Evolution of Culture*, New York, 1959; A. L. Kroeber, ed., *Anthropology Today*, Chicago, 1953; M. D. Sahlins and E. R. Service, eds., *Evolution and Culture*, Ann Arbor, 1960; A. I. Hallowell, "Personality, Culture, and Society in Behavioral Evolution," in Sigmond Koch, *Psychology: A Study of a Science*, New York, 1963, pp. 429–509; and the series of papers in the evolution of man and his society comprising the September, 1960, number of the *Scientific American*, Vol. CCIII. On the impact of evolutionary theory upon social thought in the past, see Stow Persons, ed., *Evolutionary Thought in America*, New Haven, 1950; G. W. Stocking, Jr., "Lamarckianism in American Social Science: 1890-1915," *Journal of the History of Ideas*, XXIII, April-June, 1962, pp. 239-56; Craufurd Goodwin, "Evolution Theory in Australian Thought," *Journal of the History of Ideas*, XXV, July-September, 1964, pp. 393-416.

I. THE THEORY OF ECONOMIC DEVELOPMENT

Economic growth may be said to take place whenever the output (defined in gross or net terms) of goods and services increases. It may increase under one or two sets of conditions, only the latter of which contains parallels to social evolution. First, it may increase merely because some or all kinds of inputs increase. Thus, if production in an economy is describable in terms of a production function that is homogeneous of degree one, total output will increase by a fraction k if all inputs are increased by k, and by less than k if, *ceteris paribus*, some but not all kinds of inputs are increased by k. Of course, if there were but one unit of one kind of input not subject to variation and it was being used in the stage of increasing returns, output might increase by k even though this input remained unchanged and all the other inputs were increased by k; but this is an unusual case and will be disregarded. Second, output may increase because there takes place not only an increase in the quantity of some inputs, but also a change in the quality of certain kinds of inputs (the quantity of which may or may not be increased) and an addition of new kinds of inputs to the complex of inputs being used. The increase in output is thus associated with increase in the quality and the variety of inputs, as well as with increase in the quantity of some of them; it may be associated with a change in organization. If we think of economic growth as a set, then the first and second means of growth just cited are members of this set as is the case of increasing return discussed under the first way. It is the second way that involves differentiation in the quality and the character of inputs employed and thus includes parallels to social evolution. It is also the second way that is the more important, particularly since 1800; in fact, in advanced economies most growth is of this sort. My discussion in this paper will relate primarily to the second way, and it will be referred to as economic development or complex growth, whereas the first way will be viewed as simple growth.

In the literature relating to economic growth or development, the first and second cases are distinguished at least implicitly, though not much is made of the distinction. Usually the primary concern of inquirers is the role of one, several, or more of the determinants of economic growth, or the interrelation of these roles; it is not the sequestration of those determinants, together with their interrelations and the manner in which these elements enter into processes of the sort involved in social evolution. For purposes of the present discussion, however, I shall make the distinction explicit, though recognizing that, conceptually as well as concretely, the two cases sometimes overlap.

Let (i) represent the first way and suppose that in a given large nation and closed economy output O is a function solely of economic inputs A, B, and C, and that, with technological and all other relevant conditions given, production at the macro-level proceeds as if in conformity with a production function that is homogeneous of degree one. Suppose also that recipients of output *O*, behaving invariantly, increase the stock of *A*, *B*, and *C* at some constant rate *r* per year. Under the circumstances *O* will increase at this same rate *r*, but the amount of *O* available per capita will remain constant (since the labor force [call it *C* and suppose it to be a constant fraction of the population *P*] will be growing at the same rate as *O* and the stock of co-operant factors *A* and *B*) and there will not be (because of changes in price structure or of per capita income) economic or other pressure (e.g., changes in tastes) to change the composition of *O* or the distribution of inputs among uses or employments.[2] We should then have a stable population growing at rate *r*, an economy stable as to form and rate of growth, and, if the population were large enough, stability of genetic ratios and cessation of organic evolution.[3]

Growth of *O* could not persist indefinitely at rate *r* under the conditions assumed if it were taking place in a finite world, since *A* and *B* could not continue to be made to grow indefinitely at rate *r*, and, by definition, there would not be technological changes to offset constraints upon the growth of *A* and *B* unless the population were willing to acquiesce in a reduction of per capita income and consumption. Even then, given the finiteness of the environment and the constancy of other relevant conditions, there would exist some level below which per capita income and per capita consumption would not be permitted to descend. Alternatively, even though for a time *A* and *B* increased faster than *C*, and consequently output per head increased, this movement would come to a halt when the productivity of "capital" (i.e., *A* and *B*) had fallen to a level sufficient to yield a return merely adequate to keep the stock of *A* and *B* intact. In either instance there would come into being the world of the classical stationary state, with the stock of *A*, *B*, and *C* constant at a zero rate of growth; the equilibrium characteristic of this state would have replaced the moving equilibrium described above, but, as Sorokin states, would hardly be descriptive of an empirical social system.[4]

[2] This statement also implies that the distribution of income to those who decide how it is to be spent is unchanging, or, if changed, is without effect upon the composition of final demand.

[3] "In a population indefinitely large, breeding wholly at random, not affected by selection, the proportions of the various existing sorts of genes and chromosomes will tend toward definite fixed ratios. When this equilibrium is reached, change in genetic ratios and consequently evolutionary change will cease." See Simpson, *op. cit.*, p. 227; also Hogben, *op. cit.*, pp. 106-14. Simpson's conclusion appears to be somewhat at variance with A. E. Emerson's findings (reported in this volume) and with the view that balanced genetic polymorphism tends to give rise to important genetic shifts.

[4] For a modern statement of the limits to population growth if not also to the increase of co-operant factors see W. M. Corden, "The Economic Limits to Population Increase," *Economic Record*, XXXI, 1955, especially pp. 258-60. The classical view is described by B. F. Hoselitz

Because of the finiteness of the environment in which economies are situated as well as because of the role played by equilibration in economic analysis in general, formulators of growth theories must fall back upon suitable sources of change, even as must formulators of evolutionary theory, to account for the course of events. In the theory of organic evolution, this role is played primarily by mutation and only secondarily by other sources of evolutionary change; in the absence of mutation, a kind of evolutionless-equilibrium might perhaps emerge.[5] To this equilibrium the equilibrium of a classical stationary state (characterized by essentially unchanging tastes, technology, population, and stocks of productive agents co-operant with labor) is analogous. If growth is to persist for a long time, there must be escape from the constraints of this state, and this may be provided, as suggested below, by exogenous change, or by changes which necessarily flow out of the variables, together with their interrelations, which currently maintain an economic system in a stable state.[6]

in his *Sociological Aspects of Economic Growth*, Glencoe, 1960, pp. 10-15; and by T. Haavelmo, *A Study of the Theory of Economic Evolution*, Amsterdam, 1954, ch. 1-2. "Social systems and processes are in a state of incessant flux, change, modification, transformation and movement. These may now be gradual and slow, now sudden and rapid, but they are hardly in a state of rest." See P. A. Sorokin, *Social and Cultural Dynamics*, IV, New York, 1941, p. 679, also pp. 680-81 for criticisms of various economists' notions of equilibrium.

[5] "New combinations of genes and chromosomes produce new variant sorts of organisms, but no basically new types of organisms can arise and evolutionary change cannot be long sustained, geologically speaking, as long as the genes and chromosome sets remain of the same kinds. Major and long-continued evolutionary changes therefore depend on a third source of difference between parents and offspring: mutations, which are the production of new sorts of genes and chromosome sets." See G. G. Simpson, *The Meaning of Evolution*, p. 219. Natural selection, the operative mechanism of adaptation, determines "what combinations of genes will be incorporated in individual organisms" and hence what mutations will survive; it thus serves, along with mutation and non-random breeding, to prevent the emergence of what amounts to a genetically stable population. See *ibid.*, pp. 219–27; also L. Hogben, *op. cit.*, pp. 106–14, 190–98. See also E. Mayr's account of the emergence of evolutionary novelties in response to shifts in function and C. H. Waddington's account of factors other than the "genetic system" and natural selection, in Tax, *op. cit.*, II, pp. 349–402. Lecomte de Noüy has written: "whereas adaptation blindly tries to attain an equilibrium which will bring about its end, evolution can only continue through unstable systems or organisms." See *Human Destiny*, New York, 1947, p. 71. See also Emerson's chapter in this volume.

[6] Formulators of functional and other implicitly "equilibrium" social theories usually are conscious of the need to provide escape from constraints imposed by their conceptions of equilibrium. See W. E. Moore, "A Reconsideration of Theories of Social Change," *American Sociological Review*, XXV, December, 1960, p. 811; also his *Social Change*, New York, 1963. See also G. E. Swanson's remarks in his "The Approach to a General Theory of Action by Parsons and Shils," *ibid.*, XVIII, April, 1953, pp. 131–34; Bernard Barber, "Structural-Functional Analysis: Some Problems and Misunderstandings," *ibid.*, XXI, 1956, pp. 132–34, and T. Parsons's comments on Swanson's and other critiques, "Some Comments on the State of the General Theory of Action," *ibid.*, XVIII, 1953, pp. 622, 627 ff. The limitations of functionalist approaches are treated by Ernest Nagel in *The Structure of Science*, New York, 1961, ch. 12, 14.

The economist's conceptions of equilibrium and equilibration may be less well suited to some aspects of the study of economic growth than to coping with the sorts of problems to whose solution these conceptions have been adjusted, though this shortcoming can be avoided as we indicate in II.[7] If he defines equilibration in certain ways, he can by no means account adequately for growth; if he falls back upon a process model, he may satisfactorily explain some of the past and yet not find this model correctly anticipating the future course of human events.[8] He can locate the main sources of change outside his analytical system and be content with inquiries into the manner on which this system adapts to exogenous change; but if he does this, his theory of economic development will be incomplete and may underestimate sources of change really endogenous to the system. Alternatively, he may endeavor to enlarge his analytical universe and include in it sources of change of marked import for the study of economic growth, whether stochastic in character as many social processes seem to be, or instead subject to classical economic equilibrating tendencies admixed with novelty. If he does this, he may, as noted in Part II, find most sources of change to fit nicely within his analytical system. He must, however, always allow for an analogue of mutation in the biological realm, that is, for what Whitehead calls "the conceptual entertainment of unrealized possibility," or, more generally, for sources of "novelty."[9] It is in change in the contents of men's minds and in changes associated therewith (e.g., changes in habits, institutions, and queries respecting sources of change) that technological progress, the correspondent of mutation, has its principal source.[10] The theory of economic development must allow for this. It must also allow for a possibility that is seldom present in the world of sub-human beings, even when they find themselves encased in a kind of evolutionless equilibrium. It must allow for the possibility (perhaps the probability) that the pressure men

[7] E.g., see R. G. D. Allen, *Mathematical Economics*, London, 1956, chap. 10; P. A. Samuelson, *Foundations of Economic Analysis*, Cambridge, 1947, pp. 7-10, 12, 19-20, 311-17, 319-20. 329-32. See also on quasi-and moving-equilibrium, A. J. Lotka, *Elements of Physical Biology*, Baltimore, 1925, ch. 11, 21.

[8] E.g., K. E. Boulding, "In Defense of Statics," *Quarterly Journal of Economics*, LXIX, 1955, pp. 487–88; Michael Scriven, "Explanation and Prediction in Evolutionary Theory," *Science*, CXXX, August 28, 1959, pp. 477-482; also Adolf Grünbaum, "Temporally-Asymmetric Principles, Parity Between Explanation and Prediction, and Mechanism Versus Teleology," *Philosophy of Science*, XXIX, April, 1964, pp. 146–170.

[9] A. N. Whitehead, *Modes of Thought*, New York, 1958, pp. 36, 80, 119, and *Science and the Modern World*, New York, 1947, p. 70. Concerning difficulties surrounding the concept of "novelty" see Nagel, *op. cit.*, pp. 374–80. The role of mutation and selection at the biological level is dealt with by Verne Grant in *The Origin of Adaptations*, New York, 1963; Theodosius Dobzhansky, *Mankind Evolving: The Evolution of the Human Species*, New Haven, 1962.

[10] On problems associated with the analysis of the role of ideas, see Talcott Parsons, "The Role of Ideas in Social Action," *American Sociological Review*, III, October, 1938, pp. 652–64.

are under to adapt to an undesirable equilibrium situation (e.g., that inherent in a stationary state) may in the end operate, as often as does their being confronted by other undesirable situations, to generate important changes which modify the matrix of conditions underlying this equilibrium and cause its point to be shifted.[11]

It may be noted parenthetically that since the day of Alfred Marshall (who employed natural selection and other biological concepts) and Thorstein Veblen, critic of non-evolutionary economics,[12] economists have made use of concepts drawn from evolutionary theory, thereby perhaps claiming usure on the contribution Malthus and the Ricardians supposedly made to evolutionary theory when they developed the principles of population and free competition. In an economy characterized by uncertainty, A. A. Alchian has argued, one may effectively analyze the behavior of a universe of firms by employing the "economic counterparts of genetic heredity, mutations, and natural selection," these being "imitation, innovation, and positive profits."[13] Even though one grants imitation and positive profits to be economic counterparts of genetic heredity and natural selection and allows the role of innovation to resemble that of mutation, one cannot allow innovations to be full-fledged counterparts of mutation; for innovation rates are subject to marked variation at the hands of intervening individuals, groups, etc., whereas most mutation rates are subject to little if any modification through such intervention, though exposed (as are innovations) to the sometimes countervailing influence of selection. Accordingly, while innovation is one of the possible links between economic-development theory and social-evolution theory, its determinants do not closely resemble those of mutation.[14]

[11] E.g., see E. T. Penrose, "Biological Analogies in the Theory of the Firm," *American Economic Review*, XLII, December, 1952, pp. 813-16, on how the introduction of human will makes an environment subject to modification, particularly when that environment is deemed improvable. See also Dobzhansky, "The Present Evolution of Man," *Scientific American*, CCIII, September, 1960, p. 206.

[12] See Marshall, *Principles of Economics*, 8th ed., London, 1920, pp. 247 ff., 315 ff.; *Industry and Trade*, London, 1920, pp. 163–64. Marshall's views, which reflected the influence of Darwin's work, appeared already in the 1890 edition of the *Principles*. Veblen's critiques appear in *The Place of Science in Modern Civilisation*, New York, 1919. See also my essay in Persons, *op. cit.*

[13] "Uncertainty, Evolution, and Economic Theory," *Journal of Political Economy*, LVIII, June, 1950, pp. 211–21, especially p. 220. Ramifications of the impact of uncertainty are discussed in Mary Jean Bowman, ed., *Expectations, Uncertainty, and Business Behavior* (Social Science Research Council), New York, 1958. C. R. Noyes described economics as "fundamentally a biological science" in his *Economic Man*, I, New York, 1948, p. 17. This study deals primarily with wants, real costs, preference, and natural environment rather than with the price system and inter-bargaining-unit relations.

[14] See Penrose, *op. cit.*, pp. 814–16. A number of comments on the subject of this article appeared in the *American Economic Review* in 1953–54, T. Dobzhansky reports that the mutation rate in man may vary from 10^{-3} to $4(10^{-5})$. See "The Present Evolution . . . ," *loc. cit.*, p. 206.

Haavelmo, in contrast with Alchian, has been content to treat economic evolution much as most economists treat the theory of economic growth. He has conceived of an economic system as determinate and dynamic, with its course fixed by the "production" and "accumulation" functions operative, together with the ruling "law of population growth," since randomly distributed shocks do not make for indeterminateness and since the growth and spread of education and know-how can be appropriately fitted into the system. This approach demonstrates, among other things, the source of irreversibility in economic history and the fact "that even small initial dissimilarities may in time cause very big—almost irreparable—gaps between potentially similar economic regions."[15] It does not, Haavelmo points out, indicate that the empirical future can be foreseen with a high degree of precision.

Complex growth (the second case mentioned above), or economic development, takes place when all or most of the determinants of growth are operative, and not merely increase in inputs of the sort already in use. We may classify these determinants in various ways. We may divide them into those which affect output directly (e.g., increase in inputs) and those which affect it indirectly through their influence upon the increase of inputs (e.g., increase in thriftiness) or upon the quality of inputs, especially labor. Or we may divide them into those which affect the growth of output continuously (e.g., increase in inputs, improvement in technology) and those which affect it discontinuously (e.g., redistribution of inputs among employments when the initial distribution is sub-optimal). We shall, however, classify the determinants into those operative in both cases (i) and (ii) and those operative primarily in case (ii). We have already discussed those operative in case (i); namely, increase in inputs (i.e., labor, capital, etc.) of the sort theretofore in use and upon which increase in output O was held to be solely dependent in an economic sense. We said little about circumstances governing the rate of increase in these inputs except to suggest that tastes were not very variable and that the rate of increase in inputs co-operant with labor would fall if per capita income fell, or if the rate of return to suppliers of these inputs declined. In what follows, emphasis will be put upon per capita rates, since these constitute a better index of progress than do aggregate rates.

In case (ii) increase in output, O per capita depends immediately upon increase in inputs, both old and new in form, upon the emergence of superior

[15] Haavelmo, *op. cit.*, p. 111. This finding, analogous to those of students of natural selection, recalls to mind Thorstein Veblen's conclusion that a "slender initial difference may come to be decisive of the outcome in case circumstances give this initial difference a cumulative effect." See *The Instinct of Workmanship*, New York, 1918, p. 248. On the slowness with which natural selection may work see J. B. S. Haldane, *The Causes of Evolution*, New York, 1932, ch. 4 and Appendix.

inputs and superior modes of organization and their substitution for less effective modes, and upon technical progress which facilitates such emergence and which diminishes input per unit of output and (as William Godwin anticipated) augments the extent to which the blocks of matter surrounding man (i.e., land and natural resources) can made to serve his purposes economically. Increase in input per capita or per worker of factor services co-operant with labor depends primarily upon the level of per capita income, and secondarily upon the average propensity to save which normally ranges, in a free society, between 14 and 15 per cent of "national income;"[16] it thus depends appreciably upon technical progress, particularly when such progress contributes more to growth of output per worker than does increase in co-operant factors per worker. It follows, in general, that institutional arrangements and human habits which make for technical progress, for thriftiness (i.e., a high propensity to save and make capital formation possible), and for a disposition to work effectively and skillfully[17] are essential to economic development.

Capacity for technical progress depends upon the state of science in a country,[18] upon its access to foreign sources of scientific knowledge, upon the presence of personnel with the engineering skill required to apply the findings of basic science as well as personnel with the training (usually to be had at secondary-level educational institutions) essential to carry out these applications, upon the availability of entrepreneurs able to innovate (i.e., commercialize technical progress) and both free and with incentive to do so, and upon an economy's being flexible and characterized by a sufficiently high degree of factor mobility.[19] Capacity for technical progress cannot, therefore,

[16] When coercion is present in a society and consumers are not sovereign and free, the rate of saving and capital formation may appreciably exceed 15 per cent. If, however, the presence of this coercion dampens incentive and the disposition to work, or if the set of accounting (or other) prices used to allocate inputs is defective and conducive to waste, the effect of the high saving rate may be offset at least in part by waste and depression of aggregate output.

[17] Such disposition entails both that preference for "leisure" be sufficiently limited and that the propensity to put forth effort continuously and effectively be well-developed. This propensity is much lower in quite underdeveloped than in quite advanced countries; it accounts, along with difference in skill *per se*, for great disparity in output per worker even when other relevant conditions are not very dissimilar.

[18] Growth in this capacity depends upon growth of its determinants. As this capacity increases, however, a country may become exposed to a mechanical force somewhat parallel to that which A. Toynbee has called "archaism." See *A Study of History*, VI, London, 1939, pp. 49–97. As the body of technical knowledge increases, the ratio of the best (i.e., of that on the frontier of efficiency) to the total decreases. Accordingly, if the principle of selection does not operate strongly enough and remove from use much of the inferior knowledge, relatively less use will be made of superior techniques, and this tendency will increase as the body of knowledge enlarges until its growth begins to be slowed down by this comparative non-use and its adverse effect upon the growth of knowledge itself.

[19] Flexibility on the part of consumers might also be mentioned. Its absence can be important and probably has been in some societies. In the post-1800 world and, above all, in the present-day

become significant until a society and its labor force have been appreciably modernized; it is absent from a traditional society, and it is not very notable in a handicraft society.[20] It did not, therefore, spring into being and develop independently in a number of places in the past two centuries; rather it had its modern origin in north western Europe and spread thence to other parts of Europe, to regions settled by Europeans (e.g., North America, Australia), and to those parts of Asia and Africa where European influence was great (e.g., South Africa, Algeria, India, parts of China, Malaya) or where the ruling classes were bent upon introducing modern methods (e.g., Japan).[21] Capacity for innovation and the commercialization of technical progress has depended upon the presence of persons with entrepreneurial skill, that is, upon persons with both ability to recognize the probable profitability of technical developments or improvements and access to financial resources essential to their initial exploitation.[22] Since technical progress is unevenly dispersed among industries at any given time, and since elasticity of demand for products both varies with industry and changes in time, the composition of a nation's labor force and capital structure needs to be kept adjusted to changes in supply-demand relationships associated with technical progress. Such adjustment

world, potential demand tends to outstrip supply and keep actual demand quite abreast of actual supply. I shall assume, therefore, that barriers to growth arise principally on the supply side rather than on the demand side, and that demand for income in terms of effort shifts enough to prevent increase in output per manhour from reducing annual manhours per worker below some minimum level (say, 1800–2000). However, see my "Product-Adding versus Product-Replacing Innovations," *Kyklos*, X, Fasc. 3, 1957, pp. 249–77. Computerization and automation may, however, reduce the number appreciably below 1800.

[20] See J. L. Sadie, "The Social Anthropology of Economic Underdevelopment," *Economic Journal*, LXX, June, 1960, pp. 294–303; also Hoselitz, *Sociological Aspects*, passim. On what is involved in converting a traditional or a handicraft society into a modern labor force, see W. E. Moore and A. S. Feldman, *Labor Commitment and Social Change in Developing Areas*, New York, 1960. The role of education is treated in C. S. Shoup, *The Fiscal System of Venezuela*, Baltimore, 1959, chap. 15, in *Investment in Education*, A Report of the Commission on Post-School Certificate and Higher Education in Nigeria, Lagos (Federal Ministry of Education), 1960, and currently in T. W. Schultz, *Transforming Traditional Agriculture*, New Haven, 1964, and Mary Jean Bowman, "Schultz, Denison, and the Contribution of 'Eds' to National Income Growth," *Journal of Political Economy*, LXXII, October, 1964, pp. 450–64.

[21] E.g., see G. M. Meier and R. E. Baldwin, *Economic Development*, New York, 1957, Part 2, on the emergence and intensive development of Britain and countries peripheral thereto and the spread of products, capital and labor, and technical skill from this expanding center to various other parts of the world. See also A. J. Youngson's fairly detailed account of accelerating progress in pre-1800 Britain and in nineteenth-century Scandinavia, in *Possibilities of Economic Progress*, Cambridge, 1959, ch. 8–10; also Hoselitz, *Sociological Aspects*, ch. 4–5, 7–9, and, on Japan, Henry Rosovsky, *Capital Formation in Japan 1868–1940*, Glencoe, 1961, especially ch. 4.

[22] E.g., see M. Abramovitz, ed., *Capital Formation and Economic Growth*, Princeton, 1955, Parts III–V. On the role that science might play in economic development see R. L. Meier, *Science and Economic Development: New Patterns of Living*, New York, 1956.

requires that increments in labor and capital, together with their replace-ments, be appropriately distributed among employments; it is easily accomplished if the price structure is flexible and artificial barriers are not put in the way of redistributive factor-movements.[23]

While developmental sequences have been touched upon in the literature relating to economic growth, they have not been dealt with in detail. More-over, various theses remain untested; e.g., that the autonomy of the economic sub-system of a societal system increases through time; or that (contrary to F. List's belief and in keeping with T. Veblen's) internal checks to growth develop in advanced economies and finally cause their rates of growth to fall below those of economies in earlier stages of development. It is implied that economic development presupposes the existence of appropriate ways of thought, appropriate human-habit and aspirations structures, appropriate claims and reward systems, and suitable private and governmental institu-tional arrangements. One encounters frequent mention of the importance of the money, banking, legal, tax, fiscal, property, landholding, and business-organizational systems in existence; of the provisions for the maintenance of law, order, security, and at least minimal public services and social overhead capital; of the resources devoted to education and the extent to which they are utilized in a productivity-maximizing fashion; of the attitude toward foreign capital and enterprise; of the degree to which ecclesiastical, governmental, and related forms of waste are avoided; of the course of urbanization; and so on. That these conditions are associated, that they develop simultaneously or in overlapping sequence, and that they emerge with and re-enforce economic development is generally accepted. But highly detailed analyses of the origins and of the temporal and other inter-relations of these conditions in concrete, developing economies are not yet available.[24]

[23] If an economy were essentially static, but productive agents were optimally distributed among employments, the gain achievable from flexibility and redistribution would be exhausted with the restoration of an optimal distribution. In a dynamic society, however, an optimal distribution can be maintained only if the economy is flexible and factors are mobile, since sub-optimal distributions continually come into being as a result of change.

[24] On some of these conditions see Hoselitz, *Sociological Aspects*; J. E. Meade, *A Neo-Classical Theory of Economic Growth*, London, 1961; W. A. Lewis, *The Theory of Economic Growth*, London, 1955; B. Higgins, *Economic Development*, New York, 1959; C. P. Kindleberger, *Economic Development*, New York, 1958; N. S. Buchanan and H. S. Ellis, *Approaches to Economic Develop-ment*, New York, 1955; P. T. Bauer and B. S. Yamey, *The Economics of Underdeveloped Countries*, London, 1957; H. Leibenstein, *Economic Backwardness and Economic Growth*, New York, 1957; H. F. Williamson and J. A. Buttrick, *Economic Development: Principles and Patterns*, Englewood

II. EQUILIBRATION AND CHANGE

Modern economic development is characterized by two conditions which were not very significant in the past, particularly prior to the second half of the nineteenth century. Today, more than ever, social change in general and economic development in particular are the product of deliberate change-producing action on the part of the men, groups, and agencies situated in a society; it may indeed be said that provision for continuing scientific progress, invention, and innovation is institutionalized in modern societies in both the public and the private sector. Anticipation of the future, together with action in the present to make possible what men want in the future, is the focus of a great deal of activity; it is therefore a major force in the present giving shape to the future. It is operative not only in advanced countries but also in backward countries, the leaders in most of which are turning to advanced countries, in both the "free" and the "communist" worlds, for conceptions of what their national futures should incorporate. It is these anticipations and expectations respecting the future which govern in a marked degree the ends to which current means are to be put; they help give order to some of the preference systems which are operative in both backward and advanced economies. It is possible, of course, that salutary change may be retarded by deliberate action, as when codes continue to prescribe outmoded technology, but on balance, deliberate action probably makes for the acceleration of change.

A second characteristic of the modern world is the existence, in most countries, of sizable "surpluses" which can be used to give concrete form to anticipations and plans regarding the future. In reality, of course, this surplus is still relatively small (say around or even below 5 per cent of national income) in some underdeveloped countries. Nonetheless, it is now realized that this surplus can be appreciably augmented and that what the future will bring to a people depends upon the uses to which they put this surplus. It is thus a necessary though not a sufficient condition for bringing about desired economic changes.

Even though an economy appears to be in a state of stable equilibrium, this is an impermanent state so long as it does not answer either to the description

Cliffs, 1954; S. Kuznets, *Economic Change,* New York, 1953; Margaret Mead, *Cultural Patterns and Technical Change*, New York, 1955; S. Kuznets, W. E. Moore, and J. J. Spengler, eds., *Economic Growth: Brazil, India, Japan,* Durham, 1955; also my "Economic Development: Political Preconditions and Political Consequences," *Journal of Politics*, XXIII, 1960, pp. 387–416, "Economic Factors in the Development of Densely Populated Areas," *Proceedings of the American Philosophical Society*, XCV, February, 1951, pp. 20–53, and "Sociological Value Theory, Economic Analyses, and Economic Policy," *American Economic Review*, XLIII (2), May, 1953, pp. 340–49.

of the classical stationary state (in which the stock of capital is merely kept intact), or to that of a state in which all potential increments to the stock of "wealth" are consumed in a manner not to affect future productivity. Such states are highly improbable, however. Though an economy be in a state of stable or of instable equilibrium in the present, it will be generating surpluses above current requirements which are distributed to some of an economy's income-recipients and which are variously invested in ways that make output per capita rise in the near or the less near future. Accordingly, when one views an economy over time, one finds it progressing, usually in keeping with pattern (ii) described above, and with supply curves shifting, price structures adjusting, etc.

Earlier it was noted that scientific and technological progress constitute the element most closely resembling mutation in the realm of biology. This progress, though affected by change and various unanticipatable events, is, in large part, a sequel to earlier investment of the surpluses an economy has generated. For these surpluses can be invested inter alia in the elevation of educational levels, in the training of scientific specialists, in the support of research, in the development of invention, and in the fostering of innovation. In short, the analogue of mutation in economic development is largely the product of deliberate change-producing actions supported out of the surpluses which an economy almost invariably generates. The economy, therefore, grows much as does an organism, quite subject to the requirement of appropriate degree of inter-sectoral balance, though not so constrained by internal and external limits on size which operate in respect of animals and plants. Provision for growth can even be institutionalized in the light of experience, with the result that some of the burden of decision-making can be reduced. Growth can be greater or less, even given the propensity to save; for, since some forms of investment are much more productive than others of increase in "present value," and since the uses to which a society puts it surpluses depend largely upon judgment and upon the values being stressed, a given rate of investment may generate (within limits) a higher or a lower rate of economic growth.

It is sometimes possible now, and in the future it may be even more possible, to estimate fairly accurately how action in the present will influence the rate of growth in the future. For the rate of growth today is a function, as is the rate of change in the rate of growth, of how much has been invested at various times in the relevant past, together with the uses to which this investment has been put at various times. Some forms of investment may take 20 years to bring about an increase in output (e.g., some of the investment devoted to increasing educational and scientific levels) whereas others may bring about increase within months or a year or two. In time we may have very good estimates of the concrete value of the functional connections binding various forms of investment at various points in time with the rate of growth, or the rate of change therein, at stipulated future points in time. Nonetheless, considerable error may characterize these estimates, even though estimates of the rate of diffusion of increments in technical knowledge, or of innovations based thereon, are characterized by little error. For investment in additions to the body of scientific knowledge and in their practical application may pan out much better or much worse than was anticipated at the time the investments were undertaken; results may exceed or fall short of expectations. Hence it will never be possible to project aggregate growth rates far into the future, in developed countries for the reason given, and in underdeveloped countries because information will never be adequate to permit highly probable estimates of the rate at which superior technologies can be introduced, diffused, and made to function effectively.[25] Of course, in so far as the future cannot be determined by action in the present, recourse must be had to a mode of response of primary importance in evolutionary theory, namely, that of adjusting and readjusting courses of action in the light of experiences fed back and the decision-maker's perception and interpretation of this feedback.[26]

If one is concerned with development in the quite long run, changes in a society's ultimate ends, and its value-system, become important, since these ends are by no means wholly shaped by a society's economic system, and since the selective role of profit maximization, the most useful of the economist's postulates, may vary in time and space with differences in value-system.[27] As the value-system changes, the propensity to save changes as do the uses to which a society's surpluses are put, with the result that the rate of development changes. The extent to which invention and innovation are institutionalized and somewhat insulated against transitory value changes

[25] On factors affecting the predictability of the impact of technical progress see Irving H. Siegel, "The Value of Technological Change," *Journal of Business* of the University of Chicago, XXVI, July, 1953, pp. 141–56; also the September, 1958, *Scientific American*, Vol. CXCIX, the whole of which is devoted to circumstances affecting creativity and innovation. Other circumstances than the unpredictability of the impact of technological change may also reduce man's ability to take action in the present to bring about specified results in the future. On some of the problems involved see Robert K. Merton, "The Unanticipated Consequences of Purposive Social Action," *American Sociological Review*, I, December, 1936, pp. 894–904; Emile Grunberg and Franco Modigliani, "The Predictability of Social Events," *Journal of Political Economy*, LXII, December, 1954 pp. 465–78; Herbert A. Simon, *Models of Man*, New York, 1957, ch. 5.

[26] The importance of how feedbacks are interpreted is remarked by Swanson (*op. cit.*, p. 131) when he notes that variability of response to given stimuli makes possible dynamic formulation of the connection of organism and environment.

[27] E.g., A. G. Papandreou, "Economics and the Social Sciences," *Economic Journal*, LX, December, 1950, pp. 721–23. See also Simon's papers on motivation in *Models of Man*, Part III.

may also undergo modification.[28] The theory of economic development may, therefore, draw with profit upon those branches of social science which can account for changes in value-systems and in relevant institutional and organizational structures in various kinds of societies. After all, those changes (whatever they be) which redirect the objectives and undertakings of innovators, entrepreneurs, etc., are of strategic as well as critical importance for the student of economic development.

III. EVOLUTIONARY APPROACHES

What amounts to a way of thinking that stressed the developmental aspects of culture came into being in the eighteenth century and exercised considerable influence upon nineteenth-century social thought.[29] Economics was not unaffected, but the effect was relatively less pronounced in England and France, the homes of classical economics as well as of Darwinism, than in Germany. There a combination of circumstances made for emphasis both upon developmental theory of a more or less evolutionary sort and upon the view (then less regnant than now in most of the world) that deliberate intervention by man (or the state) may greatly accelerate cumulative change, even that of the slow, Darwinian sort. In England, however, Smith's stress upon organization and a mechanical division of labor and Ricardo's neglect of the contributions of creative entrepreneurs, together with the growing practice of reasoning in terms of gradualism and equilibrating processes, made for underestimation both of growth potentials and of costs and changes attendant upon growth. Even when technical progress gave promise of abating constraints imposed by nature, optimism respecting the future did not greatly increase; after all, internal constraints of social origin might now replace receding constraints of physical-environmental origin.[30] Accordingly, belief in or concern to develop a theory of rapid growth entailing much

---

[28] Among the uses to which the surplus is put, one of the more important in respect to growth of per capita income is the rate of population growth. On the possible responses of gross and net reproduction to technological change, see Leibenstein, *op. cit.*, and R. R. Nelson, "A Theory of the Low-Level Equilibrium Trap in Underdeveloped Economies," *American Economic Review*, XLVI, December, 1956, pp. 894-908.

[29] "The leading idea behind all sciences in the nineteenth century was that of *development*." So writes Walter Eucken, who severely criticized the notion of economic stages on empirical and theoretical grounds. See *The Foundations of Economics*, London, 1950, p. 64; also writers cited in note 1 above. See also Horace Miner's discussion of the limitations of the concept of continuum when applied empirically, in his "The Folk-Urban Continuum," *American Sociological Review*, XVII, October, 1952, pp. 529–37.

[30] "Thus was the late nineteenth century generation deprived of comfort. The old misgivings about man's power to innovate and harness inanimate nature were fading, only to be replaced

collective or state intervention never became widespread in Britain. This was true also of France and (apparently) of Italy where only a century earlier (i.e., in 1725) Vico had published his *Scienza Nuova,* the first great inquiry into the nature of the rise and fall of social or societal systems.[31]

Germany, with a climate of opinion congenial to both the developmental subjectivism of Hegel and the developmental, system-superseding objectivism of Marx, witnessed the elaboration of various schema in which the course of economic development was described in terms of sequential stages. The concept of sequential stages was employed largely to epitomize different sorts of economic life and to introduce order into historical accounts of economic development. Exponents of stage theories did not at first make clear how a given stage emerged out of its predecessor, or, given that each stage was an emergent (and presumably higher and more complex) form of economic organization than its predecessor, how the organization of economic activities descriptive of any one stage differed in detail from that descriptive of an earlier or later stage.[32] They did not even specify sources of change with care, or identify such emerging internal (i.e., social) and external (i.e., environmental) barriers to economic growth as needed to be surmounted if growth were to continue and a stage of decline or stasis were to be averted. They were, of course, more interested in describing what had happened than in extrapolating the future (except in a form somewhat duplicative of experience elsewhere), or in setting down (after the manner of Vico, Danilevsky, H. B. Adams, O. Spengler, Toynbee, and others) how societies evolve only to be brought down by essentially irrational forces.[33]

In time, however, the role which the concept of sequential stages might

by fears about his inability to avoid or resolve the stresses within and between men, which far from being relieved by plenty, were often aggravated." So concluded S. G. Checkland, in "Growth and Progress: The Nineteenth Century View in Britain," *Economic History Review,* XII, No. 1, 1959, pp. 49–62, quotation from p. 62. See also my "Evolutionism in American Economics, 1800–1946," in Persons, ed., *op. cit.,* pp. 202–66.

[31] Various of these systems are described by P. A. Sorokin in his monumental *Social and Cultural Dynamics,* 4 vols., New York, 1937, 1941.

[32] As Steward *(op. cit.,* pp. 51–53) has observed, use of the concept of developmental levels, or levels of cultural integration or organization, "does not presuppose any particular evolutionary sequence." "The concept of levels of socio-cultural integration . . . . is simply a methodological tool for dealing with culture of different degrees of complexity. It is not a conclusion about evolution." Given a typology of integrational levels, it becomes possible to "examine the reintegration of simpler societies into large sociocultural systems and to make generalizations."

[33] E.g., see Sorokin, *op. cit.;* also S. G. Checkland, "Theories of Economic and Social Evolution: The Rostow Challenge," *Scottish Journal of Political Economy,* VII, November, 1960, pp. 169–81. See also my "Theories of Socio-Economic Growth," in S. Kuznets, ed., *Problems in the Study of Economic Growth* (National Bureau of Economic Research), New York, 1949, pp. 47–116.

play came to be better appreciated. This is brought out in B. F. Hoselitz's discussion of N. S. B. Gras's *schema*. The economic stage, Hoselitz writes,[34] "is an ideal-type construct" devised "to present a systematic interrelation of relevant variables" which relate to institutions; it facilitates (much as does the theory of economic equilibrium) discovery of both the manner in which "the change brought about by one variable may be traced through and related to change in other variables in the system" and of the sorts of "change in certain variables which will bring about change in the system as a whole, or at least magnitudes of changes in certain variables [which] may have this effect." Accordingly, if the concept of economic stage is to be of maximum usefulness, it must be constructed "in such a way as to minimize the likelihood that in the process of economic change illuminated by these constructs, the merely 'possible,' rather than the 'true', change-generating variables are included." The stage approach needs to be distinguished, of course, from typological approaches which suppose that certain social elements or conditions always cluster together because intercorrelated but which do not contend that clusters are ordered in certain ways because each emerges from a "lower" cluster and gives rise to a "higher" cluster.

The early expositions of economic stages did not meet these requirements. F. List identified five stages, the savage, the pastoral, the agricultural, the agricultural and manufacturing, and the agricultural and manufacturing and commercial; his purpose was to emphasize the importance of introducing manufacturing, the dynamic factor in economic growth. List's view was criticized by K. Knies and others on various grounds. B. Hildebrand, believing distribution to be the category of economic activities least influenced by physical environment, supposed that trade would evolve from a barter stage through commodity- and metallic-money stages to a stage resting upon credit. Karl Bücher supposed that politico-economic organization had passed from that of an essentially exchangeless independent domestic, or household, economy through that of a town economy founded upon limited trade to that of a national economy resting upon production for large markets. G. Schmoller identified five stages in economic development: village economy, town economy, territorial economy, national economy, and (at least by implication) world economy; and he employed parts of this pattern in his discussion of policy.

[34] See his "Theories of Stages of Economic Growth," in Hoselitz, ed., *Theories of Economic Growth*, pp. 237–38; I draw on this essay in the present section. Gras's view is set out in "Stages in Economic History," *Journal of Economic and Business History*, II, 1930, pp. 395–418. Max Weber's conception of the analytical role of stages was similar to Gras's. See Weber, *The Theory of Social and Economic Organization*, New York, 1947, pp. 223–24, and *The Methodology of the Social Sciences*, Glencoe, 1949, pp. 100-03. See also F. C. Lane and J. C. Riemersma, eds., *Enterprise and Secular Change*, Homewood Illinois), 1933, pp. 431–43; and Nagel's exposition

Later writers, when they had recourse to the concept of stages, were more alert to the methodological issues involved, though they never overcame the difficulties inherent in the use of this concept. Gras, while he made use of village and town stages, and recognized the existence of pre-village stages, emphasized the metropolitan stage as the only one truly descriptive of the distinctive qualities of modern socio-economic organization. W. Sombart, noting that patterns of economic life differed in many respects and not merely in one, shifted his emphasis from objective bases and criteria to the subjective source of these objective criteria and artifacts, and distinguished socio-economic patterns of life in terms of the spirit or cultural mentality which supposedly underlay the socio-economic behavior to which individuals gave expression. It was in the change of this mentality that major changes in economic pattern were to be sought. A. Spiethoff, critic of the notion of a sequence of stages, stressed the gestalt-like aspect of distinct forms of economic organization, identified a number of "styles" or stages of development, and indicated the complex character of the cyclical and other changes taking place within the evolving modern capitalistic world; but he did not inquire into how one gestalt is transformed into another.[35] J. A. Schumpeter came closer to supplying an explanation of the transformation process when he sought to account analytically and historically for the supposedly prospective supersession of private capitalism by collective capitalism.[36]

In recent years the stage theory has continued to have critics and advocates. Eucken has rejected the concept of stages on the ground that it divorces "economic events from the rest of the historical process" and therefore hinders "the understanding of history and of the different economic systems."[37] In a more useful critique, Kuznets has specified the minimum conditions that a sequence of stages must meet even if it is to function only as a suggestive *schema* instead of as a more demanding substantive model: 1., each stage must manifest empirically testable characteristics revealing growth on the part of units undergoing growth in this stage; 2., the characteristics associated with a given stage must, as a group, be unique to that stage; 3., a given stage must be analytically connected with the preceding stage whence it has emerged, preferably in sufficient detail to permit prediction of its emergence; 4., a given stage must also be connected analytically with

---

(*op. cit.,* pp. 464–66) of the difficulties involved in the construction of transcultural laws.

[35] E.g., see Lane and Riemersma, eds., *op. cit.,* pp. 444–63.

[36] *Capitalism, Socialism, and Democracy,* New York, 1942, Part II. Schumpeter did not make use of the notion of stages, but he recognized the contribution of historical economists who were alert to the evolving character of economies. See his *History of Economic Analysis,* New York, 1954, Part IV, chap. 4.

[37] *Op. cit.,* p. 98, also pp. 98–102, 298–99, 308–11.

the succeeding stage, preferably in sufficient detail to indicate when the earlier stage will be completed and give rise to the next stage; and 5., the social universe to which the stage theory applies must be identified, since otherwise its limitation will not be explicit.[38] H. Giersch's conception of a theory of stages, though intended to be quantitative, to allow for regular long-run variation and change, and to serve policy, does not meet Kuznets's tests. Moreover, it[39] appears to neglect what Hoselitz believes to be the[40] "crucial aspect of a theory of economic development, . . . the need to explain the transition from a stage of 'underdevelopment' to a state of 'advancement'."

Of the stage theories currently under discussion, that of W. W. Rostow has commanded most attention, largely because it is designed to delineate the emergence and course of economic development and it is supposedly adapted to rationalizing the intervention of the state in an age when collectively induced and guided growth has supposedly superseded the more autonomous growth of the sort associated with the nineteenth century. If a society would grow it must pass out of the traditional, pre-Newtonian state in which much of the world still finds itself and out of which societies now in the most advanced stages originally evolved. When a society in this stage undergoes sufficient transformation to establish the pre-conditions for the third or "take-off" stage, the great moment may be said to be at hand. For if an economy passes several decades in the take-off stage, it is likely to move into a fourth stage in which economic growth becomes self-sustaining and the economy achieves maturity in the course of four or more decades. In time this stage may give way to a yet higher fifth stage of mass consumption, suggested by such terms as age of affluence or age of opulence, used in works dealing with the problems that emerge with opulence.[41]

The locus of change in Rostow's *schema* is the system (or functions) of production operative in an economy; the points upon which inquiry should focus (even when they are less immediately apparent sources of economic

---

[38] Kuznets deals with the concept of stages in his critique of Rostow's system, "Notes on the Take-Off," in W. W. Rostow, ed., *The Economics of Take-Off into Sustained Growth*, New York, 1963, pp. 22–43. This volume, sponsored by the International Economic Association is devoted to supposedly illustrative accounts and tests of Rostow's notion of take-off. Stage theories are discussed also on pp. 315–24, and 391–401.

[39] "Stages and Spurts of Economic Development," in L. H. Dupriez, *Economic Progress*, Louvain, 1955, pp. 193–219.

[40] *Sociological Aspects*, p. 28, also pp. 42 and 78–82 on changes in social structure and sources of change. See also A. K. Cairncross, "The Stages of Economic Growth," *Economic History Review*, XIII, April, 1961, pp. 450–458, especially pp. 451–52 and 458.

[41] E.g., see J. K. Galbraith, *The Affluent Society*, New York, 1958; Harry G. Johnson, *Money, Trade and Economic Growth*, Cambridge, 1962, pp. 164–95.

change) are the elements on which the system of production rests.[42] The pre-conditions of economic development come into being when the methods of production undergo sufficient improvement and there is enough capital formation to permit some progress in output per head—changes that may be consequent upon foreign penetration or upon the ascent into positions of power of new types bent on having economic growth and allowing scope to growth-minded organizers. If these conditions are sufficiently accentuated and diffused, the critical take-off stage is at hand and social and other resistances to economic growth are being more than counter-balanced, at least for the time being, by the forces making for economic growth. This stage witnesses increases in the rate of productive investment, substantial expansion of the manufacturing sector, and the emergence of a growth-exploiting "political, social, and institutional framework." Given that the growth-favoring forces remain dominant for several decades, the economy evolves into the stage of maturity and, if per capita income continues to rise, into the stage of high mass-consumption when the supposedly plentiful flow of goods and services is competed for by the expanding requirements of the welfare state and the mass consumption of durable consumers' goods and services as well as by "the national pursuit of external power and influence."

While there is not space in which to examine Rostow's *schema* in detail, it is hardly describable as an evolutionary *schema,* even though it does illuminate some temporal aspects of economic development. The five stages are not carefully delimited and distinguished from one another in keeping with the minimal specifications laid down by Kuznets. It is not made clear how one stage terminates only to give rise to a successor stage, or why the sources of change shift from sector to sector as they do. Rostow's indicators frequently behave differently than his model requires. His suppositions also suggest that growth is less difficult to achieve and more easily made automatic than experience seems to warrant.[43] When he indicates that external

---

[42] "These stages are not merely descriptive. They are not merely a way of generalizing certain factual observations about the sequence of development of modern societies. They have an inner logic and continuity. They have an analytic bone-structure, rooted in a dynamic theory of production." *The Stages of Economic Growth*, New York, 1960, pp. 12–13. See also Rostow's "The Interrelation of Theory and Economic History," *Journal of Economic History*, XVII, December, 1957, pp. 509–23, and his paper and comments in Rostow, ed., *The Economics of Take-Off*, pp. 1–21, 311–14, 327–28, 346, 359–61, 382–84 and 409–11.

[43] See Kuznets, "Notes on the Take-Off," *loc. cit.,* also the many comments on Rostow's thesis in *ibid., passim*. In a paper presented at the International Economic Association's conference on the economic development of Africa South of the Sahara, G. J. Lighart and B. Abar of the U. N. Economic Commission for Africa observe that "steady growth" is not necessarily a normal state, at least in lands like Africa where the influence of goals is very important and one encounters mainly small pockets of development. See E. A. G. Robinson, ed., *Economic Development for Africa South of the Sahara,* London, 1964, ch. 1, especially pp. 3–5 and 20–21.

assistance may keep in motion a developmental process that might otherwise peter out, he seems to neglect that it is much easier to export capital and technology to a tradition-bound non-Western country than to modify its value-and-institutional structure. That internal stresses and constraints may arise to halt and even to reverse the developmental process in advanced countries as well as in those in the take-off stage is passed over, in large part because the inner character of the developmental forces at work is not subjected to much analysis.[44]

Respecting stage theory at least three summary statements are applicable. The sources of change are identified only imperfectly at best. The process whereby a given stage is matured and then converted into a successor stage is not carefully identified and described. The stage approach somewhat resembles a quasi-unilinear conception of cultural evolution in that it is taken for granted that economic development proceeds quite similarly from economy to economy. If the stage approach is to be made explanatory, it needs to incorporate a more fully developed conceptual scheme.[45]

IV. DEVELOPMENTAL PROCESSES

Economic development comprises two sorts of change, change in the conditions of supply and change in the conditions of demand. It is in the conditions of supply, as was implied in Part II, however, that the most fundamental changes, namely, those analogous to mutation, have their origin. While these changes vary somewhat in nature, they consist primarily in change in the content of men's minds and in the activities of innovating entrepreneurs who use some of these changes to modify conditions of supply. More specifically, important changes in the conditions of supply originate primarily in the emergence of new ways of making old products and novel

---

[44] See also Checkland's critical remarks in his "Theories of Economic and Social Evolution," *loc. cit.*, pp. 181–93. Rostow's *schema* has been criticized on Marxian grounds and his supposed misinterpretation of Marxism. Thus B. G. Gustafson writes of Rostow's theory of economic development, that "it does not contain any necessary internal dynamics." Moreover, because Rostow "is chiefly concerned with the sequential content of economic development, not its concrete form" he provides "no clear qualitative criteria for the stages of development". "But a process in stages presupposes not only continuing connection–permanence–but also qualitative changes. Without qualitative changes we can not speak of stages at all". Rostow's theory is said to be "unhistorical and arbitrary"; his "stages are at once too general and too specific". See "Rostow, Marx, and Economic Growth," *Science & Society*, XXV (3), Summer, 1961, pp. 236–37; also p. 237 where Marx's sequence of epochs (primitive, slave, feudal, capitalist, socialist, communist) is described as based on "concrete analysis" and as manifesting "determinate internal connectedness in the entire development."

[45] Papandreou's observations on "back-room" and "front-room" approaches are relevant, *op. cit.*, pp. 720–23. Even so, it is essential to heed Cairncross's criticism (*op. cit.*, p. 458) of Rostow: "He seems to me to have made the Muse of History lie on the bed of Procrustes."

ways of making new products, together with the introduction and perfection under the aegis of innovating entrepreneurs, of means and methods whereby these new and novel ways are incorporated into the industrial system. These new ways correspond to mutations; innovators correspond to the agencies that determine what mutations are to survive and that may influence the rate of mutation itself. These new ways constitute or reflect scientific and technical progress, the rate of which depends in considerable measure, however, upon the extent to which the public and the private investment of the quite regularly forthcoming surplus is oriented to the generation of such progress.

Changes in conditions of supply are reflected also in changes in the occupational or industrial composition of the labor force—that is, in changes discussed below largely under the head of demand. For, other conditions given, the relative number of persons engaged in sectors of an economy may be associated inversely with the rate of increase in output per worker. Partly illustrative of this relationship—though only partly so since demand changes are also involved—is the increase since 1900 and especially since 1929 in the relative number of workers engaged in so-called "services". Thus, between 1929 and 1961, employment in the "service" sector rose from 40.4 to 54.0 per cent of all employment whilst that in the "goods" sector fell from 59.6 to 46.0 per cent. In this same interval output per man rose 2.44 per cent per annum in the "goods" sector, but only 0.7 per cent in the "service" sector.[46]

Changes in demand are essentially adaptive in character, reflecting changes in income, tastes, price structure, etc., though they may on occasion generate new methods of production.[47] Inasmuch as technical progress probably proceeds, in the long run, at fairly similar rates in all sectors of an economy and as changes in tastes flow largely out of changes underlying increase in per capita income, we may look upon increase in per capita

[46] See V. R. Fuchs, *Productivity Trends in the Goods and Service Sectors, 1929–61* (N.B.E.R. Occasional Paper 89), New York, 1964, pp. 4, 13, also 14–15, and p. 39 on factors responsible for the differences in productivity.

[47] It is implicitly assumed, when overwhelming emphasis is placed upon supply rather than upon demand, that excess demand exists to absorb increased supply, or that demand tends to expand as a result of a variety of forces, many of them associated closely with growth of supply. Under some conditions and perhaps under many, especially in underdeveloped economies, capacity for want expansion may not keep pace with capacity for supply and hence retard the expansion of supply. See E. E. Hoyt, "Want Development in Underdeveloped Areas," *Journal of Political Economy*, LIX, June, 1951, pp. 194–202. This inexpansibility of wants is then reflected in (among other things) a greater emphasis upon leisure. However, as S. Rottenberg has shown, one cannot always interpret a seeming preference for leisure to be the result of fixity of wants; it may reflect occupational immobilities, occupational reservations, etc. See his "Income and Leisure in an Underdeveloped Economy," *ibid.*, LX, April, 1952, pp. 95–101. On various weaknesses in the "demand approach" see H. Myint, "The Demand Approach to Economic Development," *Review of Economic Studies*, XXVII, (2), 1959–60, pp. 124–32. See also note 19 above.

income as the main change to which a society's structure of demand immediately responds.[48]

For purposes of exposition, let us suppose that output in an economy is sub-divisible into three roughly equal categories of goods and services, *A*, *B*, and *C*. Let us then suppose that: (a) the income elasticities of demand for *A*, *B*, and *C* are below, at, and above unity, respectively; (b) technical progress is the same in all three branches of the economy, in consequence of which condition, together with other relevant conditions, the price structure remains substantially unchanged; (c) total output is increasing more rapidly than the population and the labor force; (d) whatever other changes are taking place do not modify suppositions (a) and (b) significantly. Now let demand *d* be described logarithmically

$$\log d = \log c + E \log i - e \log p$$

where *p* denotes price, *i* denotes income, and *E* and *e* denote income and price elasticity of demand, respectively. If, with *p* given, income *i* increases 2 per cent, demand *d* will increase 2, less than 2, and more than 2 per cent accordingly as *E* equals, is less than, or exceeds unity. For example, suppose *E* to have values of $\frac{1}{2}$, 1, and $1\frac{1}{2}$ in branches *A*, *B*, and *C* of the economy. Suppose further, for example, that the 2 per cent increase in income is attributable to an increase of 2 per cent in output per worker which reduces by 2 per cent the amount of labor required to produce given amounts of *A*, *B*, and *C*. Under the circumstances the labor requirement of branch *B* will remain unchanged; that of *A* will decrease about 1 per cent and that of *C* will increase about 1 per cent. If the increase in income were attributable in part to increase in the labor force, the occupational structure of the economy would change in the same direction but in lesser measure. The structural change flows directly from the structure of income elasticities of demand which apparently does not differ greatly from country to country when income and price-structure conditions are similar. Even when one or both of these conditions do differ from country to country, it is often likely that they will not differ enough to give rise to different tendencies than those suggested. The structural changes produced by the differences in demand elasticities

[48] This statement, even though deemed applicable to given countries, is less applicable when international comparisons are intended, since tastes, income-levels, and price structures differ internationally. Even so, the behavioral tendencies of income and price elasticities are fairly similar from country to country in respect to many categories of goods and services. H. S. Houthakker's findings regarding the response of household expenditures to income and price changes by country support this interpretation. See his "An International Comparison of Household Expenditure Patterns, Commemorating the Centenary of Engel's Law," *Econometrica*, XXV, October, 1957, pp. 532–51.

would be accentuated or reduced, should costs behave differently in different industries.[49]

During the past 150 to 200 years a number of processes have reflected a response to change in income similar to that described. (1) As per capita productivity and income have risen in various countries, the urban-rural balance has changed, with the urban component increasing absolutely and relatively and the rural component decreasing relatively and absolutely until a minimum level compatible with prevailing technology, population growth, and import-export relations has been reached. This change in the rural-urban composition of the population and the labor force, though ultimately the result of increase in output per worker, is traceable to the fact that the income-elasticity of demand for agricultural products is less than that for non-agricultural products.[50] (2) Equally striking are the changes in occupational structure issuing out of a combination of technical progress and inter-commodity differences in demand elasticity. These have been interpreted by C. Clark, following A. G. B. Fisher, to signify that the relative number of persons engaged in "primary" activities declines while that engaged in "tertiary" activities steadily increases and that engaged in "secondary" activities finally declines in relation to "tertiary" activities after having risen in relation to "primary" activities.[51] Clark's thesis has been criticized principally because it disregards circumstances which may make quite high the relative number of persons engaged in tertiary activities in under-developed countries and because it treats this category as much more homogeneous than it is in fact.[52] In general, his thesis proves inadequate in so far as any one of his categories includes activities characterized by current or prospective demand elasticities incompatible with his proposition.[53] (3)

[49] I have disregarded the fact that income-elasticity of demand tends to fall as income rises, but differently in respect of different goods. On differences in productivity see footnote 46 and text above.

[50] H. A. Simon illustrates the process nicely in a model presented in his *Models of Man*, ch. 12. As suggested above, the course of change is affected also by whether a country imports or exports agricultural products.

[51] See Clark, *The Conditions of Economic Progress*, 3rd. ed., London, 1957, ch. 9. This interpretation appeared in the 1940 and 1951 editions also. See also Jean Fourastié, *Migrations professionnelles*, Paris, 1957.

[52] E.g., see P. T. Bauer and B. S. Yamey, "Economic Progress and Occupational Distribution," *Economic Journal*, LXI, 1951, pp. 741–55; S. G. Triantis, "Economic Progress, Occupational Redistribution and International Terms of Trade," *ibid.*, LXIII, 1953, pp. 627–37, and A. G. B. Fisher's comments in *ibid.*, LXIV, 1954, pp. 619 ff.; Simon Rottenberg, "Note on 'Economic Progress' and Occupational Distribution," *Review of Economics and Statistics*, XXXV, May, 1953, pp. 168–70; N. N. Foote and P. K. Hatt, "Social Mobility and Economic Advancements," *American Economic Review*, XLIII (2), May, 1953, pp. 364–78; Martin Wolfe, "The Concept of Economic Sectors," *Quarterly Journal of Economics*, LXIX, 1955, pp. 402–420; H. B. Chenery and P. G. Clark, *Interindustry Economics*, New York, 1959, ch. 8.

[53] On this heterogeneity see H. S. Perloff, "Interrelations of State Income and Industrial

While changes in the industrial structure of economies are affected by various circumstances, they do reflect in considerable measure inter-product differences in income elasticity of demand.[54] (4) In many advanced countries the ratio of foreign trade to national income has been declining for several or more decades, though it originally moved upward in the nineteenth century and then remained essentially unchanged for some years. While this decline is traceable in part to the increasing capacity of technology to facilitate economy in the use of some raw materials and the substitution of domestic for foreign production, it is attributable in part to the evolving structure of demand elasticities. The elasticity of demand generally is higher in sectors of the economy producing goods and services into which imports in general, and imported raw materials in particular, enter in a relatively minor degree.[55] (5) It has been supposed that the ratio of public expenditure to total expenditure would grow through time,[56] and this supposition has been borne out in part, though largely for military and other reasons unconnected with the structure of consumer demand. It may be argued, however, that the elasticity of demand for goods and services that supposedly can be supplied most effectively or at least financed by agencies of the state is relatively high and that therefore the relative importance of the state's role as supplier and producer tends to rise.[57] (6) While a thesis has never been developed to this

Structure," *Papers and Proceedings of the Regional Science Association*, II, 1956, pp. 70–91 and my comments pp. 95–97.

[54] E.g., see H. B. Chenery, "Patterns of Industrial Growth," *American Economic Review*, L, 1960, pp. 624–54; W. G. Hoffmann, *The Growth of Industrial Economies*, Manchester, 1958. See also Chenery and Clark, *op. cit.*, pp. 205–11, on the implications of interindustry differences in direct and indirect demand for products.

[55] E.g., see Karl W. Deutsch and Alexander Eckstein, "National Industrialization and the Declining Share of the International Economic Sector, 1890–1959," *World Politics*, XIII, 1961, pp. 267–99. See also Alfred Maizels, *Industrial Growth and World Trade*, Cambridge, 1963, especially ch. 15–16; Jaroslav Janek, *The Natural Resource Content of United States Foreign Trade 1870–1955*, Cambridge, 1963.

[56] Adolph Wagner declared this tendency to be a "law", though he did not rest it upon precise economic principles. See his *Finanzwissenschaft*, 3rd. ed., Leipzig, 1883, Part I, p. 76; the relevant passage is reprinted in R. A. Musgrave and A. T. Peacock, eds., *Classics in the Theory of Public Finance*, London, 1958, pp. 7–8. See also *ibid.*, pp. 29, 233 ff.; Peacock and Jack Wiseman, *The Growth of Public Expenditure in the United Kingdom*, Princeton, 1961; B. U. Ratchford, *Public Expenditures in Australia*, Durham, 1959.

[57] This argument is questionable in so far as the goods and services in question can be supplied by private collectivities, or subdivided and sold in small quantities. An interpretation of the role of the state somewhat different than Wagner's is offered by B. F. Hoselitz in the light of the work of Parsons and Smelser. Hoselitz identifies four categories of societal needs, of which one has to do with goal attainment or systemic goals such as social overhead capital. While these goals tend to be supplied by the state, they vary in importance through time, sometimes commanding considerable resources and at other times but few resources. If this interpretation is correct, the economic role of the state fluctuates greatly in time; it does not steadily increase, at least in mixed and free-enterprise economies. See Hoselitz's essay in H. G. J. Aitken, ed., *The State and*

effect, it may be argued that, since price and demand elasticities for particular goods and services are inversely related to the multiplicity of goods and services, the advance of societies in opulence and in the multiplicity and variety of goods and services available tends to reduce conflict or at least the frequency of conflict situations.[58]

It is possible to explain the so-called transition and related theories of the decline in human fertility in part in terms of the structure of demand elasticities in that income growth is apparently accompanied by upward shifts in income elasticity of the demand both for quality in children and for goods and services competitive with children. This sort of explanation, though helpful, is incomplete. Whether one attempts to make use of transition theory, of theories describing essentially logistic movements, or of theories which stress an initial ascendancy of the rate of income growth above that of population growth, one must in the end account for changes in household-consumption behavior which reduce children per mother as well as for the changes which result in deferment of marriage or in non-marriage. It is these changes which help to bring down gross reproduction and crude natality and the approach of a stable population marked by low gross reproduction, high life expectancy, and a low rate of growth. It is crucial changes of this sort that the theories in question fail to account for, particularly outside one or two of the Western countries. Presumably, there is operative, besides the diffusion of effective modes of contraception, changes in tastes as well as mere adjustments to changes in price and income structures. It is doubtful whether the theory of social evolution as such can throw much light on the processes at work, though a more flexible theory of social change might. For example, it has been persuasively argued by Leibenstein and others that a "big push" in the form of heavy and sustained investment is required to lift populations out of the low-income, high-fertility, Malthusian traps in which many nations find themselves. Such investment normally serves to increase income appreciably and in time to produce changes associated with income increase. Of additional concern to the student of social change, however, are questions of this sort: Are the relevant social variables tautly or loosely interconnected? Is a "big-push" required if these variables are tautly interrelated, or will a small push suffice in that event? Is not a "big-push" required, however, if the relevant variables are loosely instead of tautly interconnected?

Economic Growth, New York, 1959, ch. 12. It is contended, however, that the state must assume an increasing role in the supply of various goods and services as a society becomes "affluent." E.g., see Galbraith, *op. cit.*

[58] While this thesis is not put forward by Mathilda Holzman, I find her discussion permitting its inference. See her "Theories of Choice and Conflict in Psychology and Economics," *Journal of Conflict Resolution*, II, December, 1958, pp. 310–20.

Time, chance, and irreversibility enter into the developmental and diffusion processes underlying economic development in general, but not in so marked a degree as in the development of economic systems. This has already been suggested in the above description of particular developmental processes resting upon the structure of demand. The development of an economic system as a whole thus resembles somewhat, as does that of many of its parts, a Markov chain process. Economic development always entails the transformation of a given state *a* into a somewhat different successor state *a'*; this is true of the development of both an economic system and many of its parts. This transformation process is stochastic, as a rule, in that at a given time it is possible for a given state *a* to become either *a'* or *a''*, or perhaps yet another state as of the next relevant period of time. Moreover, given enough information, one might in theory assign tentative probabilities to these possibilities, though in reality enough information will never be available, even in a controlled economy, to permit the assignment of such probabilities to an economy as a whole, and there will seldom be enough information available to permit such determination even for important segments of an economy.[59] As a rule, the states probable at any given point in time will not be independent of earlier states; for a developmental process, especially if it relates to a significant segment of an economy, usually is irreversible, with movement indicated in some general direction though not necessarily along any preordained path. In the light of what has been said, economic development is a cultural evolutionary process.

V. SOCIAL EVOLUTION

Inasmuch as social evolution is variously described elsewhere, it will here be defined only sufficiently to indicate what the term is taken to signify in the context of this essay. White's conception of cultural evolution is representative.[60]

"Culture undergoes another kind of change, also: a developmental or evolutionist process of change. Evolution may be defined as a temporal sequence of forms: one form grows out of another; culture advances from one stage to another. In this process time is as integral a factor as change in form. The evolutionist process is irreversible and nonrepetitive. Only systems can evolve; a mere aggregation of things without organic unity cannot undergo evolution. Culture may diffuse

[59] Uncertainty permeates every economy. Moreover, when policies are introduced to subject an economy to control, they may bring about unanticipated side effects or even aggravate the situation they are designed to remedy. E.g., see W. J. Baumol, "Pitfalls in Contracyclical Policies: Some Tools and Results," *Review of Economics and Statistics*, XLIII, February, 1961, pp. 21–66; also Milton Friedman, *Capitalism and Freedom*, Chicago, 1962, ch. 3, 5.

[60] *Op. cit.*, pp. 29–30.

piecemeal, as we have seen, but only a systematic organization of cultural elements can evolve."

Change in the availability of energy constitutes an index of and perhaps the key to this evolutionary process, for cultural systems require energy both for self-maintenance and for self-extension. "Culture advances as the amount of energy harnessed per capita per year increases, or as the efficiency or economy of the means of controlling energy is increased, or both."[61]

According to Steward, the methodology of evolution[62]

"contains two vitally important assumptions. First, it postulates that genuine parallels of form and function develop in historically independent sequences or cultural traditions. Second, it explains these parallels by the independent operation of identical causality in each case...It endeavors to determine recurrent patterns and processes and to formulate interrelationships between phenomena in terms of 'laws'."

He identifies three types of cultural evolution, *unilinear* within a particular culture, *universal* within human culture as a whole, and *multilinear* relating to often parallel development within a number of cultures. It is the study of multilinear evolution, with emphasis upon the investigation of the interrelationships of particular phenomena which are present in many if not in all cultures, that is most likely to disclose similarities and parallels and yield cultural laws and regularities.[63]

Economic development may be described as a manifestation or form of cultural evolution as defined by White or Steward. Indeed, comparison of the courses traced by economic development in many countries is likely to yield greater similarities than does comparison of the total cultures, or of noneconomic segments of the total culture, of these same countries.[64] While totalitarian, mixed-economy, and essentially free-enterprise societies may differ in respect of the methods that are employed to activate men, they are bound to resemble one another in the emphasis put upon capital, capital formation, technological progress, and (though in less measure) upon the uses to which these elements are put. They are bound to resemble one another also in so far as there are present in economies technological relations which vary little in space or time. It is open to question, however, if the concept of evolution as such is likely to be of much analytical help to the student of

[61] *Ibid.*, p. 56. Those cultures which are most superior in respect of energy transformation tend to become most dominant and extensive. See D. Kaplan's essay in Sahlins and Service, *op. cit.*; see also Fred Cottrell's analysis of the role of surplus energy, in this volume.

[62] *Op. cit.*, p. 14, also p. 26.

[63] *Ibid.*, pp. 14–15, 28–29. Sahlins assesses Steward's multilinear approach and rejects White's thermodynamic-efficiency approach for an energy conversion approach in his own essay in Sahlins and Service, *op. cit.*

[64] See Chenery and Clark, *op. cit.*, for some of these similarities.

economic development other than to impress upon him the need to take autonomous as well as built-in change for granted, and to draw upon ecology and related sciences as well as upon the study of stochastic processes to illuminate economic change and anticipate its course in part. It is possible also that the findings of cultural anthropologists respecting the role of innovation should be incorporated into the study of economic development, together with those principles of epidemiology which are applicable to the study of the diffusion of innovation.[65]

VI. ASSESSMENT

As has been indicated, economic development is an important component—probably the most important component—of social development and cultural evolution. The methods of study applicable to the study of cultural evolution are therefore applicable to it. It does not follow, however, that these methods are the ones most suited to the study of economic development as such, or even to that of non-economic factors which bear upon economic development.[66] It is likely that a less specific theory of social change founded upon an essentially functional approach to the study of society is better suited to cope with the non-economic determinants or conditions of economic development. For this sort of theory is less directionally oriented, less given to treating quasi-constants as important "causes," more disposed to allow adequate weight to the growing capacity of man to intervene and modify determinants of social change, more prone to recognize the functional interdependence of the variables composing societal systems and subsystems, and more alert to the role of communications and of what I have called "sources of novelty" which temporarily destabilize social systems only to give rise to relatively stable successor systems.

The theory of social change resembles some theories of social evolution in placing stress almost exclusively upon what takes place within a total societal system. What takes place "outside" is played down, either because it is of little import or because it has had its origin in what had previously taken place within that system. This approach must be modified, of course, when sub-systems of a total societal system (e.g., the economic system) are under analysis, for then what takes place within any given sub-system may be the result in part of what has taken place in other sub-systems, possibly because of what had taken place previously within the given sub-system. Such modification is particularly indicated when economic development is under

[65] See Homer G. Barnett, *Innovation: The Basis of Cultural Change*, New York, 1953.

[66] See B. F. Hoselitz, "Non-Economic Factors in Economic Development," *American Economic Review*, XLVII (2), May, 1957, pp. 42–56.

study, since what takes place within the economic system may be much affected by what takes place in the political sub-system, or, if a society remains tradition-bound, by various non-economic factors which need to be removed or transformed by outside agencies if economic development is to get under way.[67] When what takes place in relevant sub-systems is examined and interrelated in terms of an essentially functional approach, attention need not be confined to stabilizing and equilibrating processes. Attention may be directed as well not only to change-producing strains seemingly external to one or more sub-systems (e.g., forms of "population pressure") but also to the aleatory character of some changes that can become cumulative (e.g., the impact of deviant and unique personalities, upon values, methods, etc.), and to the essentially dialectical character of such processes as are subsumed under various polarized paradigms (e.g., Parsons' "pattern variables").[68]

A theory of social change based upon a functional approach which allows for the emergence of novelties is particularly useful to the student of economic development in that it indicates the boundaries within which capacity for development is to be found at any time. It recognizes that at a minimum certain functional requisites must be met in the political and the social as well as in the economic order (or sub-system). It recognizes also that these requisites may be met, not in one or in a multitude of ways, but in a small number of ways and within a small range of structures, and that selection of some particular way may preclude inclusion of elements peculiar to some other way.[69] It is sometimes suggested, for example, that the ways in which an economy may be *effectively organized* range along a *continuum* all the way from the pole of unfettered free enterprise to the pole of completely centralized determination. It is more tenable to suppose, however, that this interpolar range is discontinuous; points are reached when small changes in structure no longer suffice and large ones are indicated. This theory recognizes also that economic development "is simultaneously cumulative and retroactive" even as are other forms of social change. "Change is cumulative in that multiple involvements reinforce one another and yield an increased general level of commitment. It is retroactive in that a high level of commitment may be dependent on previous commitments in other contexts, but further involvement in these contexts may depend in turn on

[67] E.g., see J. L. Sadie, *op. cit.*

[68] This paragraph has been much influenced by Wilbert Moore's work on social change, *loc. cit.*; also by Sorokin's work, and by Parsons' *The Social System*, Glencoe, 1951. On the possibly development-restricting influence of specialization, see Service's essay in Sahlins and Service, *op. cit.*

[69] See Moore's work cited above; also Moore and A. S. Feldman, *Labor Commitment and Social Change in Developing Areas*, pp. 362–66.

the intermediate step. . . The initial feasible variation in paths and sequences of industrialization are fairly restricted and tend to converge substantially short of infinity."[70] Finally, this theory will in time make clear what elements in societal systems are particularly sensitive to changes in other elements or are most likely to become sources of change, and which of these elements are both manipulatable and accessible to deliberate intervention or control. It will then become more clear what sectors of economies are normally active and what ones are normally passive and hence adaptive in behavioral tendency, with the result that both the sources of economic novelty and the modes of adapting to their generative impact will be better understood.[71]

A theory of economic development must accomodate two empirical tendencies. First, the size distribution of the decision-making unit (e.g., firms) composing an economy apparently needs to be explained stochastically, "in terms of the dynamic growth process rather than in terms of static cost curves,"[72] or their analogues. Second, since economies as well as firms are complex forms of organization, hierarchical in structure and subject to natural selection, they are most likely both to evolve rapidly and to persist if they are composed of stable, intermediate sub-systems, each of which is only partially dependent upon information respecting the behavior of other sub-systems.[73] It is through the analysis of these two processes or tendencies that an evolutionary theory suited to the explanation of economic development may be formulated.

[70] Moore and Feldman, *op. cit.*, pp. 365–66. It may be added that diverging movements of the sort pictured in some cobweb and interactionist models tend to be constrained and even rendered convergent by responses set up within the economic sub-system proper or within some other sub-system of a society.

[71] Needless to say, the theory of social change serves to reveal the weaknesses in such biologic views of man's future as forecast the eventual crystallization of his society. E.g., see R. Seidenberg, *Posthistoric Man*, Chapel Hill, 1960. See also Sir Gavin de Beer's comments on obstacles to man's learning in his review of G. G. Simpson's *This View of Life*, in "The World of an Evolutionist," *Science*, CXLIII, March 20, 1964, pp. 1311 ff.

[72] See Yuji Ijiri and H. A. Simon, "Business Firm Growth and Size," *American Economic Review*, LIV, March, 1964, pp. 77–89; Edwin Mansfield, "Entry, Gibrat's Law, Innovation, and the Growth of Firms," *ibid.*, LII, December, 1962, pp. 1023–51; also Simon, *Models of Man*, ch. 9, on mechanisms suited to explain Yule distributions.

[73] H. A. Simon, "The Architecture of Complexity," *Proceedings of the American Philosophical Society*, CVI, December, 1962, pp. 467–82, and *The New Science of Management Decision*, New York, 1960, pp. 40–50.

EVOLUTIONARY THEORY AND SOCIAL CHANGE

ARNOLD S. FELDMAN

Northwestern University

I. INTRODUCTION

The purpose of this chapter is to examine the utility of evolutionary theory for the study of social change. Of course, the central concern is with those social changes that together constitute economic development. However, the study of social change *cannot* be theoretically differentiated according to the level of economic development of the units of observation. History does not end when the industrial revolution occurs. This observation may be one of the most important lessons to be learned from evolutionary thought. For surely there is no question but that societies change, and that social change is in some general sense evolutionary in character. Thus the fact that societies constantly evolve is not problematic. The only alternative is to admit to special laws of social creation.

However, although the crude fact of societal evolution of some form and in some degree is not problematic, almost every other facet of the relationship between social change and evolutionary theory is open to question and profoundly problematic. Perhaps a list of the most salient questions or problems may provide an efficient outline for organizing this essay. (At least it provides some organization, and given the excessively broad and general title, any organization is to be avidly sought and jealously cherished.)

In any case, the discussion will be oriented around the following three sets of questions:

1. What are some of the barriers preventing more adequate understanding of social change? Is it possible to suggest some ways of reducing these barriers?

2. What is understood by evolutionary theory? What elements contained in this body of thought seem most useful for studying social change?

3. What are the critical issues involved when the social changes encompassed by economic development are viewed as evolutionary? How may an evolutionary point of view contribute to our understanding of these social changes?

Of course, these questions are quite ambitious and pretentious, especially as they suggest that answers are forthcoming. Let me immediately disclaim any such aspiration. Rather, these questions can be "revived", and their importance for social science in either developing or developed societies can be indicated.

II. The Double Contingency of Order And Change.

Human societies are always ordered. Human societies are always changing. The juxtaposition of these two elemental properties of social life represents a serious problem for those who would as scientists understand the nature of societies and the manner in which they change. For both order and change should be encompassed by any body of social research that claims the adjective scientific. On this norm there is universal although most often pious agreement.

Yet it is an exceedingly rare study that simultaneously examines the character of the social order and the course of social change. Rarer still is the area of research that enjoys comparable growth and development in both of these respects. Rather, most sociological (and I suspect that one could have written "social") research displays a decided and perhaps understandable preference for one or the other of these elements as the problem for investigation. Such discretion may have been the better part of scientific valor and wisdom. However, what may have been wise scientific strategy shows signs of becoming ill-conceived doctrine, if not dogma.

The Initial Error. In sociology, the preferred strategy has been to defer the study of change until the mapping of the social order was relatively complete. This strategy is defended and justified on the grounds that one cannot adequately conceptualize social change prior to a relatively complete picture of what it is that experiences change.

The initial merit of this justification for separating social statics and dynamics is of late made dubious by the perserverance of statics and the almost total exclusion of dynamics. For this enduring separation has brought into being a theoretical and empirical apparatus ill-suited to and thus unable to cope with the crude facts of social change.

Indeed, it may be suggested that there was little initial advantage to be gained from this strategy of separation, and that perhaps the losses exceeded the gains. For if significant change is ubiquitous, any map of society that ignores change can hardly be accurate. Alfred Marshall expressed this view with typical although none the less remarkable lucidity, when he wrote: "I cannot conceive of any static state, which resembles the real world closely enough to form a subject of profitable study, and in which the notion of change is set aside even for an instance."

The extent to which the conceptual schemes derived from a concern with statics are ill-suited to dynamic analysis is most apparent when these schemes are applied to the analysis of change. Most of these applications share the following characteristics:

1) Change is always perceived as a consequence of some disturbance to some integrated status quo.

2) Thus the source of the disturbance and therefore the source of change is always exogenous to the social system experiencing change.

3) Change is a stimulus leading to the eradication of the causing disturbance.

4) The process is completed when integration is once again achieved.

There is some ambiguity as to whether these characteristics are supposed to obtain for all social change, or whether they describe a specific kind of change. In any case, the use of statically based concepts has drastically limited the kinds of social changes that can be studied. In part this severely stylized view of social change results from an incautious over-commitment to the equilibrium concept. Change is perceived as those almost pathological periods of time when societies swing away from and then back to either the same or some other equilibrium state. It seems that when in doubt, the sociologist always imagines a pendulum.

Some Variations And Their Consequences. One common variation of the distinction between statics and dynamics is the corollary one between change within a social system and change in the system itself. This distinction is, of course, between micro-dynamics and macro-dynamics. And it is argued that the former rather than the latter represents a more viable task.

As a consequence of this distinction, a considerable body of information about micro-dynamics has been amassed, while the systematic study of macro-dynamics is relatively neglected or deferred. Thus, there is increased information about such processes as the interaction within small groups, the mechanisms of childhood and adolescent socialization, the life-cycle of the family, the manner in which executives arrive at and carry through on business decisions. All of these micro-processes have come under concerted attack by various of the social sciences, and admirable theoretical and empirical progress has been recorded.

Unfortunately, the emphasis on micro-dynamics is in some degree oppositional to the study of macro-dynamics. For, the distinction between change within a social system and change of the system assumes a systems within systems conception of societies. Moreover it also assumes that the relationship between system and sub-system is uniquely hierarchical, and in one direction autonomous i.e.—change in the sub-system does not necessarily depend upon nor necessarily stimulate change in the next higher system.

It is this hierarchical and partly autonomous view of the relationship between a societies component systems that gives rise to the incredible assertion that values do not change or that they change much more slowly than any other factor. And since values are located at the most general system level, this assertion alone almost precludes macro-dynamic analysis.

In any case, micro-dynamics typically assumes the stability of macro-systems and concentrates upon adaptive and/or adjustive mechanisms to the macro-system as constituted, i.e.—changes in the means employed to achieve or maintain unchanging values.

As a consequence of its deferred status, the study of macro-dynamics enjoys a curious inflation. For like most postponed tasks, the difficulties involved multiply until they assume awesome proportions. Thus macro-dynamic social theory is inflated to the status where nothing but an encompassing theory of history will satisfy. Such inflation either leads to continued avoidance on the part of potential students, or to an embarassed self-consciousness on the part of those who undertake to work in this area as a result of the supposed pretentious character of their specialty. Of course, it can be all too easily demonstrated that the study of social change is quite as pedestrian as any other area of sociological inquiry.

Variation II. When macro-dynamics is attempted, it is usually in the form of comparative statics. This is the case for most of our current knowledge about industrialization. There are a number of excellent studies that compare the institutional morphology of pre-industrial societies with their analogues in industrial societies. The changes are deduced as the mechanisms required to get from the former to the latter. And even if one takes into account the problems intrinsic to generalizing from one version of an industrial revolution to other, possibly more exotic versions, it is clear that propositions derived in this manner are worthy achievements.

However, theory derived in this manner encounters a number of difficulties. The validity of this kind of theory rests upon the fragile assumption that processes may be inferred from static, cross-sectional relationships. Thus, while many theories of change arrived at through comparative statics incorporate attractive vocabularies of processes, in most cases, these processes are inferred from simultaneously static relationships. These theories invoke laws of change, but are devoid of direct observations of change.

The arch-type of this kind of theory is of course the theory of demographic transition. But there are other theories of change that assume the same form. For example, one might cite the theory that deals with the changing relationship between aspiration and achievement in the course of economic development.

The various changes in aspirations and achievement that accompany economic development are typically organized in terms of a three stage theory as is the case for demographic transition. Although it appears that no single writer has presented an exhaustive description of these stages, the following presentation attempts to make explicit the characteristics of each stage about which previous students seem to have achieved implicit consensus.

Stage of Social Lethargy.

This stage is characterized by exceedingly low levels of both aspirations for and achievements of improved styles of life. It is argued that the low degree of both aspiration and achievement is a consequence of an exceedingly low level of economic development and therefore, levels of consumption that just barely satisfy subsistence requirements. Lethargy results from the absence of both physical and social energy.

Stage of Aspirations Explosion.

This stage is characterized by slight economic development that minimally increase the opportunity for achievement but maximally stimulates aspirations. Thus the slight initial development stimulates all kinds of desires, the bulk of which are disproportionate to the available opportunities for the satisfying of these new aspirations. The situation is often associated with the political instability and violence that occurs in these areas as a consequence either of the frustrated aspirations and/or the desire for power in order to participate more fully in the new order of things.

Stage of Balance.

If and when the society is able to move on to more economic development and thus increase the rate of achievement, the latter is again brought into some balance with aspirations. Thus this final stage is characterized by a high level of both aspiration and achievement and the result is a new form of political and social stability.

This "theory" (obviously patterned after demographic transition) is here stated most briefly and incompletely. The point, of course, is to illustrate the general form that comparative statics imparts to the study of social change. This form might be summed up as follows: too little → too much → just right. How ancient a formula!

Variation III. The errors involved in using macro-static observations as a basis for macro-dynamic processes are compounded by the temporal extension of these processes. Many of the hypotheses about the continuing dynamics of industrial societies are the products of such temporal extensions, i.e.—the extension of processes that are thought to accompany an industrial revolution.

Marx, of course, was an outstanding offender in this regard. Much of his theory of class formation and conflict founder on precisely these grounds; i.e.—his most incorrect predictions of the increasing bifurcation, homogenization and polarization of social classes in mature industrial societies. And many share this problem with Marx. For example, the same problem is aptly illustrated by the somewhat naive convolutions of some demographers in their attempts to deal with recent and continuing increase in fertility rates of industrial societies, without departing from their apparently unshakable belief in a high correlation between industrialism and low fertility rates.

I think that it is possible to argue that all of the errors described above can be attributed to the double dogma mentioned earlier in this section: a) that one can do static analysis without dealing with dynamics, and b) that the study of macro-dynamics must be deferred until knowledge of social form is relatively complete, until the whole social territory is definitively mapped. These dogmas are so firmly entrenched in current theory, that many hesitate to make the obvious point, (if our critics are correct, such failure to deal with the obvious is rare), that it is virtually impossible to make these distinctions and preserve contact with the empirical world.

III.   Some Principles of Social Evolution

In the preceeding section, an attempt was made to indicate the illegitimacy of any enduring distinction between statics and dynamics. But, the illegitimacy of this distinction cuts two ways. If it be true that the scientific validity of social research is proportional to the extent to which dynamic factors were taken into account (whether explicitly or not), then valid social research should contain much information about social change. Re-stating this notion, if static and dynamic analysis cannot be separated in the collection of valid empirical knowledge, then the considerable fund of apparently valid knowledge about social systems that has been collected should contain much information about social change.

What appears to be lacking, is the presentation of research results in a manner that would bare its content re social change, and the means of making such a presentation. It may now be suggested that evolutionary thought, when carefully culled, provides social science with such means.

Of course, not all of the components of evolutionary thought prove equally useful for the study of social change. It is precisely this problem that has aroused the widest and most intense controversy. For all too often the literature on social evolution takes the form of wholesale attacks upon or defenses of the totality of evolutionary thought as it was stated in nineteenth century biology. Indeed, quite frequently both parties to the controversy make the surprising assumption that evolutionary thought itself has failed to evolve beyond its original nineteenth century statement.

Now, there is no single, stable theory of evolution in either the biological or the social sciences. Rather, there is a magnificent set of ideas and conceptions that have themselves experienced change, and that have been applied most fruitfully to the study of a wide range of phenomena, including social change. For, although there is little to be gained from playing the stately game of scholarly exegesis at this point, an evolutionary tone can easily be located in many theories of social change. This is especially true of what one might call the classic theories of change, e.g.—Gemeinschaft to Gesellschaft, mechanical to organic solidarity, traditional to rational-legal systems of authority, folk to urban, sacred to secular. All of these approaches to social change involved some evolutionary principles either explicitly or implicitly. This is to say that an evolutionary tone is present in the very same conceptions of social change that were previously criticized, since they are, in many ways, quite derivative from the aforementioned "classics".

Thus, it may be efficient to begin the search for some tenable principles of social evolution by re-stating in summary fashion the elements of the approach to the study of social change previously described.

1. Social systems are viewed as sets of hierarchically arranged formal, static structures.

2. Social changes are viewed as transition periods during which one variety of static structures is succeeded by another.

3. Thus, social changes are perceived as discreet incidents rather than continuous processes.

4. The specific processes or mechanisms of change are at least phrased in terms of a vocabulary of pathology, if not actually conceived as socially pathological.

5. Social differentiation, the common denominator of all theories of social change, is conceived in terms of stages (usually three-fold) and the final stage typically consists of a new static integration of the now more differentiated structures.

I think that it can be argued that a tenable scheme of social evolution involves the reversal of all of these characteristics. Thus, social evolution involves a view of social systems and the manner of their change that encompasses the following elements:

1. Systems are, in Steward's phrase, "to be viewed as culminations of predominant processes, rather than as static, formal structures."

2. Since, as Veblen put it, systems are to be defined by their processes,[26] change is incessant and not to be perceived as either temporary periods of disequilibrium or as discreet incidents.

3. Systems are perceived as experiencing permanent strains and persistent tensions. Thus social change and social conflict are associated by definition, and the association is permanent.

4. Evolution clearly involves differentiation. However, it is not a stage theory (although its vocabulary often is unfortunately) and there is no automatic assumption of the functional integration of differentiated structures.

It is now possible to use these elements of social evolution, and combine them into a theoretical posture viz-a-viz social change. This theoretical posture may be briefly and summarily stated as follows:

A. All social systems contain persistent social strains which generate social conflict.

B. The order characteristic of any social system consists of those institutions that control, ameliorate and/or cannalize the conflict produced by persistent social strains. Thus, a society encompasses both conflict and its associated change as well as a social order; that is, essentially a set of tension-management devices or systems.

C. Tension-management systems are inherently dynamic in that the persistent social strains that they manage offer most hospitable environments for social change. Although profoundly social strains may never be completely solved, they are also quite unlikely to endure unaltered. Thus social change is ubiquitous.

D. Any given social change is potentially both conflict-producing and conflict-reducing in its own right. In any case, social change and social conflict are highly correlated in some narrow sense by definition. New social norms that result from any change will necessarily be in conflict with some existing norms and will necessarily adversely affect some existing interests, even though the same change may complement still other previously existing norms and interests.

It now remains to be seen if this theoretical posture can be informative for the study of social change. Thus, the following section of this chapter will examine the character of social change at the level of the firm during the course of economic development. And while the exposition is not as "tight" as it might be, I believe that the relevance of the view of change outlined above is clear.

IV. The Evolution of The Firm.

Most theories of the firm fail to distinguish between the firm as exclusively a membership unit and the firm as the point at which a number of analytical social systems intersect and thus interpenetrate. The membership unit is one of the intersecting social systems and in its own right worthy of investigation. Indeed, membership systems are precisely the unit of observation of general administrative theory. However, when the membership system is the exclusive theoretical concern, difficulties result from the effort to "stuff" the almost infinite variety of concrete phenomena taking place within the firm into a single analytical social system with a consistent set of norms: the norms of the primary work group in the case of those who view the firm as a village and the norms of the market place in the case of those who view the firm as an actor-entrepreneur.

It will be argued here that the social boundaries of the firm are never coterminus with any single analytical social system. Thus, the firm neither has a single, all-powerful goal, nor a consistent set of norms.

The firm is more than a place of work. It is a market for both labor and commodities. It is an arena for the different occupational and union groups. The norms of the communal and societal status system are also present, and influence, in varying amounts, the behavior of the firm's membership.

In specific firms, elements from the different analytical systems may be so closely connected as to appear indistinguishable, thereby masking the multiplicity of systems that are present. For example, the line supervisor may also be the hiring agent, and thus the norms of the work place and the norms of the labor market may be combined into a single status position. But it is an error to deduce, from this empirical fact, the theoretical proposition that these norms must be so integrated or combined. Indeed, the norms that the line supervisor is most anxious to inculcate.into his work subordinates (commitment to the job, stability, indentification with the unit's task, etc.) are least like and most competitive with the norms of the labor market, (mobility, affective neutrality, universality, etc.) Thus, when these two systems are combined into a single position the person occupying that status will be performing in terms of competing norms. When these two systems, work and the market, are separated into two different positions (a special case of the separation of line and staff) the competing norms will manifest themselves as organizational conflict.

The Fragmentation-Pervasion Hypothesis

The image of the firm, projected in the preceding discussion, is the intersection and interpenetration of a number of potentially conflictual social systems. This view is quite similar to Professor Friedmann's conclusion that as technological change rationalizes the production procedures of the manufacturing firm, the result is a number of internally conflicting levels of rationalization. Thus, one social consequence of technological change within the firm is an increase in the number of conflicting levels of rationalization.

It is possible to apply Friedmann's position to the image of the firm stated above, and derive the following proposition. Technological change increases the number of analytical social systems that intersect and interpenetrate at the concrete firm. The separation of certain staff from line functions are, of course, illustrations of this process.

It was previously argued that these emergent analytical social systems are naturally conflictual, in some degree. For example, it was previously pointed out that the separation of the labor market system from the production system encouraged the overt manifestation of conflict between their respective norms.

In this sense, an increase in the number of intersecting social systems is likely to be accompanied by an increase in the salience of the particular social system to which a norm belongs. For example, "rational" selection of personnel as a labor market norm may be relatively inoperative as long as the line supervisor does the hiring. He is subject to other norms (e.g., low rates of labor turnover) that are more important for his primary social system, line production. However, once the breed of personnel men make their appearance, a "party" is formed that is precisely devoted to presumably rational techniques of hiring, partly motivated by a desire to establish a professional self-image, perhaps as a sincere belief in the value of such procedures. In any case, the salience of the particular system to which a norm belongs is increased by the very emergence of that system within the firm.

Technological change, then, increases the number of social systems that intersect at the firm by creating a larger number of more specialized social systems. The normative content of each of the emergent social systems is more limited in scope and in that sense narrower. In the previous illustration, the personnel department is narrowly concerned with labor market considerations, while the line supervisor is narrowly concerned with maintaining production schedules.

It is important to note that the narrowing of the normative scope of the intersecting social systems has a relative, as well as an absolute connotation. Thus the duties assigned to either the personnel department or to the line supervisor are a more limited segment of the firm's total duties than were previously assigned to their unitary ancestor. The specific tasks for which the line supervisor or the personnel man is responsible within his own social system may have increased, in part as a consequence of specialization. Nevertheless, such increases will now come within the narrower confines of the particular analytical social system.

The Process of Fragmentation. The preceding discussion identifies three interrelated processes that result from technological change within the firm. They can now be stated in summary form. Technological change within the firm:

1. increases the number of analytical social systems that intersect and interpenetrate at the firm,

2. increases the salience of the particular analytical social system to which a norm belongs, when attempting to explain its operation within the firm,

3. decreases or narrows the scope of social action (the normative content) that constitutes any one analytical social system.

Taken together, these three processes are aspects of a more general social change. This general social change will be subsequently called *fragmentation*.

The Process of Pervasion. Up to this point the process of fragmentation has been illustrated within the firm. Fragmentation may also begin within the wider society. Regardless of the point at which fragmentation initially takes place, the firm and the society interpenetrate each other in regard to the emergent analytical social systems. Thus, the firm as a labor market is part of a wider labor market that extends into the society.

While only one segment of the firm is narrowly concerned with the labor market, the remaining employee's have a labor market status. For example, the line supervisor, while not a part of that system within the firm that is focussed upon the labor market, is a member of the wider labor market. In this manner, the labor market, as one analytical social system intersecting at the firm, interpenetrates both firm and society.

Interpenetration also may be expressed in the following manner. The newly formed analytical social systems are bases of status allocation both within the firm and within the wider society. Within any particular firm, an employee will have a primary status. There is a particular analytical social system to which his position belongs, e.g., the production system in the case of the line manager, the labor market system in the case of the personnel man. But the total position of each of these cases will also contain elements of the other analytical social systems. Thus, the line supervisor has a status in the labor market, while the personnel man has a status in firm's authority system, no matter how marginal this status may be. Both positions will have a status in the wider occupational prestige system.

Since each total position is in this manner *pervaded* by the several analytical social systems, status comparisons within any single system are possible. Thus, positions can be separately ranked in regard to their status in the labor market, the flow of work and organizational authority, the occupational prestige hierarchy, the community, etc., etc. Moreover, the narrowness of fragmented social systems increases the accuracy of any single status comparison. However, the accuracy with which total positions may be compared decreases as fragmentation proceeds. The various possible combinations and permutations of ranks in the several fragmented systems make the global comparison of positions increasingly difficult.

Rationalized, technological changes are responsible for both of these social consequences, i.e., the fragmentation of social systems and their simultaneous pervasion throughout the society. As the bases of status allocation are fragmented into highly differentiated systems, the statuses within any single fragmented system achieve a higher degree of comparability.

TECHNOLOGICAL PROGRESS AND EVOLUTIONARY THEORY

FRED COTTRELL

Miami University, Oxford, Ohio

A good deal of today's revival of interest in evolutionary theory seems to stem from the centennial of the publication of Darwin's great work. I am, however, enough of a student of the Sociology of Knowledge to doubt that this is sufficient to account for the whole of what is happening. In fact, the reasons why the theory got such widespread notice at the time it was originally published may give us some insights into the present revival. At that time traditional knowledge was cracking under the impact of early scientific discoveries and the application of some of that knowledge which was simultaneously giving rise to new social conditions. But traditional knowledge, technology, theology and morality were so closely wed that it was very difficult for either technological changes or shift in the social structure of the society to take full hold in the absence of some defensible rationale that would explain man's relation to his Creator. The whole static model which justified things as they were could be successfully defended if only men believed that they had been created as they now found themselves to be and were rewarded accordingly. Darwin showed how the Creator might have operated—not in a single act, forever establishing what was to be, but in a series of acts taking place over time. His work was seized upon by those who stood to benefit from such a point of view with an avidity that was exceeded only by the bitterness with which it was attacked by those who relied for their security upon the preservation of things as they were.

In the Darwinian theory and its aftermath the competitive model developed by the Classical Economists was given both moral and divine sanction. Darwin's work demonstrated that the whole universe moved toward the ultimate realization of God's purposes through the survival of the fittest. To that of the Protestant Ethic was added the sanction of Science! Ruthless business and imperialism were thus scientifically demonstrated to be necessary and justified. It was only when the beneficiaries of the new age of scientific and technological progress had achieved positions of power and authority, and with it control over many of the rewards available for men of knowledge, that this competitive model became distasteful. The theory of evolution seemed to suggest that there is still the necessity for struggle, for invention and creation. But such an idea is a threat to those now thoroughly ensconced in positions of great power. It is more comfortable to adopt conceptions of a static world, where those who have engaged in struggle can pause to enjoy its fruits. Evolution was relegated into the background while less dangerous ideas, largely involving static models, became popular. The idea of progress that had, during the revolutions in the West, provided a universal symbol which justified striving, was dropped. Adaptation became the mode; each little segment was treated as a world in itself, developing local equilibrium through countervailing power.

But in parts of the world where men are not so comfortable, the model has not been dropped. Marxism supplies for many of them the ideological correlate to Darwinism. They believe that through struggle it is possible to reach higher forms of existence, and that nature ordains that through the achievement of superior science and technology Communism will provide the next superior form of man and society.

Our present concern is, of course, involved in this struggle over ideas. Is there something inevitable about the "progress" of the "underdeveloped" areas? Are there natural laws which will propel them willy-nilly into new forms of adaptation? If so, are these the laws discovered by Malthus, Smith, and Darwin and refined by the theorists of the West? Or is there something about Marx's formulations and those of his followers that effectively predicts that which must result from the interplay between what man discovers about the Universe and the way he uses it more fully to achieve his goals? Or is there still another set of requirements to be found in the Truths We Hold to Be Self Evident which will direct all men to seek what we seek, through the means we have used?

Only a little while ago questions like these were answered with extreme confidence. Science and technology can advance, we said, only along the lines and through the social forms developed in the West. Others must, to achieve our technical competence, pass through the stages we did, and once having done so they will inevitably become free; by which we meant they would internalize the values of Christianity, Capitalism, and Democracy and be able to achieve what their norms dictate. Today we are less sure that this is so, and even though our complacency has cost us dearly in many ways, we still do not like to look objectively at what has been happening in order to see why our predictions continue to be so far off the mark.

But in spite of our reluctance we have been forced to accept a revival of the idea that the world is a harsh place in which to live, one where force must be used to meet force, guile to meet guile, in the struggle for survival. We may not be so sure that the outcome of the struggle must be Progress but most of us are prepared to fight for existence, even in a worse world than this one.

So we in the Social Sciences are again looking at evolution as a model which has proved to be extremely valuable in the other natural sciences. But we are hardly equipped to use that model. Most of our research has been empirical and the bulk of it is based on observations taken in extremely limited bits of time and space. The means by which we manipulate our data are suited to deal with this kind of fact. Static and short run studies have had far more attention than historically oriented ones. The minutia which make up the bulk of our concern are selected to provide the base for such short run predictions. The business world, which has so largely controlled the development of technology, is interested in rates of obsolescence, styling, morale, limited movements of population, and so on. The educator has become extremely occupied with short run problems; the way to deal with the population bulge, the urban spread, and how to avoid teaching skills and knowledge that will be obsolete before they are mastered; even government is seldom able to support long range projects. There has been but little research money or brains to deal scientifically with the longer run social consequences of the technological changes that so often are at base the source of our immediate problems. Thus, even if it should appear desirable to use the evolutionary model, we can expect few significant findings from it in the near future. We will first have to raise a generation of students interested in, and equipped to investigate, a lot of things that have not hitherto been examined scientifically. In the meantime we have to live and deal with technological and scientific change and their social consequences by using ideas of either very doubtful worth or proved ineffectiveness.

Something of the difficulty we face is found at the very outset when we try to define what we mean by evolution. For some it is just history, nothing else. For others it means only change. One student looks upon it as the expression of Newton's Second Law of thermodynamics writ into varied forms. Evolution implies, for another set of observers, movement toward higher forms, while still another identifies it with more complex ones and yet others take the position that it is the way the greatest possible population of a given type can be maintained in a given set of circumstances. Obviously the definition chosen represents as much what the given investigator is prepared or willing to study as it does about "what is out there" to be studied.

It is on this kind of heuristic basis that I have chosen the definitions I will use here. I am not trying to synthesize or provide the greatest common denominator of other definitions. What I think of as "evolution" is a concept which implies that we are making or have made an analysis of the relationships which extend through time among a cluster of patterns to which we give our attention. We want to know what recurs and what differs during a given period; which occurs first in the system of coordinates of space in which our clock is located, and which follows. I give the name "pattern" to the complex or configuration whose recurrence or disappearance we are recording because most of us in our culture seem to make abstractions easiest in terms of geometric form. Whether this be a consequence of the fact that we communicate most of the time through arbitrary arrangements on a plane surface, or for whatever other reason, I am not prepared to say. Nor am I arguing that some other artistic form, some mathematical expression or other kind of symbol might not serve equally well. The chief point is that while events themselves have multitudinous connections with each other, extending both in time and space, the symbols which stand for some of the common characteristics of these events represent only a few of these relationships. It is only by neglecting a great many differences between specific occurrences that we can classify them as being the same thing. By "pattern" I mean to imply an arbitrary selection of this kind. To come back then to the line of thought we were following: Having chosen a number of criteria, observable with the instruments we are using, we find that these criteria assume patterns that stand in more or less persistent relationship one with another. If we are to find the conditions under which these patterns of relationships change or persist, we are forced to take samples at time intervals. When the sample has characteristics that fall outside the range of what we are willing to call "the same thing" we record change. On the basis of such samples we discover that the patterns that follow one another in time exhibit both persistence and difference. Where persistence follows persistence in all the patterns under observation there is no way that we can predict the probability of change. When some patterns change and others persist we assume that the connections between them are not revealed in such a way that they help us to increase the accuracy with which we can state the probability of change or persistence. It is only when observed changes in some patterns are regularly followed by particular kinds of changes in others that we have increased our ability to state more accurately whether change or persistence is likely, in what direction, and of what character. We look primarily at the succession of events from the past into the future rather than the reverse because the knowledge we are looking for is most useful in dealing with the future. It will be clear by this time that my definition of evolution is only a special case included in a definition of causality. "Evolution," as we shall use it is an effort to understand one series of cause and effect relationships.

Like all science it begins with the observation of specific events, but it does not stop when this history has been recorded. If we are to use it for scientific prediction evolution cannot be synonymous with history or with change. Whether or not in a given case it is useful to include the evolution of atoms and stars in the effort to understand the evolution of machines and patterns of social relationships is a heuristic problem. All we ask is "Can we, by adding the history of this pattern during the period of observation we are using, to that of the other sets of patterns also under observation, increase the accuracy with which we can state the probability of the specific kinds of change in which we are interested?" And in the interests of economy, which is important in assessing the heuristic value of any course of action, we must also ask "Is the gain in accuracy worth the cost of the proposed action?"

This has been perhaps a rather long-winded kind of justification for my definition. I have given it only because in reviewing the literature I find that a great deal of the time and effort wasted in controversy stems from a failure to lay out the premises from which the argument was made.

Darwin was concerned with the origin of the species. If we confine the use of the word evolution to efforts to solve the problem he was trying to solve we will of course have shorn off most of the substance of our present concern. But if, on the other hand, we define evolution to mean all of the causal connections that extend among those classes of things we call technological, physical, or cultural and those we call biological, we have undertaken an impossible task. This forces us back into a heuristic selection. We have to hunt through the research on how man and other organisms changed to see whether we can find knowledge useful in predicting the direction that technological change is likely to take, something of its magnitude, the effects it has had, and perhaps its specific applicability to the kind of things that go on in underdeveloped areas. In so doing we must perforce neglect a very large part of the evidence collected for other purposes by those interested in evolution for other reasons. But we will not be looking for mere analogies and parallels. The findings of evolutionists have been put into symbols that represent only a small part of what others, differently oriented and using different instruments, might have observed or did observe in the situations symbolized. Technological change was a part of, not apart from, organic and physical change also being observed. Put another way, we will not treat technological or social events as being merely analogous to biological or physical events—they are simply another among the many patterns of relationships different observers might discover among the same events.

Darwin did not have to give much attention to the class of observations that we call technological. He drew most of his evidence from a period of time in which little or nothing that we commonly call technology had yet come into existence. He could safely give limited regard to the special influence which such things as birds' nests, spider webs, beaver dams, bee hives, ant hills, and even pebbles nudged into position to block the entry into fishes' nesting places must have had on the appearance and survival of species. In a sense the use of such artifacts as these deserve to be called technological, and a thorough review of their impact on the evolution of certain biological forms might demonstrate that influence to be considerable. But certainly it would add little or nothing of concern to us. However, the habit of assuming that biological change could be understood completely in terms of physical, chemical, or biological changes in the natural environment unmodified by man was a dangerous one, once the origin of *man* became the subject of inquiry.

What in fact resulted from this outlook was this. Since physical and chemical patterns as they occur in nature can be considered to be almost constant during the time *homo sapiens* has been evolving, it must have been biological change that accounts for what he is and what he has done. Technological and social change merely represent the working out of the prior biological development. A generation or more was spent digging up the evidence to prove this point and all kinds of social policy was "justified" by the assumption that it was correct. The "fittest" were endowed by their biological superiority with the right to rule others, lesser breeds, who should be thankful "that God had in his infinite wisdom provided more able and intelligent men to govern them and prevent their being victims of their own mistakes". Of course it would be absurd to say that imperialism and colonialism were "caused" by the error in interpretation of evolutionists. There might have been other myths to rationalize and influence what was happening. The point is that this was the myth and it was bolstered for a time by what was regarded as final scientific proof.

We now know, of course, that the kind of biological organism that survived to become *homo sapiens* very probably would not have done so had there not been previous advances made in *technology* by that forbear or some of his fellows.

I suppose it will be necessary at this point to define what we mean by technology. Broadly it could be made to mean the same thing as technique, the regular way of getting things done in a society. For reasons we will explore later this is too wide a definition of technology for us to use here. But some such definition did fit the categories that the Darwinists made. For their purpose the dichotomy, heredity-environment, was necessary. Certain kinds of persistent patterns could be shown to pass biologically from generation to generation. These represent one category, heredity. The other category, environment, might consist of other kinds of recurring patterns or of irregularities. The important thing to know was that if patterns persisted they were not being preserved by biological heredity.

Regularities in environment that persisted beyond the life of a generation quickly became apparent. These were said to be due to the direct effects of the physical and biological world. Later it was found that the patterns observed operated within much narrower limits than those imposed by "nature." Side by side, in what the geographers called the same environment, were persistent patterns differing from one another. Both their differentiation and their persistence required explanation. Their persistence was found to lie in the fact that there was a kind of heredity not carried on through events taking place within the bodies of organisms. To such patterns were given the name culture. Since through the observation of culture it was possible greatly to increase the accuracy with which they could predict the probability of relationships in which they were interested, the evolutionists expanded their model to include not only biologically transmitted patterns but also persistent patterns not so transmitted. It is important for us to remember this. Whatever kinds of nonbiological factors that had the effect of producing patterns persisting through generations were for these evolutionists one category, culture.

When anthropologists got around to examining closely the actual process through which the perpetuation of these patterns was secured, they found it to be more complex than that involved in genetic transmission. Conception takes place at a single moment in time. At that moment the whole genetic endowment from the past is transferred to the organism that will be patterned by it. Obviously this is not the case with culture which has to be learned during a considerable period under quite variable conditions, from a number of sources. It may be dangerous to neglect the consequences of these differences in our effort to explain the likenesses. The great bulk of the patterns are passed on at least in part through symbols, and some anthropologists would confine the word "culture" to what is symbolically transmitted. Some patterns are transmitted through a combination of experiences. One learns to operate a lathe or ride a bicycle the way he learns to swim, by doing it. The physical objects, modified for man's use, that were passed from generation to generation contributed continuity according to their durability. Skills and judgment involved in handling these artifacts are learned, in part, from symbols, but in part learning takes place by direct feedback extending from the subject to the object and back again. It will not do to disregard this process and rely for our understanding of either change or persistence purely on the effects of symbolization—or symboling if we perhaps more accurately use the word as a verb to indicate the active process.

The scientist in field or laboratory learns from the reactions of materials directly taken from nature as well as from the symbols provided by his culture.

What he has learned cannot correctly be imputed to come solely from either source. Similarly, the experiences of those who work with artifacts give them a different meaning than would have been conveyed were symbols alone involved. The consequence of this difference in the learning process was noted by the anthropologists. Students learned that some aspects of a culture could be more clearly understood, and changes in it more accurately predicted, by studying physical and chemical facts than by observing symbols alone, while in the case of other aspects this was not the case. To the first the name "material culture" was given, and the residue was called "non-material culture". For some theorists technology is identical with material culture.

This leads to confusion. In the functional sense, in that they provide the means to carry patterns that extend from generation to generation, the categories should be treated together. The symbols that deal with material things are transmitted exactly the same way that symbols dealing with other things are transmitted. If, however, culture is only that which is symbolically transmitted, then that which is learned from artifacts through direct feedback is not culture at all.

We can't hope to undo the confusion that exists as a result of this situation. But what we want to make clear here is that "technology," as we shall use it, includes traditional knowledge gained by earlier men, including a lot of prescientific propositions developed by them and transmitted symbolically. It also includes skills and judgment learned on the job during the lifetime of those presently working. In addition there is knowledge newly invented, like science, which was not passed on to this generation but invented by it. For us, here, technology is not synonymous with material culture, nor with non-material culture, nor with culture, because it cannot be most effectively understood by trying to deal with it as if it were.

There has generally been an effort to identify technology with knowledge about and skills in using tools and machines. This could easily be accepted as our definition. But if we use it that way we must understand what this does in terms of evolutionary categories. If it is difficult to deal with an object as if it were physical or cultural, when it is both, man's control over chemical processes provides an equally confusing kind of relationship to deal with. Man's control over fire, which apparently began as far back as the early Pleistocene, has had a good deal to do with his evolution but can we call it a tool? Fire could be used for warmth, permitting man's forbears to survive in climatic zones where they otherwise could not have done so. It was also itself a weapon protecting him against predators. It could be used to cook food, making it possible for him to use for his survival plants that he could not otherwise digest. It may have been used to harden spears and to shape wooden implements at a time about which we can learn almost nothing. But more significantly for evolution it was a means to alter the whole face of a region with fire. Large areas of plant and associated animal life that otherwise could have become dominant were destroyed. This could be done repeatedly so that even the "long run" development that otherwise might have taken place never did. Similarly, certain types of plants that require considerable heat to permit them to germinate got, through man's use of fire, life chances that otherwise could not have existed, and so affected the life chances of other plants and animals.

At least at some places on earth the use of fire should be considered as a factor to be taken into account as much or more in explaining the survival of species and associated organization than the use of speech and tools, the other two human possessions which often are used to explain why an ape-like hominid could evolve into *homo sapiens.* Shall we then place the use of fire in the same classification with symbol and speech, with tool and learning-by-doing, or give it a special classification? Certainly its effects on survival are great and extend far beyond our capacity to grasp, influencing man's development in ways we know not.

For our concern here it may not matter how we classify it, but at least we ought to be put on warning that when we exclude the use of fire from our analysis of technology, we exclude from consideration a significant variable that might, if we could get evidence, greatly increase the accuracy with which we reconstruct man's history. Fire was probably used before tools were invented. But we have no way to know that. To reconstruct the past we have had to rely on stone and fossil. By its own nature fire destroyed in most cases the evidence of its use. So we cannot correlate evidence of changes in the use or extent of the use of fire with evidence of biological change. And so we are barred from using it directly. It is when we begin to make more derivative inferences from the evidence we do have that we need to exercise caution. From a knowledge of artifacts and fossils we have established certain kinds of ideas that assume that the change in tools must have caused changes in the organism. It may well be that in many instances it was the controlled use of fire in addition to or instead of the use of tools that gave rise to biological change. Perhaps some of the conclusions that we have come to with reference to the kind of social organization that must have existed at a particular time and place rest too exclusively on the idea that it was only tools, changes in symbols, or organization that gave man advantage over competing organisms.

Whether or not we include knowledge about and control over the fire as part of technology, we must include knowledge and skills connected with the use of tools and machines. So taking this as the core of our concern, let us take a look at the way technology affected and was affected by the evolution of biological types. The work of the archaeologists has established beyond doubt that changes in the form of tools and other artifacts are associated with changes in the distribution of fossils of various types dating from the same or succeeding periods. Man through changing his environment changed the conditions under which selection among types of man or his predecessors took place. Changes in environment do give rise to changes in heredity, if not directly in the old crude Lamarckian sense, indirectly, through affecting the statistical distribution of mutant types in the gene pool. Cultural invention and innovation do not necessarily give rise to mutation (though the invention of radioactive materials certainly does) but they often affect mightily who will breed and survive and so what genes will disappear from the pool. It is no longer possible to say that man became what he is by "allowing nature to take its course" to some foreordained end. We have in fact reached the point where the kind of man he was is often identified by the artifacts he left behind and his characteristics are inferred from them. What must be emphasized here is that while the scientific base for the idea of evolution through biological superiority has been pretty well destroyed, a great many elements in our culture are still what they were when it was held to be valid, and some of them are basic to our present attitudes about underdeveloped areas.

Akin to this belief in a kind of biologically natural superiority is another that denies any place to values in human evolution. By value I mean "the factors that affect choice." The early determinists, caught up as they were in a struggle with metaphysicians, theologists, and vitalists felt that they had to deny the existence of choice, lest they let supernaturalism back into their considerations. They insisted that they had found in chemistry and physics an invariate order. A caused B and that was that. Today of course it is apparent that there are a terrific number of irregularities yet to be accounted for in these sciences. Once the irregularities appear however, there is an immediate effort to create means of observation that will permit the discovery of new patterns, and if this is successful a new model which takes into account the newly observed regularities becomes heuristically desirable.

If, with the use of a model that includes means of observing the influence of choice, we can more accurately predict survival than we can using one that neglects this factor, then we are bound by heuristic imperative to use it unless the cost is greater than the gain. Once we have established the fact of choice we can proceed to examine the factors that affect choice and perhaps move still another step closer to accurate prediction in those fields in which choice matters.

Peculiarly enough there was little criticism of Darwin's use of the concept of choice in his demonstration of the way evolution takes place. His idea that sexual selection was responsible for fixing some of the characteristics of birds was crude and needed refinement, but it is not possible to dispense with it entirely. Nobody denies that when a bird chooses one rather than another as mate from among those available he affects the gene pool and that if there are large numbers of individuals carrying some specific types of genetically determined characteristics who are regularly excluded from participation in breeding the result will be to alter heredity.

The mechanism of choice is not invariate. If the single-minded pursuit of the queen bee by all the drones represents "instinct" then something else must be held to account for the fact that a particular pair of geese mate and subsequently disregard the availability of what seem to us at least to represent sex objects no different from the one chosen. Deer choose browse over hay when browse and hay are both available, but any stock raiser will testify that they will eat hay when no browse can be had. Such facts as these and thousands more that evidence preferences among animals lower than man are accepted without argument. Nor can any one doubt that in turn the choice by an animal of one plant as food rather than another affects the ecological balance in the habitat of that animal.

The mechanical model of cause and effect that has been in use in our culture so long made it very difficult to take teleology into account. The development of the theory of servo mechanisms has given us a new means to understand some of what takes place in man's behavior without forcing us to leave what we regard as being scientific ground. Although it has long been possible to observe such things as a hawk directing his flight not toward the point where the bird was first sighted, but on a course that anticipated where he would be at the moment of collision, we nevertheless avoided explanations that involved goal-directed behavior. But now that we can design a missile that will hunt a missile perhaps we can also accept the purposeful human behavior that invented it. Through the use of feedback theory we have come into possession of a model that may contribute to our understanding of processes that are going on.

It is pretty obvious that the use of a model that permits analysis of preference is heuristically justified in the study of evolution. With its use we can set about to discover the factors that affect choice using generically the same kind of process that is involved in other kinds of scientific endeavor. If anybody objects to my use of the term "value" to indicate the factors that affect choice, and the use of the term "evaluation" to indicate the process by which preference is arrived at, he is free to assign any other words that to him seem to be more fitting.

Coming back to the analysis of evolution, it appears that man is the product of evaluation as well as variation and selection by non-teleological natural forces. The consequences of choice may be such as to alter future alternatives in a way to make such choice again impossible. It may be such as to lead to the elimination of the organism choosing, or to that of some other organisms sharing the environment. It may also, through positive feedback, reinforce choice so that its future probability is increased. A great deal of culture represents the results of just such feedback. But man is led to choose not only by experience in his own lifetime but by that of his forbears on the basis of the results apparent to them.

The kind of nervous system that permitted learning in the early years so that culture could be transmitted to succeeding generations had obvious advantages for survival. Those forbears that could use tools increased their chances of survival over those who could not. So also those who had accumulated experiences, such that they need not make the mistakes others not so equipped were more likely to make, could, through the exercise of choice, modify their environment and that of future generations. The use of tools and fire and culture, and the exercise of choice, mutually affected what took place. To give priority to tools over values, biological type over culture, culture over values, or any other kind of causal assignment, on the basis of the record, is arbitrary. Imputation of causation is a function not only of the observed but the observer. If one chooses a specific point in time when a particular change is taking place in one or another aspect of the complex he can show subsequent change in other elements, but often, had another arbitrary starting point been chosen, change could have been shown to arise in the reverse order. If to get an "objective" starting point from which to impute final cause we keep going on a course, each step of which leaves out much of what in fact took place and was involved in what followed it, we continually know less, not more, of what the future will look like.

Perhaps because of the apparent futility of such a regression, perhaps because of changing concern and motivation, perhaps because of the greater availability of means, or for other reasons, those who studied organisms in relation to their environment increasingly devoted themselves to the analysis of single configurations extending through a short space of time.

This type of ecology has provided the means to discover many of the intimate interrelationships that pervade the ecological complex. It has permitted us to learn much about how, under a given set of conditions, a given plant or animal population will sort itself or be sorted. Some general propositions have been substantiated well enough that we can say that, neglecting the impossibility of mutation of invasion which will introduce organisms not now to be found here, taking into account only predictable changes in soil, climate and topography, "this kind of stable equilibrium will appear among organisms in this habitat."

Such a model has great heuristic value for those studying the impact of man for he can be treated, at least at the moment of his invasion into a habitat, as an independent variable whose presence gives rise to new hitherto improbable patterns. Man's influence in changing the face of the earth can by this process be to some degree inferred. The record shows it to be far more considerable than it was once thought to be. But again he is not apart from but a part of the ecological complex, and whether he changes the face of nature because he is the kind of animal he is, because of the culture, tools, or organization he possesses, cannot be directly known. Only where differing sets of men, using different tools, different cultures, different value systems, have invaded similar habitats can we make this inference.

In spite of a multiplicity of cross cultural comparisons there is no general agreement as to the influence of various elements of the complex. What we have come to agree upon is that the animal-man can be treated as being the same, whatever the habitat. We no longer can expect that isolation will be maintained over a long enough period of time that mutations will be differentially selected out and separate gene pools established. From now on one of our previous variables can be treated as a constant.

But if this is so, and I know of no fact more generally accepted among anthropologists, then at least part of the evolutionary model loses direct interest for us here. No matter how he got here, or what influenced the character of his heredity, we have to deal with man's gene pool as an unchanging fact during the last twenty-five thousand years or so. It is possible that there are some changes taking place in it that will become apparent to observers able to make use of a longer period of observation than we have, but they cannot be established now. Man is still one species. What we discover about the influence of technology upon man's development during the existence of *homo sapiens* is not recorded for future generations by patterning D N A. We will have to look elsewhere if we want to know about changes in the kinds of societies he builds or the psychological make-up he exhibits. It is also now possible to rule out certain kinds of patterns as being inherited. We do not have to change the gene pool either to increase or decrease this prevalence. It is also now apparent that a great deal of what we thought to be self-evident attributes of all human beings turns out to be only characteristic of a few people occupying a limited space, for only a limited time.

As a matter of fact, of course, our concern is primarily social and cultural. It gives us no comfort to know that no matter whether we regress to fairly simple hoe cultures or progress to fulfill all Madison Avenue's fantasies, man will still (barring mutations whose selection may change it) share the same gene pool a hundred years from now that he presently does. What we are here primarily concerned with is the persistence or change in certain kinds of patterns we label technological, social, political, economic, or religious.

Problems connected with the identification and the discovery of such patterns, the creation of effective typology, and analysis of their co-variance with other kinds of patterns remain very difficult. One reason for this is to be found in the nature of their transmission from one period to another. As we pointed out earlier, in biology we now know enough that we can clearly separate in our thinking the elements involved in change that derive from alterations in the gene pool from those that take place otherwise. While it is true that the nature of the species is inferred from the statistical description of a host of individuals, it is also true that each one of these organisms is endowed with all of the potential it receives genetically at one moment. A man's biological inheritance results from a single act by his parents. This is not true as it relates to his social inheritance. A long series of experiences is required to enculturate an individual. In no society is anybody endowed with anywhere near all that can be found by adding together all that is culturally transmitted by all of the individuals that make it up. What part each gets makes a difference in his behavior. Nor is there any period in the life of the individual that we can say he has received all from the past that he will ever receive. During the period that he is having symbolic experience with things from the past he is also having direct experiences, many of which are not culturally defined for him, and he may well react to such experiences in ways that modify efforts to induce him to act in culturally sanctioned ways. The deviation from cultural norms increases with the complexity of what must be learned, the order in which it is learned, and the significance attached to learning it. Those who study culture patterns find it harder to categorize them and order their appearance in such a way that cause and effect relationships among them can be imputed. Perhaps the most significant difference between the model that helped biological evolutionists see what happened and the one necessary to understand cultural evolution is the place that must be given to purposive action. A great deal of biological evolution can be dealt with effectively without taking this into account. The mechanism of choice in a great many cases is "instinct" that is transmitted biologically. Moreover, since selection is the primary process operating, the origin of non-genetic innovation is not as important as its consequences. The error involved in neglecting this source of variability is not very great. However, as we have seen, once the origin of man became involved his purposive behavior became increasingly important, and the shape of things to come often could be predicted much better if this factor were taken into account than without it. Models designed to predict cultural evolution must, if possible, discuss the bases for cultural innovation as well as the selective factors involved in their survival and that of the population in which they take place.

It is apparent that evolutionists have been concerned with the numbers of various genetic types that survive in a habitat. For many of them the study of evolution consists of an effort primarily to predict more accurately the size of each population occupying a habitat after a given period. For them, the significant fact about man is that he has increased in numbers so dramatically and has come to occupy so many different kinds of habitat. Even the explanation of why this is so is a considerable task. But most of us want to know not only how many of us there are going to be but also something about where we are going. Are we necessarily driven to increase our numbers up to the maximum fixed by the food chain in the area in which we live? If so, what will happen to our cherished values and institutions? Does evolving technology require a world different than that envisaged by our values, or can we set up values and shape technology willy-nilly so that it serves them? Or are there moral principles with which men are "endowed by their Creator" which necessarily govern, overriding both biology and technology? And even assuming that there are no such ethical principles as this assertion about man's relation to his Creator, are there some others to be found in the nature of the organism itself? For example, can the kind of man that in his childhood responds to efforts of older men in a way that permits him to be enculturated exist except in societies that induce men to teach their children? Can such an organism learn except under the influence of personal interaction that includes love and affection? And can an organism of this kind ever be taught successfully to make the choices necessary to the survival of extensive organization and advanced technology if it robs humans of the continuing opportunity for these experiences? If not, then this elementary set of ethical principles becomes a basic fact. Any culture, any technology, that attempts to function in disregard of these propositions is as certain to be adversely selected as is one that disregards other imperatives of its existence.

If then there are tendencies in humans that induce them, like other organisms, to increase their numbers up to the physical and biological limits of their habitat, and if there are technological imperatives driving man to achieve the greatest possible control over energy, there are also factors involved in organization and in learning which must be taken into account if we are most accurately to predict emergent culture. In fact, of course, a very large part of the influence of habitat and technology operate by influencing choice as well as by selecting out those choices that produce adverse results. The model we use for the analysis of cultural evolution cannot dispense with the knowledge we have about how other organisms evolve, but it must demonstrate how what we have learned through its use and in other branches of science, interacts with human purposive action. Most anthropologists will agree that man shapes his culture, and on the basis of its effects alters or retains it. The point where many of them part company lies in their interpretation of this process. Certainly to the degree that teleology is involved, we must start with the human being, the chooser who acts in ways that perpetuate the pattern or alter it. In "making up his mind," "evaluating the situation," or however we term the act of choosing, the actor responds through feedback from his previous acts, or on the basis of cultural conditioning, anticipates what the response will be and acts as he would if the response had already taken place. But after he acts he gets a response that is a result of what happens in the situation. This may or may not correspond with his anticipation. The response may so alter that situation that further choice is impossible, like destroying the chooser, or so narrowly limit the range of his future behavior that his choice no longer affects the outcome. On the other hand, the discrepancy between anticipation and realization may still permit further choice. In these cases man can respond selectively to what happens. That is to say he may react as if only part of what happened did happen. This may be due to peculiarities of his own organic makeup (like, for example, being blind or deaf) to the idiosyncracies of his own learning, or to the kind of cultural patterning common to most of the humans in the area where he is operating. Culture will have, in any case, set up a perceptive base on which the adult human must function. The response he gets will be defined by the enculturated individual selectively and the pattern of his past will be re-enforced or altered on the basis of this selective response. If the cultural definition is sufficiently adequate, the response of those sharing it permits them to initiate new acts to which in turn they will respond selectively. This may go on for a very long time. The culture provides the individual with definitions of response (meanings?) that serve to keep people acting for generations in ways that those not so enculturated may find to be fantastic. Looking at such behavior the pure culturologist says "culture can make anything good" and cultural relativists deny that there is any standard common to mankind which affects his efforts. For him there are no goals except cultural goals. No values not purely a product of culture. In a sense this is true. If culture be treated as a residue, what is left after all the factors that operate to select cultures have had their effects, then of course what is found there includes all norms, the results of all strivings, as well as all knowledge that will be symbolically transmitted. But how much of what was there yesterday is still there? How much of that was selected out by the operation of non-cultural factors? How much of what is there now is new, now to be symbolically transmitted but not learned that way? We cannot find these things out by studying culture itself. If we confine ourselves to this kind of evidence, of course we will find that the only kind of sequences there are in terms of which to impute cause and effect are cultural sequences. But if, on the other hand, our model permits us to look elsewhere, we may see that culture change was preceded by technological invention, or that certain kinds of deleterious social relationships were selected out of that culture when new knowledge made it possible to discover their influence, or that changing biological facts, like the growth of population, made what had been tolerable cultural propositions intolerable. Perhaps it is only in a comparatively short run that "culture can make anything good." (That is to say that what culture calls "good" will persist.)

For example, a physiologist or epidemiologist looking at a culture might come to a different conclusion about the persistence of certain culture patterns than one locally enculturated. He would point to the physiological resultants of the behavior that took place without reference to their cultural definition. He would show that certain culturally-ordained practices in relation, for example, to diet and sanitation are regularly accompanied by certain morbidity and mortality rates, without reference to whether or not these practices are defined culturally as being good or bad. From this information, the future size of the population, and the level of its accomplishments, to the degree that they were dependent on physiological processes, could be predicted pretty well. In turn, an ecologist viewing the ability of this population to compete with others for sustenance might well be able to predict that even though the culture lost nothing of its ability psychologically to induce its carriers to make selective response necessary to preserve it, the population itself might in a relatively short time disappear, and with it the culture it was carrying. What we have been saying is that there is goal-oriented behavior, that goals may be provided by culture, and culturally sanctioned goals may be pursued for a long time that frustrate the primary impulses of the human organism, provide technologically inefficient means to the sought ends, and are physiologically debilitating. But a culture operates in a milieu which includes other populations, often sharing other cultures, plus biological and physical elements too. Its survival depends not only on its ability to perpetuate itself psychologically in a population. It must also fulfill demands made on it by these other factors. But we must be wary in extending to cultural survival the kinds of all-or-none principle that work with the survival of genes. A gene lost from the pool is forever lost. Whatever elements it contributed to the organic pattern will from that moment cease to exert influence on the future. But cultures are transmitted piecemeal, and there is continuous alteration going on in the society using it. Soon after two cultures are brought into contact diffusion takes place and each will soon be discovered to have borrowed from the other.

What culturally is lost by the disappearance of one population may well survive in another. Natural selection operating on the biological base need not be directly accompanied by any similar or identical cultural change, and the reverse is also true. A simple way to treat this fact in the theory of cultural evolution is to assign to biological and physical phenomena a static role. We say that these factors sets limits to man's behavior, and assign to culture the whole of the basis for dynamics. Culture, we say, produces culture. One culture may have impact on another, but it is not necessary dynamically to relate cultural change to anything not included within the cultural definition. Yet we readily admit that cultures seem to interact with habitat, that for example, Eskimo Culture is different from that of the Maori, and that each is suited to the environment.

If we return to the idea that technology evolves through feedback, we get a model that permits such a dynamic interpretation. What is learned from the dynamic responses of the habitat to culture-directed behavior gives rise to choices different from those that would occur when identical limits were imposed by habitat and only symbolic interaction between individual organisms were involved. Nature does not confine itself to saying "this far and no further." Its responses are often dynamic. They become different than those anticipated in the culture and so give rise to different experiences, on the part of those acting, than were anticipated. If such experience is widespread, new anticipations develop, are subsequently transmitted by symbol and so become part of the culture. What is today deviant behavior becomes tomorrow normal, not necessarily because there is some "strain toward consistency" in the culture itself, but also because feedback from nature is selective in dynamic terms. If men fail to respond differentially on the basis of nature's responses, their survival itself may be endangered. Take for example declining plant yield from a single plot of ground. Culture can ordain that man move about and, as a result, he avoids the consequences of this natural response. Or it can provide means to restore fertility to the land. But unless it provides means to stop declining rates of plant growth, it cannot ordain that men remain there permanently and carry on in each generation as they did the generation before. Man is not wholly rational, but we cannot deny to him an element of rationality. Being a sentient, goal-directed organism, he adjusts culture through feedback. The physical and biological worlds interact dynamically with the cultural world. In the process man alters the order of his choices, some acts seem now to be more significant than they were, others less so. Values, culture, and habitat make up a network of relationship that persists in dynamic, not static, equilibrium. Not all of the dynamism can be attributed to man.

Short run stability may be followed by rapid change. This often ac-companies a mutation, an invasion, or an invention. Population which has been in stable equilibrium undergoes rapid change, but slowly it again comes into balance with the resources it can wrest from its environment. This kind of change over time provided the evidence from which our theories about evolution are derived. But recently we confront a situation in which change is far more rapid than it ever was, and continues over a longer time than did change that took place at any corresponding rate. The old idea that change could be stopped by the fact that men got tired of striving, became anxiety ridden and apathetic when change went on too long, or otherwise reached the place where they no longer willed change, will not fit the present facts.

Since nothing like it happened before, we will have to look at recent kinds of change if we are to find reasonable answers as to what is now happening in social and cultural evolution.

One theory of change assumes that what is now going on is due to the geometric accumulation of culture traits, particularly in the realm of "material culture." Certainly there is evidence that such a progression has taken place. But this fact is not self-explanatory. Why this sudden growth? Does it stem from a new kind of creativity in men? Are there an increasing number of geniuses being drawn from the gene pool? Or have we found a way to get dynamic responses from nature that men previously were unable to secure?

It seems to me that it is profitable for us to explore this latter hypothesis. Certainly a ubiquitous fact about the last five or six hundred years is the increasing mobility of men and their increasing possession of things. Both require increasing control over energy.

In the use of the energy concept we need to be careful lest we involve ourselves in tautology. Energy is a word used in the sciences to describe some regular relationships found to exist in nature. It is often also cited as being the cause of such relationships. In fact, of course, we have used the same symbol to point to two kinds of relationships among the same class of events. In spite of the confusion this generates, the energy concept has been extremely fruitful in other sciences, and we will use it here just as it is used there. We can measure energy by the effects it produces on our instruments at the moment it is converted from one pattern (or form) to another. Because this has been done, it is also possible for us now to state by formulae what the ratios between energy in two different forms are, and compute the amount of energy involved when the changes from one form to another take place.

We observe all of the patterns we observe through energy conversions.

Some of these conversions take place within the body and others outside it. All of the patterns we have been talking about can, from one point of view, be treated as arrangements of energy. Persistent relationships—(structure)— and dynamic relationships that involve describing the flow of energy through structure make up the observable world. We could use a model of this kind to deal with patterns of value, culture, organisms and things. At the moment it does not appear that such a model would permit us to predict probability more accurately than we can now do. But certainly we are required heuristically to investigate and see where it gives better results than those we now use. We are increasingly equipped to use it by the work being done in other sciences. The present concern of physicists with energy is too ubiquitous to mention. Organic chemists are increasingly using it to see how energy conversions are involved in rearrangements within the molecule. We know enough about photosynthesis to begin to unravel the energy relationships involved in synthesis and organic growth. Through the study of metabolism physiologists are beginning to understand how energy conversions take place in the body. It is now possible to trace energy from the sun—the source from which, with negligible exceptions, it comes—through the organic community to entropy. Some evolutionists have begun to evolve a hypothesis and build an energy model to study organic evolution. If it works out, it will bring together in a larger framework some scattered knowledge we already have. Most organisms taken as physical units are steady state systems. They grow to a point where energy inputs equal outputs and stop there. But taken as a class they represent expanding systems. That is, they reproduce in such ways that the only limit on growth is found in external conditions. They may be limited by inroads made on them by other organisms, or by the energy that they can control, but they are not self-limited. Organisms "capture" the radiant energy of the sun as a means to perpetuate the patterns that differentiate them one from another. Various gene patterns carry on this process of "capture" by different means. Complexes of genes result in the formation of organisms that constitute a food chain, each organism being dependent for its own supply of energy from forms created by another, performing a different operation involved in its own survival. A particular organism then is dependent for its energy control on earlier patterning by others as well as upon its own capacity to control the conversion of energy. In a particular habitat there are a number of possible combinations of such organisms. These combinations vary in pattern as well as in numbers. Together they control the conversion of part of the radiant energy of the sun that reaches them in their habitat. The total amount of restructuring that goes on as energy moves toward entropy is therefore varied. Lotka has developed the thesis that evolution is the process by which the patterns derived from variation in the gene pools to be found in a habitat are so rearranged in numbers that they capture the maximum amount of energy. Equilibrium is reached only when this maximum has been achieved. This would provide an explanation as to why the numbers of different organisms sharing an environment varies, and also give a basis for understanding more exactly why the maximum number of a particular population in a community was fixed at the point that it was, without having to account for equilibrium by talking only about equilibrium. The evidence for Lotka's position is not yet sufficient to make clear that it should be formulated into a law. But the tendency it expresses, whether or not the process ever reaches the end point he designates, fits other evidence that ability to control energy conversion is one factor involved in the persistence of patterns that require energy for their replication. Certainly the patterns of observable human activity fall into that category. Man cannot escape thermodynamics. He is dependent upon the plants that synthesize radiant energy and inorganic materials to supply the energy in the forms upon which his own body feeds. He competes with other animals for plant life, and in the process changes the life chances for various other plants. His effectiveness in controlling the conversion of energy so that it serves his needs and satisfies his values is one measure of his probable survival in a habitat. Energy flow is, of course, not an independent variable. When we say "control over conversion" we indicate that it is being directed and the social organization through which that control is effectuated and the values that direct choice are part of the energy system. But there is no gainsaying that there is a degree of variability in the response that is given by objects in nature to the same act by humans. The amount of energy flow one gets by kindling a lump of coal is altogether different than that which results if instead of coal, quartz is added to the fire. Certain kinds of response, then, derive from certain kinds of materials. There may be myriads of social arrangements that have the effect of meeting the conditions under which materials will yield this response. If increased energy flow results from any one of these arrangements, that energy becomes a new, dynamic fact to be taken into account in understanding whether it will enhance the probability that patterns will survive unchanged or the flow will change the system that gave rise to it. Obviously such an increased flow may become a factor altering choice—it may change the hierarchy of values of those who have come into possession of it. It may be feedback reinforce all of the social arrangements that existed at the moment of flow increase except those that would throttle it. Even these arrangements that limit flow may be reinforced to a degree because the human being that carried on the arrangements leading to energy flow may alter them to stop it or slow it down, if they discover that it endangers other values more important to them. The most recent case in point is, of course, the effort to control fission and fusion explosions. What we want to point up is that the increased flow has consequences and that these consequences *can* lead to further increased flow and so on. The flow is a new dynamic fact to be taken into account. It is a means that gives direction to technology and through it those complexes immediately associated with technology, and so on more derivatively. Much of a culture may be so remotely related to changing energy flow as hardly to be disturbed by it. Efforts to direct the new flow to preserve these tertiary elements of a culture may succeed while at the same time elements primarily and secondly related thereto are forced to give way as men endowed with new power by the new energy source direct that power toward their alteration. The conditions necessary to convert increasing energy flow may in some cases (as, for example, in setting fires to burn off unwanted vegetation) impose only limited conditions on the society that uses it. In others (such as, for example, controlled nuclear fission or fusion) they may be extremely narrow and the technology and social organization required to operate them be extremely precise. Here, if the flow is to be secured and maintained, most of the arrangements are dictated by the facts discovered by science to be necessary. In a sense, then, they do not flow from values or culture but from the nature of the patterns built up during the evolution of the stars and the earth and the biosphere. The direction imposed is, to a degree, permissive. That is to say, in a sense nature says "if you want this, these are the conditions under which you can have it." A culture or a value system can cause men to turn away, refusing to meet those conditions, but that culture cannot at the same time receive the benefits in increased control over energy that it would get had it met the required conditions.

Technology is involved in, but not identical with, the energy control system. But if we examine technology in terms of the effects it has on the control of energy we can see better, perhaps, why it has moved in the direction it has taken. Technological inventions that result in bringing more energy under man's control give him an advantage in dealing with other men and with the other organisms with which he must compete for energy. Among these inventions some, because they have effects that reduce his ability through organization to survive, are selectively eliminated. What is left after a time is a set of techniques and tools that increase energy control in ways that do not otherwise reduce the probable survival of other patterns in the milieu. In the broadest sense, technological "efficiency" has no meaning apart from human evaluation. But it is possible to discuss energy conversion in terms of time and energy without making an evaluation. That is, a model can be set up showing how certain kinds of results could be secured utilizing the least possible amount of energy. The results of such a model can in turn be compared with what happens using various specific real arrangements and a statement in some such measure as percentage can be used to indicate how nearly the real approaches the "ideal" system. Also given the object to be secured and the converters to be used, it is possible using an ideal model (such as a Carnot engine) to describe the rate at which it can be secured with "least effort."

At times there have been attempts to show that this is the principle behind cultural evolution. The principle has some application at certain points but it is too limited. As we have indicated, it is only when the result to be achieved is known, the converters and the energy source specified, and the rate established that the least amount of energy required can be determined. But it gives us no basis for learning what the end results are to be, and what, in terms of all the results to be secured (or the effects evaluated) is the system of least cost. It is this that we are trying to learn.

The widest framework we could use to discover where we are headed might be Newton's Second Law of Thermodynamics. According to this law, all the patterns whose survival we are interested in predicting will in the long run disappear and entropy will take their place. This answers none of our questions. Does the law work in more limited time? That is, does energy always move in the same direction, or is the law a statistical statement such that great fluctuations in direction during shorter periods are covered up by general trends? During the time the patterns in which we are interested seem to have existed, they appear more nearly to follow Schrodinger's principle of movement from order to order than in the direction of entropy. But this generalization, too, is statistical and gives no direction for short periods or specific patterns.

If we confine ourselves to the period of his existence as such, it appears that man has been engaged in producing patterns that persist far longer and involve the structuring of energy in greater amounts than was required to maintain him and the plants that originally captured for him the radiant energy from the sun. To the extent that such structures appear to be unnecessary for this biological survival (such as the pyramids for example), man appears not always to have acted on the principle of least effort. So it is not necessarily true that he acts so as to conserve energy. Certainly the fact that his control over energy is always limited forces him to choose among possible uses known to him. But regardless of his purposes he must assign a minimal amount of energy to secure the energy with which he acts on his environment. He must also use some energy to protect his energy flow from other plants and animals seeking to use it for their own preservation.

Beyond this he has choice as to what he will do with the remaining energy that is under his control, if any. Its quantity and the form it takes will have much to do with what else he can accomplish. In a given habitat the kind of tools he commands has much to do with the size of this. If he possesses only a digging stick with which to dig up roots, rodents, beetles and such like, he may have to spend most of his time and energy in this pursuit. The very limited flow of energy available will limit the complexity of the organization he can develop. Thus only limited forms of the family can be sustained in these systems.

Perhaps it is not happenstance that so very large a part of the artifacts coming to us from early man consists of weapons. With such tools it was possible to kill other larger animals and so gain control of more energy with less expenditure of his own. The development of the bow made it possible to store energy that upon its release would drive the arrow at a much higher velocity than he could attain by running. So with bow and arrow he would come into possession of the energy already captured by animals much more fleet than he, such as the deer. With the spear he was able to obtain so great a store of energy as was represented by great animals like the bison.

The analysis of the kinds of social organization that can most effectively be used to exploit energy sources of this kind has been undergoing very careful scrutiny for some time. It has become apparent that there is some degree of likeness among men in cultures using approximately equal amounts of energy from similar sources. But just how completely it will be possible to predict social patterns this way is not yet clear. Certainly the forms of social organization vary in their effectiveness, not only with the tools or weapons used but also with the plants and animals found in a given habitat. Organization and technology are inextricably combined in a complex that results in a given energy flow. A number of combinations may from this point of view have the same result. Feedback in energy terms would not distinguish between them. A broad spectrum of kinds of social organization compatible with given technology may exist. But there do seem to be "jumps" in the classifications. Certain kinds of organization require for their perpetuation minimal amounts of energy. If this is not forth-coming, the whole organization disappears. It is easy to see, to use a biological analogy, that many mice might live where no rabbit could, though they fed upon the same source. The appearance of many kinds of elaborate social organization waited upon technology that would permit control over large amounts of energy flow. If subsequently energy flow should fall below a critical point the whole system must fall apart. This thesis is not adequately demonstrated nor have the quanta of energy sufficient to maintain specific kinds of organization been worked out. There is, however, considerable historic evidence for it.

Periods during which man suddenly began to build organizations far more extensive than those he previously was able to maintain have occurred. Their incidence may be called periods of "revolution," the kinds of systems that emerged may be called "stages," or given some other name. The point is that we can show how new developments that brought sudden enlargements in man's control over energy were accompanied by what appear to be almost discontinuous change. Some cultural evolutionists give the name also to other periods when "jumps" in energy are not now apparent. In any case, there are times during which a great many of the previously regularly recurring patterns that served to show cause and effect seemed suddenly to disappear or be very greatly changed. Cultural anticipations of what should happen no longer received their accustomed feedback. Organizations previously insignificant in power and function came into control of great accretions of energy and with it the means to create choices that enhanced their own survival chances. Many others that had long been dominant began to lose power, controlled less and less energy, and became incapable of carrying on even the functions they formerly performed.

There is growing agreement that control over fire, development of weapons, and the cultivation of plants and domestication of animals represented critical points in the development of culture and social organization. For other anthropologists and historians perhaps it was the invention of the development of social organization itself that constituted means to use energy in ways so much more effective as to be classed as a new source. Childe, for example, looks upon the city in that light.

Elsewhere I have developed at some length my own conception as to what were critical points in man's use of energy and the way those who passed these points were able to expand the area over which they were dominant, reinforce or change the values that affected the choices they made, control to a degree emerging social forms, and enlarge further the flow of energy by developing science and technology. It would be a work of supererogation to repeat these findings here. But some conclusions about the way they relate to evolution and to the underdeveloped areas might profitably be pointed out.

I. First we must note that when man captured and put to use energy from sources other than that secured through photosynthesis, he introduced a factor that affected vitally the previously existing thermodynamic balance. Sometimes the quantities of energy he controlled, such as those from the use of fire for example, were greatly in excess of anything that any other organism could bring to bear in its efforts to survive in competition with man. Sometimes man, by transporting them from great distances, through the use of the wind or fossil fuel, brought plants and animals that otherwise probably never would have reached there into competition with those previously found in a habitat, completely disrupting any former tendency toward equilibrium.

The result was, of course, to create situations that could not have been predicted on the basis of the balance that existed when local patterns of organization evolved. The new energy flow provided feedback from sources so far removed from the immediate situation that no amount of adjustment between things living there could restore the previous situation. Whether we examine the flora and fauna so disturbed or the *human culture whose evolution was based on feedback from it* we find that it would be completely impossible to restore the functional relationships that once worked automatically. Where the flow of energy in a habitat is greatly enlarged, culture thus becomes more and more contrived, that is, its continuity depends increasingly on man's ability consciously to understand how it works and to be effectively able to manipulate the elements that make it work. As a consequence, discontinuity in culture becomes more common because much of what was there was never understood, verbalized, or integrated by conscious process. Under the new situation, however, "letting nature take its course" is increasingly unlikely to produce expected results. With increasing frequency *values* based on man's experience during the time he was building culture based on energy from plants and animals, induce choices that in the new situation are self-defeating, and *the more energy devoted to their preservation the less likely a workable feedback system becomes.*

II. As a derivative of this the previous relationship between dominance over an area and the growth of population becomes inverted. In societies dependent primarily upon the muscles of men for mechanical energy, the only way greatly to increase that energy is to increase the number of men. But when converters using wind or water, or fossil fuels, but requiring for their own reproduction a good deal of energy, begin to be used, it often becomes true that the flow of energy can be increased more rapidly by slowing down or stopping the increase of men than by permitting or encouraging it. The energy that might have been used to beget children and support them to maturity can then be devoted to the production of converters with a much greater capacity. The greater the disparity in the cost of producing humans and that of producing other converters of equal energy capacity, the more marked the advantage, in energy terms, of limiting the growth of population. Once a stock of high efficiency high energy converters exist, together with a reliable source of fuel, the rate of increase of high energy converters can be geometric if only the energy used to make such converters can be directed into the production of still more converters. Because the amount of energy over and above that expended to secure it (what I call surplus energy) which can be secured from coal or petroleum is so enormously greater than that which can be secured from producing food or feed, the exponential can be, comparatively speaking, very much larger for machines than for men.

III. A small population deriving its food from a relatively small amount of fertile land can, with the aid of high energy converters and fuel, become dominant over a much larger population forced to secure its food from land of declining fertility and to utilize in production many men who are in terms of input-output ratio much less efficient than the machines that might replace them. So cultures that carry values which result in enlargement of population are by those values greatly handicapped in competition with high energy cultures not so burdened.

IV. Cultures that encourage the preservation of social *organization* that limits the multiplication of high energy converters in order to preserve social organization sanctioned by low energy culture reduce the probability that they can survive in competition with those that encourage the invention of organization able more effectively to serve high energy technology.

V. In making a transition from low to high energy technology, the compatibility between already existing culture and that which must be created to operate the new technology becomes a factor. It may be that a system that depends on slow changes, undertaken only with the consent of those who must change, will prove to be more effective than does a more rapid one. On the other hand, experience with culture shock, and recovery from it, may indicate that here too there is a kind of quantum phenomena involved. A sudden shift to a new technology that is immediately able to deliver large increases in the flow of energy may be more quickly and certainly established on a feedback basis than does one initially psychologically more acceptable, but deprived by its very slowness from increasing the per capita flow of energy. The evidence is not conclusive, but it certainly cannot be said unequivocally to support the idea that democratic change will always prove to be superior to other types that do not require consent of those who will be involved in it, before change is made.

If these theses stand up, we have shown how technology is given a direction by evolutionary forces, somewhat independent of the values of particular sets of men. If all men would cease the effort to come into control of more energy, they might, by the future consequences of human and other kinds of organic reproduction, be returned to the condition in which they previously existed. But if one set of men, tired of the effort to adjust to culture changes induced by increasing energy, or satiated by its product, cease to increase their energy flow, there are almost certain to be others, who have never had control over enough energy to provide the satisfactions and the power they would like to have, who will take up the process of expansion of energy flow. It will only be when we get another response from nature, in the form of greatly diminished return in the form of surplus energy, that we can expect the present revolution markedly to slow down.

There is knowledge that leads to the conclusion that the time this will take place is not so far away as we would like to think. The results of one set of investigations led to the conclusion that if the world's population were to continue to increase at its present rate, and all of it used energy at the rate it is presently being used in the United States, all of the energy available at up to four times its present cost would be gone in a hundred years. The number of such estimates and the size is variable enough that nobody should take any specific one too seriously, but the point is that energy sources, except for solar energy, are quite finite and there will be, in a comparatively short time, an end to the technological imperative provided by the response nature gives to our search for increased energy. We are not talking about time periods similar to those that produced major changes in man's gene pool. Even if only a few more of the world's people increase, their use of energy at the rate we have, easily available energy, energy yielding very large surplus, will be gone in far less time than the duration of the Roman Empire. And then what? At the moment we are building up the size of human population at a terrific rate. Part of this has come from the elimination of diseases in places where in the past the food chain was adequate to support a population limited by those diseases. When population limitation becomes generally to depend on limited food resources, it is probable that new plants will be introduced that have higher yields than those now used. But this merely shifts the limit back to that imposed by the local nitrogen cycle. Use of great quantities of fossil fuels to activate nitrogen means more rapid exhaustion of these fuels, plus further increases in a population that cannot be sustained unless energy flow into synthetic fertilizers is also maintained.

It is possible that we will learn how to control the fusion process and get energy from sea water, but since we do not as yet know the energy costs of harnessing this energy, nor the yield, we cannot be sure that it will produce larger energy surpluses than the great bonanzas we are now exploiting. Generating equipment wears out and has to be replaced so the series representing its accumulation is convergent. Increasing amounts of energy are required just to replace existing equipment. What we can be sure is that unless some other limit is placed on the expanding system represented by human reproduction, no matter how large our stock of converters other than man eventually becomes, it will not be enough.

The social systems now in control of high energy technology are not required to diffuse them over all the earth. They can instead choose to confine its spread to areas that provide the maximum energy yield per capita, given various combinations of access to scarce natural resources, leaving large areas of the world in low energy cultures. It is possible that of two social systems, that which took the latter course might survive after the first had thus dissipated the energy necessary to maintain elaborate organization and regressed to a simpler form capable of supporting only limited technology.

At the moment, acting upon the basis of values derived from an earlier day or from pre-scientific dogma and with a naive conception of the relation of values to energy, the mood seems to be that energy shall be scattered broadcast. This is done in the effort to preserve traditional ideology, to court popularity, or to preserve the image of a benevolent and well-meaning people. Whatever the basis for such a choice, it will have consequences, and in the light of these experiences, after we have had further reaction by others to our assertions about the "Truths We Hold To Be Self Evident," we are likely to make an agonizing reappraisal of them.

Other peoples are not driven by any evolutionary principle to recapitulate the sequence of events that took place here. Nor need they use all of the ideas that we used to justify it if they did not guide our success. Some of those ideas undoubtedly did contribute to it. Others, had they alone been followed, might well have reduced rather than increased feedback from energy sources. Because we simultaneously used them, all of the ideas have been strengthened by the increased feedback that did take place. But they are not immutable evolutionary principles.

If we want to know more about the functional connections that exist between our culture and social organization and emergent high-energy technology, we will have to study them far more carefully than we have done so far. Our recent experiments in trying to introduce that organization and technology and ideology in faraway places were not carefully scrutinized, using scientific methods; so we have lost a great opportunity to discover a lot about which elements of the complex that grew up here were patterns that contributed to increase in the efficient use of energy to maintain patterns necessary for its generation, and which practices only contribute to the preservation of traditional ways that are themselves parasitic in energy terms. But it should be clear by this time that neither Smith nor Marx knew much about what he was talking insofar as it would provide a guide to emergent social organization. Capitalism's fight with Communism may be over ideology, but it will be conducted with instruments and power that were produced more often on either side by disregarding those ideologies than by conforming to what they would require in the way of organization. Our claim on the minds of men may well rest more on what happens to their bodies in terms of nourishment, disease prevention and provision against the vagaries of a hostile environment than it does on the proclaiming of truths and the shouting of slogans.

This is not to say that whatever means will increase energy flow are thereby justified in terms of cultural survival. We have already entered a caveat against the materialistic dialectic. Throughout this discussion we have asserted that values, organization, technology, and the inorganic world are together involved in producing and maintaining the patterns that govern energy flow. So in a sense it is tautological to say that patterns survive because they maintain energy flow. It would be just as meaningful to say that there is energy flow because there are patterns. Neither technological determinism nor "energetic determinism" has been demonstrated. But neither has the transcendental view of values or culture. If man makes himself, he does so in a world that includes other organisms and things that interact with man's purposes as they are reflected in his choices and resultant behavior.

There are certainly limits on the kind of organization that the kind of animal man has become imposes on evolving energy systems. Moreover, the dynamic functions of the organism are involved in the responses given to stimuli. The human infant responds not only to food and sex but also to social interaction with adults. No society can survive unless it creates values that reflect these facts. What is involved in the value system necessary to operate high energy technology is only now becoming evident as we have control of sufficient energy to discover it. But if values are, as I think they are, natural, not transcendent or supernatural phenomena, then their origin and their efforts in high energy society can be discovered and heuristically it becomes increasingly desirable that we find out what they are.

It is not our task here to talk about organization, or values or organisms in evolution except as they are involved in technological progress. What we have been trying to show is that technological progress has no meaning apart from the complex which has accompanied its evolution. It will not make sense for us to offer to others our technology, designed as it is to serve our values and our organization, on the assumption that they *must* hold to be self evident the Truths we hold so to be, and *must* be seeking the freedoms we are seeking. But neither will it make sense for them to borrow our technology on the assumption that they can take it and disregard all the other patterns involved in the complex that makes our technology work. Both we and they need to know what is necessary and what is adventitious in the relationships of technology to society.

Perhaps if we abandon our own dialectic with its all or none assertions, we can find them out.

RETROSPECT AND PROSPECT

Simply put, the question to which the authors of the foregoing essays have turned is whether or not the current interest, in various of the social sciences, in the underdeveloped areas represents a species of revival of evolutionary theory. Essentially, each author has explored the issue of whether the process about which he has written—be it cultural dynamics, political modernization, social change, Westernization, economic development, or technological progress—is at bottom some rejuvenated form of evolutionism.

It has not been easy to answer this question with a flat "yes" or "no." This is not so much because of any contributor's attempt to avoid a direct confrontation with the issue as it is due to its curious contemporary complexity. As Emerson has clearly pointed out, evolutionary theory today differs fundamentally from the older Darwinian formulation. It is no doubt improper to speak of a theoretical "revival," for if we are indeed now engaged in an evolutionary enterprise, its underpinnings are fresh and new, and a far cry from Darwinian theory.

A no doubt ludicrously oversimplified characterization of nineteenth-century evolutionism would perhaps hold that whatever comes next possesses at least four qualities. The first of these would be inevitability, in the sense that while formulators of public policy might be able to speed, retard, or otherwise influence change, they would not be able to prevent it. Secondly, it would be said that later stages in an evolutionary process tend to be more complex than their predecessors, and that a simple-to-complex model might be central to the patterns of change. It might be held, in the third place, that the change process could be traced through a series of identifiable steps and stages. Finally, nineteenth-century theory was concerned with a variety of value analysis insofar as it was held that later stages were better than earlier ones, and that the evolutionary process could in general be viewed as a process of improvement.

Examination of these propositions in the light of current social theory helps to measure the distance the social sciences have travelled since Darwinian times. The question of the inevitability of change, for example, hardly seems worth discussing within the context of contemporary theory. During the last generation or more, most social science has operated on the assumption of dynamics, as Talcott Parsons bluntly points out in asking "Who now reads Spencer?" The contemporary assumption that all things in the world of social science are dynamic, constantly moving and changing, has drastically revised the context in which the inevitability question was once asked. More than providing us with a built-in answer to the issue of the inevitability of change, twentieth-century dynamic theory has assumed the question away.

On the second point, it may well be that the simple-to-complex model is still with us to a considerable degree. Contemporary concepts such as political modernization, social change, economic development, and technological progress involve notions of movement toward increased complexity. While the complexities of many primitive or underdeveloped systems should not be overlooked or underrated, it is nevertheless true that much current developmental theory argues the movement toward ever-increasing complexity.[1] The judgment that this facet of the older evolutionism still stands as a significant contribution to contemporary research on the change processes in the underdeveloped areas deserves serious consideration.

It appears, thirdly, that the notion that the evolutionary process moves through a series of identifiable steps and stages is not dead. Such works as W. W. Rostow's *The Stages of Economic Growth*[2] constitute evidence of this. Nevertheless, stage analysis appears to exercise decreasing influence in social theory. Many of its proponents have been unclear—and some have been downright inconsistent—in the matter of identifying the theoretical function of stages. If they are to be thought of simply as convenient categories for classifying data, few will quarrel—but their explanatory value is sharply curtailed. If, on the other hand, the concept of stage is given a more active theoretical role (if, for example, each stage is defined as containing the indispensable seeds of the next one), serious problems arise. Stage theorists have not yet coped successfully with these problems. On balance, it may be said that the somewhat mechanistic steps-and-stages formulation that characterized much nineteenth-century thinking has now been relaxed to a

---

[1] See, for example, Gabriel A. Almond and James S. Coleman (eds.), *The Politics of the Developing Areas* (Princeton: Princeton University Press, 1960), *passim.*

[2] New York: Cambridge University Press, 1960. See also Rostow's "The Take-off into Self-Sustained Growth," *The Economic Journal* (March, 1956), and *The Process of Economic Growth* (London: Oxford University Press, 1953).

significant degree, and that stage theory now appears to occupy a smaller place than heretofore in the analysis of the change process.

Contemporary social scientists are no doubt more sophisticated than their predecessors in coping with problems of value analysis, but many of those problems are still with us. Darwinians were once unashamed to note that later stages in the evolutionary process were to be preferred over early ones. Similarly, the conviction is widespread in the underdeveloped areas today that economic development is a good thing and that it is better to live on a high standard of living than a low one. Indeed, it has been observed of the underdeveloped areas that "all show a passion for technology. All desire to expand the welfare state. They are concerned with efficiency and rapid change. In short, the characteristic of new nations is their desire for social mobilization, planning, and rapid change."[3] In dealing with such value questions today, it is a relatively simple and obvious procedure to make a sharp distinction between the values held by the actors in a situation under study, on the one hand, and on the other, the values of the scholar conducting the study. Once the distinction is made, it is customary to treat the former as data while arguing that the latter should be suppressed. This is more sophisticated than many nineteenth-century approaches, to be sure, but problems persist as long as scholars are reluctant to deal in a structured way with their own perceptions of the desirability of political modernization, economic development, or technological progress.

A final point remains. Concern with development or modernization in the underdeveloped areas bears a directional implication for the analysis of change. It is easy to agree that change is in process in these countries, but can we identify the direction in which they are moving? Nineteenth-century evolutionary thinking was characterized by a unilinear answer to this question—evolution was held to be a movement in one direction, toward one final end. The unilinear notion, if applied today to the underdeveloped areas, would hold that they were moving toward a common Western goal during the course of their development. Yet here, too, lies a significant difference between Darwinian and more contemporary formulations. Today we can identify two alternative directional concepts, in addition to the unilinear—random change and multilinear development.

The concept of random change has appeal for many modern social scientists. In a very real sense, it is easy to live with, since it is consonant with the assumption of dynamics, lends itself to quantitative analysis, and

---

[3] David E. Apter, "Steps Toward a Theory of Political Development" (Chicago: unpublished manuscript, 1959), p. 8. See also George I. Blanksten, "Transference of Social and Political Loyalties," in Bert F. Hoselitz and Wilbert E. Moore (eds.) *Industrialization and Society* (Paris: UNESCO, 1963), pp. 183–190.

provides one more avenue of escape from the value question. Randomness, however, would permit us to speak only of change but not of development. If there is a distinction to be made between "change" and "development," it is to be found in what these concepts say about the direction of change. The random formula, attractive as it otherwise may be, says too little about this trajectory to permit meaningful distinctions between structured development and amorphic change.

The multilinear formulation thus emerges as the most relevant of the three to the contemporary study of change in the underdeveloped areas. The multinotion lies somewhere between the unilinear and random ideas, locating considerably closer to the former than the latter. A multilinear view of development would suggest that there are a number of directions in which change could move while being regarded as development. This number, while greater than that of the unilinear notion, is nevertheless limited, and is far too small to be regarded as random. The multilinear formula would thus permit studies of development in a limited number of directions—not only toward the Western, but also toward the Soviet, and possibly a limited number of additional, models.

Each of the writers of the foregoing essays has attempted to answer the question of whether the current interest in the underdeveloped areas constitutes a revival of evolutionary theory. It would be presumptuous to attempt to synthesize those answers here in some composite fashion. Nevertheless, it would appear to be true that if we are indeed once again engaged in evolutionism, its contemporary form differs significantly and fundamentally from nineteenth-century theory.

NAME INDEX

SUBJECT INDEX